Japan Inc. on the Brink

Also by Susan Carpenter:

SPECIAL CORPORATIONS AND THE BUREAUCRACY: Why Japan Can't Reform
(Palgrave Macmillan, 2003)

WHY JAPAN CAN'T REFORM: Inside the System (Palgrave Macmillan, 2008)

JAPAN'S NUCLEAR CRISIS: The Routes to Responsibility
(Palgrave Macmillan, 2012)

Japan Inc. on the Brink

Institutional Corruption and Agency Failure

Susan Carpenter

palgrave
macmillan

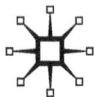

First published 2015 by
PALGRAVE MACMILLAN

Palgrave Macmillan in the UK is an imprint of Macmillan Publishers Limited, registered in England, company number 785998, of Houndmills, Basingstoke, Hampshire RG21 6XS.

Palgrave Macmillan in the US is a division of St Martin's Press LLC, 175 Fifth Avenue, New York, NY 10010.

Palgrave Macmillan is the global academic imprint of the above companies and has companies and representatives throughout the world.

Palgrave® and Macmillan® are registered trademarks in the United States, the United Kingdom, Europe and other countries.

ISBN 978–1–137–46943–4

This book is printed on paper suitable for recycling and made from fully managed and sustained forest sources. Logging, pulping and manufacturing processes are expected to conform to the environmental regulations of the country of origin.

A catalogue record for this book is available from the British Library.

A catalog record for this book is available from the Library of Congress.

Typeset by MPS Limited, Chennai, India.

To:

The Japan Policy Research Institute

Contents

Acknowledgments

I would like to express my appreciation to Ken Dickson, Investment Director, and Govinda Finn, Investment Research Writer, both at Standard Life Investments, and to Professor Jens Hagendorff, the Martin Currie Chair of Finance at the University of Edinburgh Business School for agreeing to interviews and for permitting their comments to be included in the book.

Foreword

Does it matter whether or not Japan reforms? After all, the people of Japan appear (on average at least!) to be wealthy, healthy and well-educated, with an array of high quality services and amenities to hand. Combined with its idiosyncratic culture, some geographic diversity and pockets of global leadership, there are many aspects to Japan that arguably make it a very attractive place in which to live and work, and one of the world's most interesting countries. Certainly, Japan has some problems. High government debt is one of them, but then that problem is shared with many other countries, including the UK, the USA, France and Italy. An ageing population poses a further challenge, but then many other countries are about to face a similar issue. Many of Japan's problems look quite common, even if they look rather extreme through certain lenses. So, overall, should we care too much about reform?

Well, for one type of 'stakeholder' in Japan, the answer to this question is an indefatigable 'Yes, we care!' That group is *the set of people (and entities) who invest*: shareholders, bond holders and their ilk. In a broader sense, it can include savers and future recipients of pension payments. This group *should* be intensely interested in whether or not Japan can reform. In particular, investors want to understand how share prices might behave; whether bond yields and bank interest rates might change; to understand how the price of goods and services in Japan might rise or fall; and to understand whether the Yen might rise or fall relative to foreign currencies. All these factors will help determine whether or not investors – people with capital or who draw income from pools of capital – will live well, get poorer, or even get 'wiped out' by future events.

Since the election of December 2012, the Japanese government has stated its intent to drive reform (Abe's 'three arrows' of fiscal stimulus, monetary easing and structural reform). At least part of the plan involves 'quantitative easing' (some call this 'money printing'). When practised in certain other large economies, quantitative easing appears to boost the price of risky assets and weaken the currency. Rising prices for risky assets tend to help asset-rich folk, and make the distribution of wealth less equal at the margin. A falling currency usually raises the price of imports over time, increasing general price inflation. There thus appear to be some positive and some negative investing and societal effects from monetary easing (and your starting point and perspective matters a lot in this debate!). Shareholders, though, are excited by the prospect of an end to expectations of general price falls. Shares are generally highly valued when inflation is low but positive (say, 2–3 per cent) but valuations can struggle when higher inflation becomes a problem. Shares also 'hate' price deflation, as revenue growth becomes difficult and nominal debts can eventually overwhelm firms, creating financial distress and losses for investors. Inflation rates matter!

Investors would also like to know if other, more structural, reforms can boost economic growth and firm profitability. At the time of writing, this reform seems more difficult. But some investors are hopeful: an article in the *Financial Times* on 15 April by investment analyst David Bowers is entitled: 'Sceptics underestimate Japan's policy revolution'. We shall see whether this headline proves correct or not. In her series of books on the topic, Susan Carpenter has been clear (and prescient) about the challenges for Japan to reform. She has been right so far and her message remains strong and clear. Susan also discusses the importance of reform at the firm level. Will so-called 'zombie' companies change for the better, or is restructuring just too difficult? Should investors seek out 'zombie' firms that might restructure for the better, or should they instead focus on well-functioning firms – presumably trading at higher prices? As an investor, I need to be alert to all possibilities. It is quite possible that monetary easing and asset purchases boost asset prices, weaken the currency and generate modest price inflation. Under this scenario, the stock market would likely do well over the next few years. It is also quite possible that the programme of more structural reform fails to gain traction, leaving the third of Abe's arrows behind, with Japan only superficially changed. There are other scenarios too which are far worse for investors, but these would require a separate, more detailed discussion. In the meantime, Susan's contribution on this topic should be considered essential reading for all investors: her book addresses one of the investment world's 'big issues'.

James Clunie

James Clunie is the manager of the Jupiter Absolute Return Fund, a global, multi-asset long/short fund. He holds the Chartered Financial Analyst® designation and earned a PhD in Management from the University of Edinburgh. His research interests are centered around the 'short-selling' of stocks.

Annual Average Exchange Rates

Japanese Yen per United States Dollar [JPY/USD]

2000: 106.46
2001: 122.37
2002: 124.79
2003: 115.82
2004: 107.49
2005: 110.85
2006: 116.12
2007: 117.27
2008: 102.80
2009: 93.50
2010: 94.58
2011: 83.36
2012: 82.15
2013: 93.36
2014: 103.1

Acronyms and Abbreviations

AIST	National Institute of Advanced Industrial Science and Technology
ALIC	Agriculture and Livestock Industries Corporation
ANRE	Agency of Natural Resources and Energy
BOJ	Bank of Japan
CHUDEN	Chubu Electric Power Co.
CPI	Consumer Price Index
DBJ	Development Bank of Japan
DPJ	Democratic Party of Japan
EC	European Commission
EPA	Economic Planning Agency
EPDC	Electric Power Development Co.
EXIM	Export-Import Bank
FAZ	Foreign Access Zone
FBR	Fast Breeder Reactor
FDI	Foreign Direct Investment
FEPC	Federation of Electric Power Companies
FILP	Fiscal Investment and Loan Program
FSA	Financial Services Agency
GDP	Gross Domestic Product
GHLC	Government Housing Loan Corporation
GPIF	Government Pension Investment Fund
IAI	Independent Administrative Institution
IBJ	Industrial Bank of Japan
IMF	International Monetary Fund
IRCJ	Industrial Revitalization Corporation of Japan
JAERI	Japan Atomic Energy Research Institute
JAMA	Japan Automobile Manufacturers Association

JAPCO	Japan Atomic Power Company
JASME	Japan Corporation for Small & Medium-Size Enterprises
JBIC	Japan Bank of International Cooperation
JDB	Japan Development Bank
JETRO	Japan External Trade Organization
JFS	Japan Finance Corporation
JFTC	Japan Fair Trade Commission
JGB	Japan Government Bonds
JH	Japan Highway Corporation
JHF	Japan Housing Finance Agency
JNEPA	Japan Newspaper Editors and Publishers Association
JNFL	Japan Nuclear Fuel Cycle Co. Ltd.
JNOC	Japan National Oil Corporation
JOGMEC	Japan Oil, Gas and Metals National Corporation
JP	Japan Post
Keidanren	Japan Business Federation
KEPCO	Kansai Electric Power Co.
KYUDEN	Kyushu Electric Power Co.
LDP	Liberal Democratic Party of Japan
LTCB	Long-Term Credit Bank
MAC	Ministry of Agriculture and Commerce
MAFA	Ministry of Agriculture, Forestry and Fisheries
MCI	Ministry of Commerce and Industry
METI	Ministry of Economy, Trade and Industry
MEXT	Ministry of Education, Culture, Sports, Science and Technology
MHLW	Ministry of Health, Labor and Welfare
MIC	Ministry of Internal Affairs and Communications
MIPRO	Manufactured Imports and Investment Promotion Organization
MLIT	Ministry of Land, Infrastructure and Transportation
MM	Ministry of Munitions

MOC	Ministry of Construction
MOD	Ministry of Defense
MOF	Ministry of Finance
MOFA	Ministry of Foreign Affairs
MOX	Mixed Oxide Fuel
NCB	Nippon Credit Bank
NHK	Nippon Hoso Kyokai
NPL	Non-performing Loans
NRA	Nuclear Regulatory Agency
NSK	Nihon Shimbun Kyokai
NTT	Nippon Telephone and Telegraph
OECD	Organisation for Economic Co-operation and Development
OMFIF	Official Monetary and Financial Institutions Forum
PKO	Peacekeeping Operations
QE	Quantitative Easing
REER	Real Effective Exchange Rate
SCAP	Supreme Commander of the Allied Powers
SDF	Self-Defense Force
SOE	State-owned Enterprise
TEPCO	Tokyo Electric Power Company
TIRB	Temporary Industrial Rationalization Bureau
TSE	Tokyo Stock Exchange
UDC	Urban Development Corporation
UNCTAD	United Nations Conference on Trade and Development
URO	Urban Renaissance Organization
USTR	United States Trade Representative
WTO	World Trade Organization
YODEN	Shikoku Electric Power Co.

Introduction

'Japan Inc.' was a term used by the Western business community in the 1980s to describe the intimate ties between Japanese industry and the country's Ministry of International Trade and Industry or MITI (known since 2001 as the Ministry of Economy, Trade and Industry or METI). This relationship, as well as the relationship between the Ministry of Finance (MOF) and the finance sector, was commonly perceived to be the key factor in the resuscitation of Japan's industrial complex directly after the war, for its rapid economic growth by 1972 and subsequent success in global markets by the late 1970s. On the other hand, it was also viewed as a system which perpetuated mercantile policies, unfair trade practices and institutional corruption. What was not understood at the time was that the elements in Japan Inc. together with the abiding support from the Japanese electorate promoted the rigidity of an archaic and inward system of government administration.

Based on the assessment of entrenched vested interests in Japan's political economy and the rigidity of the Japan Inc. model, this book contends that structural reforms, the essential third arrow in Abe's 'Abenomics', will not happen. As a result, Abenomics is merely a combination of reckless monetary policy and ambiguous fiscal policies which will fail to regenerate Japan's fragile economy and cut sovereign debt. It also implies that Abe is not focusing efforts on reforms but on instilling an ultra-conservative, right-wing, nationalist mind-set in the political society which lends support to a revision of the Pacifist Constitution to allow Japan's gradual re-militarization.

The book reveals the inner workings of the Japan Inc. model and the dysfunctional nature of Japan's system of government administration prompted by three major events: the floating of the yen–dollar exchange rates (1985 Plaza Accord), the bursting of the asset-inflated bubble economy and the subsequent breakdown of political cohesion. The book argues that Japan has yet to recover from the aftermath of the bursting of the asset-inflated bubble in 1989. Japan has the highest public debt among OECD countries, currently at 243 percent of GDP. Although Japan is the world's third largest economy and the second largest net creditor, it has one of the lowest percentages of inward investment of the OECD countries, a result of its post-war mercantile policies.

By the early 1990s I was convinced that Japan was locked in a system of government which was rigid and inward and that nothing significant in the political economic system would change because the very rigidity of the system prevented the accommodation to rapidly changing needs on the home front and weakened the country's ability to withstand both internal and external crises. I predicted that Japan would suffer a prolonged recession and that, due to the political turmoil and the ministries' tight control of industrial production and domestic markets, the government would not succeed in implementing substantial reforms in order to deal effectively with Japan's economic stagnation. Indeed, structural reforms and the deregulation of markets would be more in image than in substance.

This book continues the arguments stated in my three previous Palgrave texts. It confirms the prediction made in *Japan's Nuclear Crisis* (2012) of the return of the Liberal Democratic Party (LDP) and the continuation of Japan Inc. and the rigid model of government administration. Shinzo Abe who was in office in 2006 is once again Prime Minister. His right-wing political philosophy is profoundly influenced by his late grandfather, Nobusuke Kishi, who was an elite ministry official in the Ministry of Commerce and Industry before and during the Second World War. Kishi, Japan's 57th Prime Minister (February 25, 1957–July 19, 1960) was the founder of the ultra-conservative LDP which dominated Japanese politics until 1993, hence the coining of the phrase, '1955 system'. The LDP's return to political dominance and Abe's determination to resuscitate Japan's economy through traditional policies that do not tackle structural reforms while implementing right-wing policies is illustrative of the durability of the rigid Japan Inc. model and government administration.

Revealing the genuine Japan Inc.

One of the primary factors in the rigidity of the governing system was Japan's national ministries' public corporations, otherwise known as

Special Corporations or Special Status Corporations until 2003 when they were re-orchestrated as Independent Administrative Institutions (IAIs) or as government-funded agencies, some of which serve as extensions of the ministries. However, due to the opaqueness of Japan's political society there were few books or articles in English or in Japanese that had been published in the 1990s to support either my analyses or my forecast regarding the inevitable deterioration of Japan's economy. Furthermore, the consensus opinion among the foreign business community, foreign governments and journalists, both Japanese and non-Japanese, was that Japan would recover through structural reforms and the deregulation of markets as promised continuously by the Japanese government.

Special Corporations and the Bureaucracy: Why Japan Can't Reform (2003) examined the elements in the political society which frustrated the structural reforms of the public sector, which resulted in the continuation of Japan's rigid and archaic system of government administration. The book jacket states:

> In an attempt to cut public spending, which was 140 percent of GDP in 2002, Prime Minister Koizumi of Japan has targeted public corporations – in particular, Special Corporations – for dissolution or restructuring. However, he is experiencing stiff opposition from vested interest groups, among them the national ministries. They are in charge of administering reforms but have come to rely on their Special Corporations and their numerous affiliates as vehicles that intensify control over industry and local government policy and equally as a good source of post-retirement positions for elite officials. The book explains (i) why there is strong political movement to dissolve special corporations; (ii) how the corporations can perpetuate the interests of the ministries, thus inhibiting structural reforms; (iii) how the fundamental characteristics of the Japanese political economic system gives the bureaucracy the power to continue operating corporations, despite political opposition; and (iv) how the corporations function to extend ministerial control over local government.

The book gives an in-depth analysis of Japan's political economic landscape and the elements in it that engendered a system which supported and sustained the ministries' organizations and institutional arrangements while simultaneously impeding the reform of the system.

The book's conclusion 'Non-Performing Reforms' reports the stark realities of Japan's recessive economy in 2003 and that despite the continuous release of stimulus packages together with the Bank of Japan lowering its official discount rate from 6.75 percent to near zero percent in 2001, none of the measures had alleviated Japan's economic malaise. In the section 'Forecast for Japan: too little too late?' I stated: 'At the time of writing the forecast for Japan's future as a global economic power is bleak.'[1]

Special Corporations: too hot to handle

The paucity of literature regarding Special Corporations in the 1990s was related to several factors:

1. Until the Law Concerning Access to Information Held by Administrative Organs was enacted in 1999 there was a minimum of information regarding how public corporations operated in terms of annual expenditure, how the corporations used their budgets and the source of the funds. In other words, operations were concealed from public scrutiny. The information available to the public is still scanty because the organizations are not required to reveal how they receive revenue other than tax revenue.
2. The efforts of academics and journalists to access comprehensive and reliable data about Japan's political economy are complicated by the insularity of organizations and their reticence to open their doors to either Japanese or non-Japanese observers. The Japanese social-political system is relatively opaque compared to Western industrialized nations and gaining a solid understanding of a given environment can be difficult and time-consuming. This is particularly true of ministerial operations, because the ministries are very protective of their territory and control the flow of information tightly. Furthermore, there are no records of court cases, debates or hearings as there are in the US and the UK.

Nevertheless, since the early 1990s as Japan's recessive economy continued unabated, the pressure to initiate structural reform of the public sector saw an increase of books and articles by Japanese commentators and politicians calling for the dissolution of Special Corporations because they advanced the vested interests of the ministries as well as an obsolete civil service system.

The books published in the early 1990s by Japanese freelance journalists and the editorial staff of major newspapers aggressively pursued the bureaucracy because of the corruption scandals involving officials in the MOF, the Ministry of Construction (MOC) and MITI. Special Corporations were also receiving more coverage. These books supported my assessment by 1995 of Special Corporations as a key element in the Japanese system of government administration. Since Japanese commentators were beginning to write about a politically contentious subject, I anticipated that there would be more articles that revealed the exhaustion of public revenue in the continued operation of many of these organizations that had essentially become white elephants and were perpetuating an archaic system of administration. Unfortunately, there was little information on the use and the financing of budgets of Special Corporations until 1997.

A welcome endorsement

The books in Japanese concerning Special Corporations are relatively short because authors are not obliged to detail Japan's political economic environment to Japanese. However, in order to explain to a foreign readership how the system evolved and why Special Corporations were central to the system it was vital to detail the evolution of Japan's political economy since the Meiji Restoration to set the stage for Japan's post-war system. I had not read any materials in English about Special Corporations until 2002. However, *Japan: Who Governs?* (1995) by the late Chalmers Johnson provided a good source in English regarding Special Corporations as well as some of the functions the organizations provided for the ministries.

Johnson, who was a professor of political science at the University of California, is regarded as one of the foremost scholars of the Japanese political economy. *MITI and the Japanese Miracle* (1979) and *Japan: Who Governs?* (1991) were best-sellers. His books and articles credit the elite officials in the MOF and MITI as the key planners of economic and industrial policies and impacted profoundly on the perceptions of academics and practitioners of the role that the bureaucracy played in the resuscitation of Japan's post-war industrial complex and economic recovery. Both texts are encyclopedias of Japan's government institutional structure and packed with definitions and valuable commentaries about the historical development of Japan's industrial and fiscal policies.

Special Corporations and the Bureaucracy (2003) cited these texts as well as papers contributed by well-recognized academics and commentators to Johnson's Japan Policy Research Institute (JPRI) concerning the historical development of Japan's political economic system, definitions of ministerial operations, and analyses of Japan's post-war economic development, including the implementation of mercantile and protectionist policies.

While organizing the book's bibliography in July 2003 I discovered that one of the papers cited required a date of publication. I telephoned the JPRI office in Cardiff, California to confirm, expecting to speak to a secretary. A man answered the phone and kindly gave me the date. When he asked me what I was writing I told him that the subject focused on the ministries' public corporations, not expecting him to know the subject. To my surprise, he said that he had published a short book on the ministries' public corporations in 1978.[2] I asked him his name and he replied that he was Chalmers Johnson. He generously offered to publish a chapter of my book on the JPRI website. But since the book was my first effort I was reticent to contact the publisher, who, for reasons of copyright, may have preferred that I did not contribute unpublished materials. In retrospect, I should have contributed at least an abstract.

I presumed that Johnson would not remember our brief conversation and that due to his busy schedule he would not have the time to open the book but after it was published I sent him a courtesy copy. To my surprise, on February 25, 2004 I received an email from Johnson thanking me for sending him a copy of the book. He congratulated me for publishing one of the few books in English about a subject that was at the 'very heart of Japanese government' and he hoped the book would be widely read. Professor Johnson also encouraged me to continue my research on Special Corporations.

I was immensely grateful for the positive response and relieved that Johnson understood the magnitude of the subject. His encouragement made me determined to plough ahead and continue publishing books which served to provoke a realistic evaluation of Japan Inc. and which insisted that the model would remain unchanged even though after the bursting of the asset-inflated bubble the government continuously reassured the international business community that structural reforms and the deregulation of markets would be initiated.

Accentuate the positive: the Japan Inc. syndrome

Through my employment in big business and government agencies after the bursting of the asset-inflated bubble, I was privy to a Japan

Inc. which contrasted considerably to the consensus opinion among the international business community that the Japan Inc. model had propelled Japan's post-war success in the global marketplace and that after the bursting of the asset-inflated bubble in 1989 the government would take measures to deregulate markets and initiate fiscal reforms in order to stimulate a floundering economy. Nevertheless, the image of success breeds success and the Japanese elite government officials and business owners, basking in these images, became arrogant and complacent despite the financial crisis and political scandals that rocked the very foundation of Japan Inc. and forced Prime Minister Noboru Takeshita to resign from office in April 1989.

In 1991, politicians began absconding from the LDP, the party that had controlled the National Diet since 1955, to form several splinter parties in an attempt to implement political and administrative reforms. But there was no indication that the government recognized the extent of Japan's problems nor did the banks want to divulge the load of outstanding loans to virtually bankrupt companies. There appeared to be a general denial among government officials that measures were needed urgently to carry forward initial reforms of the financial and administrative systems. Furthermore, the Japanese were conditioned by government and big business to believe that they were overtaking the US as the world's biggest economy and the largest net creditor. Japan was in control. Despite promises by government to implement fiscal reforms and to deregulate markets, it was clear that the post-war system of government was too rigid to accommodate the crisis and the ensuing recession.

Japan's nuclear crisis at the Fukushima nuclear power plant on March 11, 2010 dealt the economy a devastating blow. Nevertheless, the prognosis made by the international business community, think-tanks, major asset management houses and well-known economists was that the government's planned investment for the reconstruction of the affected region would serve to kick-start the economy, which had been in deflation for fifteen years and in and out of recession for twenty years. I disagreed.

A month after the nuclear disaster I received a request from BBC News Podcast for an interview regarding the impact of the crisis on Japan's economy. The interviewer began by asking me if Japan's pre-crisis economy would be resuscitated because of government investment in the reconstruction of the northeast. I replied that it was doubtful because prior to the crisis the economic conditions of the prefectures affected by the tragedy had been fragile and were in deflation as was also the case for Japan's other regions. As significantly, the continuation of political turmoil in the National Diet would serve to inhibit the passage of disaster bills and therefore the rate of reconstruction would be very slow.

Nevertheless, the interviewer and the producer wanted to focus on the state of the macro-economy. I explained that the macro-economy had been in deflation for many years and that it had yet to fully recover from the bursting of the 1989 asset-inflated bubble. In order to understand why the macro-economy would continue in deflation it was necessary to look at the economics at the regional level. The interviewer was surprised by my response because he considered Japan as an economy that had become the world's second largest by the 1980s with exports of home electronics and automobiles flooding international markets. Evidently, he and the producer were still immersed in the Japan Inc. phenomenon and wanted only the confirmation that the reconstruction of Japan's northeast would occur soon and that the macro-economy would reap the benefits.

The producer never responded to my queries about the program's airtime and several weeks later the BBC aired a five-minute program regarding the same subject which had been recorded in Tokyo. The participants were foreign economists and commentators who predicted that the reconstruction would serve to trigger an economic resuscitation.

The creation of a Wizard of Oz economy: why did commentators get it wrong?

The conclusion in the introduction of *Japan's Nuclear Crisis* 'Perception of Japan Inc.: busting myths' states:

> Prior to 11 March, despite fiscal policies that focused on the continuous release of stimulus packages and supplementary budgets, resulting in a burgeoning public debt, and despite the Bank of Japan's soft monetary policies as well as the efforts by successive administrations to implement structural reforms of the economy, Japan was stuck in deflation. Nevertheless, it was still widely believed that the Japanese government would be able to resolve the problems that had been inhibiting stable economic growth and dig Japan out of fifteen years of deflation.

When the United States was in recession in 1981 and Japanese electronics and automobiles were flooding global markets, the American Dream model of free-market capitalism, once considered the ideal model for economic development, was no longer in vogue. The international business community saw a new model, the Japan Inc. model, which appeared to be the driver of Japan's emergence as a major technological and industrial force. The main body of literature on Japan's political economy simply defined the elements in the governing system that were considered to be the principal reason for Japan's rise from the ashes of war to become a global industrial superpower. Emphasis was placed on the power of the bureaucracy and the domination of the conservative Liberal Democratic Party (LDP) in the National Diet. *Amakudari* was defined as the migration of former bureaucrats to positions in the private sector where they forged an abiding relationship between government and business, hence the coining of the term 'Japan Incorporated'.

Like his predecessors, Kan [Prime Minister] was controlled by a rigid and inward model of administration, which was dysfunctional in dealing with the mounting problems Japan had faced since 1990. The efforts of law-makers to reform the institutions and institutional arrangements that served to keep the model in place have progressed at a snail's pace. And there is no substitute for the current model that has paralyzed the policy-making process and prevented the Japanese from accommodating the ever-changing demands on the domestic economy and dealing with the instability of foreign markets. The Japanese must depend on this system to resuscitate an economy that has experienced the worst crisis since the end of Second World War. They fully recognize that the model is archaic and inward but, ironically, they also say that it could take something as significant as a major disaster to compel reforms.[3]

In 1995 an American CEO of a large construction company told me his experiences negotiating with executives of large Japanese companies in Tokyo in the 1980s:

I found the Japanese businessmen that I dealt with who were chairmen of the boards of cable companies, Japan Airlines and Nippon Airlines, to be very aloof and arrogant. I did not find them friendly people. When the business conversation ended they had the capability of turning the switch and becoming charming at dinner, although they were still arrogant.

He also remarked that prior to 1989 and the bursting of the asset-inflated bubble there was a lack of coverage in the American press about Japan:

> The American press and business publications built this myth (and maybe the Japanese had something to do with it) of quality and better management. Now we are coming around to saying, 'Maybe this myth is a myth.'

The constraints on first-hand observation and investigation

The Japanese, pointing to the difficulty of the Japanese language and portraying it as ambiguous and grammatically illogical, tend to dismiss the common complaint by foreigners that they encounter barriers to accessing information relevant to their interests. In reality, the Japanese tend to protect their privacy and conceal themselves from outside observation through their language. Japanese organizations can use the language as a fire-wall and, therefore, impenetrable to foreign observation. Foreign media have been objecting for years about the barriers and are obliged to work within a certain context and conditions and, therefore, reporting is confined to accommodating these conditions. Their publications may not assess the entire story and their analyses of current events may also be incomplete. However, it also must be emphasized that there is little information sharing between divisions in Japanese organizations, which will be discussed in a subsequent chapter.

The efforts of academics and commentators to access reliable information is further complicated by the insularity of organizations and their reticence to open their doors to outside observation by both Japanese and non-Japanese. The Japanese social political system is relatively opaque compared to those of Western industrialized nations and gaining a solid understanding of a given environment can be difficult and time-consuming. This is particularly true of ministerial operations because the ministries are very protective of their territory and tightly control the flow of information. Indeed, ministries are not forthcoming with other ministries and even divisions within ministries are reticent to share data with other divisions. Often interviews are conducted with senior officials who prefer to speak in general terms about their organizations. Furthermore, investigative journalists and analysts have difficulty gathering reliable data concerning ministerial policies.

In an interview in 1994 Bill Whittaker, who was the chief correspondent in Japan for CBS Television from 1989 to 1993, commented on the difficulties involved in accessing information from government agencies:

> I do think that the bureaucracy controls the information, not that they manipulate the story but what they choose to reveal and when they choose to reveal it. They play it close to the vest. If they do not want it to get out, it pretty well won't get out. I think that if the bureaucracy decides that the information stays within the bureaucracy, my god, that's where it stays![4]

Foreign observers are also confronted by the language barrier. Both private and public corporations prefer to use special representatives who speak English to communicate. Many of them have been sent to universities abroad not only to study but, also, to learn how to interact with foreigners so that they can develop skills that enable them to protect and promote their organization's interests and to fend off criticism. Japanese who are not part of the organizations they wish to observe will also be accommodated by these official representatives.

Whittaker, who relied on Japanese interpreters and staff at Tokyo Broadcasting System (TBS) to access stories said:

> What I found, also, was when it came to the bureaucracy, for the press clubs that operated in different bureau, if the Secretary [of the particular bureau] said: 'No, you're not going to get that information', that was about the end of it. From what I understood, if a journalist fell into disfavor within his club and its secretary, he would get even less information the next go-around. If reporters incur disapproval from the press club they may be sanctioned. They may even be expelled from the club.[5]

Whittaker also said that if news was regarded as international relations, press clubs would open doors to foreign journalists no matter their affiliation. He was referring to Japan's press clubs, commonly known as *kisha* clubs. In *Japan's Nuclear Crisis*'s chapter entitled '"Information-Sharing" is Not a Buzz-Word in Japan: Press Clubs Insulate an Insular Political Economy' the section titled 'Press clubs: information cartels control the flow of information' explains that the formation of press clubs can be traced to 1890, around the same time Japan's new bureaucracy was established to modernize a feudal Japan. Japanese reporters insisted on entry into the sessions held by the Imperial Diet. Since then, press clubs have served as the major purveyor of information from the ministries and from the Diet to both Japanese and foreign media.

Reporters, commentators and journalists who belong to news organizations and who are covering government activities are assigned to press clubs (*kisha kurabu*) which are located in offices that are set up to gather news from major organizations such as the ministries, the Prime Minister's office, political headquarters, local parliament and police headquarters, as well as consumer, entertainment and sports organizations. The organizations offer rooms, telephones and some administrative assistance.

There are now approximately 1,000 press clubs located throughout Japan with members ranging from approximately fifteen to twenty, with the major Japanese dailies regarded as regular club members. The Prime Minister's Club can have over 500 members and the Diet Club can have as many as 5,000 members. Some IAIs and semi-private organizations such as the Japan Broadcasting Company (NHK), Nippon Telephone and Telegraph (NTT), the ministries such as the Ministry of Public Management, Home Affairs, Post and Telecommunications also operate their own press clubs. Japan Railroad (JR) and the power utilities have press clubs. Reporters and journalists representing domestic and foreign media are assigned to one club and can remain in that club for their entire career.

The members of press clubs receive information first. There is a close interpersonal relationship between reporters and their press clubs which prompts reporters to cooperate in the manner of questioning the news source and the way that the information is released to the public. As Whittaker stated, if reporters incur disapproval from the press club they may be sanctioned. They may even be expelled from the club.

The Japan Newspaper Association or Nihon Shimbun Kyokai (NSK), also known as the Japan Newspaper Publishers and Editors Association (JNEPA), plays a fundamental role in choosing which newspapers, journals and television stations can enter a specific club. The NSK was founded by Japanese media on July 23, 1946. It is an independent organization based on voluntary membership. The members include the major dailies throughout Japan and television stations, which are also affiliated with the newspapers.

The NSK website states that new members, including news agencies and broadcasters, are chosen by the board of directors and must abide by the Canon of Journalism:

> The prerequisites for membership require that the applying organization pledge to observe the Canon of Journalism as adopted by NSK at the time of its foundation and that it pass an NSK screening to determine whether its recent reporting activities are in contravention of the Canon of Journalism.[6]

According to NSK, as of November 2010 there were 113 members, including 106 daily newspapers, four news agencies and twenty-three broadcasters. The newspapers must have a circulation of over 10,000. Trade papers and political party organizations cannot enter the NSK. The NSK describes one objective as raising ethical standards and a second objective as protecting media's common interests: 'In the course of NSK history, emphasis shifted gradually to the second objective of protecting common interests, centering on the business activities of newspapers.'

Since the NSK decides on who enters which press club, accessing information is controlled and, therefore, restricted. The interlocking and vested corporate interests strengthen the press club system because the major newspapers are directly or indirectly linked to broadcasters, namely television and radio stations. Japan has five national newspapers; the *Asahi, Yomiuri, Mainichi, Sankei* and *Nikkei.* There are two major news agencies, Jiji Press and Kyodo News. Six broadcast companies constitute the government's public broadcasting system: Nippon Hoso Kyokai (NHK), TV Asahi, TBS (Tokyo Broadcasting System), Fuji TV, NTV (Nippon Television) and TV Tokyo. These organizations tend to control the activities of the press clubs. The direct and indirect institutional connections support the approach of Japanese mass media's conveyance of information to the public and Western journalists often comment on the homogeneous nature of news reporting by Japanese media. Japanese and foreign news providers who are not members of the press clubs experience difficulty accessing primary data.

The NSK's Kisha Club Guidelines states:

> Japan's media industry has a history of applying pressure to public institutions reluctant to disclose information by banding together in the form of the kisha club. The kisha club is an institution and system fostered by Japan's media industry for over a century in pursuit

of freedom of speech and freedom of press ... The fundamental purpose of the kisha club system, which has been closely involved with the general public's 'right to know', remains unchanged today.[7]

NSK claims that the press clubs enable access to information from public organizations making fast, in-depth and accurate reporting feasible.

However, the European Commission in Japan on October 17, 2002 issued *Priority Proposals for Regulatory Reform in Japan*, which called the press clubs 'serious barriers to the free trade of information'. The report stated:

> With the exception of a limited number of wire services (which, if they are members at all, often have only associate membership and, therefore, can listen but have no right to ask questions), membership is denied to journalists from foreign media organizations. It is worth noting that *shukan-shi*, or mass-circulation weekly magazines are also excluded, as well as specialized press covering sectors other than those directly related to the host body.[8]

The report delineated the root of the problem of accessing reliable data that is cited here:

1. Officials and the hierarchy of the *kisha* club have the means to prevent the spread of information that they may consider disadvantageous, on pain of exclusion of the offending journalist from the club. The system thus acts against the public interest, since it may deny or delay access to important information, including, for example, information or direct relevance to public health and safety.
2. By giving both officials and journalists a vested interest in maintaining exclusivity of a story, the system encourages over-reliance on a single source of information and lack a cross-checking, thus diminishing the quality of information available to the wider public.
3. The system encourages the widespread and undesirable practice of split briefings for domestic and foreign journalists, increasing the potential for information to be tailored to one or the other audience by the briefing party, and exacerbating the risk of spreading inaccurate and biased information about Japan.

The Commission threatened to raise the problem with the World Trade Organization (WTO). Although the NSK refuted the statement, made in its reply to the accusations, Etienne Reuter, a representative of the Commission stated at a December 2003 news conference:

> We reject the statement that our proposals are based on misunderstanding, cultural bias and misconception of facts.

The NSK acquiesced to the pressure in February 2004 and agreed to allow foreign journalists easier access to government information.

An interview with an economics correspondent from the government-funded NHK posted in New York in 1994 revealed his difficulties in accessing stories in the United States:

> When American journalists cover America, they have the advantage. When Japanese journalists cover Japan, we have the advantage, not only because of language but, also, because we have many friends. It is true that in Japan, we can visit company executives' homes at night on the so-called 'night round'. This sometimes allows us to get an exclusive or an 'off-the-record'. So, open press conferences are not as common as in the United States because the important questions have already been asked. I go to Wall Street to meet many Japanese bankers and Japanese security companies and American economists. It is very difficult to enter this silent circle. Although I can get interviews, in order to access good information I must have a friend among them. Still, as a journalist, I don't approve of any barriers to foreign journalists. We have to change our ways and make all information available to everyone.[9]

In defense of Japan's major dailies: detailed coverage but not in English

The major newspapers and political economic magazines are good sources for keeping up to date with Japan's political economy. Unfortunately, the number of news items selected by the major newspapers for their English editions are very small and do not include regional and domestic economic, political and social news coverage, including politically contentious issues. In terms of covering hard news, the Japanese press differs little from the UK press but the

Japanese editions tend to carry far more news items on regional economic and political issues, which serve to facilitate a realistic assessment of the macro-political economy. Reporting on international news is excellent and the daily news regarding China and South Korea is far more detailed. Reports on China and South Korea can be biased reflecting Japan's defensive stance with its Asian neighbors and favoring Japan's national interests, but, generally, the facts are accurate.

Foreign asset management houses also experience barriers in accessing comprehensive information in English. Govinda Finn who is a member of the global strategy team at Standard Life Investments focuses his research on Japan and emerging markets. Although he is able to read Japanese, in an interview he spoke about the gap between sources available in English and in Japanese:

> There are quite high barriers in terms of time to access a comprehensive data set. I am blessed (or perhaps cursed) with the ability to navigate through Japanese language data and it is very clear that there is a great deal more data in the Japanese sources than there is in the English language sources. In order to cover that data well requires a lot of time as it is never displayed in an intuitive fashion. We were looking at the hollowing out of Japan and overseas production ratios. METI has a good series of overseas production ratios but in the end we decided to use the Cabinet Office's data. But it is a challenge to identify this data because it is not available on our data providers, Bloomberg and Data Stream. This is fairly typical and we don't use a Japanese specialist data provider.
>
> I have a number of spread sheets which cover Japanese data which I use to follow developments in Japan and construct our forecast and most of that is partial data such as retail sales, balance of payment-type data. The other sources of information are the ministries' websites but it takes experience and expertise to understand where the duplications are. Again, the headings are not intuitive and going through them takes time. Of course, we have access to strategy economic departments at investment banks and other research companies.
>
> The broker-coverage comes from investment banks but quite often you see the gap between the English language and the key indicators that one might get through Data Stream. We don't like to use data unless we can verify where it comes from and which we can replicate. I spend a lot of my time trying to work out exactly where the investment

banks have acquired their data from. I can access more data in Japanese through Japanese brokers but there still is a lot that entails trying to verify or replicate.[10]

What you see is not what you get

The Japanese press has been accused of being homogeneous and providing readers with news that favors the organizations that pay for advertising space and allow access to their press clubs. Since its inception in 1890 the *kisha* club system has developed into an institution that is controlled through the vested interests of major media organizations, the private corporations, politicians and the bureaucracy. The system is comparable to a mini Japan Inc., paralleling the insularity and rigidity of Japan's system of government administration that was also established in the 1890s. There is an expectation among the foreign media that Japan is an open political society and that accessing political and economic information can be facilitated quickly because the country is the world's third largest economy and appears to have Westernized since the end of the Second World War through Western-style democratization. Also, Japanese multinationals have huge outward investment and automobile and electronic manufacturers have achieved astounding success in global markets.

However, after three years as a correspondent in Japan, Bill Whittaker came to the conclusion:

> I think that what fools you, what is seductive but on the surface is that it looks familiar. You've got tall buildings, freeways, subways and Western dress and all sorts of things that can lull you into feeling that you can relate to it and understand ... But if you're there for a while, you begin to realize that it is just a thin veneer, that the real Japan is behind or beneath that thought, that Western thought.[11]

Shinzo Abe's book *Toward a Beautiful Country* (*Utsukushii Kuni E*)[12] was published in 2006 a few months before he entered office for the first time and which is discussed in both my earlier 2008 and 2012 books. While bemoaning the fact that the word 'conservatism' was often considered in negative terms, he contended that the Japanese had been a conservative nation for several thousand years and that their society was a conservative society.

Ultra-conservatism together with the system of administration continues with the LDP and Abe's return to power. The elements explicit to this system are:

1. A rigid socio-political system with the bureaucracy invested with the power to plan and implement Japan's post-war economic growth without being subject to legal sanctions.
2. The close cooperation between business, the bureaucracy and the National Diet that began in the late nineteenth century during the Meiji Restoration. The finely tuned relationship continued before and after the Second World War.
3. A conservative political party that has supported the bureaucracy's policies consistently during Japan's post-war period.
4. The network of former bureaucrats and present bureaucrats throughout business and government, which greatly enhances bureaucratic power to enforce policy at both the national and local government levels.
5. Significant social pressure to accept government guidance.

The conditions stated above have impacted considerably on the sources available to foreign commentators and media, the end result being a continuous barrage for years of sound-bites in the foreign press and media and analyses by academics, economists, international think-tanks and commentators that do not take into consideration the inflexibility of Japan's political economic model and that Japan's lopsided economy has been unstable for years. But the image of success encourages the expectation that the world's third largest economy will get its act together.

Seeing is believing

In the summer of 2001 I was giving a program for Japanese small and medium-size business owners at Hofstra University located in Long Island, New York. One of the participants was a Japanese woman who had been sent by an affiliate of Nippon Telephone and Telegraph (NTT), a huge Special Corporation managed by the former Ministry of Post and Communications of which, although privatized, the government owns one-third of shares in the holding company. Several years earlier upon graduating from a university in Tokyo, she entered the company's Strategy Division. She confided that she had never really known or understood her own society until she had entered a Japanese corporation.

It was an astonishing revelation. I presumed that as a Japanese who had been raised and educated in Japan she would have adapted quickly to Japanese corporate culture. I had also presumed that having resided in Japan for seven years in circumstances comparable to middle-class Japanese prior to entering a Japanese firm and that having reasonable fluency in the Japanese language would serve to alleviate a significant degree of corporate culture shock. However, it was not until I began working for Japanese corporations and government agencies that I saw Japan Inc. unmasked.

Research methodology

An important feature of this book is how issues are introduced and addressed through the medium of work experiences in Japanese organizations which serve to highlight the integration of business and government in the socio-political context.

Fluency in Japanese was requisite to having direct access to information culled from sources within those organizations. The work involved a comprehensive knowledge of Japan's political culture and current events. Expertise regarding Japan's markets was also a requisite to gaining employment. The work in diverse organizations allowed an understanding of the nuances of the language as well as organizational behavior without relying on standard social and historical interpretations. In other words, it is best to participate as a member of the system in order to maintain objectivity. Although this book as well as the three previous texts may appear to be critical of the bureaucracy, I am among many Japanese who favor the ministries rather than the politicians to plan policies. It is the methods of implementation of these policies that serve to rigidify Japan's government system.

Objectives

The book details the reasons for the policies planned and implemented by the ministries prior to the bursting of the asset-inflated bubble economy in 1989 in order to explain their impact on Japan's current economic dilemma including: (i) why large businesses failed, despite substantial capital investment and loans from creditors; (ii) why banks continued to loan (and still continue to loan) to zombie companies while accumulating non-performing loans on their books and, as a consequence, were pressured by government to merge operations; (iii) the reasons for the reticence of banks to change banking behavior despite more regulation and monitoring by the MOF and FSA; (iv) the consequences of continued mercantile policies, non-tariff barriers and trade issues; (v) the consequences of pork-barrel policies in the rural prefectures now that the government is reducing subsidies for public works; and (vi) institutional corruption leading to agency failure.

The book evaluates the consequences of Japan's protectionist policies throughout the last two decades on issues plaguing Japan's current economic environment, including continued deflation, despite ongoing quantitative easing (QE) and low interest rates.

While the 2003 and 2008 texts focused on the mechanisms used by the ministries to implement non-tariff barriers in order to protect domestic markets from foreign competition, this book looks at some of the strategies used by domestic producers who market and distribute foreign clients' products which they consider competitive with their own brands.

The book discusses: (i) the tendency of Japanese firms to over-invest and abandon their core competencies since the mid-1980s; (ii) creditor–corporate relations (percentages of shares and directorships); (iii) nuclear power as a perfect representation of pork-barrel patronage and the Japan Inc. system; and (iv) the underlying reasons for the revision of Article 9 to allow collective self-defense and the export of weapons in the context of Japan's relationship with China and the ROK while supporting the heavy industries' alliance with foreign producers.

The book describes Japan's post-war political and economic conditions at the time the policies were made, the reasons why the policies were implemented, how these policies impacted on Japan's political economy and on the Japanese, and why the effects of these policies continue to impact today.

Much has been written about how the policies that were planned and forged by the economic and industrial ministries (MOF and MITI) expedited Japan's post-war recovery and rapid economic growth. Regardless of the hype, the United States' post-war policies and the Japanese leaders in political office during that time were equally responsible for Japan's success in global markets.

The issues have resonance with many of the issues facing other developed economies subsequent to the 2008 global financial crisis. The behavior-reaction of these economies in terms of monetary and fiscal policies and stirrings of nationalism is converging with that of Japan, increasing the relevance of the book to a wider audience. Although there are differences as well, readers will see parallels with the fiscal and economic policies and political movements in their countries. Japan is an extreme example of an economy that has not been able to adapt to either internal or external impacts. The book gives a powerful lesson about the dangers for any country where the vested interests of business and government create a self-sustaining, mutually supportive but, ultimately, destructive political regime.

1
Back to Basics?

Kishi's legacy is Abe's legacy

Prime Minister Nobusuke Kishi (1957–60) is credited with being the father of the LDP and, also, the king-pin of the 1955 political system that was based on the collaboration between politicians, businessmen and bureaucrats and banked with huge sums from the private sector. The LDP controlled the National Diet for thirty-eight years until 1993 and from 1996–2009. Abe's LDP roots and his right-wing political ideology are inherited from his grandfather, the late Prime Minister Nobusuke Kishi, whom he extols in his book *Toward a Beautiful Country*, published shortly after he entered the executive office in 2006. Now that the LDP once again holds the majority of seats in the National Diet, it is likely that the '1955 political system' will continue. With the exception of a three-year break, from 1993–6, and a five-year break, from 2009–13, the LDP has dominated Japanese politics since 1955, hence the term '1955 political system'.

In most Western countries, no single political party has been in power long enough to give bureaucrats consistent support in drafting laws and implementing policies, nor are there democratic societies where ministries can operate unfettered by legal sanction as they do in Japan, despite the well-publicized scandals involving ministerial misconduct. There are three key reasons for this support:

1. Japan's political economic system can be characterized as pork-barrel and protectionist. Big business and business federations made large contributions to the LDP coffers. The LDP received votes and large donations from traditional support groups, such as small local firms

and from businesses engaged in construction, transportation and telecommunications, in exchange for public works projects.
2. The LDP received substantial support from special interest groups, such as industrial associations and federations.
3. There is a network of bureaucrats throughout Japan's socio-political system. Bureaucrats traditionally have sought political office in both national and local government Diets and as governors and vice-governors in the prefectures. When the snap election was held on September 11 after Koizumi dissolved the Lower House in 2005 ninety-five former government officials ran for seats, fifty-seven on the LDP ticket and twenty-five on the DPJ (Democratic Party of Japan) ticket. Koizumi himself recruited a female elite career official from the MOF to stand in the election.

Toward a Beautiful Country was a best-seller. In it Abe argues that the reporting of events regarding his grandfather's revision of the US–Japan Security Treaty was misleading and should be corrected. The initial 1951 treaty inhibited the Japanese from prosecuting Americans who perpetrated crimes in Japan (e.g. military personnel). Abe claimed that his grandfather negotiated a revised treaty that gave Japan more autonomy from the United States and gave the Japanese more power to prosecute. Abe also maintained in his book that the history of Japan's war-time engagement in China reported in textbooks was also incorrect and should be revised as well. An interview conducted with a Japanese civil servant posted in New York in the 1990s included details of his education regarding Japan's military engagement in Asia during the Second World War. The official spoke about his school's textbooks.

> The textbooks in Japan do not really touch upon the Second World War. How it should be written before it is published is the problem. Historians say that the war should be written about as it actually happened (like Japan's occupation of China) but the government says that Japan is not a terrible country, so there are conflicting views.[1]

Prime Minister Abe, whose uncle Eisaku Sato was Japan's longest serving Prime Minister (1964–72) and whose father was a career LDP politician who represented Yamaguchi Prefecture in the Lower House (1959–91), was raised from birth in an ultra-conservative milieu. After the death of his father in 1991 Abe succeeded him in the Lower House. Like his grandfather, Abe's political philosophy is immersed in nationalism and his 2006–7 administration focused on promoting bills that would serve the national interest, such as the reinstatement of the Ministry of Defense and an intended revision of Article 9 in the Constitution, which renounces war, to allow Japan's military (the SDF) to defend Japan if attacked. Abe is adamant that the US–Japan Security Treaty is at the center of Japan's defense policy, which was also central to Kishi's defense policies. However, Abe's political motivation focuses on the perceived threats from China's rise as an economic and military power in Asia.

Abe, whom Koizumi had hand-picked to succeed him as Prime Minister in 2006, staunchly defended Koizumi's six pilgrimages to Yasukuni Shrine where not only Japanese military dead are interned but also Class A war criminals. The Shinto shrine was founded in 1869 and run by the military until the end of the Second World War, when the United States outlawed Shintoism. Infuriated by Koizumi's apparent glorification of Japan's military past and disregard of the suffering incurred by the Chinese and Koreans during Japan's wartime occupation, China and North and South Korea lodged vehement protests. Despite angering important trading partners and Japanese pacifists, as well as businessmen whose ventures in China and South Korea were vandalized by Chinese and South Korean protesters and who were extremely concerned about the ramifications for future Japanese–Chinese economic relations, Koizumi continued his visits to the shrine. Abe and members of his cabinet also continue the tradition despite protests from China and the ROK. He states in his book that Class A war criminals are not regarded as criminals under Japanese law.

Abe supported Koizumi's education bill in June 2006 that for the first time revised the education law that had been written in 1947. The new bill included the promotion of 'patriotism' as part of compulsory education, which had not been addressed in the 1947 education law. Although members of the DPJ voted against the bill because it might promote nationalism, the bill was passed into law in January 2007 during Abe's administration. The Basic Education Law calls, for the first time since the Second World War, for singing the national anthem and saluting the Japanese flag at school ceremonies. The law also gives the Education Minister more power over local education boards and requires that teachers renew their licenses every ten years.

On May 23, 2008 government again defied opposition to the promotion of nationalism among schoolchildren by voiding a 1949 ban on public school trips to Yasukuni Shrine. The reason given for restoring the excursions was that they would serve to educate students about Japanese culture and history.

My earlier books (2008 and 2012) included discussion regarding Abe's hands-on promotion of the *New History Textbook* for high schools which ignores Japan's Second World War military atrocities in Asia. When he was re-elected Prime Minister in 2013, Abe emphasized the need to revise Japanese history textbooks further to be less apologetic about Japan's military engagement in Asia. In January 2014 Abe's ministers announced that textbooks will be revised to emphasize that the Senkaku and Takeshima Islands are Japanese territories in order to teach Japanese children to 'properly understand our territory', an announcement which further exacerbated the already heated relationship with China and the ROK.

Deputy Prime Minister Taro Aso: Abe's side-kick

Aso's roots are directly connected to the Meiji period. His great-great-grandfather was Toshimichi Okubo who was a *samurai* in the Satsuma Clan and instrumental in the overthrow of the military ruler (*Shogun*) and one of the key planners in the Meiji government (1868–1912). Aso succeeded Yasuo Fukuda as Prime Minister in September 2008. He left office a year later when the DPJ won a landslide election to gain the majority in the Lower House. Aso wears a coat of many colors in Abe's current cabinet. Besides serving as Deputy Prime Minister, he is also Minister of Finance and State Minister for Financial Affairs.

By Japanese political standards Aso's birthright is sterling. His maternal grandfather was Prime Minister Shigeru Yoshida who was Japan's 45th Prime Minister (1946–7) and Japan's 48th Prime Minister (1948–54). Aso's wife was the third daughter of Prime Minister Zenko Suzuki (1980–2) and one of his sisters was the wife of the first cousin of Emperor Akihito. His father was the chairman of Aso Cement Company and his son joined Aso Mining where he served as president for four years before entering politics in 1979.

Compared to his deputy, Abe could be considered a 'dove'. Aso's right-wing ultra-conservative ideology and glorification of Japan's colonization days in East Asia replicates Abe's and his opinions have been well publicized in the press during his political career. Despite his frequent public outbursts espousing his neo-nationalist sentiments, he remains as Abe's second-in-command. In 2005, he touted Japan as a mono-culture with one race, one language and one civilization, excluding other ethnic groups such as Chinese and Koreans.

When he ran for president of the LDP in his bid for the office of Prime Minister in 2005, Aso's platform regarding foreign relations was 'Arc of freedom and prosperity: Japan's Expanding Diplomatic Horizons', which may also be interpreted as a reiteration of the Meiji slogan, 'Prosperous Country, Strong Country, Strong Military'. In 2006, Aso admonished the Japanese that China, with a population of one billion people, possessed nuclear bombs and had expanded its military budget by double figures for seventeen consecutive years.

During Aso's term as Prime Minister in 2008, the Western media reported that Aso Mining had forced 300 Allied prisoners to work without pay in the Aso Mining Company in 1945 and that two Australian prisoners had died. Furthermore, 10,000 Koreans were recruited to work under cruel conditions, many of whom had died. Although former laborers requested an apology, Aso refused to reply.[2]

Aso continued his nationalist rhetoric at an ultra-conservative conference in Tokyo on July 29, 2013. He criticized the lack of support for revising Article 9, stating that the Japanese should follow the example of the Nazis who, in order to avoid protests, secretly revised the Weimar Constitution to the Nazi Constitution. Aso recommended that the Japanese should learn from these tactics. He also encouraged secret visits to Yasukuni Shrine in order to avoid diplomatic outbursts. He refused to apologize or resign from office but retracted his statement, blaming misinterpretation by *Kyodo News* the newspaper which reported the event.

Birds of a feather

A number of key politicians in the DPJ share similar ultra-conservative ideologies and nationalistic sentiments. Former Prime Minister Yoshihiko Noda served as Finance Minister in Naoto Kan's cabinet (2010–11). Although he did not visit Yasukuni Shrine on August 15, 2011, marking the 66th anniversary of Japan's surrender in the Second World War, at a press conference held on the same day he reiterated Abe's contention that Japanese Class A war criminals were not regarded as criminals under Japanese law and that he saw no reason for a Prime Minister not to visit the shrine. Incensed by Noda's rhetoric, the South Korea Foreign Ministry issued a statement pronouncing Noda's words as a denial of Japan's past history of aggression.[3]

Noda, who vigorously supports the US–Japan Security Treaty, also has strong anti-communist sentiments and views China's economic expansion overseas and growing military budget as a signal that Japan is losing its competitive edge in outward investment in global markets and that China is fast becoming a military superpower in Asia.

On August 29, 2011 two days before he was elected DPJ president, at a news conference Noda alluded to China as 'a nation that is mixing economic growth and nationalism'. A week later, as the newly elected Prime Minister, he vowed to strengthen Japan's defense capabilities to protect territorial rights. Noda also pledged on September 11 that his government would continue the effort to bring all of the Japanese who were abducted by North Korea back to Japan.

Seiji Maehara was the DPJ policy chief during Noda's administration. A defense hawk, he gave a keynote speech on September 7 at a symposium for Japanese and US security experts in Washington, DC. Maehara's speech addressed exactly the same issues that Abe, his heavily right-wing cabinet and political allies were addressing. The speech, entitled 'Japan–US Alliance in Multinational Cooperation', called for a review of the five principles that strictly limit the use of weapons by the SDF in order to enable Japanese to support the United States and other foreign forces if they come under attack. He also sought a review of the three principles that formally banned the export of weapons and advocated the relaxation of regulations to enable Japan to develop and produce weapons with the United States and other countries. Maehara referred to China as 'a game changer' and a nation trying to revise international affairs.

Towards the end of Noda's administration the government purchased the Senkaku Islands from the owner, a Japanese real estate developer.

Abe's political agenda

There were major concerns among the electorate that Abe was not focusing his energy on economic recovery and his 'third arrow' of structural reforms but on establishing a solid ultra-conservative right-wing political landscape. Kishi's ideology was reflected in Abe's agenda which included the revision of the Pacifist Constitution's Article 9,[4] allowing Japan the right to collective self-defense by amending the interpretation of the Pacifist Constitution which renounces the right to wage war. Central to Abe's defense policy was the US–Japan Security Treaty (which Kishi had attempted to revise as a prelude to revising the Constitution) and the expansion of military capability in response to the Senkaku Islands dispute with China. Prioritizing the defense of the islands, Abe's cabinet approved his defense plan in December 2013 which called for a \$235– \$245 billion budget to cover a four-year period for beefing up Japan's military hardware. Abe also wanted the formal ban on the export of weapons lifted, which was expected to be included in the revised Constitution.

When Shinzo Abe's 'State Secrets Law' was pushed through the National Diet with little public debate on December 6, 2013, the Japanese media, expecting to receive gag orders from the government and to be subjected to barriers to accessing information, protested vigorously. Also known as the National Security Act, the law defined 'special secrets' as sensitive information on diplomacy and counter-espionage. Over 60 percent of the electorate, comparing it to the pre-war and wartime Peace Preservation Act which was implemented by government to quell political opposition, objected to the law because of its lack of detail of what constituted 'state secrets' and because it indicated that the government would have more control over the population.

People who are arrested on suspicion of leaking 'state secrets' can be detained in prison without trial. Those who are found guilty can be imprisoned for up to ten years and journalists who are convicted of trying to obtain classified information can be imprisoned for up to five years. Although politicians denied that the law would be used to restrict the press or the public's 'right to know', Justice Minister Sadakazu Tanigaki, the former LDP president who was defeated by former Prime Minister Yoshihiko Noda in the 2011 election, did not rule out the possibility of police raids on newspapers suspected of breaking the law.

Abe's law harkens back to his grandfather Prime Minister Nobusuke Kishi's attempt to centralize police power and restore to the police some of their former authority such as the right to search suspected criminals. In 1960 the Japanese were still enveloped in a shroud of wartime suffering and public protests erupted against what was regarded as the resuscitation of war-time 'thought control'. There were strikes and demonstrations supported by labor unions. Socialist law-makers rioted in the Diet and tried to kidnap the Speaker to prevent a vote. Three members of Kishi's cabinet resigned, forcing him to shelve the bill.

In March 2014 Prime Minister Abe's administration relaxed the law that banned the manufacturing and exporting of weapons with the intention to revise the Constitution to allow the formal manufacturing, sale and export of weapons. The United Nations approved of the use of Japanese produced weapons in countries where UN troops are stationed on condition that the weapons are not used by internal forces. Previously, Japanese firms were prohibited to sell arms to communist countries, countries that were sanctioned by the UN or countries engaged in war. The relaxation allowed Japanese industry to produce certain products related to military use such as mine-sweepers or parts for military hardware such as tanks and fighter planes. Japanese companies could also engage in joint ventures with foreign firms in the development of new weapon systems. Several reasons for loosening the law were to support Japan's defense industry to enter new markets and to beef up Japan's military spending. On July 6, *Nikkei Business* reported that Japan would approve the first arms export under the new guidelines. Mitsubishi Heavy Industries is exporting to the US its high-performance sensor used in the Patriot Advanced Capability-2 (PAC-2) surface to air missile, which the US is delivering to Qatar.

Abe's reinterpretation of the Pacifist Constitution's Article 9 would give Japan the right to collective self-defense against invasion, to allow the deployment of military personnel abroad, to substantially increase its military budget and allow the production and export of weapons. He justified changing the official government reinterpretation of Article 9 by stressing that Japan must engage in a 'proactive contribution to peace'. The change would allow Japan to aid allies who are attacked militarily, although Japan has already assisted US military operations through logistic support and participated in international peacekeeping operations. The government presented eight possible events that would require SDF deployment. Four scenarios concerned international cooperation, including peacekeeping operations (PKO) when the SDF could use weapons. Another example was that the SDF could enter combat zones on the Korean Peninsula to rescue Japanese citizens after receiving the go ahead from the ROK, contradicting Abe's previous statement to Diet members that the SDF would not engage in the Korean Peninsula. Assistant Cabinet Secretary Nobushige Takamizawa's suggestion in September 2013 that the SDF be deployed to defend friendly nations located further afield triggered concern among some Japanese that Japan could be involved in American wars. Voters also feared that collective self-defense was only the first step towards full militarization.

A survey conducted by the *Asahi Shimbun* prior to the July 21, 2013 Upper House election revealed that 75 percent of the respondents favored constitutional revision, which was more than the two-thirds majority needed to initiate a constitutional amendment. When respondents were asked if they also would favor passage of the revision with only a simple majority only 52 percent answered in the affirmative.

Constitutional revisions can only be implemented when supported by two-thirds of Diet members followed by a national referendum. However, Abe was trying to push the revision of Article 9 through a cabinet decision by September 2014. An *Asahi Shimbun* survey of 3,728 voters was conducted by telephone on May 24–25, 2014. Of those, 1,657 or 44 percent responded. The newspaper reported that 55 percent of respondents were opposed to the reinterpretation to allow collective self-defense. Sixty-seven percent of respondents considered Abe's procedure for driving through the revision of Article 9 as unacceptable. Fifty percent of respondents believed that collective self-defense would lead to more conflicts.

Abe was also facing opposition from the coalition partner New Komeito because members envisioned that the enactment of collective self-defense would lead to the abuse of the right to collective self-defense and a major revision of the Constitution. But on July 1, 2014 an agreement was reached by the cabinet on the reinterpretation of Article 9 based on three new standards, which would allow Japan to exercise collective self-defense if directly attacked, assist friendly nations which are under attack and whose enemies pose a real danger to Japan as well and to Japanese citizens' constitutional rights, and limit military action to mine-sweeping operations in mined sea-lanes which would be permitted if the lives of Japanese citizens were being threatened. Directly after the agreement, the SDF had its annual recruitment drive which was promoted through commercials using a pop idol from a girl's singing group. The campaign's slogan was 'You and Peace' and included a theme song with lyrics promoting the military as contributors to peace through engagement in humanitarian missions abroad. The recruitment drive was implemented online and through letters sent to high school students throughout Japan by the SDF

Abe's cabinet also approved a new national security strategy. Japan's defense budget included the purchase of drones, stealth aircraft and amphibious vehicles to protect the islands. The military also planned to build a new marine unit in case the islands were taken.

Japan Inc.: in the beginning

Although the term 'Japan Inc.' was created in the 1980s, the key elements in Japan Inc. have existed since the late nineteenth century and the establishment of Japan's national ministries. There is now political engagement in the selection of the ministries' personnel as Abe's administration is intent on bringing more power to the executive office in terms of planning policy, becoming more instrumental in the selection of ministry officials in top posts and weakening ministerial guidance. Nevertheless, the Japanese regard their system of bureaucratic administration as having remained relatively unchanged since its inception in 1887 during the Meiji Restoration and as steeped in semi-feudalism, despite the end of a military ruler (*Shogun*) whose xenophobic policies effectively isolated Japan from the rest of the world for over 200 years.

Discontent among the populace was already festering with the government's economic policies, which focused on agriculture and the control of over 25 percent of the land and the labor force, when American Admiral Matthew Perry entered unannounced with his warships into Uraga Bay in 1853 to demand on behalf of the United States that Japan open its shores to trade with the United States. The subsequent signing of trade treaties with America, Britain and Holland removed Japan's right to set its own tariffs and allowed foreigners the right to reside in the port cities specified in the treaties. The trade negotiators, who were the future leaders of the Meiji Restoration government, were determined that foreign powers would not occupy Japan.

Abe and Aso's political economic agenda is directly related to their national identity and to their forefathers' policies. Abe's ancestors were Choshu *samurai* who came from what is now known as Yamaguchi Prefecture. Aso's ancestors were *samurai* from the Satsuma Clan, who in league with the Choshu Clan, toppled the *Shogunate* in 1865. In 1868 the constitutional monarchy was established by members of the two clans and aristocrats. In 1871, a government was consolidated, feudal domains were abolished and prefectures were established under central government control. Okubo, one of the key planners of the Meiji government, recognized that forging economic policies was vital to bring Japan onto the same industrial and economic plateau as America and Europe. He and members of the new Meiji government traveled extensively around America and Europe from 1971–3 in the first diplomatic mission to collect information about educational systems, technologies, economic and political systems that would support Japan's industrialization.

Okubo, who served as Finance Minister in 1871, was convinced that economic prosperity was connected to national power and that the government should work closely with Japanese businesses to achieve this vision (coincidentally, his great-great-grandson Taro Aso serves as Finance Minister in Abe's cabinet). Okubo established a new military which he led as the Home Minister but members of his clan, discontented with his policies, rebelled in 1877 but were defeated by Okubo's army. The following year Okubo was assassinated by clan members who regarded him as a traitor.

Nevertheless, the seeds of Japan Inc. were sown. Okubo's economic policies focused on government-led industrial development but by the 1880s the state-owned enterprises (SOEs) were in deficit. The SOEs were subsequently divided and sold to larger businesses and the large family-owned trading companies (*zaibatsu*) who were considered to have the managerial skills necessary to develop businesses. The large conglomerates' controlling interests were dominated by a single family and engaged in merchant banking, trade, mining and manufacturing. Some of the companies such as Mitsui and Sumitomo had been established in the seventeenth century. Mitsubishi expanded its business in 1870 through a government contract to operate steamships. In return for their cooperation, the companies were granted special privileges by government, thus forging the beginning of an abiding relationship between government and the private sector.

In 1881, the Ministry of Agriculture and Commerce (MAC) was initiated to institute agricultural reforms, to promote new farming technologies brought from the West, and to guide industrialization. The Bank of Japan (BOJ) was established the following year and in 1885, the first cabinet system was created. A constitution modeled on Bismarck's Prussian constitution was passed into law in 1889 and a bicameral Parliament was inaugurated in 1890. The first general election was held in 1891, culminating in the first Diet (Japan's Parliament).

Due to the financing of the new military and the costs of suppressing the rebellion of the Satsuma Clan, the government's debt soared and the resulting inflation prompted the government to consolidate the banking system. It set a limit on the amount of yen notes that the 135 authorized national banks could print. One of the banks to receive authorization was the Dai-ichi Bank which was the first bank and first joint stock company to be established in Japan in 1873. When the BOJ was established it took over the role of printing bank notes. In 1884 Dai-ichi Bank negotiated a contract with Korea to open the Dai-ichi Bank Korea Branch to serve as the tariff management agent for Korea. When Korea became Japan's protectorate, the bank operated commercially until 1943 when it merged with Mitsui Bank to form Teikoku Bank (Imperial Bank).

The government established a number of other state banks such as Nippon Kangyo Bank (1897) to provide long-term loans to light industries and agricultural industries and the Industrial Bank of Japan (IBJ) in 1902 as a key support mechanism for industrial development to introduce foreign capital. Nevertheless, the government limited foreign direct investment in order to protect immature industries.

Although Japan's economy was undergoing rapid Westernization spurred by the importation of Western technologies and supported by American and European technicians, the military pre-Meiji mind-set remained fundamentally unchanged. Aritomo Yamagata, a *samurai* in the Choshu Clan, is considered to be the major architect of the Meiji bureaucracy. He played a number of key roles in Japan's initial military and political development. As the War Minister in the first cabinet Yamagata laid the foundation of the Imperial Japanese army. And as the Home Minister (1883–7), he worked tirelessly to suppress political parties as well as labor movements. Yamagata was Japan's third Prime Minister (December 24, 1889–May 1891) and also served a second term of office (November 8, 1898–October 1900).

The persona of the elite bureaucracy was further enhanced by Yamagata when, in 1889, he pushed through the Diet the Civil Service Appointment Ordinance regarding the behavior of civil servants that effectively kept political parties from interfering with the bureaucracy. Yamagata's amendment advanced the power of the elite bureaucracy, which he guaranteed until his death in 1922. Yamagata's tenacity led to an autocratic governing system with the bureaucracy dominating the political process. Since that time, policy-making has been guided by elite officials and the legislation written by an elite bureaucracy has been supported by elected officials in the National Diet. In other words, the Civil Service Appointment Ordinance guaranteed that ministerial misconduct would go unsanctioned by law.

The first Meiji cabinet began the task of educating the new breed of civil servants by opening Tokyo Imperial University in 1887 (rebranded Tokyo University after the end of the Second World War) and designing a special civil service entrance exam for the ministries. Until recently, graduates from the law faculty in Tokyo University have traditionally had the best opportunity for gaining entry into the elite classes of the ministries and for promotion to the top echelons in the ministries. After graduating from the university Nobusuke Kishi entered the Ministry of Commerce and Industry (MCI) in 1920.

Collaboration between the bureaucracy and big business: the beginning of a beautiful relationship (ministerial guidance and protectionism)

Determined not to let foreign powers occupy Japan, the Meiji government made an all-out effort to achieve economic and industrial equality with the Western powers. The Meiji government slogan was 'Prosperous Country, Strong Country, Strong Military'.

The MAC was instrumental in planning industrial development, managing and regulating the production of machinery, shipbuilding and heavy industry. The construction of infrastructure such as railway lines was vital for the allocation of raw materials and the distribution of goods. Since government funds were constrained and borrowing from foreign banks was limited, the *zaibatsu* joined again with the government and contributed substantial capital investment to propel Japan's rapid industrialization. In order to accelerate mass steel production, the government established Yawata Steel and the oligopolies followed suit. By 1912, Sumitomo Steel, Kawasaki Steel, Kobe Steel and the Nippon Steel Pipe companies were in full operation and producing a remarkable 44 percent of rolled steel and 64 percent of pig iron for domestic use.

Expansion and outward investment in East Asia: the beginning of an antagonistic relationship

In his book *Minshu no Teki* (*The Enemy of Democracy*) Noda argued that due to Japan's land mass (53rd internationally), mountainous terrain and lack of natural resources Japan had to extend its boundaries to seek essential energy supplies. He pointed to the importance of the Senkaku Islands as a potentially rich field of mineral deposits. Noda also expressed enthusiasm for the future mining of mineral deposits in outer space.[5]

Japan's initial attempt at expanding beyond its borders was in three successive forays. The first was in 1874 in the Ryukyu Islands (Okinawa) which extended from Kyushu to Formosa (Taiwan), a Chinese protectorate. Japan's military invaded Formosa ostensibly to punish Formosans, who had allegedly murdered Ryukyu citizens when they were shipwrecked on Formosa, forcing China to hand over the islands. A year later, in 1875, Japan seized the Kuril Islands which stretched from Hokkaido to Russian Siberia. In 1876, Japan took the Bonin Islands (Iwo Jima is among them) which are located 1,300 km southeast of the Japanese mainland. The three island chains protected Japan from the north, east and south.

Prior to its defeat in the Second World War, Japan had never been defeated in a war. The Sino-Japanese War (1894–5) marked Japan's first victory against China after a prolonged dispute over China's influence in Korean politics and the government's administration. The victory proved the strength of Japan's fledgling military as a force in East Asia. China ceded Taiwan to Japan in 1895 as a part of the Treaty of Shimonoseki and recognized Korea's independence. Although China also ceded to Japan the Liangdong Peninsula in southern Manchuria, France, Germany and Russia pressured Japan to surrender the territory. Nevertheless, Japan's navy had established a foothold along the southern Manchurian coast.

Japan was determined to develop Taiwan into a major colony by introducing Japanese education and technologies. The *zaibatsu* invested heavily in infrastructure and manufacturing facilities during Japan's occupation until the end of the Second World War. While he was serving as Foreign Minister in Abe's first administration Aso addressed an audience in Fukuoka on February 5, 2006 regarding Japan's contribution to Taiwan during the occupation. Appearing to deny that Japan's occupation was considered an act of aggression by Japan's Asian neighbors, Aso stated that he regarded the compulsory education implemented by Japan in Taiwan as responsible for the current high standards of Taiwanese education.[6]

Japan continued its expansion into Asia in 1897 by pursuing Korea, which it wanted to occupy ahead of the other foreign powers which were also expanding into Asia. A territorial dispute with Russia over Korea's autonomy led to the Russo-Japanese War (1904–5), which Japan won, giving Japan dominance in southern Manchuria. The Treaty of Port Arthur gave Korea to Japan as a protectorate in 1905, and in 1910 Japan annexed the country. The northern region of the peninsula was rich in minerals and other natural resources, which the *zaibatsu* developed. By 1910, protected by the Japanese army, approximately 170,000 Japanese were living and working in Korea. The partnership between government and the private sector was in full swing.

Japan also took over the Liangdong Peninsula and the southernmost section of the southern branch of the China Far East Railway. The military established the Kwantung army in 1906 to secure the railway and territory. A semi-private corporation was founded to operate the railroad and develop settlements and industries. The Japanese South Manchuria Railway or *Mantetsu* employed 35,000 Japanese and 25,000 Chinese by 1910. Through major investment, it became Japan's largest company and by 1916 the company was creating subsidiaries engaged in various industries including steel production, sugar refining and chemical plants. Most of the company's business related to the freight of goods for exports to Japan and Europe.

Japan's economy and big business benefited substantially during the First World War. The United States, Great Britain and France used all natural resources for military supplies, effectively halting the exports of textiles, chemicals and machinery to Japan. Therefore, the Japanese had to increase production to meet domestic demand. Equally, exports to the Allied powers of military supplies, ships, coal and steel flourished. Prior to the war, Japan was a debtor nation that imported goods and services from America and Europe. But as the export-driven economic boom continued, it became a creditor nation with a trade surplus.

Although Japan saw no action during the war, it took advantage of its position as a member of the Allied powers to expand into Manchuria. Germany's engagement in Europe reduced the number of troops in Manchuria thus weakening its military presence in the territory which had been leased from China in 1898. In 1914, Japan took over the Marshall Islands from Germany and in the same year invaded the German base of Tsingtao.

On January 18, 1915, Japan submitted to the Chinese government a list of twenty-one grievances, which included the demands that China cease leasing territory to foreign countries, that China grant Japan control of Manchuria and Shantung Provinces and that it accept Japanese officials as advisers to assist in policy-making. However, the treaty was never signed and although the Treaty of Versailles granted Japan possession of the Marshall Islands, it disallowed the occupation of Shantung, which was returned to China.

The *zaibatsu* along with other large companies entered Manchuria and invested in silver and coal mining, lumber, oil exploration and the construction of more roads and railroad lines to connect ports from where the resources were shipped to Japan for distribution to industry. Idemitsu Oil, one of Japan's major oil companies, is an example of companies that mined fossil fuels and operated refineries in central China.

A recession spurs corporate diversification into heavy industries

The end of the war in 1918 marked the beginning of a series of recessions and financial crises which tested the resilience of big businesses. With the significant decline in orders for warships and an increase in inventories Japan slipped in the ranks to ninth among shipbuilding nations. The *zaibatsu* countered by diversifying production into automobiles, aircraft and general machinery. As an example, Ishikawa Shipbuilding Company's automobile division became Isuzu Motors Co. and Kawasaki Shipbuilding Co. became Kawasaki Heavy Industries. The heavy and chemical industries were developed through joint ventures between Japanese firms and Japanese and American firms. Mitsubishi Corporation internationalized by operating through its subsidiaries in

Germany and France to import technologies and patents. Mitsubishi Shipbuilding and Mitsubishi Heavy Industries shared about 30 percent of patent rights and manufacturing licenses. Mitsubishi Electric signed a contract with Westinghouse to trade technologies.

Corporate diversification into heavy industries initiated certain systems that continued during Japan's post-war economic development:

1. Holding companies were established that monitored and audited their affiliated firms. The companies issued joint shares of stocks.
2. Large producers set up their own training facilities to train skilled labor in order to ensure that their workers did not migrate to other businesses or join labor unions which had been formed to represent workers and farmers. The seniority system (promotion and wages according to length of employment in firms) was introduced.
3. The post-war *keiretsu* system was first conceived because the smaller firms did not have the capital to finance the training of skilled labor and had to rely predominantly on unskilled labor. Unable to compete with the larger companies, they began to operate as suppliers of manufactured components, goods and services to the conglomerates.
4. The heavy and chemical industries were developed.

Although by 1919, Japan's economy was booming because of post-war construction activities, expanded exports and new business start-ups, speculation and over-heated markets triggered a stock market crash on March 15, 1920 and a panic. The government and the BOJ reacted as the lender of last resort to fund banks which enabled them to continue to provide loans to key industries.

The economy was dealt yet another blow when the Great Kanto Earthquake hit the Tokyo–Yokohama region in 1923. The earthquake was followed by a tsunami which killed 140,000 people and halted commerce in the region. The government borrowed heavily from the BOJ to implement a disaster relief bill. Additionally, due to the imports of massive quantities of goods for reconstruction, Japan's trade surplus disappeared while its trade deficit rose rapidly.

The alliance between MCI and big business: the conception of post-war industrial policy

In 1925, to deal with the mounting economic problems, MAC split into two ministries, the Ministry of Agriculture and the Ministry of Commerce and Industry. The MCI authorized recession cartels that covered the majority of industries. Recession cartels were formed to rationalize production so that major companies affected could continue to operate on a level playing field. MCI subsidized businesses to promote exports in order to counteract the trade deficit. The recession cartels, the subsidization of businesses and industrial rationalization formed the foundation of MCI's industrial policy, a term used to describe government guidance of economic and industrial development at the macro- and micro-economic levels.[7]

The third blow to Japan's economy was the banking crisis in 1927. The government was able to repay the BOJ only 50 percent of the loans that financed the reconstruction by 1926. On April 18, 1927, the Japanese branch of the Bank of Taiwan suspended operations, followed by five more banks on April 21. The *zaibatsu* took full advantage of the crisis, assuming the controlling interests in the banks and taking over smaller companies through the purchase of equities. They also placed their executives on the firms' boards. Although the financial crisis directly affected only the banking sector, the economy went in and out of recession which paved the way for MCI to assume control of Japan's industrial development.

Private industry formed the Commerce and Industry Deliberation Council in 1927 to continue until 1930. The organization was the predecessor to the current Industrial Structure Council. With the cooperation of the Council members MCI planned policy to protect industry from recession. The concept of industrial rationalization developed at this time. MCI established the Industrial Rationalization Deliberation Council on November 19, 1929, the year of the Great Depression which was sparked by the Wall Street stock market crash. The Temporary Industrial Rationalization Bureau (TIRB) was set up to operate semi-autonomously from MCI to plan policies for the control of businesses, set industrial standards and provide subsidies to support consumer consumption and the production of goods. Shinji Yoshino, the head of MCI's Industrial Affairs Bureau who established the TIRB, became MCI vice-minister in 1931.

By 1931 MCI had expanded more control over industry through the Important Industries Control Law, which was drafted by members of the TIRB and passed by the Diet on February 25, 1931. The law gave MCI the right to form cartels in twenty-six industries considered vital to national interests such as shipbuilding, iron and steel, electric machinery, rayon, paper, cotton spinning, sugar manufacturing and beer brewing. The law laid the foundation for the policy tool 'administrative guidance' which was used consistently by MITI to issue directives to industries to form cartels, to fix prices and to regulate production during Japan's post-war period.

Fascism comes to the fore

Japan's military had protected Japanese firms' interests in Taiwan and Korea since the Meiji period. As Japan's economy became more entrenched in its colonies, the military began operating independently from political intervention. By 1930, *Mantetsu's* assets were worth ¥1 billion and Japanese companies with substantial investments were dependent on the army to protect their operations. The military became increasingly aggressive in Manchuria, protecting Japanese business interests, even though the action was unauthorized by government. Using the excuse that the Chinese army led by General Chiang-kai Shek was a threat to these interests, the Kwantung exploded the railroad tracks outside of Mukden in September 1931 and blamed what is known as the Manchurian Incident on the Chinese. The army established a puppet state called 'Manchuko' in Manchuria and eastern Inner Mongolia in 1932. When Prime Minister Takayuki Inukai (1931–2) tried to rein in the military budget he was assassinated by right-wing military officers. Only a small number of the officers were convicted and imprisoned but they were considered patriots by the Japanese public.

The Manchurian Incident was the beginning of fifteen years of military and bureaucratic dominance. The military continued its forays into Shanghai, engaging with the Chinese, ostensibly to protect Japanese interests in Manchuria. The army aggressively planned the economic expansion of southern Manchuria and established SOEs that focused on one industry such as automobiles, airplanes, oil refining and shipping. Kishi was Yoshino's protégé and by 1935, the talented and ambitious Kishi was a top official in the ministry and served as key economic planner of industrial development in Manchuko in 1935. He invited his relative Yoshisuke Aikawa, the president of the Nissan *zaibatsu*, to relocate to Manchuko and establish a 50–50 joint venture with the new Manchuko puppet government. The IBJ and the BOJ guaranteed the loans for the establishment of the Manchurian Heavy Industrial Development Corporation. American steel companies also financed loans. *Mantetsu* and other Japanese industrial firms in Manchuko were connected to the company through cross-shareholdings. Japanese companies thrived in Manchuria, Korea and Taiwan until the end of the Second World War.

General Hideki Tojo, who was in charge of military operations in Manchuria, supported Kishi in Manchuko where Kishi skillfully maneuvered the distribution of capital to cultivate right-wing nationalists and allies in non-*zaibatsu* and small/medium-sized businesses. Kishi was an expert at money laundering no matter how large the amount. It was rumored that, through his connections with the opium trade, Kishi engaged in legal as well as illegal transactions for both public and personal purposes with a simple telephone call.

On February 26, 1936, 1,400 junior army officers attempted a *coup d'état* seizing key government buildings in Tokyo. Although they were foiled in their attempt to kill Prime Minister Admiral Keisuke Okada, they succeeded in assassinating three high-ranking government officials. Japan signed the Anti-Comintern Pact with Nazi Germany on November 25, 1936 and again with Germany and Italy on 6 November 1937 after declaring war on China in July.

The Second World War intensifies ministerial powers

During the Meiji period the bureaucracy was endowed with the legal capacity to operate free of political interference. However, it was during the war, through state intervention in the Japanese economy, that the ministries' institutional mind-set of management of Japan's postwar economy was established. The extra-legal authority that today's bureaucrats enjoy is connected to the war-time system of government administration.

Emergency legislation was enacted, which allowed the bureaucracy to mobilize the economy. In 1938, the General Mobilization Law was passed, giving the state complete control over political society. The three institutions that played major roles in administering the war-time economy were the two economic ministries and the BOJ. MCI and the Ministry of Finance (MOF) gained control over the industrial and banking sectors and forged a closer alliance with the *zaibatsu* which produced armaments and military supplies. A close partnership was an inevitable result of the all-out effort to win the war in the Pacific. MCI managed and regulated industry as a whole, as well as munitions production.

The Dai-ichi Bank merged with Mitsui Bank to form Teikoku Bank (Imperial Bank) which became the largest bank in Japan.

MCI merged with the Cabinet Planning Board on November 1, 1943 to form the Ministry of Munitions (MM) in order to improve the production of military supplies. When General Tojo became Prime Minister in

1941 he appointed Kishi as cabinet Minister of Commerce and Industry. In 1944, Kishi was also appointed the director of the MM.

The BOJ poured funds into both of the banks established by MCI and the MOF and to private banks (the *zaibatsu* banks were the largest) to finance the production of goods considered vital to military supplies, particularly munitions. The IBJ administered by MCI and the MOF was a crucial support mechanism, providing funds for munitions. Motor companies such as Toyota, Nissan and Isuzu produced military vehicles.

The 'main bank' system

In 1944, the 'System of Financial Institutions Authorized to Finance Munitions Companies' was established, the bill giving the government the authority to order private banks run by the *zaibatsu* to fund munitions manufacturers, thus ensuring a steady supply of armaments. Each bank was assigned to one munitions firm. In 1945, the MOF established two banks to allocate funds to cover 600 firms, assigned to fulfill their production quotas. The banks were called 'Financial Institutions Authorized to Finance Munitions Companies'. The banks were protected against risky lending through government loan guarantees. By 1945, regardless of whether firms engaged in the production of military supplies, 2,000 had been assigned a bank that would be in charge of financing. The post-war formation of the giant financial groups known as *keiretsu* was the consequence of this close relationship between the *zaibatsu* and the 'main bank' system.

Reverse reforms: maintaining Japan Inc.

Japan surrendered to the Allied powers on September 2, 1945. The period 1945–52 is commonly referred to as the Allied Occupation. The occupying countries were the United States, Great Britain and Australia but Great Britain and Australia sent far fewer troops than the United States, which was commanded by Douglas MacArthur, the Supreme Commander of the Allied Powers (SCAP). The United States was determined to create a Western-style capitalistic and democratic society. The objectives of the occupation were three-fold: (i) Japan's demilitarization; (ii) the purging of war criminals; and (iii) Japan's democratization and economic resuscitation. War-time government officials were purged as Class A criminals and executed. Tojo was among those who were executed. Kishi was purged as a Class A war criminal and imprisoned in Sugamo prison in Tokyo.

Nobusuke Kishi's post-war political career is indicative of how the (SCAP) 'reverse reforms' during the Allied Occupation effectively perpetuated Japan's war-time government administration of the economy and an ultra-conservative political environment, which enhanced the power of the bureaucracy.

SCAP intended to reform Japan's war-time economic system by systematically disbanding the military and the ministries. MM along with the Home Ministry and the Military Police were abolished in 1945. Policies also included dismantling the *zaibatsu* because of their full participation in the war effort, and initiating a new constitution to introduce democratic principles such as freedom of speech, free elections and female suffrage. Labor unions were allowed to reorganize and the Socialist and Communist Parties that had been banned during the war were given the right to reorganize. A new constitution, which removed the Showa emperor as the formal head of state, replaced the Meiji Constitution. The famous Article 9 renounced Japan's right to wage war. The Ministry of Defense was abolished.

However, the beginning of the Cold War in 1945 with the Soviet Union, the communist-backed General Strike by the Government Workers' Union in 1947, the Korean War (1950–3) and the perceived threat of communist expansion in East Asia persuaded SCAP to reconsider a number of the intended reforms in order to cultivate an economically strong and politically conservative ally in the Pacific where the United States could base its military operations in the Pacific and its military hardware. In 1947 the Diet banned strikes by government workers and in 1948 the Wage Control Program replaced free collective bargaining.

SCAP recognized that fundamental to a swift recovery for Japan's devastated industrial complex was the expertise of the ministry officials who had managed Japan's war-time economy. It reinstated former ministry officials, thereby preserving Japan's pre-war institutions and the economic system. SCAP's staff ignorance of the Japanese language and the social system compelled them to rely on existing institutions, namely the bureaucracy, to implement policies. The nature of bureaucratic rule and the persona of the ministries remained intact because the officials who planned Japan's post-war industrial policies were former MCI and MOF officials.

Forty-two officials who were Kishi's colleagues from MM took upper-management positions in MCI, which was re-established in 1946, and then in the Ministry of International Trade and Industry (MITI), which was formed through the consolidation of MCI and the Board of Trade in 1949. But it was a double-edged sword. The bureaucrats who had run the war effort were deeply humiliated by Japan's defeat and the subsequent occupation. Refusing to capitulate spiritually to American occupation, they worked vigorously to plan and implement policy. By rising from the ashes of defeat and overtaking the United States on the economic front the Japanese would demonstrate to the world that Japan was a power to be reckoned with.

On the other hand, the officials' loyalty to their ministries' reticence to release control of their administrative territories and deregulate markets created rigidity and insularity in the administrative system. The rigidity was further exacerbated by the consistent support of the National Diet and by the electorate who believed that Japan's success in global markets was the consequence of the policies planned by the elite ministerial officials and that the bureaucracy's policies were impervious to failure. Only a minority of Japanese questioned the wisdom of these policies.

SCAP dissolved the *zaibatsu's* holding companies so that the family owners no longer held the controlling interests but the reforms were negligible. The Cold War convinced SCAP to reverse its initial objectives and follow a more lenient course, sanctioning the return of the conglomerate. The conglomerates reorganized into groups of enterprises (i.e. *keiretsu*) with the *zaibatsu* main banks at the center of capitalization thus preserving the pre-war and war-time main bank system. The financial groups that funded the domestic economy included Mitsui, Mitsubishi and Sumitomo. Centered on one bank, a 'main bank' that funded corporate investment, the corporations had cross-shareholdings and directors in common. The main bank system remained fairly intact until the 1997 Asian financial crisis when banks, both state and private, were pressured by government to merge due to the load of non-performing loans on the banks' books.

Many of the small and medium-sized firms that had been suppliers to the *zaibatsu* during the war were put on extended contracts to supply parts and services. Some firms were partially owned and produced parts solely for one *keiretsu*.

The Anti-Monopoly Law was enacted in 1947, but relaxed by 1953 to allow financial companies within each conglomerate to own as much as 10 percent of the shares of the firms not connected with finance. The law also allowed MITI to form import-export cartels, price cartels and production cartels, legally sanctioned by the Japan Fair Trade Commission (JFTC). MITI's Industrial Rationalization Council requested that the *keiretsu* invest capital in domestic firms.

After the war and prior to 1955, the Liberal Party was the main political party. Its president Shigeru Yoshida served as Japan's 45th Prime Minister (1946–7) and Japan's 48th Prime Minister (1948–54). Taro Aso's grandfather was a former official in the Ministry of Foreign Affairs and served as Japan's Ambassador to Italy and to Great Britain during the 1930s. He was imprisoned briefly in 1945. Yoshida's policies emphasized the rebuilding of Japan's industrial complex through rapid economic growth while depending on the United States military alliance which allowed Japan to pour all its resources into the resuscitation of the economy. Known as the Yoshida Doctrine, the policies impacted significantly on Japan's future domestic and foreign political economic policies.

The San Francisco Peace Treaty, signed on September 8, 1951 between Japan and forty-nine countries, officially ended the war, divesting Japan of occupied territories and confiscating Japan's overseas assets. The US–Japan Security Treaty, signed a month later, ensured an economic and military alliance between the United States and Japan.

'The 1955 system': Kishi, the renegade power-broker

When Kishi realized that he would not be executed, he planned tactics that would lead a right-wing conservative party to power, an organization which would also include right-wing socialists and conservatives. Before the outbreak of the war, Kishi had formed the Association for the Defense of the Fatherland. When he returned to Tokyo in 1939, he extended his network and won a seat in the National Diet in 1942. In 1944 he established the 'Kishi New Party'. Its members were Kishi's political and business right-wing associates from Manchuria and elite control bureaucrats and right-wing military personnel who had planned the 1931 *coup d'état*. His money power base were the directors of the public companies in Manchuria and the non-*zaibatsu* independent businesses that had reaped profits through Kishi's agendas.

When he was released from prison in 1948, he was forbidden by SCAP to enter public office again. However, the order was soon rescinded by SCAP as a part of its 'reverse reforms'. Kishi first re-established his Kishi New Party and integrated it with his 'Association for the Defense of the Fatherland' to form the 'Japan Reconstruction Federation', which included some of the former members of a pre-war conservative party and elite bureaucrats. He consolidated the federation with the well-established ultra-conservative party whose objective was to revise the new constitution and the security treaty to allow Japan to rearm in order to defend itself. His younger brother Eisaku Sato, who was Yoshida's protégé and chief cabinet secretary, urged Kishi to enter the Liberal Party, which was established by Ichiro Hatoyama, who was slated to become Prime Minister in 1946 but was purged by SCAP and prohibited to enter politics for five years. Kishi understood that in order to realize his ambitions he had to enter mainstream conservative politics and requested an introduction to Yoshida.

Yoshida had numerous confrontations with Kishi over ideological differences and tried to dissuade SCAP from allowing him to enter public office again. On the other hand, the Prime Minister recognized that Kishi's connections with business brought substantial contributions and that he had become, through his political connections, a force to be reckoned with. He invited Kishi to become a member of the party and to run for election. Kishi won a seat in the National Diet in 1953.

Kishi made a power-play within the party by accusing Yoshida of being in the lap of the Americans and the British. He succeeded in undermining Yoshida's leadership by courting senior members of the party as well as business leaders to form a new government. Calling for a new conservative party, together with 200 politicians he created the 'New Party Formation Promotion Council'. Yoshida reacted by expelling him from the Liberal Party.

In 1954, Kishi and his party joined Hatoyama and other Liberal Party members and combining the strategic alliance with the Socialists formed a separate faction, the Democratic Party. Together they won 185 of the 467 seats while the Liberal Democrats lost almost half of their seats in the Diet. Hatoyama succeeded Yoshida as Prime Minister in 1954. However, Hatoyama was reluctant to merge the parties with the Democratic Party faction because he sensed that he could lose control, but Kishi's political acumen and determination paid off and the Liberal Democratic Party was established in 1955 with Kishi at the center.

Kishi had finally achieved his goal. He had succeeded in incorporating the existing conservative parties, right-wing and more moderate factions into a single conservative political party which would dominate Japanese politics for thirty-eight years. Hatoyama suffered a stroke in 1954 but continued to serve in office until 1956 before resigning. He was replaced by Tanzan Ishibashi, who, also due to illness, resigned after just sixty-three days. On February 25, 1957, Kishi, who was Foreign Minister in Ishibashi's cabinet, became Japan's 56th and 57th Prime Minister. Sato served as Minister of Finance in his brother's cabinet.

Kishi shrewdly manipulated America's intense fear of communism in the United States (1947 Truman Doctrine) and communist expansion in Asia to push his ultra-conservative party to power. America was instrumental in guaranteeing that LDP politicians would dominate the National Diet in the first election. Communist-backed labor union protests were suppressed and the CIA funneled money to the LDP in the 1950s and 1960s in order to ensure a strong, conservative government. The CIA had created a fund, known as the 'M Fund', which was organized from the sale of confiscated Japanese military supplies, industrial diamonds, platinum, gold and silver which had been stolen in occupied countries and the sale of shares of the dissolved *zaibatsu*.[8] Kishi, who was strongly supported by the United States as Prime Minister, was a recipient of CIA funds which were funneled through LDP coffers. The US State Department announced in July 2006 that by 1964 President Lyndon Johnson had officially stopped payments for 'covert programs of propaganda and social action to encourage the Japanese to reject the influence from the left'. However, the fund effectively continued during Japan's post-war period to support the LDP.[9]

Kishi the money-man

Kishi's Manchurian experiences were integral to his methods of operation while in political office. He was masterful in amassing funds for the support of his right-wing ideologies as well as for personal gain. Before he became Prime Minister, Kishi drew in funds from his business networks cultivated during his Manchurian days and from right-wing nationalist businessmen who used their vast wealth to support right-wing politicians.

Kishi was practiced in ritualizing corruption. He used public resources to produce public works contracts for businesses that supported the LDP while simultaneously reaping kick-backs for himself and members of his faction. The use of public resources was regarded as an innovative way of raising political funds that were difficult to trace. It was also an effective route for sourcing political funds connecting the LDP with the private sector. Kishi established the Overseas Economic Cooperation Fund to facilitate repayment of losses experienced by Japanese firms operating in Asia during the war. The fund was designed to aid developing countries but the distribution was determined by the countries' officials receiving the aid, LDP politicians and conservative Japanese businesses. Kishi's finesse for manipulating public funds and money laundering was legendary in the LDP. However, he was never implicated in any of the corruption scandals that involved LDP politicians after he left office.[10]

During his three years in office, Kishi's only major defeat was his attempt to centralize police power and restore to the police some of their former authority such as the right to search suspected criminals. Public protests erupted against what was regarded as the resuscitation of war-time 'thought control'.

Kishi's major success but, also, the cause of his resignation in 1960 was the revision of the US–Japan Security Treaty, which nationalists considered to favor the United States. Although the Self-Defense Force (SDF) was formed in 1954, the nationalists were adamant that Article 9 in the Constitution be revised. The negotiation did not include the revision of Article 9 but Kishi convinced the Americans to agree to a revision of the terms of the treaty, including the curtailment of America's right to quell domestic disturbances and giving the Japanese more control over their defense. The treaty committed the United States to help Japan defend itself from attack while Japan provided bases and ports for the US military. 'Mutual defense' became central to Japan's national defense policy.

In his book Abe reported that thousands of Japanese were opposed to a military alliance with the United States and angry crowds surrounded the Diet buildings where his grandfather and uncle were forced to remain until they were escorted by police to Kishi's residence where he and his brother met them. The LDP passed the revised treaty at a special midnight session and when only a minority of Socialist parliamentarians were present. However, President Dwight D. Eisenhower's state visit to celebrate the signing of the revised Security Treaty was canceled due to the public protests. Kishi resigned from office and was replaced by Hayato Ikeda.

Japan's economy was helped considerably by the Korean War. Through the production of munitions for America's military, Japan's exports increased by 26 percent. Equally, due to the Korean War, followed by the Vietnam War which was in full swing by 1966, America's military presence at naval, army and air bases located throughout Japan was a constant reminder of Japan's defeat, demilitarization and occupation. Nevertheless, in order to stabilize Japan's economy and to promote rapid economic growth the US opened its markets to Japanese exports, which the Japanese government took full advantage of.

2
The Sign of the Times: Japan Inc. (1955–1974)

MITI's long-term industrial policies concentrated on the development of the heavy industries, namely the petrochemical industry and other energy-intensive industries such as aluminum and plastics. Between 1955 and 1973, Japan's annual GDP increased almost six times to 11.5 percent. The MOF, MITI and the Economic Planning Agency's (EPA) policies were considered to be the drivers of this rapid economic growth. Nevertheless, it is difficult to quantify the extent to which ministerial policy actually drove the economy. Besides SCAP's 'reverse reforms' other factors should also be considered:

1. Joseph Dodge, the chairman of Detroit Bank, was SCAP's economic adviser who planned policies to stabilize Japan's economy. Known as the Dodge Line, the yen was set at the cheap rate of ¥360 per dollar to assist Japanese exports and to promote Japan's economic revitalization.
2. Mercantile policies.
3. America's open markets.
4. Access to cheap technologies, especially from the US.
5. Prime Minister Hayato Ikeda (1960–64) whose 'double income' economic policies focused on the development of the heavy industries as opposed to small businesses.
6. Low military spending (Yoshida Doctrine).
7. High savings rate.
8. Consistent support for policies from the National Diet and business community.
9. Industriousness of a literate workforce.

Money doesn't grow on trees

At the end of the war, there was a shortage of capital. In order to support rapid economic recovery, the state created a number of banks to provide long-term, low-interest rate loans to industries. After the end of the war, Nippon Kangyo Bank was privatized to become a commercial bank but the division that had served to provide long-term, low-interest rate loans was nationalized during Prime Minister Shigeru Yoshida's administration in 1952. The Long-Term Credit Bank of Japan (LTCB) together with the IBJ and Nippon Kangyo Bank and the Nippon Credit Bank (NCB), which was established in 1957, were important financiers of industry.

MITI established two state banks in the early 1950s: the Japan Export Import Bank (EXIM) and the Bank for Overseas Economic Cooperation. Since MITI exercised capital outflow even the purchasing of cheap technologies corporations which applied for EXIM loans required direct approval from MITI, which could prove to be problematic if the corporations were not considered amenable to MITI's directives.

MOF established the Japan Development Bank (JDB) to provide loans for capital investment for the expansion of domestic operations and for the rationalization and modernization of the coal and steel industries.

The BOJ was at the center of Japan's economic development, keeping discount interest rates lower than the market price. The bank initially controlled net lending of metropolitan banks and by 1957 the lending of regional banks also, dictating to each bank the amount acceptable through the extra-legal policy tool of 'window guidance' (*madoguchi shido*). The BOJ decided the quota according to the ranking of the banks from the metropolitan banks down to the regional banks. The state banks were also ranked. The IBJ ranked first and assumed an even more important role than it had played during the war, providing low-interest rate loans to firms to support rapid industrial growth. The LTCB and the NCB were ranked second and third respectively. Banks adhered to the dictates because through this policy they could achieve an equal market share and simultaneously be protected by the BOJ, as the lender of last resort, and MOF, the ministry that protected the banks against losses.

The Teikoku Bank's business deteriorated, due to internal friction caused by differences in Dai-ichi and Mitsui's corporate cultures and in human resource management. As a consequence, in 1948 Teikoku Bank reorganized into two separate banks – the Dai-ichi Bank and the Teikoku Bank. The Teikoku Bank was then rebranded the Mitsui Bank in 1954.

Dai-ichi Bank and Nippon Kangyo Bank merged in 1971 to form the Dai-ichi Kangyo Bank (DKB). The bank surpassed Fuji Bank as Japan's largest bank in terms of assets and deposit market share. It was the only bank to have branches in all of the prefectures. The bank also managed the national lottery system (*takarakuji*).

Fiscal Investment Loan Program

The Fiscal Investment Loan Program (FILP) was established in 1953 as a huge financial organ operated by the public sector to channel funds to key industries through newly established institutions known as FILP institutions. FILP received its capital from the Trust Fund Bureau (TFB) funded by the deposits from the Postal Savings System (PSS) and by the premiums from the public pension scheme.

FILP designated institutions were state banks such as EXIM and the JDB and Special Status Corporations or Special Corporations (*tokushuhoujin*) which were established after the Second World War to aid in the reconstruction of infrastructure destroyed during the war to resuscitate Japan's industrial complex. The ministries began to establish public corporations in 1947 during the Occupation at the encouragement of the Supreme Commander of the Allied Powers (SCAP). Four of the corporations were designated for foreign trade, eight supported domestic distribution, one served to control price adjustment and two were for economic rehabilitation. Special Corporations received funds through FILP Agency Bonds for contracts to corporations for the construction of public works, for infrastructure, for housing, loans to small and medium-size companies, mortgages and life insurance.

The government had difficulty defining the exact characteristics of Special Corporations other than that they assisted the government in promoting national interests. Nevertheless, they can be viewed as corporations that were based on a national law, which had been approved by the National Diet. Special Corporations were established according to certain establishing procedures through a special law, the Law of Establishment Act, Article 4-11 subject to the Ministry of General Affairs (renamed in 2001 the Ministry of Public Management, Home Affairs, Post and Telecommunications). The law was neither civil nor corporate.

The corporations were linked to the industrial sectors under the administrative jurisdiction of each ministry. By the early 1990s the ministries had established over one hundred Special Corporations. It was a simple procedure because all that was needed to establish a new one was the writing of an 'establish law' in the name of the corporation and a request to an obliging Diet to sanction it.

The Ministry of Construction (MOC) (renamed in 2001 the Ministry of Land Infrastructure, Transport and Tourism – MLIT) initially established ten corporations. By 1955 there were twenty-six. During Japan's period of rapid economic growth, ten further public corporations were established annually by the MOC. By 1960, the number had increased to fifty-two and by 1970 there were 144.

The largest corporation was the Japan Highway Corporation (JH) which was established by the former MOC in 1956 to award contracts through bidding procedures to construction companies to rebuild highway networks throughout Japan. Japan is often referred to as the 'construction country' because of the increasing construction of infrastructure and public works since the early 1960s. The MOC established the Hanshin Expressway Corporation in 1959 to construct highways to connect Osaka and Kobe and the Metropolitan Expressway Corporation in 1962.

MOC established the Government Housing Loan Corporation (GHLC) in 1950 to provide finance for the rebuilding of homes devastated by the Second World War. As Japan's biggest home lender, the GHLC financed 30 percent of all houses constructed since the end of the war. The MOC established the Urban Development Corporation (UDC) in 1955 to engage in the supply and maintenance of housing.

The former Ministry of International Trade and Industry (MITI) (renamed the Ministry of Economy, Trade and Industry in 2001) established the Electric Power Development Company (EPDC) in 1952 to provide electricity nationally. The Metal Mining Agency of Japan (MMAJ) was established in 1963 to manage the mining of non-ferrous metals.

Japan imports over 80 percent of its fossil fuel. The ministry established the Japan National Oil Corporation (JNOC) in 1967 to oversee the energy-producing industries and manage imports and refining through federations of importers. JNOC assisted Japanese oil companies with exploration and drilling for oil. The federations connected MITI to the oil refiners, who distributed to the retailers. The domestic companies cooperated with foreign firms, such as Indonesia Oil, Mobil, Shell and Dhabi Oil, usually holding the larger share of the investment.

MITI established the Japan External Trade Organization (JETRO) in 1956 to promote small business exports to overseas markets.

Special Corporations were re-established in 2003 as Independent Administrative Corporations (IAIs) under a special law and as Incorporated Administrative Agencies under another special law but are still government funded and managed by the ministries. In 2008, the banks that were originally Special Corporations were re-established as 'special corporations' or *tokushugaisha* which were slated for privatization within three years but they remain as state banks to support business development.

The hollowing out of rural Japan: building frenzy

At the end of the war Japan's primary industry was agriculture. In the late 1950s when Japan began its period of rapid economic growth, thousands of young high-school graduates living in farming and fishing villages left for the Tokyo–Osaka–Kobe regions to seek better-paying jobs in retail shops, factories and small businesses. The mass migration resulted in the loss of population in communities outside of the industrialized areas and the overpopulation of big metropolises. The majority of farmers who remained in the rural areas were middle-aged or older.

By 1970 it was difficult to believe that Japan's industrial complex and infrastructure had been devastated by the war. The 1964 Tokyo Olympics had witnessed a spurt of infrastructure construction and industrial development in the metropolitan areas and rural areas. Towns were connected by haphazard arrays of new small dwellings which were constructed without consideration of design and which blighted the once lusciously green countryside and farmland that had been snatched up by land developers. Farmers, who had profited from the sale of their property, replaced their centuries-old farm houses with new-builds complete with modern conveniences, including flush toilets. The toilets were manufactured by Toto, a company founded in Kitakyushu in 1917 which became the world's largest toilet manufacturer by the 1990s.

Nixon's shock: the end of the Gold Standard and fixed exchange rates

The 'Nixon shock' refers to the end of the Bretton Woods system of fixed exchange rates and the Gold Standard on which currency standards were based. The Bretton Woods Agreement in 1944 established the US dollar as the only national currency backed by gold. The other currencies were valued against the dollar and countries could trade their dollars for a fixed amount of gold held in the US. In the early 1970s, the Vietnam War caused a rapid rise in inflation in the United States, which was also experiencing pronounced trade and budget deficits. The dollar that had been valued at $35 per ounce of gold was weakened by America's inability to cut government spending and reduce its trade deficit and budget deficit, which Nixon claimed was causing the inflation. As the government continued to print more money to fund operations in Vietnam and inflation continued to rise, countries began exchanging dollar assets for gold and America's gold coverage dropped to 11 percent. In August 1971, President Richard Nixon imposed ninety-day wage and price controls as well as a 10 percent import surcharge. This action effectively made the dollar non-convertible on the open market. Even though the import surcharge was dropped five months later, there was a general revaluation of currencies. By 1976, there was no longer a fixed exchange rate.

The MOF suppressed the yen, which had been ¥360 per dollar for twenty-two years to ¥308 per dollar. The government's fiscal stimulus together with the BOJ's lower interest rates acted to prevent the yen's rapid appreciation. The currency finally stabilized at ¥300 per dollar. Although the yen appreciated almost fifty cents to the dollar the prices of exports to the American market were relatively unaffected. MOF officials felt that as long as Japan ran a trade surplus with the United States, they were in control of the economy and their administrative territory. Japan continued to hoard its dollar assets in the United States, considered a safe haven, while controlling the yen in Japan. The yen's appreciation did not seem to affect the Japanese people who, encouraged by the government, were saving much of their income. By the 1970s, the savings rate had peaked at almost 30 percent, the highest in the world.

Big shock: 1973 oil embargo shakes up MITI's industrial policies (but not for long)

The 'oil shock' which began in October 1973 virtually put an end to the focus of MITI's long-term industrial policies. The Organization of Arab Petroleum Exporting Countries (OAPEC), consisting of OPEC, Egypt, Syria and Tunisia, announced an oil embargo to protest the United States' military support of Israel during the Yom Kippur War. The embargo lasted until March 1974 but it was considered by many countries, including Japan, to have been caused by the United States which had controlled oil prices. The end of Bretton Woods and the dollar's devaluation impacted negatively on oil exporting countries, namely the Arab States.

In January when Prime Minister Kakuei Tanaka (1972–74) met with Henry Kissinger he was unable to receive a guarantee from the United States for a steady supply of crude oil in return for Japan's support of American policies. The Japanese government felt compelled to take a pro-Arab stance and Japan was thereby recognized by the Arab nations as pro-Arab. Although the embargo ended in March, the price of crude oil rose from $3 to $12 per barrel and the yen appreciated to ¥260 per dollar.

Contrary to expectations that the sudden rise in prices would cause inflation, Japan's economy slumped into recession.

Temporary hysteria

The oil embargo triggered a stampede by housewives to supermarkets where they emptied the shelves of sugar and toilet paper. Despite the appreciation of the yen and steep rise in the price of petrol, some business owners seemed relieved that the oil shock had occurred because they assumed that the sudden decrease in oil imports would force the government to slow down the pace of rapid industrial development and that the Japanese would have a brief respite from continuously pushing their economy forward.

MITI at the controls

But the government had no intention of slowing down. Steel, automobiles, heavy and home appliances, petrochemicals, auto-tires, synthetic fibers, aluminum, non-ferrous metals, plate glass, pulp and paper were the industries that were among those directly affected by the oil embargo and the subsequent increase of petroleum prices. The crisis forced the government to recognize the county's vulnerability and take immediate measures to rationalize oil in order to decrease the demand for both gasoline and electricity. Former Prime Minister Yasuhiro Nakasone (1982–86), who served as the Minister of International Trade and Industry in Tanaka's cabinet, implemented the policy instrument 'administrative guidance' for 'the Conservation of Oil and Electricity in the Private Sector'.

MITI had been using this tool since 1952 in order to form cartels of industries designated as important to national interests, protecting them from foreign competition. The tool can be used *ad hoc* at the discretion of the ministries. There are no laws that limit the number of times the guidance can be used, giving the ministries uncommon powers to regulate. Companies will usually receive notification that they are to follow ministerial regulations. The directives are either transmitted in writing or by telephone, although a law in 1997 officially curtailed the use of the telephone.

MITI's Agency of Natural Resources and Energy (ANRE) drafted the Petroleum Supply and Demand Normalization Law (PSDN) which was passed by the Diet in December 1973. After the embargo was lifted in February, 'administrative guidance' was replaced by PSDN. The law gave MITI control over the supply and the consumption of oil for both large and small companies and oil products and dealers reported their production and sales to MITI. MITI could direct companies to change plans and to keep supplies in stock or to sell. MITI could 'guide' the Association of Petroleum Dealers to secure the national oil supply. Production and price cartels were included in MITI's control policies. MITI officials managing JNOC and MITI's industrial associations such as the Japan Gas Association and the Japan Petroleum Institute facilitated the use of 'administrative guidance'.

Nuclear power: the pillar of Japan's energy supply

In 1973, the government announced that nuclear energy was a national priority. In order to continue economic expansion and overtake the US economy the government had to reduce industries' reliance on fossil fuels. In 1974, the 'Three Power Source Development Law' was enacted to subsidize local authorities that were willing to host nuclear power plants. The law called for a tax, which was included in consumers' utility bills, to be used by government to subsidize public works in communities that hosted the plants. In the 1950s the United States had fully supported the introduction of nuclear in Japan as an integral part of its global strategy, and the Japanese government's long-term energy policy targeted nuclear power as the major provider of electrical power. Nakasone had proposed the Atomic Energy Basic Law which was passed in 1955 and served as the second chairman of the Atomic Energy Commission founded in 1956. Also in 1957, the Japan Atomic Power Company (JAPCO) was formed by the electric utility companies and MITI's Electric Power Development Co. (EPDC KK) was established to spur on the commercial use of nuclear power. As a division of MITI, EPDC regulated the electric power companies.

A number of Special Corporations were formed in the 1950s for the development of nuclear power. In 1959, MITI established the Japan Nuclear Fuel Corporation, the forerunner of the Japan Nuclear

Development Corporation (PNC) which was the major fuel cycle research institute in Japan. The PNC engaged in numerous activities, including uranium exploration, high-level nuclear waste disposal, spent fuel reprocessing, MOX fuel fabrication and the development of a fast breeder reactor for the use of MOX. The Science and Technology Agency established the Japan Atomic Research Institute (JAERI) and the Atomic Fuel Corporation.

MITI, together with the regional utility companies and the heavy industries involved in nuclear power such as Mitsubishi, Toshiba and Hitachi, aggressively chose sites for the construction of nuclear power plants in rural, depopulated municipalities with inadequate tax bases, where the civil societies were considered weak and where subsidies to support local small businesses and maintain employment would promote the acceptance by local authorities of nuclear power plants in their areas. Japan's arable land, which represents only 15 percent of the total land mass and agriculture, and which is highly subsidized and protected by government, accounts for roughly 1.5 percent of Japan's GDP.

MITI's industrial policies restructured but not MITI's mind-set

MITI continued to maintain substantial control of its administrative territory through protectionist policies. By 1978, the structurally damaged energy-intensive industries were considered 'sunset' or 'slump' industries. The policies included doling out subsidies to the depressed 'sunset' industries and the continuation of 'administrative guidance' to form anti-recession cartels, rationalization and price cartels under the Structurally Depressed Industry Law. The cartels played a primary role in limiting competition from foreign manufacturers and were merely a continuation of the policies that had promoted rapid growth. The LDP supported MITI's policies because politicians needed contributions from businesses for their campaigns. The policies benefited MITI officials as well. Some officials, motivated by the prospect of receiving post-retirement positions, favored the largest firms.

Akio Mikuni is the president of a Japanese investor-supported bond-ratio agency and a former executive at Nomura Securities Co. He has criticized the bureaucracy's policies in an array of commentaries and books. In 1998, he wrote about the role that industrial associations played in the formation of cartels, as was also the case during the 1930s:

> These industrial associations and the implied promise of government intervention had helped maintain the viability of member companies,

thus obviating the need for individual companies to accumulate the sufficient capital on their own to withstand downturns. Anti-trust laws do exist, but they are largely empty.[1]

Cartel-like policies continue today to protect domestic markets even though the government insists that many import barriers used in the past, including tariffs, have been eliminated. Informal guidance may be given by the ministry through trade and industrial associations, whose members feel obliged to follow policy, such as purchasing solely from domestic producers. It was suspected that members of industrial associations, such as petroleum, colluded in the 1990s to fix prices while the Japan Fair Trade Commission (JFTC) turned a blind eye. It is interesting to note that MOF officials have been among the members of the JFTC board and although there are anti-monopoly laws, they are considered relatively ineffective.[2]

Japan's steel industry also benefits from these policies. The increase of former MITI officials in the steel industry between 1983 and 1988 suggests that MITI used 'administrative guidance' to implement the formation of cartels among steel manufacturers under the same Structurally Depressed Industry Law. Apparently, MITI's cartel policy for the steel industry in the 1990s was supported wholeheartedly by the steel companies because they were fearful that the industry would fail without protection from foreign competition.

MITI's Fujitsu vs. IBM: David and Goliath

The 'oil shock' acted as a catalyst, intensifying the focus of industrial policy on the development of high-tech information systems and the coddling of Fujitsu through major investment and support of Hitachi, NEC and Toshiba. Although prior to the war the government had engaged in the development of computer technology, directly after the war MITI, along with NEC, Fujitsu and NTT, engaged in R&D for computer technology. However, these efforts produced computers that were technically inferior to computers that were being manufactured by well-financed computer companies in the West.

IBM was the only wholly-owned subsidiary in Japan during the 1960s. Foreign firms could enter the market but only through technology-sharing agreements. In other words, foreign firms had no control over direct market entry and held only the minority share in the joint venture. When IBM asked MITI for a permit to allow the company to create a wholly-owned manufacturing subsidiary to produce computers in Japan, MITI refused. In 1960, through a series of complicated sets of agreements of patent rights and percentages of royalties to individual Japanese companies (to prevent competition between companies) IBM was allowed to open operations. However, MITI continued to tightly regulate IBM Japan's sales and to protect domestic manufacturers through levying tariffs of 15–25 percent on imported computers and 'buy Japan' directives. Japanese companies which purchased only Japanese computers received tax breaks and, also, their acquiescence to MITI's directives gave them better access to MITI's patent office and the facilitation of new patent permits.

Despite the fact that Japanese companies preferred the superior foreign computers to Japanese computers, MITI's protective policies effectively reduced the purchases of imports from 90 percent in the late 1950s to 40 percent by the mid-1960s.

In 1966, MITI founded the Japan Software Co., a joint venture between its fledgling Fujitsu, NEC and Hitachi and funded by the Industrial Bank of Japan (IBJ) to develop software for MITI's concerted effort to match the IBM 360 computer, which was ready and waiting for launch in Japan. However, the effort failed because the players had considered only domestic sales and not foreign markets. Also, since the joint venture was essentially government-funded, other domestic software companies were reticent to enter the software market. By 1972 orders had plummeted and the corporation was on the verge of bankruptcy, forcing MITI to terminate the project.

By procuring technologies and parts from foreign suppliers, the technology gap began to shrink. IBM was the Goliath in global markets but when a designer for IBM established a start-up to produce a mainframe which was IBM compatible, he approached Fujitsu for investment. Fujitsu purchased 40 percent of the company and began to produce computers which were compatible with IBM business systems. Other Japanese companies took the same route and soon Japanese customers were purchasing domestic brands and IBM was struggling for market share.

US–Japan relations: unwilling bedfellows

Although the Occupation had ended, the Korean War followed by the Vietnam War and the constant presence of the American military throughout Japan was a painful reminder for many Japanese of Japan's defeat and the Occupation. There was a palpable anti-American sentiment.

Yukio Mishima (1925–70) was one of Japan's greatest writers of the twentieth century and nominated three times for the Nobel Prize for literature. He was born into a family of bureaucrats and was a nationalist. He enlisted in the Ground Defense Force in 1962. In the same year, Mishima formed a small private army of which most of the members were students and pledged to protect the emperor, whom he felt exemplified the Japanese spirit. On November 25, 1970, Mishima, accompanied by four members of his army, tried to instigate a *coup d'état* at the Self Defense Force headquarters in Tokyo. They broke into the commandant's room and held him hostage. When Mishima read his manifesto to the soldiers who had congregated below, he was jeered. Humiliated, Mishima returned to the room and committed suicide.

Mishima was one of former Tokyo governor Shintaro Ishihara's closest friends. Ishihara's initial exposure to the United States was during the war when his neighborhood was strafed by American aircraft. Ishihara claimed that the aircraft flew so low that he could see pictures of naked women and cartoon characters painted on the sides of the planes. His book *Japan Can Say No* (*No to Ieru Nihon*) was a collaborative effort with the late Akio Morita who was Sony Corporation's founder and chairman. Published in 1989 the book was a best-seller. Ishihara argued that the United States regarded Japan as a subordinate and that this attitude was related to racism.

Interviews conducted in 1994 with Japanese civil servants who were children in the 1960s included questions related to their impressions of America during their childhood.

A MITI 'elite' career officer aged 46 stated:

> The Japanese saw America as the ideal country. Japan was supported by a large amount of American aid. Men from the Occupation Forces were in the town where I was living so I saw American troops often. The men had splendid physics. I thought that the bases were very luxurious. My main impression was the gap between the poverty in Japan and the abundance. I didn't see any resistance to the Occupation but the Japanese, who were attending elementary school and who were of a slightly older generation than I, felt great sadness at the loss of Japanese traditional values. Some authors like Yukio Mishima and Shintaru Ishihara saw the Occupation Forces as conquering devils and Japan as a pitiful nation. The Japanese, particularly at that time, were simply trying to survive so there was a strong feeling that America was supporting Japan. Social values completely changed. In a word (and this is true for the entire world), Americanization was taking place and, consequently, Japan was inside this giant wave.

A MITI non-career officer aged 36 said:

> Although I was born quite a while after the end of the Second World War, the American Occupation Forces were still in Japan. My first sense of America was that America defeated Japan in the war. Until Japan's definitive defeat, Japan had never lost a war. There was an army base in my neighborhood. I was very small so I don't remember seeing soldiers, but I saw many American civilians in my area. My impression was that Americans were very large and that America was a powerful and wealthy country. Americans lived very wealthy existences with big cars and shopping centers. They were independent! The Americans who lived in my town looked well-off and lived in spacious quarters. On the other hand, Japanese lived in a small area in overcrowded quarters.

An officer who was 31 spoke as follows:

> My father was in the Second World War. I didn't hear specific things about the war, but I often heard about Japan's poverty because of the loss of the war and how everybody suffered. Rice and food were at a premium and it was wasteful to leave anything on one's plate. Subjects such as war dead [and] the peace pact were not discussed much. Only after Japan became richer was there talk about how Japan broke the peace. There was also ambivalence about the US. The Japanese lost self-confidence because of the loss of the war. Self-confidence was also lost because everyone stopped telling their children about Japanese culture, Japanese values and how they wanted their children to live. My father kindly taught me various things but he didn't speak about Japanese culture, civilization or social values. I think that this was true for most Japanese households.[3]

A local government officer, who was 35, said that his childhood impressions about the United States were influenced by the stories his grandmother told him about the American B-29 bombers that flew over their home during the war.[4]

To market, to market

Preparations for the 1964 Tokyo Olympics included catering to the needs of the thousands of foreign visitors, most of whom had never held chopsticks or chewed on a morsel of sushi. Foods from abroad such as cheeses, biscuits and cereals, chocolates, canned goods, wines and spirits were imported to Japan by the large trading companies. The Japanese, feeling the first flush of prosperity since before the war, also purchased these imports. They liked what they tried and the demand for imported foods increased.

Dutch cheeses, Bulgarian jam, American cornflakes and instant coffee, English biscuits and tea and rice were in great demand. The rice was called 'Specially Chosen Rice' (*tokusen mai*). The name was ordinarily given to rice grown domestically in prefectures renowned for rice such as Niigata Prefecture but claims were made that the rice was actually from California and sold on the black market. Because imported rice was banned due to strong lobbying by rice farmers who were receiving substantial subsidies from government, the claims were difficult to confirm.

In the metropolitan areas, clothing and food stores supplied products comparable to goods sold in American metropolises. Daiei Inc., established by Isao Nakauchi as a budget retailer for food, apparel and home furnishings in 1957, was beginning to embark on expanding operations throughout Japan. By the late 1970s, the company had opened stores in Asia, America and in Europe and was one of biggest employers in Japan. The trading company Marubeni also engaged in Daiei's operations.

Nevertheless, Japan's mercantile policies protected industry from foreign competition and Japanese consumers' choice of products was limited primarily to goods produced in Japan. Domestically grown fruit was relatively expensive compared to that produced in the US, although US grapefruit were sold at almost the same price as in the US. The Japanese *mikan* controlled the markets while Navels and Valencia oranges – priced at £3 per orange – were left to rot on the shelves. *Mikan* juice from Ehime Prefecture, one of the primary orange-growing regions besides Shizuoka Prefecture, was sold in cans but foreign residents considered that there was no substitute for Valencia from Florida. The high tariffs on Navel and Valencia oranges were the result of the policies of the Ministry of Agriculture, Forestry and Fisheries (MAFA) and the Japanese orange growers' associations who donated liberally to the LDP political coffers.

The domestically produced foods suited Japanese palates and Japanese kitchens where most meals were prepared on propane burners. The small homes lacked storage space and freezers were out of the question. Refrigerators were half the size of the American brands and without freezing compartments. Refrigerators with freezer space for ice cream and ice cubes were considered luxury items.

There were inexpensive canned goods from Romania and Bulgaria, although not sold in the US due to the Cold War. Imports of processed foods, tea and coffee were distributed by the large trading companies such as Itochu, Mitsui and Marubeni, all of them in MITI's administrative jurisdiction. Occasionally the products' labels indicated that the distributors were manufacturers of goods unrelated to the food and beverage industry such as steel companies which were also within MITI's administrative jurisdiction.

Food plays a central role in Japanese society and housewives traditionally spent a good portion of their household budget on food. The quality of food was more important than the amount on the plate and it was obvious that frugality dominated household budgets. Shoppers habitually examined products, comparing one piece of fruit with another or a vegetable with another vegetable for several minutes before deciding on a purchase. In the 1970s this practice extended to purchases of packaged meats and fish because the additional import duties made the imported products too expensive for daily consumption. Meat was very expensive and, although beef imports from Australia and lamb from New Zealand could be sourced, US beef was almost non-existent.

Japanese wine and liquor producers were importing and distributing foreign wines, fortified spirits and blended whisky in the 1960s. Bottles of Johnny Walker Red and Black labels and Chivas Regal were much sought after for corporate gifts and for special friends. The importers and distributors were the large major wine and liquor producers such as Suntory and Sanraku Inc. Wine produced in Japan was generally considered inferior to the wine imports because Japan's weather was not conducive to the cultivation of grapes for wine and producers mixed their wine with grape juice from Hungary and Bulgaria.

Although the majority of consumers' expendable income was still limited, foreign luxury brands had already entered Japan through either licensing agreements with Japanese producer-distributors or through joint ventures with the Japanese company controlling 51 percent of the shares. Christian Dior licensed Kanebo, the venerable textile company and the oldest listed company on the Tokyo Stock Exchange (TSE) to produce and sell its fashions in its flagship store in the Ginza. Dior also licensed Kanebo the rights to manufacture nylon stockings for the Dior brand. Since foreign apparel entered the market through licensing agreements and was manufactured in Japan, the clothes were produced specifically for the Japanese stature. Foreigners as well as Japanese with larger statures were obliged to purchase more expensive foreign imports or visit tailors.

MITI's administrative territory included textiles and retail and wholly-owned foreign subsidiaries were tightly regulated to protect domestic companies from outside competition.

The struggle to take control of distribution

Entering Japan's tightly controlled agricultural markets was problematic unless the produce was being imported for ingredients in processed foods. Blue Diamond Almond Growers' (BDG) direct entry into the Japanese market in the 1970s explains the route taken by some foreign companies.

The California cooperative is the world's largest almond grower. However, the Japanese were unfamiliar with the nut until it was introduced in Japanese Western-style confections after the war. Initially BDG entered the market through bulk exports of almonds to the Japanese confectionery industry in the late 1950s, employing distributors to handle shipments and sales. Realizing that the distribution system was complex and was frustrating sales, BDG opened a market development office in Tokyo in 1969 to promote an increase of sales.

In order to link up with a strong distributor, BDG Japan had to promise a viable market. In Japan, traditionally many women do not cook until they marry because their mothers prepare meals to allow their children to concentrate on their school work and to prepare for college entrance exams. Women will attend cooking classes for a quick study and culinary schools are a vibrant business in Japan. In the 1970s, BDG established a good rapport with many of the schools throughout Japan and demonstrated through classes to novice housewives the attributes of almonds in various recipes.

In 1971, BDG introduced almond snacks and by 1974, the Japanese began to consume more almonds. BDG was able to convince thirteen Coca-Cola bottlers to let it piggy-back on their sales and distribution system. The partnership assisted BDG's business considerably. In 1975 California almond exports to Japan were 16 million pounds. Twenty years later exports had more than doubled.

Hello Japan Inc.!

By the 1970s Japanese car manufactures were aggressively going after the US market with compact, fuel-efficient cars. Even though the US government reacted to the oil crisis by rationing gas and introducing a 55 mile-an-hour speed limit, Japanese producers offered prices that were very competitive with the American 'gas-guzzlers' and the dealers were reliable, offering good repair services. Americans, who considered that Japanese manufacturing was imitative and inferior, began to recognize that Japanese products were more than just plastic toys and cheap metal tools. As consumers were scooping up Sony television sets, they were becoming curious about Japan's corporate management style and techniques which were widely believed to be the most efficient in the world.

3
The Route to Heaven-on-Earth

Amakudari ('decent from heaven') is a primary component in Japan Inc. *Amakudari* began informally during the 1930s when the government started to strictly regulate the economy for the war effort. Business owners employed bureaucrats in order to determine future government directives as well as to lobby interests. It was widely believed in the 1970s and 1980s that the interlocking relationship between business, the bureaucracy and politicians was the secret to Japan's success in global markets. The system seemed to work well while Japan was emerging industrially. However, what was not generally recognized was how the interlocking relationships created a mutuality of vested interests of the stakeholders, a very insular environment that protected domestic businesses from foreign competition and a rigid system of ministerial administration of the economy, a model that would consequently impede the efforts by successive administrations since the 1990s to implement structural reforms. Although the practice has been regarded as encouraging corruption and sloppy regulation, it was not until the beginning of the 1990s after the asset-inflated bubble burst and scandals emerged involving *amakudari* and the ministries' collusion with companies in their administrative jurisdiction that *amakudari* was no longer condoned. However, despite some reform measures initiated by the LDP in 1998 and 2001, the system continues.

Japan's post-war civil service system includes *amakudari* which is an institutionalized practice through which the National Personnel Authority (NPA) formally places elite bureaucrats who have reached retirement age into private and public organizations. The arrangement provides officials with re-employment in top level management positions where salaries are often higher than their previous salaries in the ministries. Many positions are in the corporations whose industries are within the officials' ministries' administrative jurisdiction. The relationship between bureaucrats and former colleagues who have migrated to businesses in a sector under their ministry's administrative jurisdiction automatically tightens the ministry's grip on that sector. The officials have a direct link to their former ministries and, therefore, can lobby their employers' interests and concerns. The companies reciprocate by acquiescing to ministerial policies thus enhancing the ministries' regulatory controls. 'Administrative guidance' is easily facilitated through *amakudari* which serves to connect retired ministry officials employed in the companies that are receiving directives from MITI.

The system has served as a mutual back-scratching mechanism because the companies that hire bureaucrats have a direct pipeline to the ministries and accept officials with the anticipation that they will be treated favorably and receive useful information and subsidies, contracts for public works, as well as swift approval for license and patent applications. Companies may be reticent to employ officials but will acquiesce to pressure from the ministries because of the concern that they will not be able to compete with other businesses that do hire officials.

Although the NPA actively seeks upper-management positions in the private sector for retiring officials, the ministries also search on behalf of their staff usually in companies and other entities in the sector they administrate using their budgets and authority to exert pressure. MOF officials will find employment in the financial industry, while METI officials find employment in manufacturing, retail, energy industries and power companies.

Kent E. Calder stated in his paper 'Elites in an Equalizing Role: Ex-Bureaucrats as Coordinators and Intermediaries in the Japanese Government–Business Relationship' that Special Corporations supplied the overwhelming number of positions for former bureaucrats, many of the corporations being involved in the aid of small businesses. Calder explained that the owners of smaller businesses relied on former bureaucrats more than the owners of larger businesses because they had less access to central government. A former bureaucrat on the board or in an upper management post of a smaller firm could 'equalize' the competition with the larger firms. Calder also proposed that firms located further from Tokyo relied more on former bureaucrats because they were more isolated from central government than companies closer to the capital, and therefore less capable of sustaining tight relationships with officials in the ministries.[1]

A pertinent example is the case of the CEO of a medium-sized chemical firm based in Tokyo's Suginami Ward, which was established in 1941 as a producer of special chemicals for the war effort. After the war, the founder continued operations, avoiding competition with large manufacturers by producing a small range of specialty chemicals. MCI administered the chemical industry during the war, and since the company had produced during the war, it retained a good relationship with MITI after the war. The founder's connections with ministry officials undoubtedly helped to secure subsidies. Between 1952 and 1977 the company received a number of subsidies from MITI for research and development. The CEO also hired an officer from JASME (Japan Finance Corporation for Small & Medium-Size Enterprises) as Senior Managing Director and General Manager of Executive Affairs, thus placing the company in a more favorable position to receive long-term, low-interest loans. His interpersonal network in government helped him to import new technologies in the 1950s and the 1960s. His connections in MITI also may have expedited his application for patents, licenses and permits.

When the CEO died, his son-in-law succeeded him as CEO. The company tied up with a major pharmaceutical firm and a clock manufacturer, supplying them with chemicals. The CEO, looking ahead at foreign markets, opened a sales office in Hong Kong in the early 1980s. Eyeing markets in Europe and the United States, the CEO engaged in a joint venture with a major Japanese trading company, a wise move because the trading company had long-established distribution channels. The trading company did not manufacture the same kinds of chemicals and thus the relationship was mutually beneficial. The company supplied technical information and production acumen, and the trading company supplied investment and distribution. To ensure an enduring relationship, the CEO hired an employee from the trading company who had been based in Europe for many years, who knew how to conduct business in European countries and who was an appropriate figure for liaison with his former employer. Another pay-off was that the vice-chairman of the trading company had been an elite official in MITI, giving the company additional connections to the ministry.

The CEO never took his connections for granted, working tirelessly to maintain and to extend his interpersonal network in business and government. He was the friend of a former prime minister who graduated from the same university. He was the president of his district's Chamber of Commerce and Industry, a chartered corporation managed by MITI's Industrial Policy Bureau. The CEO also served simultaneously in other small and medium-size business organizations managed by MITI. Through this participation, the CEO was in constant contact with other business owners and with elite officials.

To put the story into the context of the Japan Inc. model, the CEO needed a solid interpersonal network with central government officials and owners of big businesses in order to ensure long-term growth and maintain stability.[2]

Amakudari in IAIs and affiliated institutions: theme and variation

The National Public Service Law stipulates that bureaucrats cannot, for a period of two years, legally move directly to positions in private companies attached to the sectors their ministries regulate. However, they can move immediately to their ministries' corporations, industrial associations or research institutes supported by their ministries or by the other ministries where they linger for two years with pay before going on to the private sector. Most officials will wait out the two-year period of grace in public corporations and then slip into higher management positions in private companies although some officials may elect to remain if there are no offers from the private sector.

The ministries can cleverly manipulate the system to provide jobs for their staff in their corporations:

1. Bureaucrats can be sent by their ministries to work in their ministries' IAIs, agencies, research institutes and industrial associations while they are still engaged by their ministries (and drawing salary). This practice is known as 'on loan to another company' (*shukko*). Although the officials are still connected to their ministries they are identified as officers of the organizations where they have been transferred. And while the posts are considered to be temporary, they can develop into permanent positions. Essentially *shukko* can be the catalyst for *amakudari* in the public corporations.
2. The ministries are not required to apply to the NPA in order to 'loan' an official to an organization. Officials who are 'on loan' to an organization can then migrate to the private sector without waiting out the two-year period of grace.
3. Bureaucrats can remain attached in some way to their ministries' public entities through their subsidiaries (as advisers or members of boards) while working for private businesses, receiving salaries simultaneously from both public and private sectors without waiting out the two-year period of grace.

4. Positions in IAIs may be given to elite bureaucrats who have not reached retirement age, but are considered to be nearing the end of their careers. The 'gift' is actually a signal to officials that they will not be promoted much higher in their ministries, but that their loyalty is appreciated.
5. The lucrative salaries that top management in the public entities receive make the positions enticing to retiring officials and to officials who had left their ministries to work in the private sector. As an example, on October 24, 2009, Kyodo News Service reported that ninety-eight public corporations hired officials who had retired from the ministries which managed their respective corporations. Eleven were operated by METI and seven of them, including the Japan External Trade Organization, were headed by former METI bureaucrats. Of the seven, six were officials who had left the ministry to work as executives and advisers at major private companies. The average annual salary of twenty-nine chiefs for FY 2009 was $226,470.
6. The ministries operate research institutes where officials are 'loaned' for a two-year period of grace before migrating to the private sector.

These variations of *amakudari* have evolved over a fifty-year period and are regarded as the norm and not as corrupt practice by ministry officials. The system has continued for many years and, although the Japanese do not condone the system, they have become inured to it. *Amakudari* offers a strong incentive for entering the ministries.

The following case illustrates how secondment to the corporations has traditionally assisted MITI officials to migrate to the private sector after retiring from the ministry and then, via the *amakudari* system, return to three public corporations before a final stop in a fourth corporation:

1. The official entered MITI in 1957 directly after graduating from Tokyo University with a law degree. He was posted in the Industrial Policy Bureau in MITI's Agency of Natural Resources and Energy and then in the Minister's Secretariat, Economic Cooperation Division. He moved on to the Japanese Embassy as a member of the delegation for the EU in Brussels and later was seconded to JETRO Paris as second in command. He returned to MITI to serve in the Economic Planning Agency (EPA) for two years. He served for one year as the Minister of Trade and Industry's press attaché in 1977 before

migrating to the Japan National Oil Corporation (JNOC) for three years. He returned to MITI for one year as the General Director of Basic Industries Division in 1982 before retiring.

2. A second case illustrates how secondments can lead to full-time employment in an industrial association. An official entered MITI after graduating from Kyoto University Law Faculty. He was the director of Policy Planning in the Minister's Secretariat and served as Secretary in the Japanese embassy in Indonesia. He was seconded to a JETRO overseas branch office to serve as president for two years after which he returned to MITI. He served as Deputy-Director General for Global Environmental Affairs and a director of the Research Institute of International Trade and Industry, a MITI research institute. Upon retirement he took the position of president of the Electronic Industrial Association of Japan (EIAJ), a MITI industrial association.

3. The third case represents how officials' repetitive secondment to a ministry's public corporation can ultimately lead to a job in the private sector. After graduating from the Law Faculty at Tokyo University the officer entered MITI. He was 'loaned' to JETRO Tokyo headquarters in 1986–89 where he was in charge of planning policy. After returning to MITI for a two-year stint he was seconded to a JETRO American branch office, where he served as president for three years. While residing in the United States he received a Green Card which enabled him to move directly to a second JETRO branch office in the United States as the president for two years. After retiring from MITI he entered an affiliate of an American company in Japan.[3]

Amakudari in IAIs: bid-rigging

The *amakudari* system is a breeding ground for bid-rigging activities and collusion among bureaucrats and businessmen. The ministries' corporations grant government contracts for public works projects to private industries and are the vehicles that connect the ministries to these industries. Former bureaucrats can choose the recipients of the lucrative contracts that are funded by tax revenue, and in return, receive employment in the corporations to which they have awarded the contracts. A Lower House survey showed that in 2006 alone, of the $17.1 billion in disbursement for state projects, 98 percent was contracted to those entities without bidding procedures.

Former Prime Minister Junichiro Koizumi (2001–6) entered office on a platform that promised public spending cuts, which focused on downsizing FILP and abolishing debt-ridden Special Corporations that were receiving the major funding from FILP. One of the first corporations Koizumi planned to abolish within five years was the Japan Highway Corporation (JH), a Special Corporation managed by the MOC, with sixty subsidiaries throughout Japan. Koizumi succeeded but not without a significant struggle. Traditionally its presidents and vice-presidents were elite retired officials from the MOC who received retirement allowances while they served in the JH. The JH distributed contracts to the construction companies and bid-rigging involving large construction companies was commonplace. Even though an anti-collusion bill was implemented in 2003 to prevent bureaucrats from positively influencing the outcome of bids from corporations, collusion continued to be a common practice.

On September 29, 2005, the Japan Fair Trade Commission (JFTC) ordered forty-five Japanese steel bridge-builders to cease bid-rigging contracts from government and from the JH. The JFTC alleged that twenty former officials in the JH, including former Vice-President Michio Uchida and a former executive board member Tsuneo Kaneko, had received jobs in forty-five companies due to their involvement in bid-rigging. Among the forty-five firms named were Mitsubishi Heavy Industries Co., Ishikawa-Harima Heavy Industries and Kawasaki Heavy Industries Ltd. The JFTC announced that the contracts procured through illegal bid-rigging were worth approximately $2.35 billion. Former JH officials who were employed in the bridge construction companies had accessed unpublished information in the JH regarding toll road bridge construction projects.

Consequently, Uchida and Kaneko, along with officials from twenty-six corporations were indicted on December 8, 2005 for bid-rigging. Some of the officers had been officers in the JH before their employment in the firms. Besides the companies listed above, other companies accused of bid-rigging included Mitsui Engineering and Shipbuilding Co., Sumitomo Heavy Industries Ltd., Hitachi Zosen Corporation and Nippon Steel Corporation.

Uchida and Kaneko were charged with instructing subordinates to carve up contracts for an elevated highway bridge in Shizuoka Prefecture in May 2004. The contracts inflated JH's costs by $445,000. Uchida was arrested on July 25, 2005 and later fired from his position as vice-president of JH on August 22. Kaneko was arrested on August 1. On December 7, 2007, Kaneko was found guilty of violating the Anti-Monopoly Law and sentenced to a two-year prison term, although it was suspended for three years.

On December 17, 2005, they entered a plea of not guilty to the charges. However, the private corporations pleaded guilty. In December 2006, reacting to reports of bid-rigging by local government officials together with bureaucrats in their ministries' corporations, a revised law was enacted by government that would bring stiff punishment to officials in these corporations who were convicted of involvement in bid-rigging. The revised law included officials in the expressway corporations that were the result of the privatization of JH.

Japanese dailies go after *amakudari*

In 1993, the editorial staff of the *Nikkei Shimbun* ran a series of in-depth articles that delved into the bowels of Japan's bureaucracy. The articles were collated for a book that was published in June 1994. *A Creaking Giant Power* (*Kishimu Kyodai Kenryoku*) examined the relationship between the bureaucracy and the National Diet as well as the power of the bureaucracy itself. It explained why bureaucrats were more influential than politicians in Japan's governing system, and why the Japanese did not believe that politicians could plan effective legislation and thought that there was no real leadership in the Diet. The reasons given for their lack of confidence were: (i) politicians were subservient to the whims of special interest groups; (ii) there was ongoing friction between political factions; and (iii) politicians did not have the expertise or experience to plan effective policies because bureaucrats had been given the power to draft laws since the Meiji period.

The interviews with politicians and bureaucrats reported in the book illustrated the ministries' struggle to retain power during that time. The foreword began with the contention of a former MOF administrative vice-minister that elite bureaucrats were motivated by their belief in democracy. His conviction reflected the mentality of bureaucrats who served with him during Japan's post-war period of rapid economic growth. The book also related the views of young officials in the MOF and MITI, who seemed to be aware that their ministries must become more egalitarian and that the relationship between the bureaucracy and politicians should be made more transparent.

Susumu Takahashi, a former administrative vice-minister in MOC, was interviewed about his views on *amakudari*. Takahashi admitted that there was an alliance between politicians and the MOC and that there was indeed a relationship between the ministries and industry. However, he emphasized that denying bureaucrats post-retirement positions in industry was unrealistic because bureaucrats generally retired earlier than corporate executives and they needed supplementary income. He was disturbed that elite officials, who were commonly referred to by the press as 'Old Boys' or 'OBs', received benefits while they were working in post-retirement positions. Takahashi, who became the president of the Government Housing Loan Corporation (GHLC) in 1990 after he retired from MOC, claimed that the number of positions in Special Corporations was limited. However, he omitted to mention the number of positions available in the subsidiaries of Special Corporations or in other institutions operated by the ministries.[4]

The results of a public survey conducted by the newspaper in 1993 regarding how the electorate felt about their bureaucracy are included in the book. A significant percentage of people questioned revealed their discontent with elite civil servants, reflecting their reaction to the disclosures of scandals involving the ministries. The perception of bureaucrats was: (i) they had a strong elitist mentality; (ii) they were irresponsible; and (iii) they were clever and shrewd. Twenty-two percent answered that bureaucrats were cold and uncaring. Only 3 percent believed that bureaucrats should be entrusted to plan policy independently, and an overwhelming 70 percent agreed that bureaucrats should join forces with politicians to plan policy.

The newspaper conducted another survey at the end of October 1993 of 200 bureaucrats on their views of the governing system; 147 officers answered questions ranging from devolution, and the deregulation of markets to *amakudari*. The questions about devolution brought negative answers concerning the ability of local government to plan policies. The respondents insisted that the national ministries must always bear the responsibility of governing the regions.

As for the loosening of regulations and opening of Japan's markets, 63 percent of the respondents in their twenties wanted deregulation. Fifty percent of the respondents in their fifties were also in favor of more deregulation.[5]

Not to be outdone, the editorial staff of *Mainichi Shimbun* entered the fray as well in 1994 with a book focusing on *amakudari* in both private and public corporations. *Kasumigaseki Syndrome* (*Kasumigaseki Shindoromu*) was a surprisingly frank account of the deterioration of values among bureaucrats in terms of their objectives in establishing corporations and research institutes for the sole purpose of providing post-retirement positions for the elite retirees.

The book's most significant contribution is the reporting on how *amakudari* and the temporary posting of elite officials in branch offices of their corporations in the prefectures (*shukko*) helped the ministries to monitor local government policies. Since the bureaucratic hierarchy places officers from the national ministries above local government officers, the positioning of ministry officials at the local government level automatically induces acquiescence by local government to ministerial guidance. The book was also critical of temporary postings because there was every likelihood that the positions would become permanent.

The *Mainichi* staff detailed how the ministries maintained control over their sectors by placing conservative retirees into management in both private and public corporations. In addition, they revealed how the ministries used their corporations to distribute contracts to companies for public works and how *amakudari* not only tied ministries to businesses but also facilitated connections between businesses and former bureaucrats, who moved first to public entities before moving onto the private sector.

The book included a public survey in December 1993. Although 77 percent of the subjects questioned credited bureaucrats with Japan's rapid economic growth, 41 percent of the respondents regarded bureaucrats in the 1990s as being greedy for power. Thirty-one percent asserted that bureaucrats worked for the benefit of their ministries, but only 18 percent felt that bureaucrats worked for the good of their industrial sectors. A mere 3 percent felt that bureaucrats were hard working, and only 3 percent considered bureaucrats to be honest and sincere.

Of the people surveyed, 60 percent wanted *amakudari* abolished while only 12 percent wanted the system maintained; 38 percent wanted the system abolished for political office and 43 percent of the people polled wanted the companies that hired bureaucrats to be subjected to strict regulations.[6]

The *Nikkei Shimbun* also conducted a survey in 1994 of 1,780 employees in seven Special Corporations that had been established by the MOC. The employees were questioned about the *amakudari* of staff members, who comprised 80 percent of the employees. The 7 percent of the employees who answered that *amakudari* was necessary were in the minority; 38 percent felt that the system was a bad influence and should be abolished; 29 percent felt that nothing much could be done about the situation because of the recession; 33 percent claimed that the former bureaucrats were useless; and 50 percent answered that the retired officials were helpful to some extent. Again, a minority of 3 percent maintained that the former officers performed their duties well.

Amakudari: a no-win situation?

In March 2007 during Abe's first administration, plans were submitted that would prohibit the ministries finding post-retirement positions for their officials and would create a new body that would centralize job-hunting for all of the ministries. But it would take three years to begin operations after its establishment. Abe's comments at the panel discussion summed up why the curtailing of *amakudari* practices would prove difficult:

> I have said that we have to root out the ministries' somewhat forcible job-hunting tactics that are backed by their budgetary power and authority.

In April, Abe's cabinet approved a bill that would end *amakudari*. When the bill was submitted to the Diet in June, the Prime Minister touted it as the biggest reform of the administrative system in sixty years. Besides opposition to the bill by Abe's LDP colleagues, the opposition parties were also against it, contending that the bill did not guarantee the end of collusion between government and the private sector. Abe's coalition government, frustrated by the opposition, temporarily withdrew the bill.

Nevertheless, the struggle continued a year later in April 2008, when Prime Minister Yasuo Fukuda's administration announced that a draft bill for further reform and regulation of 101 IAIs would be submitted to the Diet. If passed, the bill would be law in 2010. Applicants from outside the ministries would be able to apply for positions in the ministries' organizations, but appointment would be approved by all ministers in the cabinet. Also, retired bureaucrats working in the ministries' public entities would be prohibited from side-slipping ('side-slipping' is the term used to define this particular behavior) into businesses that had connections with the organizations. However, opponents were skeptical that the new law would act to eliminate *amakudari* since traditionally the cabinet had systematically approved the appointments of senior ministry officials to positions in the organizations.

Fukuda's successor Taro Aso established in 2009 the Center for Personnel Exchanges between Government and Private Entities in order to integrate job placement of civil servants. The center is operated by the NPA in the Ministry of Internal Affairs and Communication (MIC). Aso's objectives were to put a stop to the continuing rampant bid-rigging for public works at the initiative of government officials which led to wasteful spending of tax revenue, and to prevent ministries and agencies from directly contacting interested companies and other entities to find jobs for officials. However, the measure has proven toothless since its inauguration.

On August 30, 2009, when the DPJ won the majority of seats in the Lower House, which had been dominated by the Liberal Democratic Party (LDP) since 1955, it called for the eradication of *amakudari* for the ministries' corporations. But the ministries that were in charge of implementing reform procrastinated because not only did the system provide positions in the private sector but, as importantly, the system allowed easy migration to jobs in their organizations where the number of jobs vastly outnumbered those in the private sector. Furthermore, jobs in these organizations enabled officials to migrate smoothly to positions offered by the private sector.

By trying to bust bureaucratic rule and bring more power to the executive office, the DPJ were the odd-men-out and, consequently, their policies were not enthusiastically supported by the ministries. Indeed, former Prime Minister Naoto Kan (2010–11) and his DPJ cabinet finally came to terms with the fact that in order to implement economic reforms and trade agreements, they had to rely on ministerial support and began back-tracking on promises to weaken the bureaucracy.

Former Prime Minister Noda devotes an entire chapter to *amakudari* in the ministries' corporations in his book *Minshu no Teki* (2009), entitled 'Elite Ministry Officials: the system that is sponging off the country'. Noda praises elite officials for entering their agencies with the best of intentions and civil servants for working tirelessly for their country. Noda then connects *amakudari* to the ministries' corporations and pronounces the system a waste of human resources and an appalling waste of public funds. He states that even though bureaucrats expect to migrate to positions in the corporations their skills are not conducive to the jobs and that they randomly choose work that is not specific to the needs of the corporations. Noda claims that anyone who accepts the use of tax revenue for the financial support of the ministries' corporations and their officials' salaries in IAIs is incredibly generous. Noda points out that since the subsidiaries of large companies provide many of the jobs, the number of bureaucrats in post-retirement positions in the private sector is escalating.[7]

Although Noda's claims are justified, the national ministries also use *amakudari* to attract university graduates into the ministries. Before eliminating the system, there must be other mechanisms in place that act to incentivize talented graduates to enter the civil service.

4
Pork-Barrel Politics in the Prefectures: The Winners

In 1982 Chalmers Johnson stated in his best-seller *MITI and the Japanese Miracle*:

> Most of the ideas for economic growth came from the bureaucracy and the business community reacted with the attitude of what one scholar called 'responsive dependence'.[1]

Nevertheless, during the 1960s and 1970s one of the key ingredients in Japan's rapid economic development, especially at the local level, was the mutual obligation/mutual protection relationship between LDP politicians, businessmen, and ministerial officials.

Prime Minister Kakuei Tanaka: Mr. Japan Inc. and the art of pork-barrel patronage

Japan's political economic system can be characterized as pork-barrel and protectionist. Big business and business federations made large contributions to the LDP coffers. The LDP received votes and large donations from traditional support groups, such as small local firms and businesses engaged in construction, transportation and telecommunications, in exchange for contracts for public works projects. Elected officials who represent poorer regions can remain in office for many years on the condition that they bring public works contracts for local businesses.

Prime Minister Kakuei Tanaka (1972–74) is considered the strongman-strategist in Japan's post-war politics and key organizer of the LDP political machine. After entering the LDP in 1955, he quickly established himself as the godfather of pork-barrel politics. Tanaka was the antithesis of Kishi not only in terms of his blatant and often crude methods of raising capital and the use of public funds, but also with regard to his political career which was peppered with corruption scandals, one of which ended his political career and the Tanaka faction. Deliberate in his methods of collecting political contributions while simultaneously lining his own pockets, Tanaka created a well-oiled political faction in the LDP, which survived until the late 1980s

Born in Niigata Prefecture in relative poverty, Tanaka left school to work as an errand boy in a local construction company. His service in Manchuria was cut short due to illness and he returned to Niigata. In 1942 he married a divorcee seven years his senior whose father owned a medium-size construction firm. When his father-in-law died Tanaka inherited the company, naming it Tanaka Civil Engineering and Construction Industries. Tanaka entered politics in 1945 when SCAP planned the first post-war election in 1945. Tanaka knew that conservative voters would regard him as an outsider without proper political lineage and that winning votes could be problematic. Despite using personal funds for his campaign, Tanaka lost the election.

He relied again upon his wealth to campaign in Niigata a second time in 1946 and courted the socialist farmers who, due to SCAP's land reform, had received the land they had previously been renting. Tanaka pledged to bring public works projects for schools, highways and tunnels, railroads and land reclamation projects to the region in exchange for their votes but he lost the election. When he tried for a third time in 1947, he lost again but by a far smaller margin due to his cultivation of the rural vote. Nevertheless, Tanaka remained true to his promises to bring public works projects and subsidies to Niigata during the rest of his years in politics.

His organization in Niigata, the Etsuzankai (Niigata Mountain Organization) was established during this time to serve initially as a local chamber of commerce. The organization soon became a formal political organization and as Tanaka's personal association it was his strongest support group. By the 1980s there were 313 district organizations which included the majority of construction and transport companies as contributors. Tanaka himself owned several of the companies. At its peak, the association boasted over 100,000 members and the tightly knit group perpetuated Tanaka's image as the quintessential political boss.

Before he became Prime Minister, Tanaka had survived a series of corruption scandals that ordinarily would have ended any career in politics. Regardless, Tanaka served in Kishi's cabinet and also in Sato's where he was MITI minister. In 1953, he devised the Volatile Oil Tax Law, which was the first in a series of tax-related laws specifying the tax revenues that would be used for road construction, which later developed into the biggest public works expenditure after the Tokyo Olympics. In 1966, the LDP-dominated Diet passed the Public Demand Law, which called for both central and local government to increase distribution of procurement contracts to small and medium-size companies.

Tanaka understood that the key to political power was making money and gifting money and that the accumulation of personal wealth was integral to financing the LDP machine. His career was equally divided between policy-making in government and pork-barrel transactions. His record in maintaining his elite position in government despite allegations and indictments for illegal business dealings is the ultimate master class for survival in Japanese politics and in the uninhibited use of public funds.

Tanaka was the consummate user of FILP directed towards public works projects. His interpersonal relationships with the construction industry, MOC, MITI and the Ministry of Transport (MOT) facilitated a multitude of land deals and public works infrastructure projects, reaping enormous profits for both big and small businesses and large sums for their families and for the LDP's treasure chest. As significantly, due to the loyalty of his constituents in remote, agrarian-based Niigata Prefecture, he remained in political office well after he was implicated or indicted in corruption scandals.

In the early twentieth century, Niigata was a densely populated, agricultural prefecture, which supplied the Japanese with the finest rice and sake. At the end of the Second World War, Tanaka's Niigata ranked among the poorest prefectures in Japan. Less than a decade later, Tanaka had become a major figure in Japan's government and his generous contributions to LDP politicians and ministry officials helped him secure for his prefecture bountiful subsidies from central government.

When members of his political organization petitioned Tanaka with requests for business he answered by bringing in public works. The funds were funneled through his association. There were numerous allegations against Tanaka by public prosecutors regarding kick-backs to his Niigata-based political association. Usually, he emerged unscathed. By the 1980s Niigata was the beneficiary of large public works projects, courtesy of Tanaka's interpersonal networks with ministry officials, the construction industry, the utilities, telecommunications and heavy industries.

In 1962, Niigata ranked fifth among the forty-seven prefectures, receiving $33.6 million from the national budget. In 1965, Niigata ranked fourth with $66.94 million and in 1970 Niigata had achieved third position with an allocation of $177.7 million. By 1983, Niigata ranked first in the nation for per capita expenditure for public works.

Besides Tanaka Civil Engineering and Construction Company and the Nagaoka Railroad Company, Tanaka – often referred to as 'the human bulldozer' – was also the chairman and later vice-president of Echigo Kotsu, a transport company, as well as of several electric wire companies. Tanaka established dummy companies with no staff or offices to purchase real estate in Niigata for the sites of a nuclear power plant, the bullet train passage, a university and land reclamation, to name only a few. The profits from the land-flipping deals were extremely lucrative.

In 1972, directly before Prime Minister Sato's resignation from office, Tanaka published *Plan for the Remodeling of the Japanese Archipelago* which highlighted the crowded cities and pollution associated with rapid industrialization. Tanaka's plan called for connecting rural areas with large cities so that Japanese could move to cleaner and healthier environments in the countryside. Tanaka's book served to boost his popularity among voters and, as importantly, it also presented him with the opportunity to profit considerably from future infrastructure projects and real estate transactions.

On the other hand, Tanaka's plan can also be viewed as an innovative method to raise land prices and to use funds for pork-barrel patronage in the prefectures, specifically in Niigata. During the period 1967–70, three of the six ministers in prime ministers' cabinets were members loyal to Tanaka. From 1970–76, the seven ministers of construction and four ministers of posts and communications were in Tanaka's domain.

There were allegations against Tanaka by public prosecutors regarding kick-backs to Etsuzankai for the Tadami River hydro-electric project and for the reclamation of the Shinano river-bed, which Tanaka had purchased from farmers in the 1950s. Usually he emerged unscathed from the series of allegations.

Tanaka left office as Prime Minister in December 1974 amidst yet another scandal. When the press criticized his business dealings with the land and real estate companies the Diet held a public inquiry. When the committee called the secretary of Etsuzankai with whom he was having an affair, Tanaka resigned from office rather than having her take the stand. Two years later in 1976 he was pursued by the well-documented Lockheed bribery scandal which should have ended his career in politics but, instead, the event revealed the unwavering loyalty of his constituents in Niigata who stood by him throughout the investigation.

Tanaka was released on $690,000 bail in August. He was convicted not on bribery charges but for violating foreign exchange laws and was given a four-year prison sentence. Tanaka remained free on appeal until his death in 1993. Nevertheless, Tanaka and his faction continued to receive substantial support from the electorate and Tanaka kept his seat in the Diet representing his Niigata constituency until 1985 when he and his faction finally lost power to Nakasone.

During his term as Prime Minister, Tanaka took more control over MOC and the Ministry of Transportation. Additionally, all of Tanaka's 1972 cabinet were to become future prime ministers. Takeo Miki (1974–76) was Deputy Prime Minister, Takeo Fukuda (1976–78) was Minister of Finance, Masayoshi Ohira (1978–80) was Minister of Foreign Affairs and Yasuhiro Nakasone (1982–87) was MITI minister. Post-war Japan Inc. was thriving.

Noboru Takeshita: a Tanaka protégé

Prime Minister Noboru Takeshita (November 6, 1987–June 3, 1989) was Tanaka's chief fundraiser while he was in the Tanaka faction. He tirelessly combed the countryside collecting money for the LDP treasury. Takeshita was chief cabinet secretary from 1971–74 in both Eisaku Sato's and Kakuei Tanaka's cabinets. Under Tanaka's tutelage, Takeshita forged tight networks with the construction industry and MOC. The large general contractors were particularly fond of Takeshita because his projects brought lucrative contracts. When he was Minister of Construction in Takeo Fukuda's 1976 cabinet subsidies soared to Shimane Prefecture, which Takeshita represented in the Lower House.

Shimane Prefecture, the second least populated prefecture in Japan, has a land mass of 6,708 km^2 but the population is a meager 0.74 million. Located on the southwest of Honshu, its coast lies on the Sea of Japan. The terrain is mostly mountainous with only 6 percent of arable land available for agriculture, of which 80 percent is devoted to rice farming. The primary industry is fisheries. Shimane also includes the Oki Islands and it claims the territorial rights to the South Korean controlled island of Takeshima. Recognized by the ROK as the Dokdo Islands, the territorial dispute is a source of constant friction between Japan and South Korea.

Takeshita's commitment to bringing home as many public works projects as possible was pragmatic because the projects served to keep his small business constituents in Shimane and the construction industry satisfied and the LDP coffers full. Takeshita was able to retain his seat in the Diet long after he resigned from office because of his continuous effort to supply his constituents with subsidies, which funded about 60–70 percent of public works projects. During the 1970s and 1980s Shimane's infrastructure was substantially upgraded to include three airports, tunnels and four expressways, land reclamation projects and numerous dams. There is also a national university and a prefectural university.

Shin Kanemaru served as an aide and key fundraiser for the Tanaka faction. However, after the Lockheed bribery scandal he and Takeshita left to form their own faction in 1985. When Takeshita became Prime Minister in 1987, Kanemaru assumed the post of Deputy Prime Minister. After returning from Manchuria where he had served in the army, Kanemaru returned to his home in Yamanashi Prefecture where he owned a successful liquor business before entering politics. Known as the 'kingpin of the LDP' following Tanaka's resignation from office, his back-room politicking and skill at bringing in huge sums of money to LDP coffers due to his network with industry and the underworld made him a potent leader in the LDP and the Takeshita faction the wealthiest and the largest in the LDP. As was the case for the Tanaka faction, construction companies that wanted to expand operations through public works projects contributed the major share of political contributions to the Kanemaru/Takeshita faction.

Big bucks for big business

The development of Japan's electric power companies and the nuclear power industry through the close collaboration of businesses, ministry officials and elected officials and the intimate roles that Special Corporations, research institutes and industrial associations played during the process is a superb representation of the post-war Japan Inc. model. There was conjecture that Kan's political demise was due, in part, to his attempts to reform the model, in this case the nuclear power and electric power industries, which are of prime importance to national policy as well as to the interests of politicians, bureaucrats and businessmen. The return of the LDP and the restart of the plants illustrate:

1. A rigid hierarchical socio-political system.
2. The long-term vested interests of politicians, ministries and big businesses which perpetuate the unforgiving rigidity of Japan's government model of administration.

3. The poorer prefectures' reliance on the continuation of public works projects, which is illustrated by the nuclear plants.

The world's biggest nuclear power plant: Tanaka's treat

The Kashiwazaki-Kariwa Nuclear Power Plant (KK) in Kashiwazaki, a major city in Niigata and in Tanaka's third district constituency, is a classic example of land-flipping and pork-barrel patronage in the rural and poorer prefectures and why, despite serious accidents and the 2007 earthquake, the plant continued to operate until March 2011.

KK, which is operated by TEPCO, was constructed on land which had been purchased from Hokuetsu Paper Company in 1966 by the mayor of Kariwa, a village adjacent to Kashiwazaki. The mayor, who later confessed that he was acting on Tanaka's behalf, sold the land to Muromachi Sangyo, one of Tanaka's dummy companies, which, in turn, sold it to TEPCO for far more than the original price. Tanaka's political association realized a profit estimated to be $11 million. In 1969, Tanaka convinced the government to plan the construction of a nuclear power plant on the site. FILP supplied the funds and the ministries' Special Corporations distributed the contracts and licenses to industries that were mainly in MITI's and MOC's administrative jurisdiction.

It's not nice to fool Mother Nature

KK is the largest power plant in the world and built on 4.2 km² of land on the coast of the Sea of Japan near the epicenter of the strongest earthquake to occur at a nuclear power plant prior to Fukushima. The case of KK is representative of other power plants throughout Japan. Kashiwazaki had a population of 93,000 and the local residents were worried even before the first reactor was constructed that the ground of the site was too soft for a nuclear power plant. In the KK design, TEPCO only took into consideration land faults and not submarine faults. Since there were no seismic guidelines when KK No.1 reactor was approved in 1977, a government panel of experts guaranteed that the plant would withstand a quake of a 6.9 magnitude despite some experts disputing their claims.

KK's seven reactors became commercially operational between 1985 and 1997. In Japan, generally the six biggest construction companies build the reactors and the giant heavy industries design and supply the reactors. The first three reactors at KK were designed by Toshiba, which also supplied the reactors and the steam generators. Kajima constructed the reactors. Hitachi designed and supplied No. 4 and No. 5 reactors as well as the steam generators. Shimizu Takenaka Co. constructed the reactors. Toshiba designed No. 6 reactor and, together with General Electric Co., supplied the reactor. Kajima and Kumagai Gumi were the contractors. Traditionally, retired officials from MOC served as presidents and executive directors in these construction companies.

When the Niigata–Chuetsu–Oki earthquake struck in July 2007, killing eleven people and injuring over a thousand, all of the reactors were shut down for twenty-one months until the damage that the plant had sustained was repaired. Two reactors went on line again in 2009. All operations were suspended after the Fukushima nuclear crisis.

The most dangerous power plant in the world

The New Komeito Party (NKP) is in the coalition government with the LDP. Although the party has evolved to include other right-wing parties since the 1990s, the original party was an offshoot of the Sokka Gakkai, a lay Buddhist organization based on Nichren Buddhism and founded in the 1930s. The organization developed rapidly after the war primarily because of sponsorship from Japanese with low income. The Buddhist organization published magazines and brochures advocating devotion to the church's precepts and promising that praying to the head of the church would prevent or cure baldness as well as other diseases. Believers (that is, contributors to Sokka Gakkai coffers), would also achieve successful careers.

The political party was established in 1964 as the New Komeito Party. (On September 26, 2014 to celebrate the 50th anniversary of the establishment of the party the 'New' was removed from the English title). According to NKP officials, the Sokka Gakkai and the NKP are independent organizations. Nevertheless, the Sokka Gakkai and the NKP meet biannually and the majority of NKP members are also Sokka Gakkai members. In the 1960s the Sokka Gakkai built a pagoda as a symbol of Nichiren Buddhism near the town of Gotemba on the outskirts of Hakkone National Park and Mount Fuji in Shizuoka Prefecture.

The town of Hamaoka (merged in 2004 with Omaezaki) is located in the Tokai region at the southern tip of Shizuoka Prefecture and 125 miles northeast of Tokyo. Tokai is Japan's major industrial and manufacturing region with densely populated cities where economies are supported mainly by the manufacturing sector. Car manufacturers with extensive operations are Toyota Motor Corp., Honda Corp., Mitsubishi Motors and Suzuki.

Hamaoka was impoverished when the residents accepted to host a nuclear power plant in 1969. Seismologists had warned the government in 1970 before the license for the construction of Hamaoka Nuclear Power Plant No. 1 reactor was granted to the Chubu Electric Power Company (CHUDEN) that the proposed site was near two seismic fault lines and that a major earthquake in the Tokai region was overdue. Regardless, CHUDEN received the permit and commenced construction and the plant was commissioned in 1976. Three more reactors were commissioned and, despite seismologists' claim that Hamaoka was the most dangerous plant in Japan, a fifth reactor was commissioned in 2005. Although two reactors have been decommissioned since 2009, a sixth reactor has been under construction since December 2008 despite seismologists' insistence that an earthquake of the magnitude of 9 (such as the one that occurred in 2011) would trigger the evacuation of more than 28 million residents in Tokyo. Operations were suspended after the Fukushima nuclear crisis.

Aomori Prefecture's no. 1 industry: nuclear power

Aomori is located in the Tohoku region and is the northern-most prefecture on the main island of Honshu. With a population of about 1,437,000 people, its primary industries are forestry, aquaculture and agriculture. But the nuclear power industry has become a dominant part of its economy and nuclear facilities are located in some of the most scenic areas along the Pacific coast. With four more power plants currently under construction, the prefecture will be host to more nuclear-related installations than any other prefecture in the country.

In 1980, the electric power companies established Japan Nuclear Fuel Ltd. (JNFL) to commercially recycle spent fuel. The ten domestic electric power companies and seventy-seven other firms are among the larger stockholders but TEPCO is the largest. The government designated the village of Rokkasho-mura for a uranium enrichment plant and for a low-level radioactive-waste disposal unit. In July 1984, the Federation of Electric Power Companies (FEPC), one of MITI's electricity-related industrial associations, asked Aomori Prefecture and Rokkasho-mura for permission to locate nuclear facilities in the village. In April 1985, a basic agreement on the location of the nuclear facility was reached. JNFL financed and operated the Rokkasho Uranium Enrichment Plant which began operation in 1992. JNFL's second installation, the high-level Radioactive Waste Storage Center, was completed in 1995 and began operating in the same year.

In 1998, JNFL received a request from the FEPC to begin studies regarding the development of a MOX fabrication plant (J-MOX). Subsequently, in 2001, the Aomori government received a request from METI to build Japan's first nuclear fuel reprocessing plant in Rokkasho-mura. The complex, which is financed and operated by JNFL, includes a MOX fabrication plant and a high-level nuclear waste facility. The investment in the development of the complex ballooned to $20 billion by 2001.

Operations were delayed when ANRE revealed in 2002 that, taking into consideration the costs of construction and equipment, the cost for reprocessing the fuel in-house was 1.5 times more expensive than importing it from Great Britain or France. METI apologized publicly, stressing that it had not known of the data and that the ministry never intended to conceal it. FEPC met with Aomori government officials as well to explain why in 1996 it had concealed information that indicated that the cost of burying spent fuel was about 30 percent less than recycling it. The FEPC claimed that the data were not considered important enough to publish and that there was no need to review the national nuclear fuel recycling policy or to change the current strategy for recycling spent fuel. Three years later the Aomori governor finally acquiesced to government pressure to allow operations to proceed.

The utilities sweeten the pot for political parties

The power utilities have been linked closely to the LDP and have contributed millions of yen to LDP politicians, first through direct contributions from the companies until 1976 when that route was formally curtailed, and then through individual contributions from the companies' top executives who purchase tickets to political campaign events. Nevertheless, DPJ politicians also have interpersonal relationships with the electric power companies and through the acceptance of campaign contributions. TEPCO's union established a political league in 1976 specifically for the collection of campaign funds for politicians. TEPCO's labor union belongs to the Federation of Electric Power Related Industry Workers' Union of Japan. The federation's political action committee also contributes funds to the DPJ. At least 112 DPJ members in the Lower House have been supported by TEPCO's union. As an example, the DPJ Upper House member Masao Kobayashi, a one-time member of TEPCO's labor union, received ¥30 million.

Masashi Fujiwara, a DPJ member of the Upper House, was employed as an electrical engineer at the Kansai Electric Power Company (KEPCO) which operates a number of power plants. Fujiwara, who had served as secretary-general of KEPCO's trade union, stated in April 2011 that since 2007 the DPJ, as a part of its 'Basic Energy Plan', considered nuclear power to be fundamental to a stable energy supply. Fujiwara reportedly had received during 2007–10 ¥36 million in campaign contributions from TEPCO.

The utilities continue to purchase fundraising party tickets to lobby their interests. *Asahi Shimbun* reported on April 21, 2014 that nine utilities which operated nuclear plants had bought tickets to Deputy Prime Minister Aso's fundraising parties for at least ten years but their names were not revealed in Aso's political fund reports.

Asahi Shimbun also reported on July 20 that a former director of CHUDEN told the paper that during the period 1980–2004, the company had donated ¥30 million ($290,000) from a slush fund to four gubernatorial candidates. Former Aichi Prefecture governor Masaki Kanda, who had served as governor for three terms (1999–2011), admitted that he had received political donations from CHUDEN in 1999 and in 2003 before his election campaigns. Although he was never asked to reciprocate, Kanda served as a member of CHUDEN's utility policies panel and was considered to be among the influential people at the local level. Furthermore, CHUDEN had requested that five major construction companies contribute ¥1 million each to the 2003 donation. The former director revealed that he had divulged the names of the companies to Kanda. However, Kanda told the *Asahi* that he could not remember if he had received funds in 2003.

The former director alleged that in order to raise the slush funds, CHUDEN embellished the amount of orders it placed with the construction companies. There was also reason to believe that CHUDEN had used the revenue from consumers' electricity bills to encourage politicians to support utility projects. Since the utilities must gain approval from governors and local officials before they can proceed with the construction of new reactors or the restart of idled reactors it is essential that the companies remain on good terms with local governments which host nuclear power plants. The director admitted that often CHUDEN was approached by local government officials for political contributions. CHUDEN denied the allegations, stating that there were no records of the transactions.

On July 28, the *Asahi* reported that Chimori Naito, a former vice-president of KEPCO, also revealed that KEPCO contributed huge 'top secret' donations to prime ministers over a twenty-year period which were funded by taxpayers.

The price of pork-barrel patronage: the towns that can't say 'no'

Tanaka's *Plan for the Remodeling of the Japanese Archipelago* and the Land Development Policy did not stem the migration of the population from the rural areas to bigger cities and industrialized regions. On the contrary, instead of a more devolved society, Tanaka's plans acted to engender more dependency on central government and on ministerial guidance. Moreover, Tanaka's pork-barrel system justified the plundering of FILP by politicians, ministry officials and big business. However, while Japan's economy was expanding and tax revenues were feeding the treasury and Japan was overtaking the US economy, the Japanese preferred to ignore the spending spree.

In 1974, the 'Three Power Source Development Law' was enacted to subsidize local communities that were willing to host nuclear power plants. The law called for a tax, which was included in consumers' electricity bills, to be used by government to subsidize public works in communities that hosted the plants. Since 1966 local governments hosting nuclear reactors have received altogether ¥2.5 trillion in nuclear-related subsidies. ¥915 billion in subsidies was distributed after the law was passed and the host cities, towns and villages charged plant operators ¥892 billion in fixed property taxes. The utility companies are said to have donated ¥53 billion to local governments. However, according to the *Mainichi Shimbun*, which conducted a survey in August 2011, supported with ANRE data, the total amount could well be higher because local governments were reticent to release data that confirmed the sum total of nuclear-related fixed property taxes and donations.

The local communities that host nuclear power plants and which have been the beneficiaries of numerous public works projects are structurally dependent on the power industry and on central government to improve living standards, to provide employment and to procure support for small businesses. Pork-barrel patronage paved the way for the entry of nuclear power plants and for the massive investment by power companies and heavy industries into these communities.

The local authorities came to accept central government directives usually with little protest because of the ministerial controls over local government officials and because, if the directives by the state agencies were refused, the communities might forfeit future subsidies for public works projects on which they had come to rely. The communities became addicted to the subsidies, as the local governments connected hosting power plants with the subsidies for the future construction of schools, free and improved welfare services and lower taxes. It was not until the late 1990s after a series of accidents occurred at power plants that the Japanese began to recognize the implications of building nuclear plants in earthquake-prone zones and to question safety regulations.

Kashiwazaki-Kariwa

There were demonstrations, petitions and referendums in Niigata before 1985 when the first reactor was scheduled to go online. Even in the 1980s and prior to the earthquake in 2007, the Niigata governor personally visited the MITI cabinet minister to present a letter requesting that MITI's Nuclear Industry Safety Agency (NISA) ensure the safety and security of KK. The minister promised.

After the earthquake, the struggle by anti-nuclear protesters to have KK decommissioned lost momentum, the reason relating to Niigata's need for government subsidization of the local economy and the pressure from the ministries, from TEPCO shareholders and from manufacturers with big investments in the Tohoku region on local government officials to continue to host KK. Also, the majority of Kashiwazaki City and Kariwa residents felt obliged to accept the plant because the government had generously poured more than $2 billion in subsidies into the economy and the plant employed hundreds of people.

At a news conference on April 23, 2014 Niigata governor Hiroko Izumida accused central government of claiming that the newly established Nuclear Regulatory Agency's (NRA) safety regulations were 'safe' even though they failed to address issues related to protecting residents against nuclear disasters. Also, the government is transferring to local governments the responsibility for the evacuation of local residents when an emergency occurs. Izumida, who met with US nuclear regulatory director Gregory Jaczko in March, argued that local authorities will not be able to make effective evacuation plans until the central government reassesses the structure of its disaster management. Izumada proposed building nuclear shelters in residents' homes.

Ultimately, the residents and the local authorities are controlled by the concern that if they refuse to accommodate KK, government support for public works will either decline or cease altogether.

Hamaoka

Omaezaki (Hamaoka) has received $700 million in subsidies since the 1970s and the power plant employs 3,000 people. The reaction by the local authorities was similar when Kan decreed a shut-down of the Hamaoka Nuclear Power Plant following the nuclear crisis. Shizuoka governor Hetia Kawakatsu, while praising Kan's sudden deviation from the DPJ's 'Basic Energy Plan' also requested that the government assume responsibility for any negative impact on the local economy from the suspension of Hamaoka's operations. Shigeru Ishihara, the mayor of Omaezaki, also requested that the state promise financial support for the 1,200 people who worked at the plant and to guarantee the city's budget, which relied mainly on hosting Hamaoka's operations.

With the exception of two plants, the suspension of operations for all of the other power plants has acutely affected local economies. Residents reacted in June 2013 by re-electing Mayor Ishihara, who ran for another term against an anti-nuclear candidate.

Rokkasho-Mura

In April 2005, Aomori governor Shingo Mimura acquiesced to METI's request to approve the construction of the MOX fabrication plant (J-MOX). When he signed the agreement together with the mayor of Rokkasho-mura and the head of JNFL he urged FEPC to speed up its efforts to implement the MOX program. The construction was delayed due to protests lodged by anti-nuclear activists and due to safety issues. Operations were slated to begin in 2012 but were postponed until the NRA gave the go-ahead. JNFL has filed a new application, which is expected to be approved.

A nuclear power plant, which began operating in 2005, is located in the small town of Higashidori where the primary industry was fishing before TEPCO arrived in 1992 to ask the local government for permission to build a nuclear reactor. The area had seen the emigration of hundreds of construction workers who had been laid off by contractors. Since then TEPCO has injected massive funds into the area and the reactors have become the town's primary industry. The construction of the other reactors at Higashidori power plant complex brought subsidies for construction of a new elderly care home, a new clinic, a school and a childcare facility.

Oma is a village near Higashidori where the economy was also constrained and the 6,300 residents wanted to receive the same treatment as Higashidori. In 2008, METI gave a permit to J-Power (the former EPDC) to operate a plant in Oma. Currently under construction, the pluthermal reactor with 100 percent MOX fuel is expected to be in commercial operation this year (2014). The subsidies have provided a school, a care home for the elderly and a fishing facility. In May 2011, two months after the Fukushima nuclear disaster, the majority of residents declared that the Oma plant was an absolute necessity and hoped that the construction would continue. There was also hope among the residents that more reactors would be constructed in the future.

Governor Mimura, who won a third four-year term in office on June 4, 2011, campaigned for safe nuclear energy and promised to put in place an independent panel of experts. However, his campaign avoided mentioning the power plants currently under construction. Running as an independent, he was supported by the LDP and the NKP. Mimura's opponent in the election, Takashi Yamauchi, who was a former prefectural assembly member and also ran as an independent, was supported by the DPJ. Yamauchi, calling for the end of nuclear powered energy, promised voters that he would freeze the existing plans for the construction of more reactors in Aomori.

Shimane

Noboru Takeshita's pork-barrel patronage brought Shimane Prefecture a nuclear power plant with two reactors. Shimane-1 (commissioned in 1974) and Shimane-2 (commissioned in 1989) have brought the prefecture larger subsidies. It is calculated that No. 2 reactor provided over 75 percent of the local tax revenue during the 1990s. CHUDEN owns and operates the plant. The workforce's abiding reliance on public works projects and concerns among local authorities that the subsidies would ebb encouraged the request for the construction of a third reactor. The construction, designed by Hitachi, was underway in 2011 and was to be commissioned in March 2012. No. 3 reactor has brought local residents $90 million in public works funds and a guarantee that $90 million in property tax revenues will be allotted over a fifteen-year period when the reactor is commissioned. After the Fukushima disaster, the residents were very worried about the safety of their nuclear facility but the need for government funds overrides the concerns for safety and residents accept the risks.

Pork-barrel patronage: the beggars

Some local government officials claim that central government views prefectures as 'beggars' and that they must court ministerial favors by offering gifts to top government officials. They also complain that they are 'slaves' to central government.

Ehime is a prime example of how large subsidies for public works are accessed by local governments. It is also an illustration of the failure of the national ministries to consider the frequency of use of the infrastructure projects, the outlay of tax revenue for the upkeep of the infrastructure and, most importantly, the projects' cost-effectiveness.

Ehime is the largest of four prefectures on Japan's fourth largest island of Shikoku. The prefecture has 5,672.5 km of coastline, the fifth-longest in Japan. The population is approximately 1.4 million with about 500,000 living in Matsuyama, the capital. The primary industries are agriculture (citrus), forestry and fisheries. Secondary industries are ship-building, chemicals, machinery and paper pulp. In terms of per capita income, Ehime ranks 35th among the forty-seven prefectures, 32nd for personal income, 25th in industrial output, 25th for agricultural produce and 30th for the size of the budget (as of 2005). Although not mentioned in the prefecture's literature, Shikoku's only nuclear power plant is located in the fishing village of Ikata which supplies the island with most of its electricity.

Before he entered office, Governor Iga had been an officer of the Ehime local government and a staunch member of the LDP. As vice-governor under the previous administration, he was in line to succeed as governor. At the beginning of Iga's administration, one of Ehime's representatives in the Lower House in the National Diet was an LDP politician who entered Prime Minister Takeshita's cabinet in 1987 for one year as Minister of Construction. Ihei Ochi was in the right place at the right time and, as a consequence, the applications for public works in Ehime were accepted in the first Takeshita budget.

Iga took full advantage of Representative Ochi's connection with the MOC and the construction industry and during his twelve years in office he cultivated an interpersonal network with top officials in the ministries to promote Ehime's needs. Ehime is one of the most scenic areas in Japan and tourists flock to Matsuyama Castle and to Dogo Onsen, Japan's oldest hot spring which is the site of Natsume Soseki's famous novel *Botchan*. Besides being the birthplace of Kenzaburo Oe, the 1994 Nobel Prize winner for literature, Ehime is reputed to be the home of Haiku.

Governor Iga established Ehime's presence in the United States through Iyo Bank, Ehime's regional bank. Like a number of prefectural banks in the late 1980s, Iyo Bank also opened a one-man branch office in Manhattan to provide offshore services to Ehime businesses in the United States. However, since Ehime businesses were SMEs transactions were intermittent. The branch office was closed in 2004 to be replaced with a representative office.

Iga's close ties to the ministries enabled him to access large subsidies for public works which included a network of highways and tunnels throughout Ehime's mountainous terrain, and the Kurushima Bridge that links Ehime with Hiroshima on the main island of Honshu and which was under the management of the Honshu-Shikoku Bridge Authority, one of the debt-ridden public corporations that were merged with the JH. Iga's efforts also brought an international airport, a convention center, a modern art museum and, his biggest triumph, a Foreign

Access Zone (FAZ) in Japan. By the end of his final term in office, Iga had gained the reputation among residents as a governor obsessed with self-glorification.

MITI initiated FAZ installations in response to the United States' demands that Japan open its markets to more imports. In 1992, MITI wrote the Law on Extraordinary Measures for the Promotion of Imports and Facilitation of Foreign Direct Investment in Japan, setting the stage for the construction of Foreign Access Zones throughout Japan.

In January 1993 before the inauguration of FAZ in Matsuyama, MITI International Vice-Minister Yuji Tanahashi met with foreign business executives in Tokyo to discuss the implementation of FAZ and MITI's plans to modify customs laws, create a fund for industrial structural adjustment, subsidize foreign investment, defray investment coasts, guarantee loans, provide additional investment information and support employee recruitment. When asked if the difficulties experienced by foreign companies to access Japan's markets were due to lack of effort, Tanahashi replied that the Japanese language could be problematic but he did point to the successful entry by large international firms such as Motorola and Texas Instruments.

In April 1993, a company comprising government organizations and private corporations was established to manage FAZ. The Ehime Foreign Access Zone Co. Ltd. constructed a distribution center for the handling of imported goods and three exhibition halls, one of which was the largest exhibition hall in the Shikoku-Chugoku region. The hall was suitable for numerous events with conference rooms fitted with projection and simultaneous translation equipment. The entire exhibition area covered 7,300m². JETRO set up a JETRO FAZ Support Center in the facility to provide FAZ-specific information.

Iga also established a prefectural representative desk at JETRO New York where his son served as the first representative. When Iga's son returned to Ehime, he was given the post of director of Ehime's Foreign Access Zone. The desk was transferred to Hong Kong after Iga lost the 1999 election.

After his resignation from office in September 2011 former Prime Minister Naoto Kan made the famous pilgrimage of the eighty-eight Buddhist temples on Shikoku. Immediately after Kan became the Prime Minister in 2010 his wife Nobuko published *What on Earth will Change in Japan now that you are Prime Minister?* (*Anata ga Soori ni Natte, Ittai, Nihon no Nani ga Kawaru No?*), detailing her marriage and her husband's political background, which focused on politics at the grassroots level, challenging the traditional political system and environmental issues. Mrs. Kan wrote that her husband enjoyed person-to-person contact, pressing the flesh, drinking and back-room politicking but not the homework. The book's objective was also an attempt to inform readers of Kan and his DPJ colleagues' continuing struggle to implement structural reforms of a rigid administrative system.

5

The Japanese Economic Miracle: Japan Inc. on Center Stage

The United States' open markets to Japanese imports and the continuation of the favorable exchange rates put Japanese producers on an even playing field with their American rivals. By the mid-1970s the Japanese automobile industry was taking full advantage of the oil shock and, hot on the heels of Chrysler and GM, aggressively pursued American consumers who were beginning to appreciate the fuel-efficient engines as well as the lower prices. Honda first entered the American market via its motorcycles, which proved to be very competitive with the heavier Harley-Davidson. German car manufactures also benefited with sturdy and reliable fuel-efficient Volkswagens and Audis.

MITI had tried in the late 1950s to convince car manufacturers to engage in the 'People's Car Program' which was similar to the Nazi 'People's Car' that was designed by Porsche for the Weimer Republic in 1934 when Japanese engineers were sent to Germany to study automotive technologies. Suzuki and Subaru complied, producing several mini-models with 150cc engines. However, Toyota and Nissan, who were keen to produce models that were competitive in the United States, postponed participation.

Commentators have assessed the Japanese auto manufacturing industry as having developed aloof from MITI's regulations but the ministry's policies and government subsidies effectively protected them from foreign competition in the domestic market. Furthermore, MITI officials routinely received post-retirement positions on the boards of auto manufacturers.

MITI's Large-Scale Retail Store Law protects Japan Inc. but not Japanese consumers

Until recently the wholesale-distribution system was regarded as feudalistic and very insular. The relationship between manufacturers, wholesalers and retailers was based on networks that were established between the parties prior to the war and which continued after the war. The relationship still continues but has loosened considerably not through deregulation but through the changes in the wholesaling business. Since the cost of goods sold in shops includes wholesalers' fees for services rendered, including storage facilities and direct delivery to retailers, consumers pay more for goods that would be cheaper if the wholesalers were not the third party in the distribution channel. Also domestic products can be more expensive because of government subsidization of a particular sector, particularly agricultural products such as rice. Traditionally, rice farmers are paid by government to leave their fields fallow. The government also stores rice stocks which act to inflate wholesale prices. In the long run, consumers shoulder the extra costs.

Small businesses, including agriculture, account for 99 percent of business activity in Japan and for the employment of 70 percent of the workforce. As stated previously, during Japan's post-war period, small business owners were the strongest supporters in the LDP politicians' constituencies and the most influential in local communities. They contributed substantial funds to political coffers in return for public works projects. Until 1997 Japanese small retailers were partially protected from the encroachment on their businesses by the Large-Scale Retail Store Law (LSL) which was implemented in 1974 by MITI, the ministry that regulates the retail sector.

The LSL can be traced to 1937 when the MCI began to regulate large stores in response to the demands of politicians in power to protect their small business retailer constituencies from the competition of larger retailers who were beginning to expand operations. Although the MCI had regarded the regulation of the retail industry as an impediment to its development, it finally gave in to political pressure when self-regulation by the larger stores failed. The Department Store Law (DSL) remained in place until it was terminated by SCAP in 1947 because it was considered to contradict the new Antimonopoly Law.

However, after the Occupation ended, the DSL was reinstated, disallowing department stores from building over 1,500 square meters of floor space without first obtaining a permit from MITI. The permit could be refused if the structure was considered an intrusion on the businesses of small retailers in the area. The applications for permits were often sent to members of small store associations in the location where the store would be built for deliberation, and MITI requested that large stores consult with these associations. The DSL also enabled MITI to control the closing times and the number of days for holidays of department stores which enabled the small retailers to remain open for longer hours.

After the war, MITI's objectives were focused on the development of industries but the ministry was pressured to accommodate LDP politicians' request to protect their small business constituents from large retailers who could threaten businesses by undercutting prices.

However, it can be argued that in return for MITI's response to the LDP's request, the ministry received full support in the Diet for planning policies related to the regulation of other sectors, thereby preserving MITI's administrative territory. Also, the LDP would be keen to allow the creation of more public corporations without questioning the motivations (i.e. *amakudari*) and the utilization of public funds. The mutual protection/mutual obligation relationship was fundamental to the Japan Inc. model. Despite the DSL, by the late 1960s the birth of chain superstores began to change Japan's retail landscape.

Retailing not only food but also non-perishables the superstores were beginning to encroach on small business retailers and department store territory. The stores avoided applying for permits by operating in installations with less than 1,500 square meters floor space, creating separate entities which operated on separate floors in the same building but which were controlled by a single corporation. The small retailers as well as the department stores lobbied MITI to keep the superstores at bay. MITI tried to ameliorate the tricky situation by asking the Department Store Council, local Chambers of Commerce and small retailers to discuss the effectiveness of the DSL system and to arrive at a consensus regarding the planning of optional regulations.

The DSL or permit system was subsequently replaced in 1974 by the LSL, which offered a simpler notification procedure requiring companies to notify MITI of plans for new stores and to obtain approval of their plans from the associations of the traditional shopping arcades (*shotengai*). Although department stores were usually located near or adjacent to railway stations and at a good distance from the small business arcades, the LSL did not stop the growing number of superstores which were slowly becoming an integral part of Japanese consumer culture. Convenience stores were also locating in the vicinity of train stations. The pioneer of the superstore phenomenon was Isao Nakauchi, the founder of Daiei Inc.

Isao Nakauchi the renegade retailer

Isao Nakauchi led the way by procuring in bulk and retailing goods for mass consumption. Nakauchi's initial venture was a discount pharmacy in Osaka known as 'Housewives Store, Daiei'. The parent company was Daiei Pharmaceutical Company and financed with capital earned from selling penicillin at inflated prices directly after the end of the war. Although his brother and some of his colleagues were arrested, Nakauchi emerged unscathed and continued his journey to build an empire encompassing Japan's first discount retail-supermarket outlets and domestic and international operations that included hotels, shopping centers and a baseball team.

The Daiei Pharmaceutical Company was successful because customers appreciated the discount pricing at a time when household savings were limited (about 10 percent) and budgets were constrained. Nakauchi refused to engage in the cartels formed by the owners of small retail shops which artificially raised the prices of goods and which contradicted the objectives of his business model.

Nakauchi, emboldened by the success of his first venture, opened more discount stores in the Osaka region, introducing candy, cosmetics, toiletries and foods. By 1970, Nakauchi had transformed Daiei Pharmaceutical Company into a general discount retail store, rebranding it Daiei Inc. By 1972 Daiei had become Japan's second largest retailer with a chain of discount superstores located throughout Japan.

Nakauchi, who regarded Daiei as the 'Sears Roebuck of Japan', introduced the concept of in-house brands when he acquired a Japanese firm that manufactured radios and televisions which were sold overseas at lower prices than in Japan. Nakauchi sold the same goods under the Daiei label for half the price. Nakauchi kept his overheads low not only by selling in bulk but also by expanding operations of outlets located in less populated areas where rents were much lower than in the cities.

Nakauchi goes full-speed ahead

Nakauchi regarded the LSL as one of the main obstacles to expansion in Japan because of the powerful influence on the political society by the small store associations. Often proposals for establishing branches entailed negotiating with more than seven *shotengai* simultaneously which might involve reducing store hours and limiting the kinds of products sold. Furthermore, approval could often take as long as seven to eight years. He also recognized that foreign importers were frustrated not only with tariffs and the distribution system but also by the LSL which, by limiting floor space, also limited the number of foreign products sold in the shops.

When Nakauchi took Daiei Inc. in the 1970s to the United States and Honolulu to open a subsidiary Daiei USA in the Pearlridge Shopping Center he found a welcoming environment. Since he was not confined by the LSL the 17,000 square foot store was the largest Japanese food store in Hawaii with 60 percent of the food imported from Japan. In 1975, Daiei expanded the store to a three-story structure which included a restaurant.

In 1972 due to the loosening of regulations regarding foreign retailers entering Japan, Nakauchi engaged in joint ventures with Joseph Magnin, a San Francisco department store, and Swift and Company, an American meat packing firm established in 1855, that also produced processed dairy and meat products such as pork sausage and ham. Daiei operated Swift's ice cream concession. Although Daiei had become Japan's largest retailer by 1974, Nakauchi continued to drive his business full-speed ahead.

Taking advantage of the growing market for Western goods, in 1976, after doing a successful trial run selling the apparel of American retailer J. C. Penny in Japan, Daiei engaged in a joint venture opening stores in Japan under the J. C. Penny name. The contract gave the trading company Itochu 5 percent of equity. In 1978, Daiei became the sole agent in Japan for the British retailer Marks & Spencer, which already had a presence in Hong Kong, a British protectorate. In 1981, Nakauchi engaged in a joint venture with the prestigious French department store, Au Printemps, opening branches in Kobe (1981), Sapporo (1982) and Tokyo (1983).

Daiei's joint venture with the American fast-food chain Wendy's International in 1979 in steakhouse restaurants proved unsuccessful because the large portions of food and the shops' interiors were not conducive to Japanese consumers who preferred less on the plate and dining in more intimate surroundings. Due to hasty expansion the venture was heavily in debt by 1988. Nevertheless, Hub, the British-style pub chain, proved more popular. The first pub was opened in 1980 in Kobe and, in the same year, a second pub was opened in Tokyo's fashionable nightclub district of Roppongi. In the same year, Daiei also purchased three Holiday Mart stores in Honolulu, converting them into Daiei stores. Altogether there were four Daiei outlets in Hawaii.

Nakauchi reorganized his company in 1981, merging one of its affiliates with the food company Maruetsu. Daiei now controlled 25 percent of Japan's total retail food business. In the same year, through the purchase of 10.5 percent equity in Takashimaya, Daiei became the largest shareholder in one of Japan's oldest luxury department stores.

In 1982, Daiei, in a partnership with a Japanese insurance company, purchased the Ala Moana Center in Honolulu, one of the world's fifteen largest shopping centers which quickly became a popular destination for Japanese honeymoon couples.

By 1984 Daiei's superstores numbered 160 but the expansion was funded with heavy borrowing. Surprisingly, unlike Nakauchi's previous objectives to cut overheads, Daiei opened a branch store in the Ginza, one of Japan's most expensive districts. Financing its debt created a huge loss and despite mass sales, Daiei continued to experience substantial losses in 1985. However, contrary to the majority of Japanese firms which borrowed from a single bank who was the principal shareholder, Nakauchi spread Daiei's debt among four banks, which provided him with a degree of independence regarding business strategy and investment.

Daiei returned to the black in 1987 and bought Riccar, the bankrupt sewing machine manufacturer, at MITI's request, thus beginning a tradition of buyouts. Also that year, Daiei announced its five-year plan to introduce the electronic information network Point of Sales (POS) in its superstores. Nakauchi was creating an empire that seemed unstoppable.

Kanebo Ltd.: the oldest listed company on the Tokyo Stock Exchange

The early Meiji economy was supported by rice cultivation and light industries such as cotton and silk yarn spinning and small tool production. Kanebo Ltd. was established in 1887 in Kanegafuchi, Tokyo. Known at that time as the Tokyo Trading Company, it began spinning raw cotton into thread in 1889. In 1893, the company's name was changed to the Kanegafuchi Spinning Company.

The textile industry experienced rapid development and by 1897, exports exceeded imports as Japan became entirely self-sufficient in cotton textiles. By 1907 large textile companies had joined to form textile oligopolies, driving British yarn from the domestic market. The Kanegafuchi Spinning Company began weaving cotton textiles in 1905. It diversified ventures to raw silk spinning in 1908, opening a plant in Kyoto City, the center of kimono production. The raw silk was transported from the silk farms in northern Kyoto Prefecture. Later in 1921 the company expanded to raw silk reeling operations.

Kanebo went international in the 1920s and 1930s when it launched new businesses and opened new distribution channels. The South American Colonial Company was established in 1928 which entered the United States in 1935. Kanebo established the Kanebo Service Company in 1931 to manage retail outlets throughout Japan. By 1934 Kanebo began to produce woolen yarn, chemical fiber and flax fiber.

The company's chemical engineers invented Japan's first synthetic fiber in 1939.

Kanebo began diversification into cosmetics, producing soap from oils extracted from silkworm cocoons, which it distributed domestically and abroad. Although most of the company's installations were destroyed during the war, Kanebo rebuilt operations by 1947 and restored operations in South America under the corporate name Kanebo do Brasil S.A.

During the 1960s and 1970s, Kanebo began to enter new business ventures while simultaneously expanding its textile divisions. In 1961 it formally launched its cosmetic production facility and marketed and distributed the cosmetics through fourteen sales offices. The following year a laboratory was opened in Paris as well as a plant south of Yokohama. In 1964, Kanebo began producing and distributing fashion merchandise, including hosiery for Christian Dior through license agreements. In 1968, Warnaco Inc., the American manufacturer of men's apparel, entered Japan through a license agreement with Kanebo to produce and distribute men's shirts under the Hathaway brand.

Kanebo's unrelenting diversification

Kanebo entered the processed food market with the acquisition of a Japanese producer of frozen foods in 1964 to launch Kanebo Harris Inc. Besides frozen desserts, the new division produced chewing gum and chocolate. Kanebo expanded the division by buying yet another frozen dessert manufacturer in 1971. The list of processed foods increased with the buyout of a company which manufactured instant *azuki* beans (red beans), soups and rice cakes.

The acquisition of a pharmaceutical company in 1966 allowed Kanebo to diversify into herbal medicines, building a laboratory for product R&D in 1976. Two years later, Kanebo introduced a product line of Chinese herbal medicines which was being imported from China and used extensively in Japan.

Kanebo expanded its synthetic textile fiber and chemical materials operations and began to produce nylon in 1963 and polyester filament in 1969. Pursuing the increasing demand for synthetic materials Kanebo engaged in a joint venture with Asahi Kasei, a synthetic textile company. In 1975, another joint venture with the National Starch Company produced and distributed chemical products with industrial applications.

Kanebo's most profitable venture was cosmetics and the company expanded operations internationally during the 1970s. Kanebo first entered markets in Thailand, Indonesia, the Philippines, Singapore and Hong Kong.

Kanebo Hawaii was established in 1975 followed by entry into the European market in 1979 with the introduction of a single brand in Harrods London before forming a joint venture, Kanebo Cosmetics Europe Ltd. with UTC International in Zurich for marketing Kanebo cosmetics throughout Europe. The company initiated improvements to customer service by developing sales techniques that were specific to local consumer cultures.

Capital was invested in new product lines and beauty salons in Japan where Kanebo's cosmetics were exclusively used and sold. Establishing a new cosmetics plant in 1991 in Europe, new products were designed solely for the European market. Entry into South Korea in 1992 was followed by the launch in Japan with a fade-resistant lipstick which was introduced into the European, Taiwanese and Thai markets in 1993. Kanebo engaged in numerous licensing agreements to import European fragrances and toiletries.

One-third of Kanebo's capital was invested in the expansion of the pharmaceuticals division with a facility opening in 1989. R&D was restructured, and cardiovascular, dermatological and immunological drugs were developed. Kanebo also acquired patents for drugs developed by other pharmaceutical companies, which entailed major investment.

Kanebo increased production and distribution for textiles and fibers and Kanebo Cotton Spinning Company went to Georgia USA to build a facility for spinning cotton. The food division introduced new ice cream products. The electronics division, established in 1985, was also entering software joint ventures with an Indonesian software company. Kanebo's diversification into other sectors was unremitting.

Japanese tourists proliferate: the buying spree

By the mid-1970s, many Japanese had sufficient expendable income for a honeymoon to Hawaii or a trip to the US and Europe. The explanations written in Japanese at key tourist attractions in the larger cities on the east and west coasts indicated a major increase in the number of Japanese tourists. By the early 1980s Japan had become the world's second biggest economy and producers of luxury goods such as Tiffany and Cartier began catering to Japanese tourists and hiring Japanese staff to ease sales transactions.

Americans could be forgiven for thinking that the Japanese were wealthy because they were flocking to jewelry, handbag and shoe shops to purchase expensive brand names. However, if Americans were to travel to Japan and purchase the same items they would have understood why most Japanese consumers were confined to purchasing domestic brands while spending their income on luxury goods overseas. The high tariffs which were levied on imported goods, including leather products, jewelry and apparel, made the same luxury products unaffordable to the majority of Japanese. Besides import duties, the wholesaler's costs were incorporated in the price of the imports. The importer's agent met the shipment at the port of call to take the goods through customs and, as stated previously, the wholesaler collected the goods to store in warehouses because often the importers' facilities were not large enough to store the inventory.

Since footwear produced in Japan was sized according to Japanese feet, Japanese or foreign residents with longer limbs were at a disadvantage and experienced difficulties sourcing domestically produced apparel, lingerie and shoes.

After the war the Japanese textile industry was a sunset industry and subsidized by government. Japanese apparel manufacturers were equally protected by MITI's policies and foreign apparel manufacturers entered the market through licensing agreements with Japanese companies which produced and marketed the goods. However, apparel companies which had strong brand name recognition in the country of origin where Japanese travelled or worked managed to enter Japan and establish independent subsidiaries after the government loosened regulations in 1971.

As an example, in the United States and Europe Levi's were synonymous with jeans. The Levi Strauss Company was established 1853 in San Francisco during the California Gold Rush. In 1965 Levi Strauss began to enter Asian markets, including Japan. It opened a branch sales office in Tokyo in 1965 and in 1971 established its wholly-owned subsidiary. Nevertheless, it encountered stiff competition from Japanese manufacturers. Levi Strauss decided to initially concentrate its efforts on establishing a strong brand image with which the Japanese consumer could identify, enabling them to differentiate Levi from other brands on the market. The company succeeded through a television ad campaign called 'Heroes Wear Levi's' launched in December 1978 which targeted the age group from fifteen to twenty-nine and focused on legendary Hollywood film stars such as John Wayne, Clark Gable, James Dean and Marilyn Monroe. The campaign developed into 'American Legend, My Mind Levi's' in 1982 when Levi Strauss opened Levi Strauss Japan KK, impacting positively on sales of jeans. The company's innovative distribution and logistics center in Tokyo also served to help Levi Strauss to capture a sizable share of the outerwear market from 1985.

Japanese corporate culture: the secret ingredient?

The common perception among Westerners during Japan's economic expansion was that the Japanese corporate system was one of the major strengths of Japan's political economy, that the system fostered loyalty among staff, and that the constant effort to integrate staff into the corporate culture secured a stable working environment. The lifetime employment system initiated after the war by big business to ensure a stable workforce promoted the image of a caring and nurturing employer whose fate was tied to that of the workers. The popular notion of Japanese corporate life was that it inspired group unity and commitment to hard work to achieve corporate goals. Employees sang the company anthem and participated in morning exercise routines before work, management gave daily pep-talks to inspire commitment to the company, year-end bonuses were distributed to deserving staff, and directors were personally involved in their staff's welfare. Division managers also took their staff out drinking at the company's expense after hours to encourage good communication and group harmony.

The Matsushita effect

Two of Japan's major industrialists, Konosuke Matsushita, founder of the Matsushita Industrial Electric Co. in 1929 (now Panasonic Group) and Kazuo Inamori, founder of Kyocera Corporation, were devout Zen Buddhists. Matsushita's style of management became popular among foreign businesses in the 1980s, particularly in the US. Even though the methods did not altogether suit Americans, companies imitated them because they symbolized the perceived strengths of the Japan Inc. model. The Matsushita style also significantly influenced the management models of Japanese firms.

Konosuke Matsushita is regarded as the mentor of modern Japanese industrialists. Matsushita was born into middle-class comfort in Wakayama Prefecture in 1985 but a typhoon destroyed the family estate. His father, a gentleman landowner who preferred local politics and working at city hall to managing his property, was forced to sell the ancestral home. He invested the proceeds in a sandal shop, but inexperience and inept management brought bankruptcy within two years and he was forced to sell his entire estate to pay off the remaining debts.

Matsushita was removed from grammar school at the age of ten to work as an apprentice for a year in a brassier shop and then in a bicycle shop for five years in Osaka to supplement the family income. The family's reduced circumstances as well as his experiences as a middle-aged novice merchant supported the father's theory that a formal education was likely to prevent his son from grasping the gritty realities of business. A practical, on-the-job training was elemental to understanding the ins-and-outs of operating a successful enterprise. And a wealthy merchant could inevitably hire the best and the brightest to deal with the intricacies of his business.

The Japanese victory in the war with China in 1895 gave the Japanese a sense of confidence and prompted economic optimism. The industrial expansion generated a need for faster transportation. By the time Matsushita was ten years old, the bicycle and trolley had replaced the conventional horse-drawn carriage and bicycle shops proliferated. However, when Matsushita saw that Osaka was being connected to the suburbs by an electric transit system, he predicted that this new power source would profoundly impact on daily life.

When he was sixteen he managed to gain entry into the Osaka Electric Light Co. and became, within five years, a fully-fledged professional electrical engineer and a pioneer in a rapidly growing industry. Frustrated with the tedium of his position as an inspector, he decided to leave the company to set up operations in his tiny home in the Osaka suburbs. Sales of his newly designed screw-in light fixtures were poor during his first two years in business but he continued inventing and manufacturing new devices in order to sustain his company.

In 1923 Matsushita set up Matsushita Electric Houseware Manufacturing Works and, riding a bicycle, sold his products door-to-door. He was convinced that there was a market for bicycle lamps sustained by batteries that lasted longer and were more cost-effective than the candle-lit lanterns that were commonly in use. After contacting a manufacturer of dry-cell batteries to develop a battery which would last for forty-five hours, he designed the body. Unfortunately, for six months he was unable to sell even one battery through wholesalers. He decided to avoid wholesalers altogether and set up his own agents in three cities to sell directly to dealers. The strategy was successful and the battery was the foundation of his business.

Matsushita's youth as an apprentice recalls Charles Dickens' days of long hours, meager wages, few holidays, and a diet of rice and pickles, interrupted twice a month with the addition of a slice of fish. He had no particular interest in religious practice until he was aged thirty-seven.

At the urging of a friend, he attended a service at a Buddhist temple. The atmosphere and the sincere devotion of the congregation brought him great consolation and inspired him to develop a personal ideology which supported his own propensities to push himself into overtime. Spiritual benefits could be reaped not only from prayer but also from the daily, diligent execution of one's duties.

He attended religious retreats at Buddhist monasteries, prodding his employees to participate in order to restore inner peace and to improve concentration. What was good for the soul was also good for sales. The enthusiastic found solace but the less willing realized only pain, sitting in cross-legged silence for eight hours a day.

As an engineer, an inventor and a businessman, Matsushita was intimately involved in all aspects of his company. His treatises on management, productivity, employee development, employee welfare, and guiding an enterprise through crisis were the bibles for Japanese businesses. Many of the books were published by the Peace and Happiness Through Prosperity (PHP) Institute, which Matsushita founded on November 3, 1946, in order to resuscitate the Japanese psyche crushed by the war. The institute provided a positive environment in which professionals from the public and private sectors could conduct research, collect data on economic trends, engage in business consultation, and create educational programs. As president, Matsushita poured his efforts into the institute and he thrived on a non-stop lecture circuit to preach his methods until his death at the age of ninety-four.

Kazuo Inamori: the Matsushita effect

When Kazuo Inamori retired as chairman and founder of Kyocera Corporation in 1997, he entered the priesthood at a famous Zen Buddhist monastery in Kyoto. Nevertheless, he continued to be very active in business. In 2011, he was asked by the DPJ government to become the chairman of Japan Airlines (JAL) to help salvage the bankrupt airline, which was nationalized. He held the post until 2013. JAL is reported to be solvent.

Inamori had wanted to become a pharmacist because he, as well as other members of his family, had suffered from tuberculosis. But he failed the entrance exam for medical school and ended up going to Kagoshima University in Kyushu where he had been born. He graduated in 1955 with a degree in chemistry.

Since the university was not considered first-rate, Inamori struggled to find employment after graduation. He finally was accepted by a small chemical company in Kyoto City where he worked for three years researching high-tech ceramics. He recognized that there was no competition in the market for light, inert, heat-resistant ceramics but his employer did not want to progress with the research. Frustrated, Inamori left the company to join six friends to start a tiny business in a small factory shack with an investment of $30,000, producing ceramic components for silk screening and paper-making machinery. Inamori was unable to get a loan to expand operations because the old boy establishment regarded Kyocera Corporation as a maverick and Inamori, who was twenty-seven, as an intruder who lacked social grace and business savvy.

Due to poor sales, Inamori decided to go abroad to seek greener pastures. After a visit to California to look at possible new markets, he decided to open a sales office there in 1968, courting the American semiconductor industry. In 1971, Kyocera purchased the ailing Fairchild Camera Semiconductor ceramic packaging plant in San Diego and began its well-documented climb to the top as the major supplier of ceramic (silicon) chips in the world.

Although Kazuo Inamori has often been described as aggressive and creative in the American mode, he is also referred to as being similar to Matsushita because of his concerns regarding employee development. However, while Matsushita's company had the reputation of handling its employees with tender loving care, Inamori originally ruled his roost with a rigorous and regimented boot-camp style of personnel management. Employees who were dedicated to the Kyocera cause could even expect to receive a proper burial in a ceramic coffin in the company plot which Inamori had established at a famous Buddhist monastery in Kyoto.

Inamori followed Matsushita's lead by publishing books which promoted his corporate philosophy such as *A Compass to Fulfillment: Passion and Spirituality in Life and Business* and *Elevate Your Mind and Expand Your Business*. Inamori travels the world lecturing to enthusiastic audiences on corporate management. Some of his Twelve Management Principles point to Matsushita as a mentor:

1. Clearly state the purpose and mission of your business. Set high objectives that are noble, just and fair.
2. Keep a passionate desire in your heart. Your desire must be strong and persistent to penetrate into your subconscious mind.
3. Strive harder than anyone else. Work steadily and diligently, one step at a time, never relenting in tedious work.

4. Success is determined by willpower.
5. Possess a fighting spirit. Business management requires a persistent 'rock-piercing' will.
6. Always be cheerful and positive; hold great dreams and hopes in the pureness of your heart.

The DPJ and the Matsushita effect

Matsushita established his Institute of Government and Management in 1979.[1] The Institute incorporates Matsushita's personal philosophies and values that were promoted by the PHP. The Institute's 'Basic Principle' encourages 'deep love of our country and our people' and the contribution to the 'peace, happiness and prosperity of all people'. The curriculum includes Zen meditation and the martial arts.

Former Prime Minister Noda deeply admires Matsushita. After graduating from Waseda University in political economics Noda received a degree from the Matsushita Institute. Several of his cabinet members were also graduates of the institute. Noda, who has a black belt in judo and enjoys combat sports, is considered a fiscal conservative and a defense hawk (his father was in the SDF) and strongly supports the US–Japan Security Treaty. He may disagree with members of the LDP about methods of reform of Japan's political system but his ideology reiterates Abe's nationalist values. Fifteen days before he won the election for Prime Minister on 29 August 2011 he contended at a press conference that the Japanese Class A criminals interred at Yasukuni Shrine were not criminals and that there was no reason for a prime minister not to visit the shrine. Incensed by Noda's rhetoric, the South Korean Foreign Minister stated that his words were in denial of Japan's past history of aggression.

Thank you Plaza Accord?

The United States, due to high government spending during the Vietnam War and a stock market crash in 1973, suffered a recession from 1974–5. The United States also suffered a double-dip recession in 1981–2 while Japan was becoming the second largest economy in the world. Although 'overtaking the United States' economically, the Japanese felt obliged to continue to rely on the ministries and politicians to tightly regulate their industries and to continue mercantile policies, accumulating a large current account surplus while holding the yen within Japan.

After the termination of the fixed exchange rate in 1971 the currency market was unregulated and controlled by supply and demand.

Although economic growth was rapid and inflation was low in 1985, the US was experiencing a large and growing trade deficit. On the other hand, Japan and Germany held a large trade surplus. Protectionist trade policies and the appreciation of the dollar against the currencies of its primary trading partners, Japan and Germany, threatened to destabilize the foreign exchange market. The US pressed its trading partners to agree to a multinational intervention to control the gradual devaluation of the dollar against other currencies in order to make American goods competitive in global markets.

In September 1985, the United States together with Japan, France, West Germany and Great Britain agreed on the Plaza Accord which effectively intervened in currency markets, floated the dollar and appreciated other currencies, including the yen. The US promised to reduce its government deficit and lower interest rates. Japan agreed to loosen monetary policies and initiate financial sector reforms. During 1985–7, the yen appreciated 51 percent against the dollar. In FY 1986 Japan's exports plummeted from 4.5 percent to about 3 percent, a blow to its export-driven economy. To counteract the expensive yen the BOJ reacted by easing interest rates in early 1986 from 5 percent to 4.5 percent and gradually to 2.5 percent by February 1987.

Ken Dickson, Investment Director (Foreign Exchange), Standard Life Investments, explained that the US dollar remains the reserve currency of choice. 'Although they prefer not to have all of their money invested in US dollars, there are not many countries around the world in which they might invest reserve assets that are big enough, wide enough or deep enough to be classified as safe or to be able to invest without moving the price.'[2] For Dickson's overviews of the current connections between foreign exchange and monetary policy which directly relate to the BOJ's monetary policies directly after the Plaza Accord see note 2 on p. 300.

During the post-war period the central bank had dictated to each bank quarterly the amount acceptable for net lending (i.e. quotas) through the extra-legal policy tool known as 'window guidance'. The banks were ranked accordingly, from the large metropolitan banks to the regional banks. The BOJ's easy money policy triggered what is referred to as Japan's 'asset-inflated bubble economy'. Corporate over-expansion in Japan during the bubble years of 1986–90 was funded by substantial loans from national and regional banks. Many of the loans were under-written by the spiraling value in real estate. This trend was accelerated by fiscal policies which included lowering taxes. Unfortunately, the banks lacked the skills to assess collateral and based the approval of loans to valued customers on the same collateral because they assumed that the BOJ provided a safety net as lender of last resort since the late 1950s.

On the other hand, the extra-legal 'window guidance' could pressure banks to hire retired officials. The BOJ would 'punish' banks by reducing loan quotas, while taking no action against the borrowers to recover collateral, leaving 'zombie' borrowers effectively bankrupt but still in business. Many retired bureaucrats from MOF and retired executives from the BOJ were employed in top management positions in metropolitan banks and financial institutions. As of 1992, there were 78 former MOF officials and 64 BOJ officers on the boards of 115 listed banks through *amakudari*.

During the 1990s a series of scandals linking the failure of financial institutions with MOF officials in the regulatory agency that monitored the *keiretsu* main banks and other financial institutions were covered extensively by the Japanese media. Nevertheless, *amakudari* continued.

Bubble, bubble: all you need is cash

Japanese businesses were caught up in a wave of prosperity but misinterpreted the 1988 bubble as a benchmark for future rapid growth in consumption. Unaware, or perhaps in denial, that the economy was over-heated and that the markets would not be able to sustain the momentum, they continued to plough capital investment into the expansion of their affiliates and the diversification of their businesses.

Daiei expanded internationally to cater to Japanese companies which were expanding operations overseas. However, the company was deviating significantly from its core competencies by diversifying into hotels and shopping centers at home and abroad such as the Aloa Moana Shopping Center.

While closing the Pearlridge store in Honolulu because of poor sales, Daiei purchased the Nankai Hawks baseball club from Nankai Electric Railway in 1986 and moved the team to Fukuoka. Daiei built the Fukuoka Dome Stadium in 1992 to house the team, rebranding it the Daiei Hawks. The stadium stood adjacent to Daiei's Sea Hawk Hotel and Resort. Even after the bursting of the economic bubble, Daiei continued to borrow and to deny debt, as did its creditors, two of which were Mitsui Bank and Sumitomo Bank.

Nakauchi, copying Wal-Mart's founder Sam Warton's 'Wal-Mart' and 'Sam's Club' stores, created Japan's first wholesale membership club using the name Kuo, his nickname. Nakauchi also attempted to copy Aldi's international success with his Daiei's Big-A-Box Co., marketing a limited selection of non-perishable goods in warehouse-type installations. Nakauchi, who was already undercutting the prices of Daiei's competitors who were trying to get into the discount market by the early 1990s, announced in 1995 that by 2010, he intended to cut the prices of goods by 50 percent.

But Daiei was not alone. Forecasting a rise in domestic consumption during the 1980s and 1990s other firms were also expanding beyond their core competencies, despite growing debt and the loss of profits due to the financing of the debt.

At the height of the bubble in 1987 consumer spending was vibrant and Kanebo forecast rapid growth. In tandem with the celebration of its centennial anniversary, Kanebo announced a Ten-Year Management Program. The program's objectives were to develop its textile division, to consolidate operations further and to diversify into other businesses. Kanebo restructured the company into separate subsidiaries – Kanebo Cosmetics, Kanebo Cosmetics Europe, Kanebo Home Products Company, Kanebo Textile Company Ltd. – while continuing significant capital investment in all of the divisions.

In 1986 Kanebo began to increase activities in fashion operations by manufacturing and distributing shoes and apparel for the Italian fashion house Fila. Kanebo went to China in 1987 to produce nylon stockings, which accounted for 50 percent of the market. The remaining stock was exported to the United States, Japan and Southeast Asia. Kanebo joined with Warnaco Inc. again in 1988 through a second licensing agreement to form a new brand, 'Charles F. Hathaway', and designing and manufacturing men's suits, jackets, trousers, shoes, belts and accessories in Italy. In FY 1988, Kanebo achieved revenues of $3.6 billion and net earnings of $21.5 million, an increase of almost 23 percent from the previous financial year.

6
The Roaring 80s: The Bicycle Economy Out of Control

In 1988, Tokyo was a capital of opulence and reminiscent of the Roaring Twenties and the 1929 stock market crash. Clearly, Japan's economy was over-heated. Famous designer-brand boutiques were installed in every department store. The large trading companies, in league with the retailers, imported apparel and leather goods. Despite prices that were far more expensive than in the country of origin, shoppers were willing to spend hard-earned income on famous brand names. To promote their brands as synonymous with imported luxury goods Japanese designers priced their apparel at almost the same rates as their foreign competitors.

There were new office buildings and four-star hotels operated by Japanese retailers. New products displayed on shelves were removed after only three months if sales were slow and replaced with new products. As an example, the first issue of a youth-oriented magazine *Hey Tom!* appeared on the newsstands only once. A second issue was never published because the number of subscriptions and sales were considered to be too low.

The Toto bathroom showroom, located in an exclusive shopping area in Tokyo, was illustrative of the bubble economy. Toto had developed from a manufacturer of utilitarian toilets to a designer-manufacturer of toilets and bathrooms that were fit for emperors and for sultans. The showroom was a museum of decadence which provided visitors a brief respite from the tedium of the workplace. The toilets on exhibition were covered with gold- and silver-leaf. Some of the toilet lids were embossed with semi-precious stones and the baths were inlaid with intricate ceramic tiles.

The elaborate wrapping paper and packaging of products, and the plethora of small Japanese boutiques, Michelin star French restaurants and Italian bistros suggested an economy that was vibrant and expanding. The streets were dotted with foreign fashion and jewelry boutiques, elegant Japanese stationery shops, home-ware shops and Japanese traditional cake shops which also sold selections of French and German freshly baked goods to compete with the French and German patisseries. Some of the stores sported marble floors and pillared interiors. The counters in the immense food halls in department stores were laden with expensive specialty regional foods produced by venerable Japanese establishments and well-known European producers, samples of which were offered to customers, many of whom returned several times to indulge. Bottles of imported French and German wines, along with brand-name spirits and liquors lined the shelves of the liquor sections. The branch of the Seibu Department Store in Hibiya devoted an entire floor to wine and wine tasting. Elegant and expensive Japanese-designed Western apparel and Italian shoes were on display to entice the nouveaux riches.

Consumers could not resist the foreign luxury brand foods and Champagne boutiques in the large department stores. Customers stood patiently in long lines before the Fauchon Bakery in the luxury department store Takashimaya Nihonbashi to purchase a single loaf of French bread or to spend hard-earned income on a bottle of Champagne at the exclusive Clicquot Champagne Boutique in Mitsukoshi Department Store. Japanese would even wait in long queues in front of the counters of famous Japanese bakeries to purchase newly released pastries, which could be equally as expensive. Maxim's was also a place to be seen with corporate clients.

Supermarket shelves displayed almost everything that a Japanese housewife could wish for, including domestic cheeses and butter from Hokkaido produced by Trappist monks. There was Kobe beef for a price, and New Zealand and Australian lamb (but no US beef). Domestic companies were also copying foreign brands but these products were also sold at premium prices.

Tokyo was a world unto itself and did not represent the economic conditions in other cities, especially in regions that were distant from the capital and in agricultural prefectures. Foreigners who visited Japanese cities and towns either on business or on holidays saw the glitter of opulence and assumed that the Japanese had achieved astounding success economically and that the Japan Inc. model was infallible. The general consensus among the Japanese who were receiving large year-end bonuses was that they were enveloped in an era of prosperity.

Beer boom: signs of an over-heated economy and overkill

The research and development of new products and marketing strategies by the domestic food and beverage industries were indicative of the
economic environment during the 1970s and 1980s. There was intense
competition between domestic producers for a piece of the domestic
market and producers, sparing no expense, went to extremes to carve
out a niche in an already crowded market.

Besides sake, beer has been the beverage of choice among the majority
of Japanese males since German beer brewers entered Japan during the
Meiji Restoration to teach the Japanese beer brewing. Traditionally, a
meal commenced with a glass of beer.

The big four beer brewers, Kirin, Asahi, Sapporo and Suntory, have
been engaged in an ongoing battle for the domination of the beer
market. Their marketing strategy has encompassed not only a wide
range of promotional activities but also the continuous launch of new
brands. Competition became more heated in the late 1980s. In 1982,
costs for advertising and promotion were approximately $350 million.
By 1991, these expenditures had jumped to $1 billion.

In 1987 when Asahi Beer launched 'Super Dry' Kirin, Sapporo and
Suntory decided to court both male and female consumers through
newly constructed beer halls. Sapporo's Bavarian-style Sapporo Lion had
been a popular after-hours gathering place for many years. Sapporo's
new establishments were giant beer hall/restaurants which were creative versions of the traditional beer hall and where patrons could escape
from the pressures of the workplace, eat reasonably priced food, and
drink Sapporo Black Label. While promoting the producers' beers, the
halls simultaneously promoted beer as a perennial beverage.

Kirin and Suntory opened beer halls near Osaka's main train station.
The Kirin Lager Jungle-da was a cavernous 21,000 square feet and seated
600 patrons who could meander through a tropical rain forest and cross
rushing streams via rustic bridges. Customers enjoyed listening to a live
band while eating a variety of cuisines and drinking the house specialty,
Kirin Lager. Kirin also opened a huge complex in Nagasaki which was
modeled after a Dutch village. Its Beer Village in Yokohama sported a
mini-beer museum, a video library, a beer-tasting corner, a restaurant
where eleven kinds of beer were served and two garden areas. The public
could tour the plant to view how the beer was brewed.

Kirin also introduced a new service which enabled customers to order
draft beer through local liquor stores which was then delivered directly
to them within three days. During 1986–91, the four companies had

collectively released sixty brands which served not only to confuse consumers but to overcrowd the market. Producers eliminated many of the brands after only a few years on the market.

Confection madness: signs of an over-heated economy

By the mid-1970s the confectionery industry was releasing a bevy of reduced sugar (but chocolate-covered) products onto the market, targeting a new breed of consumer – the young, single, working woman. Japan's economy, continuing its expansion, created better job opportunities and rising salaries. However, in order to avoid the burden of paying notoriously high rents, many young people opted to remain at home with their parents, taking advantage of a free room and board. Their disposable income was spent primarily on clothing, cosmetics and comestibles. The confectionery industry began wooing women with a host of products, going the gamut with ad campaigns, innovative packaging, test marketing and sampling at supermarkets and department stores. Marketers used mass media effectively with television personalities promoting the products.

If products failed to receive quick acceptance, they were pulled from the shelves and replaced with new products such as chocolate-covered pickled white radish. In the 1980s Lotte marketed single-servings of chocolate ice cream served in gold kimono-like covers. Meiji marketed 'Fresh', a milk chocolate bar. The Belgian chocolate manufacturer Godiva gained entry to the market by introducing solid chocolate golf balls to Japanese golf-lovers.

Japan's wine boom

In 1976, the only place one could buy a decent bottle of wine in Japan was a Western-style hotel. As an alternative, diners could bring their own to the restaurant and pay corkage. Wine-lovers could also find imports in department stores or they could go to a local liquor shop to buy domestic vintages produced by the two largest producers in Japan, Suntory Inc. and Sanraku Inc. Imported wines and blended whisky, such as Chivas Regal and Johnny Walker Red and Black went for premium prices.

However, Japanese employees, who were seconded to corporate offices in the US or in Europe for three to five years, were exposed to fine wines that were not yet available in Japan. Also, Germany, Austria and France were gradually becoming tourist destinations for Japanese who would enjoy sipping a glass of wine with their meals. It was simply a question of exposure to options.

Suntory's classic was a sweet red or white wine similar to the Communion wines which were introduced to the Japanese in the six-teenth century by Portuguese and Spanish Catholic priests. Imported German and Austrian wines also catered to the preference for sweet wines, which remained popular until the mid-1970s. In 1972, a Suntory television commercial urging people to 'drink wine on Fridays' triggered a mini-wine boom. By 1979, the younger generation, especially women, were drinking a glass or two of wine at bars and in restaurants, usually of the sweet variety.

Ironically, although the rise in wine consumption raised profits, it created a shortage of Japanese grapes. There were not enough grapes to go round and bulk grape juice from Romania, Hungary, Germany and Austria was blended into the domestic wine. The labels of bottles of domestic wines do not indicate that 90 percent is reconstituted grape juice and water.

The Japanese would have continued to savor wine if it had not been for the scandal in the mid-1880s when Austrian wine was contaminated with antifreeze. This discovery spelled disaster for the wine trade in Japan. Since the Japanese are fastidious consumers, the wine market withered and it took several years and much effort on the part of for-eign wine associations and domestic importers and producers to revive trust among Japanese consumers. Following the scare, the wine market began to recover because more Japanese were working and traveling abroad and developing a taste for foreign cuisine. By the mid-1980s, French, Italian, German, Spanish and Italian restaurants proliferated throughout Japan.

Confident of an expanding market for foreign wine during the next decade and taking advantage of low interest rates, Japanese wine produc-ers began purchasing or investing in vineyards located in famous wine producing regions such as the Bordeaux and the Burgundy regions of France and in the Napa-Sonoma Valley in California. In 1986, Suntory, a family-owned firm,[1] considered to be the producer of the finest domes-tic whisky and wine, purchased a Sonoma winery and invested millions of dollars in replanting vineyards and grounds, which it later divested in 1996. In order not to be out-classed by Suntory, in 1987 Sanraku Inc., Japan's second largest wine producer, purchased Markham Vineyards.

Although not engaged in wine production, Otsuka Pharmaceuticals, Japan's third largest producer of pharmaceuticals and the first to build a research facility in the US in 1983, purchased a California winery.

Established in 1921, the multinational company also has a food and beverage division which produces snacks and drinks for the health-conscious. CEO Akihiko Otsuka referred to wine as a healthy alternative to hard liquor and kept a collection of Bordeaux in a cellar in the Otsuka Pharmaceutical Research Center at Lake Biwa, near Kyoto.[2]

In 1986, Otsuka purchased Ridge Winery, which is located at an elevation of 2,600 feet on top of Monte Bello Ridge in the Santa Cruz mountains near San Jose. Two of the owners who were former presidents of Syntax, a pharmaceutical firm which had a joint venture with Otsuka Pharmaceuticals, knew that Otsuka was a collector of Bordeaux. When Otsuka visited Ridge, he liked what he saw and purchased it.

Orange juice glut: too much of a good thing

The Japanese, while enjoying eating *mikan* fruit, preferred drinking the bottled or canned varieties of Valencia-based drinks. As stated previously, the *mikan* growers successfully lobbied for years for strict import quotas on foreign citrus, protecting what they considered an already saturated market. Despite their stalwart efforts, consumers' increased exposure to cheap, fresh Valencia orange juice created a demand and significantly helped to support the US–Japan Beef and Citrus Agreement, signed in July 1988, which technically removed restrictions on imports of single-strength orange juice mixtures as of April 1, 1991. The quota on orange juice concentrate was also eliminated on April 1, 1992. The tariffs ranging from 25 percent to 35 percent remained.

However, due to consumer demand for Valencia orange juice in 1989 the government expanded the import quotas three years ahead of schedule. In 1989, import volume was double the agreed level for that year. By 1990, imports exceeded the established quotas. In 1990–1, cheaper Brazil Valencias were being imported, accelerating the over-supply of orange juice. Sunkist introduced a quart of California fresh orange juice at $4 per quart. In April 1992, a number of producers and retailers including Suntory, Kagome, Asahi Beer and Daiei, were jostling for a piece of the orange juice market. No expense was spared with a range of innovative packaging products, ad campaigns and test marketing. By mid-1992, only four months after quotas were formally lifted, there was already an over-supply of orange juice in Japan. The miscalculation of the mass market and consumer demand resulted in price wars between suppliers and prompted the development of new products and beverages such as orange juice blended with other fruits to coax consumers to drink more orange juice.

Dazzle in Tokyo, the Big Apple and London Town: the sky's the limit

During the bubble years, Japanese companies invested heavily in the purchase and construction of commercial and residential properties in Japan. As a consequence, the value of real estate throughout Japan, particularly in Tokyo, appreciated over 50 percent. Japanese companies purchased high-profile properties in Manhattan and Los Angeles. In October 1989, Mitsubishi Estate, an affiliate of Mitsubishi Trading Group, initially invested an estimated $846 million in cash for a 51 percent interest in Rockefeller Center, joining other business owners with whom it had previously purchased 6.1 percent of shares in 1984. The Exxon Building was purchased by Mitsubishi Real Estate Development Company of Tokyo for $620 million in 1986. Identifying itself as Japan's second largest real estate company, it also invested $500 million in Citicorp Plaza in Los Angeles, which it developed with the Prudential Insurance Company.

Aoki Corp. at the Algonquin and regional banks: more bubble stories

The Algonquin was the venue for the renowned 'Algonquin Round Table', which was established after the First World War in 1919 by a group of illustrious journalists, authors, literary critiques, playwrights and humorists who met daily for lunch. Among the members of the mutual admiration society were Dorothy Parker, Robert Benchley and Pulitzer-prize winners Robert Sherwood and George Kaufman. They played games, gossiped, and spouted witticisms and ideas. Since some members wrote newspaper columns the group became famous in the national press. The round table continued until 1929. The hotel earned the status of New York City Historic Landmark in 1987. The Aoki Corp., a large Japanese construction firm, purchased the property with the Texas-based Bass Group in 1987 for $29 million. During the same year Aoki also purchased with Bass the Westin Hotel and resort chain for $1.53 billion with the IBJ financing the transaction. The fifty North American hotels included the Plaza Hotel in Manhattan where the Plaza Accord was signed.

Japan's big banks opened retail branches in the US during the 1980s. Daiwa Bank opened branches in New York City and in Los Angeles. However, the bank's management was haphazard and in late 1995, it suffered a $1.1 billion loss due to a rogue bond trader at the New York branch. Toshide Iguchi, who admitted to 30,000 unauthorized trades during twelve years in New York, was sentenced to four years in prison. Daiwa was accused of covering up the loss and ordered to shut down its US branches. Sumitomo Bank subsequently took over Daiwa's operations.

Iguchi published *Confession* in 1997 in which he condemned the bank for covering up the loss and accused prosecutors of a sloppy investigation. In an interview with *Bloomberg News* on April 30, 2014, Iguchi claimed that only 5 percent of unauthorized financial trading cases are reported.[3]

In an attempt to emulate the metropolitan banks, Japan's regional banks such as Kyoto Bank and Iyo Bank (Ehime Prefecture), anticipating that the Japanese economy would continue to expand, opened tiny branch offices in New York and Los Angeles with the objective of providing offshore support for small businesses based in their prefectures. Some of the banks operated offices for no other reason than to be seen as having 'internationalized'. The new branches also served as an illustration of Japanese overconfidence and the need to be recognized as an economic force in international markets.

Sushi anyone?

The wave of Japanese corporate investment and operations in the US and Great Britain also brought opportunities to Japanese retailers and to small and medium-size business which were setting up shop to provide services to the large corporations. Japan's most venerable department stores opened stores in New York and in London to provide Japanese foods and accoutrements to Japanese corporate executives. Mitsukoshi Department Store operated a branch in London, serving elegant and expensive Japanese cuisine to a devout Japanese clientele working in Japanese ministries, banks and large corporations.

Manhattan and Los Angeles were the most sought-after destinations for small businesses which included office suppliers and real estate agencies who offered rental properties and relocation services at inflated fees to Japanese executives who were bringing their families with them during their secondment. There were small Japanese businesses that catered for corporate events and delivered the standard Japanese lunch boxes to offices daily. Japanese sushi restaurants along with tempura and noodle houses proliferated and were not only a popular lunch-time destination for Japanese but for non-Japanese as well.

A branch of one of Tokyo's finest traditional noodle restaurants opened a branch in Soho, Manhattan in 1991. The owner had graduated from the University of California with a degree in city planning and was confident that his noodle restaurant would be successful. His family invested substantial capital to finance the refurbishment of a small installation and cover costly overheads which included sending to New York the chefs from the Tokyo restaurant to cook the dishes and most of the ingredients, including the buckwheat from Hokkaido for the noodles. An article in the *New York Times* promoted the new establishment to the rich and famous from the world of art, music and fashion, and to Japanese corporate executives. The restaurant became the hot spot to go for Japanese haute cuisine.

Pop goes the bubble: fallout

In May 1989, the BOJ began to boost the official discount rate from 2.5 percent to 3.25 percent and then to 5.5 percent. Due to the first Gulf War, the BOJ tightened interest rates further. Stock prices fell to 50 percent of their value during the peak in 1989 and by 1991 the value of real estate fell heavily.

The banks, which were very exposed to the real estate market, were left with a substantial body of non-performing loans or 'bubble loans'. It was estimated at the time that the top twenty-one banks were carrying $100 billion at the end of September 1992, escalating 50 percent from the end of March and constituting one-third of their total capital.

Until the 1990s, all Japanese banks were assured that the government would support them unequivocally. But the banks lacked the skills to evaluate borrowers who were poor credit risks. Furthermore, the banks regarded both the BOJ and MOF regulators as their protectors who shielded them from close scrutiny by outside auditors. The banks were reticent to disclose the extent of their non-performing loans because it would be tantamount to admitting mismanagement.

With property values plummeting 50 percent, Japanese corporations who invested billions of dollars in foreign properties lost billions of dollars in the fire sales of their properties during the 1990s because of the recession and continued economic stagnation. In 1994, a debt-ridden Aoki sold its stake in the Algonquin to Starwood Capital and Goldman Sachs & Company for a mere $561 million. Mitsubishi Estate also suffered a one billion yen loss in FY 1995 when the operator of Rockefeller Center declared bankruptcy, Mitsubishi's first lost since its establishment in 1953. After selling its share in twelve of the fourteen buildings within Rockefeller Center, it managed to hold on to the McGraw-Hill Building and the Time-Life Building. A major reason that prevented the banks from calling in the loans was that the banks owned equity in their corporate borrowers and had members on their boards.

During the real estate bubble, Japanese corporations were buying up art masterpieces, mainly Impressionist and Post-Impressionist, at international auctions in London and New York at inflated prices without regard to quality. One motivation was that art was regarded as a speculative investment because in Japan art works do not have to be registered and can be handed over to other parties anonymously. By investing in paintings companies could avoid paying taxes and use art as collateral for loans, money laundering, bribery and even as political donations. In the 1990s, as the recession continued, some companies that declared bankruptcy were pressured to hand over their art to their lenders who were said to be storing the art in their vaults because the art was revalued at deflated prices.

Daiei by the early 1990s was depending on its major creditors for rescheduling the repayment of a huge tranche of outstanding loans. Daiei was on its way to becoming a zombie company and its decline was becoming evident in some of its US operations. As an example, a large Daiei market was located in New Jersey which catered to Japanese expats who were seconded to the branches of Japanese corporations and government agencies. Many chose to reside in New Jersey and make the daily commute to Manhattan because the rents were cheaper.

New Jersey was a prime area for a Japanese supermarket but since Daiei was heavily invested in other businesses and real estate internationally Daiei was struggling to manage and maintain its supermarket chain overseas. The market's expansive first floor was devoted to Japanese foodstuffs. The facility was comparable to the Japanese outlets but the installation was shabby and rather bleak with bags of rice and other grains placed unceremoniously on the floor while many of the foods, ordinarily sold fresh in Japan, were stored in long freezer spaces. Rice crackers and sweets were displayed in boxes set on shelves. Although Daiei was a discount retailer in Japan, the prices of the same goods sold outside of the country were more expensive because of tariffs and shipping costs. A Japanese-style restaurant located on the second floor served mediocre but expensive fare and customers were not prepared to pay for cuisine that they could easily prepare at home.

When the BOJ pulled the rug out from under the real estate market the reaction by banks and their borrowers was remarkably low-key. It was business as usual. Sanraku Inc., Japan's second largest wine producer and an affiliate of a large Japanese corporation, was a prime example of how parent companies, flush with success in international markets during the 1980s, were investing capital to expand subsidiaries in ventures that were beyond the subsidiaries' core competencies and using strategies based on predictions of continuous growth in foreign and domestic markets. Their loyal banks, who also owned equity in the companies and in their subsidiaries, were willing to continue lending without assessing collateral or the risks involved regardless of the accumulation of significant debt. Furthermore, the regulation of the banks both private and state by the Ministry of Finance and the Bank of Japan, the lender of last resort, was almost non-existent. The banks continued to lend to their borrowers and the borrowers continued to expand operations while disregarding debts which they kept refinancing.

Sanraku Inc. is also a good example of Japanese companies that expanded and diversified operations during and after the economic bubble without considering the consequences and context of the bursting of the bubble, such as the deflationary impact on consumerism as well as a maturing consumer market and aging population.

Sanraku represents:

1. A company's rapid over-diversification during the bubble years, the miscalculation of Japan's economic stability and the impact of the continuing recession on the domestic consumer market during the 1990s.
2. The problems experienced by a subsidiary's parent company when taking over the management and operations of a company that had operated fairly independently for many years and which had a separate corporate culture and different objectives.
3. The problems encountered by foreign producers entering the Japanese market through a third-party distribution system.

7
The Metamorphosis of Sanraku Inc.

Sanraku Inc. was formerly known as Showa Brewery, established by the Ajinomoto Corporation in 1934. In 1935 Showa began to produce alcohol and in 1946, *shochu*, a popular Japanese distilled spirit made from sweet potato or rice with 25 percent alcohol content by volume. In 1961 Showa Brewery purchased Mercian Winery and then merged in 1962 with Nisshin Brewery to purchase Ocean Co., a whisky producer.

In 1985 Showa's name was changed to Sanraku Inc. The English translation of 'Sanraku' is 'three pleasures' – the company produced wine, a blended whisky and *shochu*. Consumers classified the blended whisky as a 'working man's whiskey'. The English translation of Ajinomoto is 'essence of taste'. The company produces the flavor enhancer 'Accent', otherwise known as monosodium glutamate (MSG), and holds the sole patent on the fermentation process for its production. MSG is commonly used in Asian cuisine.

Saburosuke Suzuki established Suzuki Seiyakusho, a pharmaceutical company, in 1907. When Dr. Kikunae Ikeda, a chemist, acquired a patent for his invention of the fermentation process for MSG, Suzuki purchased a joint share in the product and received a permit from the Ministry of the Interior to produce MSG under the label Lady & Aji-No-Moto. Suzuki began production in a small factory in Zushi, a town located two hours south of Tokyo. In 1909, after the company won a bronze medal at the first Japanese Invention Exhibition, it launched its brand Aji-No-Moto which became the corporate name as well.

Aji-No-Moto entered Taiwan in 1910 and in 1912 began selling wheat starch to spinning companies. The company expanded operations in China in 1914 and in 1917, Suzuki established S. Suzuki & Co., the origin of the present Ajinomoto Group. Although Suzuki opened sales offices in China, Singapore, Taipei and New York in the 1920s and 1930s, the offices were closed at the end of the war. After the war, in 1947, Ajinomoto resumed exports to the United States and began to trade publicly in 1949.

From 1951 onward Ajinomoto developed into a multinational company, its group of subsidiaries manufacturing a full range of products, including salad dressing, soups, seasoning, cooking oil, pharmaceuticals, fertilizer and animal feed. It launched Knorr's Cup-a-Soup in 1964 and engaged in numerous joint ventures with foreign food producers in Japan to produce such products as Kellogg's Corn Flakes, General Foods Maxim Coffee and DANON dairy products. In 1982, it began exporting its product Aspartane to the United States and NutraSweet to Switzerland.

Tadao Suzuki, Saburosuke's grandson, was Ajinomoto's vice-president before moving to Sanraku as its CEO in 1987. Suzuki intended to rapidly convert Sanraku Inc., a conservative and unsophisticated producer of low-end Japanese spirits, whisky and wine, into a market leader, focusing on wine, and with name recognition to rival Suntory, the whisky and wine producer which has traditionally been considered by Japanese consumers as the premier whisky and wine maker in Japan. Although Suzuki intended wine and spirits to be Sanraku's core business, he also intended to expand Sanraku's fish feed and chemicals business, which were specific to Ajinomoto's business interests. Suzuki apparently, unconcerned about Japan's economic outlook, was confident that he would achieve his objectives swiftly through substantial financing from Sanraku's parent company and Ajinomoto lenders. Realistically, the transformation of Sanraku Inc. into a company which rivaled Suntory would take several decades.

Mr. Suzuki and Sanraku's new corporate strategy

Prior to Tadao Suzuki's entrance, Sanraku had been importing and distributing wines and liquors. It was the agent for Tio Pepe Sherry (Portugal, 1972), Gustaf Adolf Schmidt wines from Germany and Tokai wine from Hungary (1973), Jim Beam Brands (1977), and Remy-Cointreau and Maison Albert Bichot (1982). Louis Martini Vineyards located in the Napa Valley, California had been a recent addition to the wine portfolio.

Suzuki was determined to give Sanraku Inc. a full corporate make-over as rapidly as possible. For moral support Suzuki brought along with him some of his former colleagues from Ajinomoto to manage various divisions, including the wine division, the liquor division, general affairs, finance and human resources. The new director of the wine division had been the former director of Ajinomoto's mayonnaise and soup division.

The loosening of restrictions for obtaining a liquor license had opened up the flow of liquor onto the general market and Sanraku's business was concentrated on sales to restaurants, hotels and bars. The market for ordinary consumers had experienced rapid growth due to a change in eating patterns such as dining out rather than staying at home and entertaining guests outside of homes which were too small to accommodate a large number of people. Suzuki intended to promote wine as a part of the daily meal because the Japanese diet had come to include many gourmet and international foods and beverages. Due to Sanraku's affiliation with Ajinomoto, Sanraku had the means and funds to enhance its strong relationship to the food industry and, therefore, promote wine as an accompaniment to food.

1. Domestic wine: Suzuki planned to capture the first-time wine drinker by producing wine-based beverages, targeting its Select Brand for household use.
2. Suzuki wanted to raise the Mercian Brand image and 'cost merit' by strengthening its Mercian network overseas and establishing the quality controlled Mercian wine within the imported wine market.
3. In the midst of the expanding import market, Suzuki planned to increase Sanraku's share by rapidly expanding its portfolio of world famous brands.

Considering these factors, Suzuki intended to acquire the top share in total wine sales not only for Mercian domestic wine but also for imported wine. But Suzuki had a tough task ahead. Prior to Suzuki's entrance the wine division staff oversaw everything related to wine: marketing, promotion and distribution to on-premise establishments, department stores, markets and liquor shops. Wine awareness was low at Sanraku, which Japanese identified as a liquor company producing alcoholic beverages for mass consumption.

Suzuki wrote in the March 1990 issue of Sanraku's in-house magazine *Ferment* that he envisaged a company which would concentrate most of its efforts on wine production. He also intended that the production of *shochu* and alcohol be decreased while the production of Western-style liquor, food-stuffs and chemicals would be increased two-fold. Sanraku also manufactured animal feed and some pharmaceuticals, and similarly to its parent company, produced through the fermentation process.

Suzuki also would focus more energy on controlling distribution and more emphasis on corporate relations.

Prior to Suzuki's entry, Sanraku's budget for R&D was small compared to Suntory's because Sanraku was engaged in other businesses while Suntory's core competence focused on alcoholic and non-alcoholic beverages. The winery and its vineyards were also on a smaller scale compared to wineries in foreign wine producing regions.

If Suzuki had been a fly on the wall

Suzuki entered Ajinomoto in 1951, after graduating from the School of Economics at Keio University. He became a director in 1971 and then vice-president in 1981. In 1987 he assumed the post of president of Sanraku. Despite his education abroad, his business acumen and his former position at Ajinomoto, Suzuki was still a member of the traditional Japanese corporate establishment.

As Sanraku's president, and later its chairman, Suzuki represented the company at corporate events and entertained corporate clients. He delegated daily operations to division managers and attended only high-level corporate meetings on strategies which were planned at the division levels. He was remote from internal affairs and it appeared that significant information relating to operations was being filtered out by middle management. Suzuki would have been wise to take more control of the restructuring of the company and corporate management.

The men who emigrated from Ajinomoto were hardly wine aficionados. The new director of the wine division who had been the former director of the mayonnaise and soup division at Ajinomoto had a penchant for sake and karaoke bars. His second-in-command who was seconded from Ajinomoto was a marketer for Cup-a-Soup and was out of his depth when it came to persuading Japanese to drink more and better wine. However, Suzuki was supported by the expectations of future success because the 1970s and 1980s economy had created consumers with a growing disposable income and who were willing to be wooed by imaginative marketing and promotion of high-end goods.

The wine division staff could not be considered wine connoisseurs but they were Sanraku old-timers who had forged tight sales networks with businesses. A woman in her mid-fifties was the only female middle-manager or *kachoo* in the wine division or, indeed, in the entire company. There were three male employees in their late twenties, two full-time salesmen and one secretary, a girl in her early twenties. Suzuki was content to rely on their expertise as well as on Sanraku corporate staff until he found people who were better qualified.

Suzuki and his colleagues from Ajinomoto were approaching retirement age, which gave them seniority in the management. After they had retired as directors of their assigned divisions they would serve as executives on Sanraku's board of directors. Cliques (*batsu*) or old boy networks exist in every society and can create a back-scratching, mutual obligation/mutual protection system in both business and government, especially in Japan where relationships are often forged during university years. The institution itself is a brand and future employment and even social status can hinge on where one has been educated.

In terms of business education, the private universities, namely Keio, Hitotsubashi or Kyoto, traditionally outranked the other universities and the technical colleges from where the majority of the Sanraku employees had graduated. The Keio old boy network was specific to certain industries such as the finance sector. Presidents and upper management in the retail banks are often graduates of Keio University, a private university recognized for its economics faculty. Mr. Suzuki and Ajinomoto directors, some of whom had moved to Sanraku with Suzuki, had economics degrees from Keio.[1]

If Suzuki had sat at desks in the various divisions observing Sanraku staff six months prior to his decision to diversify and expand operations, he would have recognized the significant differences in the corporate culture of Ajinomoto and its affiliate. He would have been better able to gauge the pace by which Sanraku staff would adapt to the change of management and their new responsibilities and the timeframe for achieving his goals. However, Sanraku staff, who had graduated from regional universities and technical colleges on much lower incomes, would be uncomfortable sitting next to Suzuki whom they regarded as elite, urbane, wealthy and second in command at Ajinomoto, Sanraku's parent company. They would be reluctant to share information about personnel in the other divisions and their private personal concerns. Therefore, bringing in former colleagues from Ajinomoto to chair some of the divisions in order to restructure Sanraku would prove to be ineffective unless Suzuki himself was intimately involved as well.

In order to modernize Sanraku's corporate culture, its management and working practices Suzuki immediately employed two staff from McKinsey and Co. to engage with the wine division staff for a year. However, the consultants, a man and a woman, did not communicate with staff but observed daily operations in silence for one year before departing. Whether or not McKinsey's recommendations were deemed applicable, Suzuki had sent out a clear message to personnel that the times were indeed changing. But old habits die hard and the Sanraku old-timers were not anticipating any significant changes. There was also palpable anxiety among staff who regarded Suzuki as an interloper who was frustrated with his lack of responsibilities at Ajinomoto and had taken Sanraku as a 'toy' to mold into his version of Suntory.

Mercian's corporate culture: true to form

The Japanese social system is a rigid hierarchy built from group upon group but there is no single group that is directly on top of another. In other words, the structure of the system resembles a pyramid of horizontal groups. First and foremost, the Japanese identify themselves as members of groups (for example, organizations such as corporations, government and educational institutions, divisions within organizations and even home towns). They may not identify themselves through their occupation but through the institutions where they work. When workers are questioned about their professions they often refer to their employers first. Even university degrees are not as important as the ranking of the institution where the individual received the degree.

To external observers, mutual trust and cooperation play a significant role in the interaction between individuals. This perception is an ideal. Realistically, the Japanese social system dictates that, in order to ensure a stable, secure and predictable environment, individual desires must remain subordinate to the needs of the group. A hierarchical corporate structure and the seniority system prevail in most institutions. Top management is usually composed of the oldest members of staff who have worked their entire careers in the same organization. Upper management will delegate daily operations to division managers. The divisions are structured as a hierarchy as well. The division managers delegate the work to division staff.

Japanese corporate headquarters can be a high-pressure workplace because of the monitoring by upper management and high expectations of staff. Branch offices that are located in other cities or, better still, in other countries, may be the preferred option because the further the distance from corporate headquarters, the more release there is from scrutiny. The less communication there is between branch offices and headquarters, the more freedom there is from the constraints of corporate regulations. However, the opportunities for promotion within organizations, including government institutions, are often based on forging a strong interpersonal relationship with upper management in corporate headquarters.

Besides hiring the consultants from McKinsey and Co., Suzuki made some token gestures such as replacing the morning exercise routine with soft, languid music piped through loudspeakers at 3 p.m. But instead of energizing staff, the music signaled a post-lunch siesta. Also, employees were no longer required to wear uniforms. However, these changes were superficial at best.

Mercian's internal structure was hierarchical and human resource management was based on the seniority system with promotion generally unrelated to merit. Sanraku guaranteed lifetime employment and staff received generous welfare benefits. With the exception of the wine division *kachoo* who had worked in Sanraku for some years there were no other women in management positions and there were few opportunities for females for promotion up the corporate ladder. Two women were recruited by the wine division as 'wine advisers' to receive on-the-job training but it was doubtful that they would be promoted. With the exception of a few external officers, most members of the board were appointed internally. The traditional rotation system (also found in the civil service) required that the directors of the divisions and some staff were transferred every three years to different divisions, to train them as 'generalists' on their way to positions in senior management. The technical staff usually remained in the same division during their entire careers.

Even though there were four divisions in the same room and about seventy staff, Sanraku's divisions were entities unto themselves with the directors forging strong relationships with their staff. There was a liquor division, a spirits division, a special products division and a wine division. With the exception of the wine division, which had about nine staff, the other divisions had ten or more staff who sat at long tables placed in close proximity to each other.

The rotation of staff was one of the more intriguing aspects of Japanese corporate culture. When a director received notice that he would be transferred to another division, he prepared psychologically by gradually disengaging himself from his division several months prior to the actual transfer. After moving to the new division, he would no longer communicate regularly with the staff in his former division, even though the division was located in the same room.

In *Why Japan Can't Reform* (2008) an interview conducted in 1994 with a vice-president of the North American branch of a major trading company was included. He had previously been seconded to the

Chicago branch. When asked why the Japanese could not internationalize he addressed the issues experienced by Japanese corporate personnel who are seconded abroad to corporate branches:

> The rotating staff, even if they spend five years here, upon landing at Narita Airport, once they go through the doors of Narita, they forget everything they experienced during the last five years. They must be real Japanese. That's the only way to live in Japan. The only way to live in Japan is to forget everything one has experienced. It is not only true in ordinary Japanese society, but it is also true in Japanese companies (even in my company). No matter how many thousands of workers are sent to no matter how many countries, the Japanese will not develop an international point of view and will not become international. If one considers that the Japanese people live entirely on trade, Japan cannot afford to be isolated.[2]

After Sanraku purchased Markham Vineyards in 1988, a male member of staff in the wine division, who had entered the company several years earlier, was seconded to the winery for two years with his wife and child. During that period he studied the winery's daily operations, and assisted in the refurbishment of the plant, the replanting of the vineyard and the finances. As importantly, he was able to integrate into American society through his experiences working with Americans of various ethnic origins and improving his English.

Upon his return to corporate headquarters he visited the wine division and other divisions where he was welcomed by staff. He returned a week later after he had relocated his family and, although he sat at his former desk, he remained idle. He commuted daily to the office only to remain idle without assignment. The same routine continued for three weeks before he was transferred to the finance division where his responsibilities were only superficially related to his training in the Napa Valley, which was a loss to Sanraku of knowledge-transfer and also a waste of human resources.

The truth about overtime

The foreign media often report that Japanese corporations pressure employees to work long hours and that doing overtime is common in the workplace. This is a general misconception. Payment for overtime for full-time staff is considered the norm in medium to large corporations. Mercian staff who remained in the office after 6 p.m. received time-and-a-half. Often, directors of divisions and *kachoo* disappeared at lunchtime to return to the office around 4 p.m. They would then stay at their desks until 8 p.m. or later, receiving overtime pay. The absent staff may have been attending to business outside of the office but often they attended to private affairs. The overtime pay supplemented their salaries and was vital to their family's welfare. The downside was that doing overtime reduced the time with their families because many men had long commutes home, some of them arriving as late as 11 p.m.

Interaction on the workplace

A usual reply from staff when asked if they enjoyed their working environment was, 'Human relationships are difficult', illustrating the ongoing struggle to control behavior in order to preserve group unity and harmony. The director of the luxury goods division, whose family had owned the Mercian Winery prior to it being purchased by Showa in 1961, became the deputy director of the wine division in 1989. Realistically, he should have been the director because he had in-depth knowledge of Mercian Winery operations but the hierarchical structure of the company, his age and his relationship with Suzuki dictated the position.

Although the rigidity of the system could be stifling and discourage personal development, some employees were satisfied. However, others expressed the desire to have the option of migrating to another company but they were reticent to make the move because they would be forced to start again as new staff members at the bottom of the ladder in the new corporation and accept a much lower salary, regardless of their maturity and the skills that they had acquired while working for their former employer. They also inferred that the company to which they were applying might consider them with suspicion and question their motivations for leaving a company mid-career and their willingness to take the risk. There might also be issues of loyalty to a new employer and technology-transfer. Another concern was that the employee's company might be informed about their application to other companies because of the connections between the corporations through interlocking directors and stock shares.

Information-sharing

Group unity and loyalty to a higher authority are indicative of the Japanese social system. However, group unity tends to encourage group insularity thus preventing staff from sharing information with staff working in different divisions. 'Information-sharing' is not yet a buzz-word in internal corporate operations.

Getting to know you

Communication among members in divisions improved considerably during the after-hours bar hopping arranged by their directors. The forays were ostensibly planned to promote team spirit. Staff would congregate first at a restaurant for a meal, toasting first with beer followed by wine. The first destination was usually a karaoke bar. The second destination might be another karaoke bar for another song fest and more whisky accompanied by bowls of a potpourri of dried cuttlefish, rice crackers, peanuts and chocolate. The women members preferred Japanese tea with roasted barley. Its pale brown hue is similar to the color of whisky, which they disliked intensely. Most of the staff were able to avoid a third round because the last trains home departed by midnight.

The directors also took their divisions for the traditional annual week retreat at the company's country estate to build team spirit and loyalty through group training, which included team games and long walks. The staff returned to the office unshaven, exhausted and hoarse from shouting their pledges of loyalty to each other and to the company. Their exhaustion may have been partially due to late-night drinking and toasting each other, which was probably the most enjoyable part of the retreat.

December is a busy season for corporations because of preparations for year-end events and staff parties. Mr. Suzuki organized ice-skating parties at a Prince Hotel, which most of Sanraku's staff felt obliged to attend. The New Year holiday began on December 31 and ended on January 5. Even though Mr. Suzuki was trying to modernize HR management methods, he still adhered to custom and Sanraku employees were required to arrive at the office on January 3 at 8 a.m. to hear Suzuki give a formal New Year's greeting, a tradition in many Japanese corporations. After a few hours of toasting to the New Year and to Mr. Suzuki, everyone returned to their homes. Most employees, especially those who had over a one-hour train commute, would have preferred to have spent the day with their families.

Suzuki hits the ground running: catching up with Suntory

Due to the BOJ's low interest rates during the bubble years, and Ajinomoto's and Ajinomoto's lenders' financial support, Suzuki was able to purchase two old and dilapidated wineries. In 1987 Sanraku purchased Markham Winery in the Napa Valley, California followed by Chateau Reysson in the French Bordeaux region in 1989. The vineyards in both wineries had to be replanted and the structures refurbished, involving a huge capital investment. Sanraku staff, worried that the budgets for their divisions would be downsized because of Suzuki's commitment to wine, grumbled that Sanraku was serving as Ajinomoto's real estate agent.

In 1988, Sanraku entered into a number of import and distribution third-party ventures with the luxury brand Champagne Pommery, Scotch whisky maker William Grant, Torres, the largest producer of Rioja in Spain, Cordinu Cava and Cruz de Domaine de France which was one of France's largest wine merchants and represented many of the smaller French vintners internationally. Their attitude towards the Japanese could be arrogant, regarding the Japanese as wine novices and unable to appreciate fine wine.

Since Suntory was importing Freixenet, Sanraku courted Cordoniu, playing the catch-up game. Champagne Pommery was a valuable client because Suntory was also marketing and distributing a top-end Champagne. Suzuki was also considering Gallo, California's largest wine producer and known at that time for jug wine produced mainly for home consumption and which was in a lower price range than Louis Martini. Robert Mondavi and Rolling Rock, which were being imported and distributed by another Japanese company, were also brands being considered for an expanding portfolio.

Until 1989 there was no consumption tax in Japan. Instead, a luxury tax was included in the retail price of the goods. In 1989, the luxury tax was revoked and replaced with a 3 percent universal income tax. The wine division re-evaluated the pricing of imports, especially Champagne Pommery, one of the more expensive items in the wine portfolio. The discussion focused on Suntory's pricing strategy and the consensus was to raise the price of Pommery to make it slightly higher than Suntory's Champagne import in order that the Japanese would regard the higher priced wine as of better quality.

Taking advantage of Ajinomoto's presence in China, a key market where it had manufacturing facilities and excellent distribution channels, Sanraku began to import wine from Gu Yue Long Shan located in Shaoxing Province in 1990. The company also invested in a joint venture with an Australian winery in the Hunter Valley, New South Wales to produce wine for export to Japan.

Peachy keen on OLs

In the late 1980s young women between the ages of eighteen and twenty-six, who were mainly support staff in companies, were vigorously courted by not only confectioners but also by liquor producers. Known as OLs (office ladies), the women were earning a good income but in order to economize many lived with their parents instead of renting their own apartments, an expensive proposition in Japan. Frugal (but only up to a point), they invariably spent some of their monthly salaries on sundries, mainly food and clothing. The wine and liquor industry, anticipating that OLs would acquire a taste for fruity white wine and low alcohol beverages, dashed off an array of products.

In the summer of 1988, in anticipation that Sanraku would be importing and distributing Peachtree Schnapps, two enterprising young male employees in the spirits division concocted samples of a drink with slightly different ratios of Peachtree to alcohol. After taste testing samples of the mixtures on young female staff they settled on the formula for a carbonated drink with 6 percent alcohol content.

Merchandised in a four-ounce pink can, a television commercial featuring a popular starlet was used to launch Peachtree Fizz on the market. Supporting print advertisements and hot-pink vending machines featured the same starlet. Some Sanraku executives questioned whether consumers preferred the starlet to the drink. Nevertheless, Peachtree Fizz was a resounding success. Following the launch, the inventors were presented at a brief ceremony with jackets bearing the Peachtree logo.

The Beaujolais Nouveau debacle: Suzuki's worst nightmare

Unfortunately Sanraku's first triumph was tempered in November with a major crisis revolving around the late delivery of Beaujolais Nouveau from France and which impacted negatively on Suzuki's plans to redesign Sanraku's corporate image.

Japanese wine producers and importers had made a concerted effort during the 1980s to encourage the potential wine-lover to buy that first bottle, to sip their first glass of wine. Marketing and promotion were sometimes extremely creative, as in the 1988 and 1989 big, pushy promotional campaigns for the introduction of Beaujolais Nouveau on to the market.

Although Takashimaya and Daimaru, two of Japan's most prestigious department stores, had been carrying Beaujolais Nouveau for over fifteen years, sales were unremarkable. However, in order to introduce wine to Japanese who preferred beer and sake, otherwise known as 'wine-beginners', in June 1988, Sanraku brought in a Summer Nouveau from Australia. Sales were so successful that feverish preparations were made by the domestic wine producers, including Suntory, to launch an all-out media campaign for Beaujolais Nouveau. It not only appealed to the agrarian roots of the Japanese, but also to their traditional love of festivals and celebrations dedicated to the first arrival of new crops of the season such as rice and tea. The Beaujolais Nouveau party was considered a logical extension of a festival welcoming the first sake.

The campaign progressed on schedule and complete success was anticipated for not only the 1988 season but for subsequent seasons as well. Wine importers placed large orders with wine merchants in France. The wine was scheduled to arrive from France on November 15 (November 14, French time) and delivered to hotels, restaurants and department stores, which geared up for record sales. The countdown to 12:01 a.m. began. But Suzuki's worst nightmare commenced when the wine failed to make an entrance at customs.

Given the Japanese sense of timing, it was of crucial importance that the new vintage would be flown directly from France in time for the celebrations. And because the sun rises in the East, Japanese celebrants would be the first to taste the new wine before everyone else in the world. Unfortunately, it was too much too soon for the French and for the Japanese companies. The French were overwhelmed by the coordination problems of air-lifting thousands of cases of the wine half way around the world in a single day. The Beaujolais Nouveau did not arrive until the following day. Sanraku also had simultaneously launched a Mercian brand Beaujolais Nouveau to take advantage of the event.

When the director of the wine division realized that the Beaujolais Nouveau from France would not arrive at customs on time for distribution to Sanraku's customers he called an emergency meeting with all wine division staff, including Suzuki, and a *kachoo* from the distribution division who was overseeing the logistics of the delivery from France. Since Suzuki had not been advised of the situation earlier, he was outraged that he had not been informed either. The incident was a specific example of Suzuki's isolation from Sanraku's daily operations and key decisions taken by middle-management without first conferring with the CEO.

Evidently, the distribution division, which was located in the room adjacent to the wine division, delayed informing the wine division that the wine would be delivered a day late. In other words, there was no coordination between the wine division and the distribution division (i.e. 'information-sharing'). The distribution division *kachoo* intimated that the French wine merchant may have delayed the arrival of the wine in Singapore where the flight from Paris had to refuel because the French did not want the Japanese to be the first to drink the wine. However, there was no evidence to corroborate his suspicion.

Mr. Suzuki and the director discussed options that would minimize the damage in terms of large financial losses suffered by Sanraku's clients and Sanraku's reputation and corporate image. It was decided that Mr. Suzuki, the directors from other divisions and corporate executives would travel throughout Japan to personally apologize to Sanraku's clientele.

After the crisis Sanraku conducted surveys at twelve Tokyo department stores with managers in the liquor departments to get their assessment of Beaujolais Nouveau. The managers were unanimous about the boom being the result of the push by mass media and that Japanese were significantly influenced by media. The manager of Takashimaya's liquor department explained:

> College students want to give the impression that they are wine experts so they drink Beaujolais Nouveau on November 17. It gives them status, the same as when they are drinking Corona Beer or Wild Turkey. The mass media latches on to this and takes the message to consumers who then request that restaurants, which would not ordinarily carry such low-class wine, serve Beaujolais Nouveau. In France, the restaurants control what its patrons drink ('This is what we offer so please choose from our selection'). Restaurants in Japan cater to the whims of their clients. The customer controls what the restaurant offers. Beaujolais Nouveau has snob appeal.

The manager at the liquor division at the elegant and venerable Mitsukoshi department store said that Japanese were wine snobs and that Beaujolais Nouveau resembled Valentine's Day, a mass media event:

> The Japanese are extremely conscious of doing something within a time frame and of deadlines. Therefore, if one doesn't drink Beaujolais Nouveau on the third Thursday in November, there is no significance, no importance. The event is a good excuse to have a party.

The manager of the liquor department at Seibu Department Store in Ikebukuro said:

> Sanraku should know why Beaujolais Nouveau is so popular. It is one of the companies which pushes and advertises it. Its popularity is mainly due to mass media. It is not good wine and the wine department tries to persuade people to drink better wine. The wine beginner tries local wine. Mercian is watery, has no bouquet and is high in alcohol also. The company shouldn't even try to produce it!

The grave illness of Emperor Hirohito necessitated the postponement of the Beaujolais Nouveau festival by one week in November 1989. Staff seemed unconcerned about the Emperor's health and complained that waiting for his impending demise was a major inconvenience and a loss of business. The Emperor succumbed the following weekend. Department stores and supermarkets were opened for business as usual, although the dirge from Tchaikovsky's *Sixth Symphony* was piped through loudspeakers.

Shoppers could be forgiven for their apathetic reaction to the Emperor's death because the majority of them were born after the war. SCAP had removed the Emperor as Japan's head of state and the constitutional monarchy was dissolved along with the military. The old constitution was replaced with a new democratic constitution, courtesy of SCAP, which prohibited Japan from waging war and exporting military hardware. Emperor Hirohito was a reclusive figurehead who symbolized the past, the war and much suffering. Also, after the war, he was even more remote from society because he was no longer the head of state.

Hirohito's passing announced the end of an era spanning a turbulent sixty-three years of history. Due to government policies to overtake the United States economically and show the world that Japan was a force to be reckoned with, the less-is-more frugal society that once was a primary attribute of Japanese culture along with traditional values had become within twenty years a nouveau riche throw-away society. The younger generation was focusing on the future and the creature comforts, travel and shopping afforded by new wealth rather than on a past that for many was bleak and highly controlled by the government. The present represented the loosening of strictures on the society and far more freedom.

Getting to know the third party in the party: non-tariff barriers

Exporters to Japan usually enter a 'third-party distribution' arrangement with a Japanese company which shares the costs of promotion while marketing and distributing the goods. Some distributors manufacture products that are similar to those of the importers and, likewise, distributors are not necessarily engaged in the same business but are linked through equity and directors to large trading companies, which serve as the importers. Foreign liquor and wine producers usually depend upon the third-party distribution system.

However, the national wholesalers (there are also regional and local ones) were also entering the wine market during the bubble years with their individual labels. Foreign producers were beginning to contact wholesalers directly to sell and distribute their brands while wholesalers were also contracting foreign producers to produce wine for their own labels. The foreign firms were located mainly in Hungary or Romania where production costs were far lower than in the more popular wine-producing regions. The quality of the wine was questionable but the price per bottle undercut both domestic and imported brands because price did not include the wholesalers' fees. Nevertheless, the wholesalers' long-term relationship with their importer clients dictated that goods were delivered as promised. The signs that the old distribution system would gradually change in favor of the consumer were undeniable, not because of government deregulation but because wholesalers wanted a piece of the market and were competing with the importers for whom they were also providing services.

Foreign producers of food and beverages who want to enter the Japanese market generally do not contact a prospective importer directly but will appoint agents to represent them. The agents may have a number of clients on their roster and scout foreign markets for potential importers. The agents are concerned primarily with the initial stages of entry with the objective of sealing a transaction on behalf of their clients. Large trading companies that have international operations, such as Mitsubishi, Mitsui and Marubeni, will search for products deemed suitable for the Japanese market and will introduce the producers to importers. However, producers of brand-name products may make direct contact with importers or be contacted directly by importers who manufacture goods comparable to the brand-name products and can offer not only distribution and sales channels but also marketing expertise.

Foreign companies, while regarding Japan as a potentially lucrative market, also recognize that the distribution system can hamper penetration and that relying on importers who also produce similar products is the fastest route to entry. However, relying on importers who produce competitive products may not be entirely in their interest. Although the initial entry may be successful, sales may dwindle due to circumstances that could have been avoided if, prior to entering into an agreement, the foreign companies had sent staff to Japan to observe how the potential importers were marketing and distributing their foreign clients' products in conjunction with their own goods. Additionally, doing some research on the importers' corporate management and corporate strategies concerning the development of their domestic business would provide a better understanding about a future relationship, which can be costly in terms of output for advertising and marketing, 50 percent of which is often assumed by exporters. Private visits to Japan to assess the effectiveness of distribution and marketing of their products is also advisable.

Producers of famous brand names often travel to Japan to meet with the importers after contracts are signed for the market launches. When Sanraku's clients paid visits to corporate headquarters, Suzuki promoted the image that Sanraku was a sophisticated company with expertise in marketing foreign wine and possessing well-established sales and distribution channels. There were media events, elegant meals at French and Italian restaurants and traditional Japanese inns, site-seeing tours throughout Japan and market tours of retailers located in key cities to show how Sanraku was planning to promote their clients' products. In other words, Suzuki was the epitome of a Japanese CEO who was polished, literate, well-educated in Western consumer culture and a bon vivant.

8
The Martini, Glenfiddich and Babycham Marathons

Louis Martini Vineyards was one of Napa Valley's oldest and most revered family-owned wineries that had been established in 1933 in anticipation of the end of Prohibition. Well-recognized for its Cabernet Sauvignon, the winery owned over 900 acres of premium vineyards in the Napa-Sonoma Valley. Louis Martini was reputed to be among the finest of California wine makers. The winery is a popular tourist attraction with daily wine tours and tastings. Coincidently, Markham Vineyards is located directly across the road from the Martini Vineyards whose wines were already in Sanraku's portfolio when Markham was purchased.

When Mr. Martini and his wife visited Sanraku in November 1988 for the promotion of his wines, he had retired as the CEO, leaving his daughter Carolyn to manage operations, but he remained on the board as chairman and figurehead of the winery for several years. The Martinis stayed at the five-star Imperial Hotel. Unfortunately, the original building designed by Frank Lloyd Wright had been removed and replaced by a modern structure that was indistinguishable from other hotels in the city but Martini was pleased with the accommodation.

On the first day of his visit to corporate headquarters, Martini was greeted warmly by Suzuki at a press conference organized for the wine trade. After many photographs were taken, Martini was interviewed by the wine and liquor magazine *Wands*. Following the interview, Mr. Suzuki hosted Mr. Martini and his wife, who had accompanied him, for lunch at an elegant French restaurant which served (at Sanraku's request) several of the Martini wines being introduced on the market.

In the afternoon there was a second interview with the wine publication *Vinotheque*. Suzuki entertained the couple and members of the wine division, who were to escort Martini around Japan for ten days, at dinner at a fashionable Italian restaurant. The following day, Martini was taken on a tour of Tokyo department stores and liquor shops to view how Sanraku was planning to market his six varieties of wine. The bottles were proudly displayed on the shelves in full view of Japanese wine lovers which Mr. Martini presumed was the way Sanraku intended to promote his wine. After the market tour Martini and his wife were driven in a chauffeured car around Tokyo and environs for sight-seeing.

On the third day the director of the wine division played host at a luncheon which was followed by a presentation to the Japanese Sommelier Association by Martini at the New Takanawa Prince Hotel which was followed by another dinner again hosted by the wine division director and accompanied by Louis Martini wine.

The itinerary was well choreographed. Throughout the whirlwind ten-day tour Martini visited a number of department stores and liquor shops to be shown how Sanraku would be marketing and distributing the brand. Wherever Martini visited, his bottles of wine were always displayed in full view on the shelves, in front of the bottles of domestic wine, including Mercian. Martini wines accompanied every meal, including the ones hosted at traditional Japanese inns.

The Martinis were escorted by members of the division on the bullet train to Osaka for another wine seminar conducted by Martini at a restaurant which had been organized by Sanraku's Osaka branch office. The salesmen were old-timers whose territory covered most of the Kansai region. Before Suzuki's takeover they had been selling mainly Sanraku-produced spirits and Mercian wine besides the small portfolio of imports to bars, restaurants, small retailers and department stores. Martini visited liquor shops and department stores in the Kansai region where consumer preferences in terms of food and drink differed from the Kanto region, where Tokyo is located. The branch manager hosted a dinner for the Martinis at a Japanese inn where Martini wines were served alongside the traditional sake.

The following day was spent in Kyoto to meet the branch manager of Sanraku's Kyoto branch and for a short tour of the city and another formal dinner at a traditional Japanese inn in Kyoto hosted by the branch manager to introduce Martini to the rest of the Sanraku sales staff.

Martini was taken by bullet train to Okayama City for a brief drive on the Seto Bridge, which connects Honshu to Kyushu. The bridge was fairly empty of traffic. He was told that commuters between Honshu and Kyushu preferred riding the train because the tickets were less expensive than the bridge toll. Martini rode the bullet train from Okayama to Hiroshima where he also conducted a wine seminar and visited department stores and liquor outlets. There was another bullet train to Fukuoka, Kyushu for the last wine seminar, which was organized by the Sanraku branch office. Martini was chauffeured to Kumamoto to see Sanraku's large *shochu* plant.

Before returning to Tokyo, the Martinis were revitalized at a traditional Japanese hot spring resort in Beppu to relax in the sulphur baths. An enologist was sent from Sanraku's R&D facility near Tokyo to meet with Martini and converse about grape growing and wine making.

During his time with the wine division staff, Martini asked for their assessment of the California wine market in Japan. He was surprised to learn that California wine accounted for only 17 percent of the market in contrast to French wine which accounted for over 30 percent. He was even more surprised when he was informed that total wine consumption occupied only 1 percent of Japan's alcoholic beverage market.

Martini asked how Sanraku planned to market California wine in general and to promote his brand. The staff explained that Japanese considered French wine to be more elegant and that preparing a meal to accompany the wine took major effort. On the other hand, California wine was considered inferior to French wine, and this negative image persisted. They proposed that Sanraku publish a small cookbook to promote his brand as an elegant addition to a meal which could be prepared at home on top of the stove within thirty minutes, using inexpensive ingredients that were easily available at the neighborhood market. In other words, the cookbook would promote the brand as informally elegant. The cuisine together with Louis Martini wine would transport the housewife and her husband, who had returned home after a stressful day at his office, to sunny California. The cookbook would be distributed to liquor shops and department stores where the Martini brand was being retailed. Martini enthusiastically supported the concept and as soon as he returned to Tokyo, he informed Suzuki that his company would assume 50 percent of the cost of the cookbook.

If Louis Martini had been a fly on the wall: Martini revisited

Key to Suzuki's objectives was the upgrade of the Mercian Brand image and 'cost merit' by strengthening its Mercian network overseas and establishing the quality controlled Mercian wine within the imported wine market.

If Louis Martini or his agent had returned a few weeks following the launch to the department stores and liquor shops in Tokyo, Osaka, Kyoto and Fukuoka anticipating that they would see bottles of Martini wines on display as they had been displayed previously, they would have been disappointed. The bottles were tucked behind Mercian wines (labeled Chateau Mercian and Bon Marché) on the shelves and barely visible to shoppers. Clearly, Sanraku's marketing strategy for foreign wines was secondary to the promotion of its domestic brands.

Martini's agent, who also represented the American beef industry, was the agent for other California wineries. At his annual meeting with the Sanraku wine division to discuss the sales for 1990 and future sales for FY 1991, he was informed that the stock of Louis Martini wine was no longer sufficient to support the increasing sales of California wine and that Sanraku was expanding its California presence in the market. Perhaps aware that Martini's price and quality were comparable to the soon-to-be released Markham merlot, the agent offered to introduce his other California wine producer clients whose wines were cheaper. On the other hand, perhaps the agent was unaware that Sanraku's Mercian wines, which were cheaper than both Martini and Markham, were competitive with cheaper California brands and were receiving star treatment.

Sanraku snares Glenfiddich: a third-party – party

Suntory was importing and distributing Ballantine's Scotch whisky before Sanraku was approached by the agent for William Grant and Sons, an independent family-owned distiller, to import and distribute Grant's, its blended whisky. It was a coup for Sanraku because the distiller was said to be the third largest Scotch whisky producer in the world with over 10 percent of market share. But Suzuki did not stop at a blended whisky and managed to sign a deal with the company to import and distribute its popular Genfiddich single malt Scotch whisky.

Alexander Gordon, the Chairman of Glenfiddich, attended the Glenfiddich launch in Japan with his wife in March 1989. The budget for the high-profile four-day launch of the brand was sizable by any standard but Suzuki was intent on upgrading Sanraku's image as rapidly as possible.

The four-day event was choreographed similarly to the Martini visit. When the Gordons arrived in Tokyo they went directly to the Okura Hotel, a five-star hotel comparable to the Imperial Hotel where the Martinis had stayed. The director of the liquor division, who had formerly been a director at Ajinomoto, escorted the Gordons everywhere in Suzuki's personal chauffeur-driven silver Mercedes Benz.

The initial reception at corporate headquarters was attended by media and photographers. Mr. Suzuki gave a welcome speech and Gordon responded in kind, posing with Suzuki for photographers sent by the media to cover the event. A series of formal events followed announcing to the media and to the trade the entry of one of the first single malt whiskies on the Japanese market. Until then the Japanese primarily enjoyed blended whisky as did Americans. In the evening Mr. Suzuki hosted an elaborate dinner, serving Glenfiddich and cheese as the final course. Mr. Gordon, who was the part-owner and figurehead of Glenfiddich, was duly impressed.

The following day was devoted to sight-seeing in Tokyo since it was the Gordons' first trip to Japan. With the exception of business meetings, wherever he went, Gordon wore binoculars and was raising them constantly to his eyes. Evidently, he was an avid bird watcher and traveled all over the world to view birds. Suzuki hosted yet another lavish meal that evening.

The director of the liquor division accompanied Gordon by bullet train to Kyoto for more sight-seeing followed by a visit to the Sanraku's Osaka sales office where Gordon appeared at yet another launch reception hosted by the branch manager. He was escorted to large department stores and liquor shops to view Glenfiddich displayed on the shelves and to speak with sales staff about the future marketing of the brand.

Upon their return to Tokyo, the Gordons were escorted to see a famous Zen Buddhist monastery located in a town one hour south of Tokyo. It was their first visit to a Buddhist monastery. Enraptured with the natural beauty of the ancient cemetery, they appreciated the opportunity to see the graves of venerable politicians and writers.

The liquor division director, who was a devout Catholic, presumed that since the Gordons were Christians that they would prefer visiting his church in Tokyo. However, he had not been informed that the Gordons were devout Scottish Presbyterians and did not want to attend a Catholic service.

Before his departure to Hong Kong, Gordon visited corporate headquarters to thank staff and Suzuki for their welcome. He expressed confidence that Sanraku would provide fine support for Glenfiddich in Japan. Gordon delegated the responsibility for monitoring operations to the William & Grant agent.

Glenfiddich revisited

The William & Grant agent's territory covered the company's Asian markets and trips to Japan to assess Sanraku's marketing and distribution of Glenfiddich were intermittent. If the agent had visited the same outlets where Gordon had been escorted in Tokyo, Osaka and Kyoto, shortly after Gordon's departure, he may have questioned the presentation of the first single malt whisky to enter the Japanese market. The bottles were displayed alongside bottles of domestic blended whiskies.

Babycham: my one and only?

In 1989, Hiram Walker Allied Vintners which was a part of Allied Lyons (now Allied Domecq) approached Sanraku regarding marketing and distributing Babycham. Allied Lyons was the world's second largest producer of wine and spirits, including Ballantine's whisky, which was being distributed by Suntory. The company owned Showerings, the British company that was producing Babycham and Britain's third-largest producer of pear cider. The beverage was a pear-based sparkling cider with a 6 percent alcohol content served in 800cl dark green bottles with a cute chamois logo on the label. In Britain the drink had an aura of post-war life when men took their dates to the neighborhood pub for an after-dinner drink. The popular phrase 'I'd love a Babycham' was used for years to market the drink.

The wine division was unfamiliar with Babycham but after a tasting the consensus opinion was that Babycham would be popular among women aged 18–30, or older, but for different reasons than in Great Britain. At the time, there were few foreign imports of low-alcohol drinks targeting women who could not tolerate higher alcohol beverages and who were not beer drinkers. Babycham's fruity flavor and carbonation and, as importantly, the green bottle with the chamois logo on the label as well as the fact that it was 'British' would definitely appeal. It would be the first pear cider to enter the market

Sanraku announced to its branch offices that samples of Babycham were to be tested for two weeks to calculate the drink's popularity. At the end of June, the Showerings International Marketing Development Director visited the wine division to discuss the logistics of distributing samples of both the sweet and dry Babycham to various outlets. Sanraku salesmen began promoting sales to on-premise establishments (i.e. bars, restaurants and hotels).

As was forecasted, acceptance of the brand among young women was positive. The following October, the Showerings Managing Director accompanied the International Marketing Development Director to the formal launch of Babycham and for meetings with the wine division to discuss the fall promotional campaign.

The wine division chose similar choreography that was used for the Martini and Gordon visits but since Babycham was not regarded as a luxury brand or as a wine, Suzuki was not as involved with the proceedings. Wine division staff attended to the Showerings directors, escorting them first to Tokyo and Yokohama retailers, including bars and convenience stores where the green bottles of the pear cider were on full display. The directors were taken to Osaka to meet with the salesmen in the Sanraku branch office who guided them to various outlets and who suggested marketing strategies and the types of outlets and on-premise establishments where Babycham would experience good sales. The Osaka branch manager hosted a dinner for them which included toasting with Babycham.

The following day was spent in Kyoto for meetings with salesmen at the Kyoto branch and for lunches and dinners at traditional Japanese inns. The elegant Japanese cuisine was accompanied with Babycham. Again the directors were escorted to the usual venues to view displays of Babycham. There was an afternoon of sight-seeing, first at several famous Zen Buddhist monasteries followed by a tour of the War Museum (now known as the Kyoto Museum for World Peace). The exhibits included Japanese submarines and aircraft with the old version of the Japanese flag painted on their sides, torpedoes, various types of Japanese military hardware and uniforms from the Second World War. There was also the body of a British fighter plane that had been shot down over the Pacific.

After returning to Tokyo, the directors were entertained with a lavish dinner at which Suzuki presented them with expensive gifts to commemorate their visit to Japan and to celebrate Showerings' subsequent relationship with Sanraku.

In March 1990, the marketing development director paid a fourth visit for a meeting with the wine division followed by a dinner hosted by the director of the wine division. He targeted convenience stores and on-premise establishments as the most important market for Babycham and again visited bars in Yokohama that were said to be popular among young office workers. Sanraku also opened a booth for Babycham at Japan's largest annual food and drink exhibition. Afterwards the director was taken for a meal by wine division staff to an Italian restaurant for pasta and Babycham.

Babycham revisited

Showerings had invested considerable capital at the initial stages, assuming over 50 percent of the expense for promotional materials, which included tokens stamped with the Babycham logo and flyers in Japanese. Nevertheless, if the director of international marketing and development had returned to Japan to monitor sales at the outlets and on-premise establishments in the cities where he had been escorted, he would have seen that Babycham was not the one-and-only fruit-based, low alcohol drink and that it was often lost among other similar drinks that had been launched by domestic producers, including Sanraku's Peachtree Fizz, which contained the same alcohol content.

9
Marketing and Advertising Strategies: What's it all About?

Suntory's marketing strategy: sipping sophistication, sipping elegance

Suntory was an entirely different animal to Sanraku. Since the 1890s Suntory's core competence had been alcoholic and non-alcoholic beverages and later foods and some pharmaceuticals. The company is owned by the Torii family who established their winery in 1899. Suntory built Japan's first whisky distillery in 1923 and is considered Japan's finest whisky producer. In 1963, although Suntory entered the beer brewing industry as a latecomer, initially producing a draught beer in 1967, the company quickly became recognized as a major contender in the competitive beer market. Suntory also has a line of non-alcoholic beverages. In 1984 it engaged in a third-party venture with the premium ice cream producer Häagan-Dazs, one of its numerous joint ventures with foreign producers in the food and beverage industry. In 1985 Suntory entered a partnership with Château Lafite Rothschild and also purchased Château Lagrange and over 50 percent of Château Beychevelle. Suntory Vineyards and research center are located in Yamanashi Prefecture where the other large Japanese wine producers' vineyards are located. Suntory's wine is said to be made from their domestically cultivated grapes.

In terms of marketing and promotion Suntory concentrated its huge marketing and advertising budget on wine, whisky, beer and soft drinks. The advertising and marketing campaigns for wine and whisky had focused on the arts and culture since the 1920s when the Torii family initially began supporting educational and social welfare programs. As the years progressed, Suntory's commitment came to encompass the full-fledged funding of the arts and literature. Suntory's intense patronage of music, fine arts, and literature extended to its involvement in the 1980s in wildlife conservation. The corporate identity is immersed in a potpourri of cultural activities. The Suntory corporate philosophical theme 'Enjoyment of Daily Life', together with its advertisements, cleverly exploits its corporate identity to promote its products. As an example, a well-known Japanese author approached Suntory in the 1980s suggesting that he do a commercial for whisky in Japan. His theory was that Suntory and writers were intimately related because both were producers of 'Culture'. The spot was successful. The writer's recently published novel received valuable publicity and the writer's calm soliloquy about the 'Enjoyment of Daily Life' stamped an indelible literary image on a bottle of Suntory. Other writers have since joined his ranks, further enhancing this image. A scene in the film *Lost in Translation* replicates the television advert with the protagonist, played by the American actor Bill Murray, sitting in a chair, holding a glass of Suntory whisky and mouthing a few words in Japanese.

The Suntory Museum of Art was opened in Tokyo in 1961 and the Château Beychevelle International Center of Contemporary Art was opened in 1989. In 1986, Suntory Hall was inaugurated in Tokyo and is regarded as one of the finest concert venues in Japan. The 2,006 seat hall was built to commemorate Suntory's 60th anniversary of its whisky production and the 20th anniversary of its beer brewing operations. The hall includes a 450-seat recital hall as well. Suzuki copied Suntory by opening an art museum in 1990 in Nagano Prefecture naming it the Mercian Musée d'Art Karuizawa.

Sanraku's marketing mix: cheap but cheerful

Suzuki's strategies were designed to: (i) expand the portfolio of mid-to-high-end imported wine and spirits and (ii) purchase wineries in famous wine producing regions. The Sanraku wine division had been promoting wines for many years but the rapid expansion of the line of alcoholic beverages and the purchase of two wineries within a year was proving a strain on the wine division's personnel and Sanraku's advertising and marketing budget. The marketing was uncoordinated and went over-budget.

The wine division was also developing wine-based drinks, which targeted young women and men with limited income. In 1988, Suntory, which also operated a flower business, released a wine instilled with the essence of flowers in bottles that were painted with the specific flowers such as cherry or lemon blossom. While Suntory was marketing flower-infused wine, the wine division was marketing wine in milk cartons ('bag in box') and several drinks targeting young women. Vino 5 was a concoction of wine diluted with fruit juice and water and packaged in a pint-size carton and sold mainly at convenience stores.

What's really cooking?

Sanraku's marketing budget had traditionally included setting up booths at various trade fairs and exhibitions for the wine trade in areas where Sanraku's sales offices were located. Sanraku joined with other wine producers for wine tasting events for its retail clients to promote Sanraku's most recent imports and domestic blends. Similar to other liquor producers Sanraku also published print adverts in trade publications and popular magazines for both its domestic and imported brands. However, other types of promotion were rarely considered.

The wine division was caught by surprise when Martini immediately embraced their proposal for a cookbook devoted to the promotion of his wine. Suzuki's reaction was tepid but he felt compelled to continue promoting the Martini label. Generally, Japan's two largest advertising companies, Dentsu and Hakuhodo, engaged in the majority of projects but the shoe-string budget allotted for the cookbook allowed the services of a tiny marketing firm, which had minimum experience in the advertisement of foreign products.

In January 1989, discussions regarding the design of the cookbook commenced. The staff assigned to participate in the implementation of the cookbook explained the objectives. The meal would consist of one dish served with a salad and rice or bread and coordinated with a specific Martini wine. With the exception of one dish, the ingredients would be void of meat because beef, due to the import quotas and tariffs, was too expensive for household budgets and Australian and New Zealand lamb was still unpopular. The recipes would be ostensibly Mrs. Martini's and the preparation time for the meal would be no longer than thirty minutes. The food would be prepared on gas burners because most households did not own ovens because of the high electricity bills.

The staff presumed that the marketing firm would provide an attractive layout but two weeks passed before the second meeting. Staff were shocked to see that the layout did not resemble anything they had envisioned because the agency's employees had never been to California and perceived the golden state in the context of a Disneyland or a Fisherman's Wharf. Although a cheap option, the firm was unsophisticated and totally out of its depth and the wine division staff realized that if they did not engage directly, the cookbook would never evolve.

The production for a seven-page format took three months. Since Japanese imagined French cuisine as elegant and California cuisine as McDonald's and Kentucky Fried Chicken it was a cost-effective solution to changing this image and a few staff promoted the use of the booklet as a prototype for other imported California wines and for Markham. However, when the copies arrived at corporate headquarters, the wine division's middle management were reticent to part with them, despite the requests from Sanraku branch offices. Although the cookbook had been authorized and Louis Martini was footing over half of the bill there was no desire to promote an import that Sanraku intended to slough off. Eventually, copies were duly sent to Sanraku branch offices and to the Martini Vineyards winery. The Martinis were exceptionally pleased, reporting that a Japanese woman tourist touring the winery had burst into tears of joy when she saw the cookbook, claiming that no other winery she had visited had offered literature conceived especially for Japanese.

Gustav Adolph Schmitt wants the cat but Sanraku doesn't

Rudolph Schmitt, the CEO of the German wine maker Gustav Adolph Schmitt, which was established in the seventeenth century, visited the wine division in 1990 to discuss improving promotional methods for his new brands that Sanraku was launching on the market. Since the wine had been in the wine division's portfolio since the 1970s Schmitt was candid about his concerns about the expansion of his brand amidst the rapid addition of other brands. The discussion focused on the design of a label and the promotion of a new Liebfraumilch. Mrs. Schimtt who also attended the meeting mentioned that she owned cats. Several members proposed a label with a black cat and a short storybook-pamphlet with the cat as the hero. It was also proposed that Mrs. Schmitt send family recipes for a small cook booklet, mimicking the proposal made to Louis Martini.

Mr. Schmitt enthusiastically endorsed the recommendation and sent the family recipes. However, after Schmitt returned to Germany, the wine division was less positive. The wine division director sent a letter to Schmitt thanking him for his enthusiasm and for the recipes but that he would appreciate more detail regarding how the CEO wished to proceed. The promotion did not progress beyond the preliminary stages.

Misjudging market trends: Sanraku's *shochu*

Sanraku was one of four major producers of *shochu* and instantly recognized as a producer of excellent *shochu* and very competitive in the
market. But Mr. Suzuki's strategy for Sanraku targeted the reduction of
shochu production because he considered it to be an unsophisticated,
blue-collar drink. This strategy was a miscalculation of the future *shochu*
market because the strategy did not consider *shochu*'s growing popularity and *shochu*-based drinks among Japanese youth because of the
introduction of tequila. The Japanese enjoyed ritual and the salt on the
rim of the glass and the sucking of the lime after drinking was a ritual
which also provided a virtual trip to Mexico.

I christen thee Mercian Inc.

Although Mercian was the second largest wine producer in Japan, consumers still regarded Suntory as the premier wine maker whose wine
was considered to be superior to Mercian wine. Suzuki realized that
something significant had to be done to hammer a new corporate name
into the minds of consumers.

Before changing Sanraku's name, in the spring of 1990 surveys were conducted throughout Japan on Mercian's name recognition and Mercian's
corporate image. Ninety-nine percent of the 358 people surveyed recognized Sanraku as an old and traditional Japanese liquor producer and
Suntory as the wine producer. Fifty-eight percent of 210 respondents did
not know that Sanraku produced wine and that Mercian was a part of
Sanraku. Suzuki felt that because Mercian already had name recognition,
creating an entirely new name would confuse consumers and was convinced that if the Mercian brand was to vie for top position in the wine
market, the Sanraku corporate name would have to be Mercian. In June,
Suzuki announced at a press conference that Sanraku would henceforth
be known as Mercian Inc. Nevertheless, the survey sample was not large
enough to allow a solid assessment of the name-change and executives in
upper-management were concerned that the name 'Mercian' would have
a negative connotation among wine consumers.

New digs and new PCs

Suzuki's takeover and corporate make-over included moving offices to
a new building in the posh section of the Ginza by the end of 1988.
In January the company moved to Ajinomoto's newly constructed

headquarters, located in the center of the Ginza within walking distance of Japan's flagship department stores, premier restaurants and hotels. A larger-than-life color photograph of a starlet holding a glass of Mercian wine was draped over one side of the building. The press was also invited to attend the lavish inaugural reception. Although the configuration of the office had been altered, all of the divisions remained in the same room. The meeting rooms and reception rooms were well designed. The new wine tasting room equipped with individual spittoons was used regularly by the wine division to taste and assess the quality of the wine samples sent by foreign producers who approached Mercian for sales and distribution in Japan.

New IBM computers replaced the computers manufactured by the Nippon Electric Company (NEC) which had been used for many years. Evidently, the director of HR, without consulting Suzuki, had decided to replace all NEC with IBM which signified that in the 1980s IBM, along with other subsidiaries of foreign multinationals, had placed large numbers of retired bureaucrats on their board of directors. IBM hired officials from MOF, the BOJ and the Science and Technology Agency. Indeed, IBM Japan employed more retired senior bureaucrats than any domestic firm, including three elite MITI officials, in order to ease entry into the information service business sector and to compete with Fujitsu for a larger market share.

All that glitters is not gold

Despite Japan's economic instability, Mercian Inc. continued to expand the wine business with the acquisition of Calpis Co., the producer of a yogurt-based drink, a comfort-food beverage in Japan like Ovaltine in the United States. Calpis had previously purchased top-of-the-line California boutique wines in anticipation of a domestic wine boom and Ajinomoto considered Calpis a good investment because of its yogurt operations.

Unfortunately, Suzuki was diversifying into activities that were exposed to the economic slowdown and he overestimated the pace of consumption and the rate of growth. Some of the business risk was spread by expanding the animal feed business and adding foods to Sanraku's roster of products. However, the diversification also served to muddy the water during a bumpy economic period by going beyond the company's traditional core competencies. Furthermore, Suzuki's ambitions for Mercian Inc. pulled former Sanraku staff out of their comfort zone. It was not a winning formula.

Within three years, the number of staff in the wine division had increased to twenty. Four of the original staff had either retired or had been sent to work in branch offices, which was considered a humiliating step down the corporate ladder.

Sanraku was engaged in other businesses entirely unrelated to wine or spirits, and fish feed and fertilizer did not have a symbiotic relationship with wine. There were growing concerns about Sanraku's core competencies and marketing strategies and although Suzuki could rely on Ajinomoto for some support and on loans from the major metropolitan banks, he could not rely on the management unless he observed operations and Mercian's accounts directly. Regardless, even in the best of times it would have taken a number of years to develop Sanraku's business as a premier wine producer in the same league as Suntory.

By 1999, within a decade after Sanraku had been rebranded Mercian Inc., the company was experiencing significant problems with choppy sales and questionable management. Suzuki's message to stockholders in the 1999 annual report included:

> In fiscal 1999, the year ending December 31, 1999, Japan's economy, unable to make a full-fledged comeback, continued to be hampered by high unemployment rates and a prolonged lull in consumer spending. To acclimatize to the age of change, a series of large-scale mergers started taking place in the financial industry. Over the next few years, the nation's economy on the whole will likely experience a huge transformation.
>
> During the period under review, Japan's alcoholic beverage market, affected by the trend for lower selling prices, continued to encounter intense sales competition. The Japanese wine market retreated, following an exceptional performance in the previous term. Fiscal 1999 saw a sharply growing demand for low-priced Chu-hai drinks, while wine sales declined, affected by inventory adjustments.

(*Chu-hai* is a *shochu* highball beverage. Suntory was competing successfully in the *chu hai* market as well.)

Suzuki's message to stockholders in the 2000 annual report revealed a continuing contraction in profits and Mercian's management problems which had been evident ten years earlier.

> Conditions in the alcoholic beverage market were harsh owing to the trend toward lower selling prices, reflecting the stagnant economy ...

despite rationalization measures, consolidated sales in fiscal 2000 fell 10.1%. Operating income fell 39.6% ...

To enhance corporate governance, we have improved the board of directors and appointed external directors, and introduced economic value added (EVA) as a key management indicator, adopted a new personnel system and a performance-based system ... Price reductions are expected to continue hampering alcoholic beverages market, intensifying survival among companies. The Mercian Group is undertaking to enhance its management base ... the board of directors will concentrate on policy making and operation monitoring. To this end, we have appointed external directors.[1]

Yoshihiko Miyauchi: Mr. Japan Inc.

Yoshihiko Miyauchi was appointed an external director on the Mercian board in 2000. His intimate networks with government and big business since the 1960s are indicative of the Japan Inc. model. Miyauchi, who is 78, retired in May 2014 as Chairman and CEO of Orix Corporation, Japan's largest leasing firm and major provider of general financial services in Japan.

Miyauchi received an MBA from the University of Washington in 1960 before entering Nichimen & Company (now Sojitz) in 1961, a general trading company that was established in 1892 as the Japan Cotton Trading Company. He learned the leasing business when he was sent on a training program in the United States. Miyauchi established the Orient Leasing Company in 1964 together with three trading companies and supported with the backing of a group of financial institutions, including the IBJ and Dai-ichi Kangyo.

Miyauchi expanded the company into areas related to the core business and diversified to financial services that included real estate and life insurance. Although Orix fell into deficit during the bubble economy, the Asian currency crisis and the Lehman Brothers shock, Miyauchi always managed to resuscitate the company. However, Bloomberg reported on April 29, 2011 that Orix Corp was Japan's third-largest borrower in 2010 and one of the first companies to issue bonds when its sales declined after the March 11 earthquake.

Besides Mercian Inc., Miyauchi served on the boards of numerous companies, including Sony Corp whose founder Akio Morita collaborated with former Tokyo governor Shintaro Ishihara to publish the bestseller *Japan Can Say No* (*NO to ieru Nihon*) which argued that the United States regarded Japan as subordinate and this attitude was indicative of racism in America. Although Ishihara's controversial, xenophobic, bigoted and neo-nationalistic remarks often angered the public, his unwavering stance cultivated among many Japanese a sense of stability during unstable times and, hence, a huge following. Ishihara's victory for his fourth term in office in April 2011 was partially attributed to his support of Japan's development of a nuclear arsenal. He also advocated the manufacturing and sale of weapons. In July 2014, Ishihara, together with ultra-conservative politicians, formed the New Generation Party (*Jiseidai no To*), advocating the drafting of a new Constitution and denying non-Japanese residents the right to vote.

Orix was one of thirty-five corporate investors, including NTT Communications, Hitachi and Kajima Corporation that bankrolled Ishihara's pet project, a commercial city bank, established in 2005 to provide unsecured and unguaranteed loans to small and medium-sized businesses. Eighty-four percent of the investment was tax revenue from the Tokyo Metropolitan Government. Shinginko (New Bank) had extended loans and loan guarantees totaling $2.165 billion despite the default of $22.55 million by the end of 2005. In September 2007 Shinginko reported a loss of $868 million of which $79.8 million had accumulated during a six-month period. The reason given for the loss was poor assessment of collateral and mismanagement. In February 2008, 'Ishihara's Bank', as Shinginko was often called, received a government bailout of $371 million. The bank is still operating and reported to be in the black.

Miyauchi, who is a strong advocate of structural reforms, is the chairman of the government's Council for Regulatory Reforms. He financed the businesses of friends whom he regarded as entrepreneurial such as Yoshiaki Murakami who shared the same beliefs about the need for regulatory reforms in business operations. Miyauchi was one of the chief financers of the Murakami Fund (M&A), which was established by former METI official, Yoshiaki Murakami in 2002 (worth $3.6 billion). Murakami was popularly known as a flamboyant, aggressive and successful entrepreneur in the same style as Takafumi Horie who was also a brash, young entrepreneur and president of the Internet portal operator Livedoor. A close friend of former Prime Minister Koizumi, Horie was arrested for securities fraud on January 23, 2006 but released on bail the following April. He was subsequently convicted to serve a two and a half year prison sentence beginning on March 17, 2007.

Murakami's relationship with Horie resulted in his conviction for insider trading and a subsequent two-year prison term. Murakami escaped the prison sentence by moving his fund and residence to Singapore.

Miyauchi, whose company was engaged in real estate during the bubble years, may not have forecasted that the BOJ would suddenly raise interest rates but he did understand that nothing in the government–business system had changed basically since the 1970s, or even in the social system, and that the industries in the financial sector were still being regulated and closed to many foreign companies. The exhausted expressions of passengers riding subways showed a deep fatigue from the frenetic peddling of an over-heated economy. Japan was entering an unsavory period of daily revelations of political and corporate corruption but the façade of well-being continued.

10
Bubble, Bubble, Turmoil and Trouble

The year 1988 saw the beginning of a rash of political scandals that served to unhinge Japan's political system because of the involvement of numerous high-ranking members in the LDP and elite civil servants. The Recruit scandal hit the front pages of the major dailies. The massive insider trading and corruption scandal that brought down Prime Minister Noboru Takeshita's entire administration, the resignation from office by many key politicians, and the arrest and indictment of powerful businessmen are pertinent examples of collusion between cross-party ultra-conservative politicians, bureaucrats and big business and of money politics during Japan's post-war period. The Recruit scandal, involving 155 prominent figures, was regarded as the most pervasive of all time and much bigger than the Lockheed scandal. It was also credited with spurring the defection of members of the LDP to form the New Japan Party in 1992 and Morihiro Hosokawa's installation as prime minister in August 1993.

The scandals that plagued Prime Minister Kakuei Tanaka before, during and after he was in the prime minister's office were regarded as political corruption, involving primarily politicians. The Lockheed bribery scandal in 1976 was covered by the international press because the case went to trial and Tanaka was sentenced to four years in prison for accepting $3 million from the Lockheed Corporation for convincing ANA to order passenger planes from Lockeed instead of from McDonnell Douglas. Former Prime Minister Eisaku Sato was also implicated with Lockheed officials in separate bribery cases. On the other hand, the Japanese electorate regarded politicians as corrupt and not in the same league as bureaucrats who were in charge of the economy and who were considered above reproach.

Hiromasa Ezoe established Recruit with $2000 as an advertising-sales agency in 1969. Ezoe, whose motto was 'In This World Money Comes First', built the tiny company into a $3.2 billion conglomerate with subsidiaries that engaged in human resources, real estate, supercomputers, restaurant and hotel management, information-publishing, property and telecommunications. Throughout the years, in order to expand the company's business, Ezoe habitually offered his company's unlisted shares before they went public to politicians, bureaucrats and businessmen who made substantial gains when the shares were released on the open market.

From 1984–6 Ezoe sold shares of the real estate subsidiary Recruit Cosmos for $20 per share before it went public to politicians, bureaucrats, business leaders and journalists. When Cosmos went public and the shares were sold on the over-the-counter, asset-inflated stock market the price per share tripled and the purchasers reaped millions of dollars. It was a common practice for Japanese companies to sell stock to influential buyers at reduced prices but the magnitude of the sale of more than 850,000 shares was unprecedented.

Ezoe was arrested, and during the eight-month investigation Ezoe told prosecutors that he had spread millions of dollars in cash and unlisted stock to 100 politicians, bureaucrats and businessmen. Prosecutors arrested or indicted nineteen people, among them the former chairman of Nippon Telephone and Telegraph, Hisashi Shinto, and two of the corporation's top executives, Kunio Takaishi, the former Vice-Minister of the Ministry of Education, and Takaishi Kato, the former Vice-Minister of the Ministry of Labor.

Nippon Telephone and Telegraph (NTT), a Special Corporation managed by the former Ministry of Posts and Telecommunication, was the domestic provider of telephone networks and was in the process of undergoing partial privatization. Ezoe needed strong political connections to ensure that the regulators would not break up NTT's networks into smaller private companies that would be competitive with Recruit. Offering shares was an innovative and cost-free method of promoting influence. In 1986, Ezoe met with Shinto to arrange two business transactions with NTT. The first was getting Recruit into the lucrative market of reselling special telephone circuits to businesses. The second was NTT's procurement from Recruit in 1988 and 1989 of two US-made Cray Research supercomputers, which NTT would resell to Recruit at a reduced price. At the same time, Mr. Shinto, who was a close friend of Takeshita's predecessor Prime Minister Yasuhiro Nakasone, was given 10,000 shares of Recruit Cosmos. Shinto used the shares for two NTT slush funds for direct contributions to prominent politicians and for purchases of tickets to political fund-raising events.

Takeshita had been in office since November 1987. The implication of bribery among a number of Takeshita's cabinet ministers did not help his public approval rating which had already sunk below 30 percent. Takeshita's finance minister, Kiichi Miyazawa, resigned in December 1988, claiming that an aide had purchased stock using his name. Takeshita quickly reshuffled his cabinet, replacing fifteen of his twenty ministers. When Miyazawa resigned, Hisashi Shinto also admitted his involvement in the stock deal and resigned his post as chairman of NTT.

When Takeshita was questioned by prosecutors in October 1988 he denied misconduct, but in April 1989, he conceded that he and members close to him had received $1,000,000 from Recruit. Although he denied making any profit from the Recruit shares he admitted that Recruit had purchased more than $570,000 worth of tickets to two fund-raising events for him in Tokyo and Iwate Prefecture in May 1987. Although such contributions were legal, the Recruit contribution exceeded the limit that had been set after the Lockheed scandal.

Other well-known figures involved were the chairmen of two major dailies. Nakasone also conceded receipt of Recruit shares and resigned from the LDP to become an 'independent'. He escaped indictment as did a number of other prominent government leaders. The Daiei Group purchased 35 percent of Recruit shares in June 1992.

On April 25, 1989, Takeshita announced that he would resign from office. A former aide committed suicide in penance for his leader's humiliation. Prosecutors concluded that there was not enough evidence to indict Takeshita. On October 10, 1990, the eighty-year-old Shinto, considered one of Japan's most powerful business figures, was convicted of receiving bribes. He was fined $170,000 and sentenced to a two-year prison term but the sentence was suspended because of his age.

The beginning of the end of the '1955 system'

In 1989 LDP politician Sasuke Uno succeeded Takeshita as Prime Minister but resigned within three months after taking office due to a sex scandal involving his relationship with a geisha. Uno's successor was Toshiki Kaifu, another LDP politician (1989–91) who attempted reform measures but political scandal in the LDP again obstructed his efforts. Ironically, in November 1991 Kiichi Miyazawa took office and tried to persuade the Diet to implement a 5 percent consumption tax for the first time in Japan's post-war history.

The bursting of the economic bubble was followed by more scandals encompassing members of the LDP, ministry officials, the construction industry and banks. However, Kanemaru, the LDP major-domo, was enveloped in a series of corruption scandals that ended his political career. In October 1992, he publicly admitted that he had received $4.1 million in illegal contributions from Sagawa Kyubin, a trucking company that had relations with construction companies and the underworld. However, he avoided public questioning through behind-the-scenes politicking and escaped prosecution with a small fine. Kanemaru, who was seventy-eight, was arrested with his secretary and indicted for tax evasion in March 1993. When public prosecutors raided Kanemaru's residence they discovered in his safe-deposit box gold bars and $50 million in cash and securities. The public outcry and the continuing media attention on the collusion scandals involving politicians, bureaucrats and big business forced Kanemaru to relinquish his seat and tender his resignation as LDP vice-president. A prison sentence was suspended because of his age. The governor of Niigata Prefecture also resigned from office amid allegations that he received $2.4 million in unreported campaign contributions from Sagawa Kyubin.

After the BOJ suddenly raised interest rates and real estate prices plummeted, the reaction by the Japanese was very low-key, bordering on denial. There also was confidence in the established model of government administration and the belief that the economy would stabilize.

However, the struggle for power among factions in the LDP due to the recession and the acknowledged need for action to ignite Japan's lagging economy destabilized the political system. Some government members, wanting to distance themselves from scandal and attempt to initiate political reform, defected to form new parties. Morihiro Hosokawa, the former governor of Kyushu, founded the reformist New Japan Party with Hiroshi Kumagai, a former MITI official who had left MITI in mid-career to enter politics on the LDP ticket. Former Prime Minister Yoshihiko Noda was also a member. The party joined forces with the Japan Renewal Party, which was founded by another LDP political kingpin Ichiro Ozawa, and Tsutomu Hata.

In August 1993, Prime Minister Miyazawa lost the no-confidence vote in the Diet (purportedly due to his proposed tax hike) and resigned from office, which marked the end of the thirty-eight-year reign of the LDP over post-war politics. Hosokawa became the Prime Minister and formed an eight-party coalition government. His domestic policy focused on the reform of the electoral system and confronting political and corporate corruption. His international policies were the antithesis of Abe's and other right-wing politicians' views when he formally recognized that Japan had waged a war of aggression in the Pacific. He also made a formal apology to Korea for Japan's colonization. The charismatic prime minister cut residential and income tax to alleviate the impact of the bursting of the economic bubble on the economy but was pressured by MOF to raise the consumption tax from 3 percent to 7 percent by 1997 to compensate. Hosokawa could not bring consensus in the coalition, and reneged.

After only eight months in office Hosokawa was compelled to resign because he received a loan from Sagawa Kyubin for ¥100 million yen. His claim that he had repaid the loan was not believed by LDP members. Also, there were problems within Hosokawa's administration, which had been weakened by political infighting among factions. Japan Inc. was beginning to slip into a political black hole.

Ozawa, like Hosokawa, aggressively pushed for more autonomy for local authorities and for the reform of the electoral system that would encourage fairer representation in the Lower House and result in a true two-party system, which was achieved when the reform bill was passed during Hosokawa's administration.

In order to preserve the Hosokawa coalition government, Tsutomu Hata, who had served as deputy prime minister, stepped in as prime minister but held office for only three months because of Ozawa's habit of alienating colleagues by pressuring them to accept policies he vigorously promoted like raising the consumption tax to 10 percent and more devolution for local authorities. After failing to convince the Socialists, whose party was a member of the coalition, to agree to certain policies, they left Hata's coalition and the LDP regained seats in the Lower House general elections forcing Hata to resign the following June.

In July, Tomiichi Murayama, a Socialist, assumed the post, forming another coalition cabinet composed of members of the Socialist Party of Japan, New Japan Party and the LDP. He began a push to reform the political system itself in order to end the relationship between politicians, bureaucrats and businessmen. This movement prompted a power struggle between politicians and bureaucrats, who were intent on maintaining control over the regulation of the economy.

Murayama's administration suffered from a sequence of events that served to end Murayama's term in office in 1996. There was the Kobe Earthquake on January 17, 1995, which brought harsh criticism of the government's handling of the aftermath, the continuing recession, political infighting and the opposition of Socialist Party members to

Murayama's support of the Japan–US Security Pact, which the prime minister contended was in accordance with Japan's Constitution. Furthermore, the Sarin gas-attack by the religious cult Aum Shinrikyo in the Tokyo Underground on March 20, 1995, which killed twelve people and injured 6,000, increased Japanese anxieties about the country's socio-economic stability. Voters returned to the LDP fold and the Socialist Party lost many seats in the Lower House in the 1996 election. Murayama resigned as prime minister making way for the LDP president Ryutaro Hashimoto to enter the executive office. Frustrated members of the new parties either returned to the LDP or joined other parties.

Ozawa ploughed ahead to form the New Pioneer Party in 1995, merging it with the Renewal Party. He defeated Hata in the election for secretary-general in the party but it was a meaningless exercise because Hata and the majority of members left the party to form other small parties.

Ozawa went on to form the Liberal Party, which participated in Prime Minister Ryutaro's LDP coalition government (1996–98). He cultivated a devout following of young supporters throughout the 1990s. Many of his lieutenants were first employed to perform menial chores in his home such as cleaning and walking his dogs. If they proved to be hardworking and loyal, they were promoted to secretarial positions in his Tokyo office.

Ichiro Ozawa, the spoiler: protégé of Tanaka and Kanemaru

Ozawa represented Japan's mainstream ultra-conservative political environment during Japan's post-war period that evolved through interpersonal connections between politicians and businesses to become a tangled web of vested interests, collusion and corrupt practices. In October 1992 Ozawa was also implicated in the Sagawa Kyubin scandal.

Although ministry officials were not concerned that Ozawa would be a serious threat to the ultra-conservative LDP, he was very involved in shaking up the political status quo. On the other hand, he was not a team player. Known as the 'shadow shogun' he was regarded as a key political strategist, back-room deal-maker and a fund-raiser in the same mode as Kakuei Tanaka, his mentor. Tanaka taught Ozawa the importance of establishing strong relationships with smaller firms that were trying to compete with big established companies for a share of tight markets. He also taught Ozawa that a close relationship with the construction industry was essential to a politician's purse.

Ozawa was born in the rural and agrarian Iwate Prefecture in northeast Japan. His father, who had owned a construction company, held a seat in the Lower House. When his father died, Ozawa stood for election in 1969 as a member of the LDP and won. He joined Tanaka's faction and rapidly gained popularity as did future prime ministers Tsutomo Hata and Ryutaro Hashimoto with whom he jostled for position in the Tanaka faction. He impressed leaders with his skill at manipulating opposition parties to pass unpopular bills in the Diet but because of his unfettered ambition, and dictatorial methods, he was also disliked by many members in the LDP.

A right-wing reformer, he transferred to the Takeshita–Kanemaru faction after Tanaka left office in 1974. As was also the case for the Tanaka faction, construction companies who wanted to expand their operations (e.g. contracts for public works projects) contributed the major share of political contributions to the Kanemaru–Takeshita faction. Ozawa was taught by Tanaka and Kanemaru how to garner the support from local electorates and grass-roots politics.

Ozawa, who had been implicated in the Recruit scandal in 1988 for his involvement in insider-trading sanctions, was interrogated in October 1992 when Kanemaru was arrested over the Sagawa Kyubin affair. He was questioned about escorting Kanemaru to meetings with Sagawa management. His retort to prosecutors was that he was merely going along to act as barman. In December 1992 when he was still an LDP member Ozawa was implicated in a money scandal which involved Kajima Construction, one of the big six general contracting companies that had been charged with bribing numerous politicians in order to win contracts. Ozawa called a press conference to deny reports by the *Asahi Shimbun* that the contributions were illegal.

In 2003, Ozawa merged his Liberal Party with the DPJ. He became the DPJ secretary-general but his imperiousness lead to confrontations with party members, especially with Naoto Kan. He was elected as president of the DPJ and his campaign tactics, which focused on cultivating voters and collecting campaign funds in rural areas, led the party to its biggest victory in the Upper House. Although he resigned in protest after the LDP Prime Minister Yasuo Fukuda (2007–8) proposed a coalition between the LDP and the DPJ, Ozawa was persuaded to remain in the post. He won the presidency three consecutive times. But a number of DPJ politicians considered him a spoiler and a trouble-maker and in May 2009, Ozawa was pressured to resign due to his alleged involvement in a political funding scandal. When he masterminded the DPJ victory in the Lower House, DPJ Prime Minister Yukio Hatoyama (2009–10) rewarded Ozawa by appointing him secretary-general of the party in 2009.

The loyalty of two Ozawa lieutenants and their willingness to support him regardless of the methods involved resulted in the arrest on May 3, 2009 of Ozawa's chief political secretary Takanori Okubo for allegedly accepting illegally $250,000 in political contributions from the construction company Nishimatsu. The firm was already being investigated for other corruption scandals. Private firms are allowed to contribute to political parties but not to individual politicians. The contribution was passed through Ritsuzenkai, Ozawa's fund body. Although Ozawa claimed ignorance of the contribution, the public prosecutors pursued the case and relentlessly investigated his alleged financial irregularities.

Ozawa, as the new secretary-general of the DPJ, kept an indignant silence and denied the requests from the Diet to appear at hearings during the rest of 2009, relying on his popularity among voters to defuse the situation. However, 75 percent of voters thought that he should resign as secretary-general after prosecutors raided Ritsuzenkai to discover $4 million in cash in illegal contributions from Kajima Corp, a major construction company. Prosecutors also searched the office of former aide Tomohiro Ishikawa in the Diet members' office building as well as Kajima Corp's offices. Ishikawa was a member in the Diet's Lower House. Ishikawa and Okubo were also charged with not registering contributions in the Ritsuzenkai books in order to hide the receipt of ¥50,000 each from Mizutani Construction related to a dam construction project in Iwate Prefecture.

Ozawa brushed off accusations of any wrongdoing stating that, although he and his aides may have misjudged conditions, there was no intention to violate the law. Ishikawa, aged thirty-six, was indicted for accepting illegal contributions and resigned from the National Diet on December 2, 2010. On January 31, 2011, a special panel of lawyers who had been assigned to investigate the case returned with an indictment. But Ozawa's continued resistance to face questioning in the Diet and Kan's administration's shrinking public approval rating (17 percent) forced the DPJ Standing Officers Council to officially suspend Ozawa from the DPJ on July 20. Nonetheless, like his mentor Tanaka, despite his indictment and pending trial, Ozawa maintained his power base. His group of 120 supporters in the DPJ was significantly larger than the groups supporting the other DPJ politicians. When Kan was about to resign in late August, some candidates sought Ozawa's support, suggesting that his suspension from the party be reconsidered. However, Ozawa did not support Yoshihiko Noda, who assumed the office of Prime Minister at the end of September.

A few days before the election, Ozawa, who was struggling to make a comeback as the kingpin in the DPJ, was informed that Ishikawa, Okubo and Mitsumoto Ikeda, who had succeeded Ishikawa as an aide, were convicted in Tokyo District Court of falsifying Risuzankai's financial reports in 2004, 2005 and 2007 concerning a land purchase in Tokyo's Setagaya Ward and given suspended prison sentences. Ozawa continued to refuse to appear before Diet members.

Ozawa vehemently opposed Noda's tax hike bill, which was passed in July 2012. Never a team player, Ozawa left the DPJ, taking some party members with him, to establish yet another small political party. Ozawa was cleared of all charges in April 2012.

Ishikawa had also proven his loyalty to Ozawa by shoveling snow and scrubbing floors in his house and doing clerical work at Ritsuzankai before entering politics. While awaiting his trial after which he was expecting to be imprisoned, Ishikawa published *Serving Ozawa Ichiro, the Rascal (Akuto Ozawa Ichiro Tsukaete)* in July 2011. Ishikawa describes his painful decision to resign his seat in the Lower House after his arrest in 2009. His book also relates Ozawa's penchant for treating his aides with arrogant detachment. On the other hand, Ishikawa expresses his respect for Ozawa's political acumen, his driving political ambition and his single-minded back-room politicking to promote his policies.[1]

Bureaucrat bashing

After the revelations of collusion between ministry officials and the construction industry, the bureaucracy became fair game for Japanese journalists and for politicians who were trying to wrest power from it.

During Prime Minister Hosokawa's brief administration, Hiroshi Kumagai served as the Cabinet Minister of Trade and Industry. Kumagai was a career officer in MITI and was serving as director-general of the Small and Medium-Size Enterprise Agency when he left in 1976 to run for political office on the LDP ticket. He won a seat in the Upper House of the Diet in 1977 and then took a seat in the Lower House in 1983. In 1991 he served for one year as the Parliamentary Vice-Minister of the Economic Planning Agency before assuming several high-ranking positions in the LDP. He was one of the founders of the New Japan Party with Hosokawa in 1992 and after serving as MITI Minister served as Minister of State in 1994. Kumagai was also one of the founders of the DPJ in 1998 but after a power struggle with Naoto Kan, he, along with three of his colleagues, defected in December 2002 to form the tiny New Conservative Party (NCP) where he served as president. After the November 2003 elections only four members remained in the right-wing reformist party and Kumagai accepted Prime Minister Koizumi's invitation to merge with the LDP because he considered Koizumi a right-wing reformist.

Kumagai's and Ozawa's political objectives were similar, especially in regards to wresting regulatory powers from ministry officials and bringing more power to the executive office. A classic example of efforts by politicians to poke holes in the bureaucracy by further inflaming public opinion against elite ministerial guidance occurred in December 1993. Although Kumagai was the front-man in instigating the incident, Ozawa was rumored to be involved as well.

When Kumagai was serving as MITI Minister in Hosokawa's cabinet he demanded the resignation of Masahisa Naitoh, who was said to be in line for the post of MITI International Administrative Vice-Minister. Ostensibly, Kumagai's reason for demanding the resignation was that Naitoh had arranged a promotion in MITI for the son of his close friend and patron, Yuji Tanahashi, MITI International Vice-Minister. Yasufumi had entered MITI in 1987. The promotion was intended to enhance his image, thus improving his chances of winning a seat in the Diet when he entered the election as an LDP candidate of Gifu Prefecture, a seat that his grandfather, a former governor of Gifu, had occupied for many years. Despite his newly polished image, Yasufumi lost the election.

Kumagai, who reportedly wanted to stop 'favoritism' in the ministries, accused Naitoh, a civil servant, of failing to abide by the principle of non-partisan politics but realistically the affair was related to the power struggle between factions within MITI and between special interest groups in the LDP and the New Japan Party. There was also the possibility that Kumagai's ulterior motives were personal because during his time in MITI his relationship with Naitoh was said to be fractious.

Hideaki Kumano, the Administrative Vice-Minister and the head of MITI, was responsible for implementing the dismissal. Although he was against Naitoh's resignation, in order to keep the peace, he pleaded with Naitoh to resign quietly. Initially Naitoh refused to resign, calling the stand-off a test of the independence of the bureaucracy. However, on December 23, he resigned without apology at a news conference, telling reporters that he had simply followed the long-established custom of giving titles to ministry officials who ran for office. Although Naitoh's admission was not welcomed among the general public, who were questioning the integrity of ministry officials, it also illustrated that many ministry officials opted for political careers (as did Kumagai in 1976) and that the ties between bureaucrats and politicians could be very close.

The affair was covered extensively by Japanese media as the drama was unfolding. The February 1994 issue of the political economic magazine *Sentaku* printed a four-page spread with photographs of both Kumagai and Naitoh.

The incident shook the halls of MITI. It was only the second time in the history of the ministry that a high-ranking official was dismissed (the first was in 1952). Naitoh's subordinates objected to politicians interfering in MITI's affairs and vociferously opposed Naitoh's resignation.

Kumano, who had been caught in the middle of the dispute, submitted his resignation from MITI in June to take responsibility for the upheaval in the ministry. Upon his retirement Kumano moved to the Industrial Policy Research Institution (IPRI) where in 1993, Yuji Tanahashi had also migrated upon his retirement.

Masahisa Naitoh was well connected in the United States because he had been posted as a director of the Industrial Research Division at the largest North American branch of the Japan External Trade Organization (JETRO) in New York in the mid-1980s while he was negotiating with the United States Trade Representative (USTR) on behalf of the Japanese semiconductor industry.

When Naitoh formally resigned on April 1, 1994 he moved to Georgetown University as the Marks & Murase professor in the Asia Law and Policy Institute (ALPS) program. Japanese businesses and government and government agencies are among the clients of the law firm Marks & Murase.

On April 7, 1994, Naitoh gave a lecture at the Georgetown University Law Center. He reflected on the motivations of ministry officials who worked during Japan's rapid economic growth period and who seemed inspired by their roles as the administrators of Japan's economic rebirth. He lamented the changes in attitudes of current bureaucrats, who, he felt, had become inward and 'turf conscious', working to protect their ministry's territory rather than making policy to deregulate markets.

Naitoh told the audience that the Japanese people, who had relied for centuries on either an emperor or a military to govern them, did not want to take the initiative to plan their own destiny but preferred to entrust responsibility to a bureaucracy. He explained that the submission to bureaucratic rule gave the ministries much power which was further enhanced by the close contact between bureaucrats and businessmen, who feared retribution if they did not comply with guidance.

The following June, Naitoh was reinstated by MITI as a consultant. *A Creaking Giant Power* carried an interview with Naitoh before his dismissal. When he asserted that bureaucrats operated independently of politicians he was asked if he thought that bureaucrats could work together with politicians to forge policies. Naitoh felt that it might prove feasible if politicians could plan strategies and the bureaucrats did the legwork, implying that administrators knew more about managing industry and economy than did politicians. He expressed disappointment that, although bureaucrats were the servants of their country, they had become isolated from society and had forgotten their mission.

Naitoh claimed that the multitude of rules and regulations did not act to effectively support MITI's control of industrial policy but, rather, the trust between bureaucrats and private businesses facilitated the implementation of policy.

Kumano was also interviewed. He objected to the interviewer calling MITI the 'Number Two Ministry of Finance' (*Dai-niji Okurasho*) which implied that MITI was taking over MOF's territory by executing duties that usually fell within MOF's remit.

Despite his frank rhetoric, Naitoh did not mention the fact that the ministries had extended power over the political economy through their corporations and the *amakudari* system which served MITI and the other ministries to persuade businesses to accommodate their policies. Indeed, Naitoh participated in this very system, as is also the case for the majority of elite civil servants. Naitoh's post-MITI career, although more prolific, represents the post-retirement careers of ministry officials, who have found upper management and directorships in corporations linked to their ministries' administrative jurisdiction.

In 1997, Naitoh served as an advisor and then as Vice-Chairman, Executive Vice-President, and Senior Managing Director at Itochu Corporation, one of Japan's leading trading companies, which together with retailers are in MITI's administrative jurisdiction. Naitoh was also a Vice-President of Meiji Seika Pharmaceutical. From 1995 to 2007 he served as a director at Molex Inc., an electronic component manufacturer whose clients include Nippon Electric Company (NEC), one of Japan's largest producers of semiconductors. Naitoh has been a director at Dupont Qualicon Inc. since 2000.

In 1994 Naitoh became the chairman and CEO of the Institute of Energy Economics in Japan (IEEJ), which was established in 1966 by MITI as one of its corporations. Under the umbrella of the IEEJ are the Oil Information Bureau (established 1981), the Energy Data and Modeling Center (1984), the Asia Pacific Research Center (1986), JME

Center (2005) and the Green Energy Certification Center (2008) in which Naitoh remains a director.[2]

The current chairman and CEO is Mazakazu Toyoda who was METI's Vice-Minister of International Affairs in 2006. Some of his other METI posts included director of the International Economic Affairs Division and also the Director-General for Manufacturing Policy. Toyoda's career in METI which focused on energy and international relations is pertinent to the operations of the IEEJ. His post-retirement positions in the private sector included serving as the outside auditor for Murata Manufacturing Co. Ltd. and as Corporate Auditor for Nitto Denko. Both companies are in METI's administrative jurisdiction.

Since 2008 Yuji Tanahashi has served as chairman of the Japan Petroleum Exploration Co. Ltd., which prior to 2003 was an entity in JNOC.

Japan bashing/America bashing

The term 'Japan bashing' was first used by Robert Angel in the 1980s while he was the president of the Japan Economic Institute, which was the organ for the Japan lobby in Washington, DC and funded by the MOFA. The term was coined to counteract anti-Japanese sentiment in the US regarding Japan's trade surplus with the US and the USTR's demands to Japan to commit to numerical quotas on its exports to the US.

The three Japanese automobile manufacturers (Honda, Toyota and Nissan) agreed in 1981 to limit the number of cars exported to the US, but by 1985 they had opened production facilities in the southern United States to produce larger models where workers were not union members. As the American auto industry was losing market share to Japanese car imports, American auto workers, fearful of losing jobs, protested by physically bashing Japanese cars with sledge hammers and burning Japanese flags, despite the fact that the cars parked in the staff parking lots of US car manufacturers were packed with Toyotas and Hondas.

The purchases by Japanese companies of high-profile real estate and American movie companies during the bubble years also triggered a spat of public protests. Sony Corp purchased Columbia Pictures in September 1989 and Matsushita purchased MCA Entertainment in 1990. The $6.6 billion MCA deal included the concessions in Yosemite National Park which, after considerable public outcry that Japanese companies were buying up pieces of the American landscape, US Interior Secretary Manuel Lujan launched an inquiry into whether entertainment giant

MCA Inc. had violated its government contract to operate Yosemite concessions when it sold Yosemite Park and Curry Co., the concession operator, to Matsushita without Lujan's approval. The unwelcome publicity and pressure from Lujan pressured Matsushita within two years to sell off the concessions, which included a hotel and tents, for $49.5 million to an American non-profit foundation where Lujan served as a member of the board. The foundation donated the concessions to the National Park Service. In 1995, Matsushita parted with 80 percent of its stake in MCA for $5.7 billion. Matsushita did not refer to the bursting of the real estate bubble as a reason for the sale but, instead, pointed to differences with MCA management.

When he was interviewed, the NHK correspondent maintained that, although there had been good coverage by American media on Japan, there had also been articles by American commentators who appeared to have no fundamental knowledge of Japanese culture. Exaggerating one tiny aspect, they insisted that it represented Japan and connected these issues to trade friction.

The United States Trade Representative: who is the fairest of them all?

Japanese ministry officials grumbled that due to the end of the Cold War, the US no longer considered Japan as indispensable in terms of a military alliance and that the USTR was taking a much tougher stance at trade negotiations by demanding numerical quotas because US military bases in Japan were no longer considered vital to US interests. Officials also complained that one of the ways that the US was reducing the trade deficit was by selling older models of military aircraft to Japan for its self-defense forces, but not the state-of-the art models to limit technology transfer.

In 1993 the USTR was pressuring Japan again to open up markets to more processed foods, home electronics, automobiles and car parts. The automobile and car industries that were well represented by powerful lobby groups and labor unions were relentlessly pursuing the members in Congress whose constituents were businesses engaged in these industries. Trade deals seemed to relate to political need rather than to reducing American trade deficits. The USTR was also pressuring Japan to open markets to the financial, insurance and pharmaceutical industries.

American news media were covering the heated US–Japan trade talks beginning in 1993 which included the increase of exports of cars and car parts. There were reports that even though Japanese markets were wide open to American pop culture and fast foods, including Coca-Cola and McDonald's, Japan's markets were closed to American automobiles. Although Japan's inward investment was a measly 2.5 percent of the annual GDP, the second lowest among the OECD countries, importing American cars with the steering wheels on the wrong side and which were too big for Japan's narrow streets was not a logical solution to lowering the US's trade deficit with Japan.

The NHK correspondent admitted that mass media reported news in a way that it thought the public wanted to hear, putting the emphasis on trade friction rather than on the efforts by both sides to reach a compromise. He repeated the same claims made by Japanese government officials that Japan was not as important to the United States as the United States was to Japan because of its markets. He was amazed at the paucity of information about Japan Americans received, including staff in President Clinton's administration, and was critical about the fact that there were no representatives in the USTR who spoke Japanese or understood Japanese culture and psychology. The correspondent was concerned that since Clinton regarded China as America's future market pro-Japan representatives would be absent at the negotiation table.

Bill Whitaker had a similar view. He admitted that media hype sold papers and raised ratings but because television news reported the news as it was happening the reports could be inaccurate and, at times, false. He gave as an example the US media's biased coverage of American auto workers smashing a Japanese car which failed to include that American car manufacturers had become complacent, producing cars that were no longer competitive with Japanese manufacturers whose cars were better designed and who were aggressively entering the American market. He also thought that there was a real danger of overemphasizing the role the press played in fanning the friction between the two societies and that the people themselves should assume responsibility for the state of affairs.

The Japanese resented being America's whipping boy because they felt that America's economic problems were of its own making and were unrelated to Japan's economic rise and clout in international markets. Without referring to Japan's protectionist policies, a MITI official related his government's stance in an interview conducted in 1994 at the time of the negotiations and which is still relevant:

> The latest pronouncement of the US Trade Representative is that the reason for the continuing huge trade surplus is because of Japan's position as a nation. This problem, really in terms of numbers [quotas], clearly must be solved. But if you turn things around and look

at it from Japan's perspective, the United States had a huge trade surplus up until 30 years ago. Americans worked very hard and made excellent products. The trade surplus was natural. If the Japanese wanted a trade surplus, they had to develop excellent products. When comparing how open the door is to Japanese products and American markets, America's markets are far more open than Japan's. Compared to the present time, there are far more American products in Japan than before because American products are excellent. When Americans during negotiations negotiate with the contention that Japan is devious, from our point of view, it is Puritanism. Big decisions based on one standard![3]

A ministry official also interviewed was concerned that because of the trade friction the United States would abandon Japan in favor of China due to China's economic expansion, potential vast markets and its growing influence in global markets:

Concerning America's request to Japan about the trade imbalance, America has so much it only has to think of itself. The US is now looking at China instead of Japan because it's easier to enter the market. The Chinese language has more similarities to English than Japanese. Chinese resembles English in grammar and communication is easier between Chinese and Americans. Chinese resemble English because there are many phrases and sayings that are common in both languages. In Japanese, special terms must be invented in order to communicate. Also, Chinese and American preferences are more similar than Japanese and American preferences.[4]

Digging up the dirt

The Japanese press and television broadcasting stations began reporting news about the United States that was often provocative. Japanese newspapers and branches of television stations that were located on the east and west coasts sent local staff around the United States to gather news stories regarding crimes perpetrated against Japanese tourists and racial discrimination, drug culture, prostitution or abortion issues which could be construed as 'scare-mongering' and creating the impression that the US was racked with social problems and a dangerous place to live.

Bill Whitaker was often disturbed by how Americans were portrayed on Japanese television. Reports focused on racism, crime and the deterioration of American society. Whitaker himself was affected by what he saw on the tube in Japan and was initially afraid of returning to the US in the early 1990s. Although he recognized that gun crime was 'outrageous' he soon realized that the he would not be a victim when he drove downtown to his office.

A former reporter for *Nikkei Weekly* expressed concerns about biased reporting by both Japanese and American media. While Japanese media focused on racism and drugs issues in the United States, American media's coverage of Japan was equally inflammatory, particularly in regard to the trade friction. He was dismayed when he saw the televised report by a newscaster who held up a Motorola mobile phone, complaining that despite its small size, it was not sold in Japan due to Japan's closed market.

TV Asahi is one of the largest commercial new stations in Japan and operates bureaux in Washington, DC, New York City and in Los Angeles to cover US news. The station has collaborated with the American Broadcasting System and CNN. In the 1990s the Manhattan office was located on the twenty-seventh floor of the International Building in Rockefeller Center, when the building was owned by Mitsubishi Estate but later moved offices to Third Avenue.

The first Gulf War began on January 16, 1991 when the US declared Operation Desert Storm to counteract Iraq's invasion of Kuwait on August 2, 1990 and its refusal to withdraw its troops from Kuwait territory. The declaration was accompanied by an airstrike by the US coalition warplanes on Iraqi military targets, including Baghdad.

TV Asahi sent reporters based in the United States to the Middle East to cover the war. Simultaneously they continued covering US news. The political cartoons published in the Japanese newspapers were not US-friendly regarding the United States' involvement in the war. A cartoon by a well-known political cartoonist depicted President George W. Bush in cowboy gear on a bucking bronco and lassoing a terrified Saddam Hussein. Another cartoon depicted weeds growing abundantly in front of a dilapidated White House with the words 'The New World Order' scribbled beneath.

It was rumored that, in order to counteract President Bush's visit to Honolulu on December 7 to commemorate the fiftieth anniversary of the bombing of Pearl Harbor, TV Asahi was attempting to uncover information regarding atrocities committed by American GIs in Iraq against Iraqi soldiers such as burying them alive in the desert. Ironically, George Bush canceled his trip to Honolulu to avoid friction with its key ally in the Pacific.

An interview conducted in 1994 with a staff member of a large Japanese trading company who had been posted as vice-president for five years in his company's Chicago branch office and then as vice-president in the New York branch office for another five years is also pertinent to current events:

> I hate mass media! The Japanese press does not transmit correct information about the US to Japanese. For example, Prime Minister Hosokawa came here a few months ago and stayed at the Waldorf Astoria. President Clinton also stayed there. There was very tight security. The heavy police protection was for Clinton, not for Hosokawa. This is not done to such an extent in Japan. The Japanese press reported that the police blocking off the street didn't give Hosokawa adequate security like it did to Clinton. The newspapers from other countries in attendance didn't complain. I wasn't there, but wherever President Clinton goes, security is always tight and very disruptive. This unimportant news became fodder for criticism.
>
> However, things that happen in Japan are very important. Everyone knew that Mr. Kanazawa [Kanazawa was a top official in MOC] accepted large bribes from the construction industry but no one wrote about it! Everyone writes about the Waldorf Astoria and Clinton! However, the *Washington Post* did write about the scandal.
>
> I don't feel that Japan and the US are equal. The interest and concerns that the Japanese have for Japan are completely different. Japan is not important to the United States. It's all right that ABC doesn't report news about Japan. But for Japan, America's very big. Trade with America is tremendous because the population in the US is tremendous and America takes huge amounts of imports. America's need for news about Japan is much less than Japan's need for news about the US.
>
> In both countries inaccuracies in reporting are made on various economic facts. There is the excuse that reporters want to report on things as fast as possible and, therefore, cannot get the complete facts. Because of this, I don't like to read the reports. I have not seen much news on Japanese culture here. Even though Japan is the US's leading trading partner, Japanese companies produce cars and electronics here. If America's markets disappear, Japan could not exist. It would be a pitiful state. It would be ludicrous to be angry about the degree of interest Japan has for the United States and the degree of interest that the US has for Japan![5]

An interview also conducted at the time with a MITI ministry official is indicative of how, not only Japan, but also many other countries, regard their relationship with the United States. It also reveals Japan's defensive stance regarding the US–Japan relationship:

> Wherever one goes in the world, English is understood and, therefore, Americans do not have the desire to learn about other foreign countries. That's because America's bounty, America's words and America's system supports the world. It's just the way things are, I guess. America is vast, the great supporter, America, the great provider, America. We are always aware of its presence. I think that the recognition of whatever relationship Japan has with the United States is within this context.[6]

11

Special Corporations: Insatiable

When SCAP permitted the formation of a public corporation to support the development of the match industry, representatives, fearing tight controls over their sector, issued a petition on August 10, 1947 to SCAP in protest. The protest claimed that the corporation was being formed not to support the industry but to provide jobs for bureaucrats. SCAP rejected the petition because it assumed that the industry did not want ministerial controls. Later reflecting on its decision, SCAP believed that public corporations could resuscitate Japan's war-time system of autocratic controls.

Another forty corporations were added to the list by 1975, by 1980 the total was 240 and by 1990 the number had grown to 326. Throughout the post-war era numerous subsidiaries ('children corporations') and subsidiaries of these subsidiaries ('grandchildren corporations') were established by ministry officials. Special Corporations, their 'children' and 'grandchildren' corporations and branch offices served to place officials from the national ministries throughout Japan. As an example, among 322 of the corporations MOC had established, 34 percent employed fewer than five people, 54 percent employed fewer than ten people, and only 9 percent had more than one hundred staff.

Nevertheless, there was one corporation employing over 700 employees. Japan Highway (JH) had over sixty subsidiaries with such names as New Japan Highway Patrol, Sapporo Engineer, Hokkaido Highway Service, Sendai Highway Service, Number One Highway Service, Western Japan Highway Service, Highway Service Research, Japan High Car, and Highway Toll System.

The development of Japan's electric power companies and the nuclear power industry through the close collaboration of businesses, ministry officials and elected officials and the intimate roles that Special

Corporations such as EPDC, research institutes and industrial associations played since the mid-1950s is a solid representation of Japan Inc.

As an example, MITI's EPDC's subsidiaries included the EPDC Environmental Engineering Services Co.; EPDC Coal Tech and Marine Co.; Kaihatsu Co.; Kaihatsu Computing Service; Kaihatsu Denki Co.; KEC Corporation; KDC Engineering Co.; and EPDC Overseas Coal Co. The EPDC also had a holding company and an industrial company. Until the EPDC was privatized in 2003 the branches served to provide posts for local government officials as well. Some of the corporations also operated representative offices overseas.

By 1972, Japan's GDP was 10 percent and it had become the world's third largest economy. Realistically, many of the corporations were no longer needed to support economic development and should have been dismantled. However, the ministries had come to rely on their corporations, because not only did they provide temporary post-retirement positions for officials while they had waited for the obligatory two years before migrating to positions in the private sector (*amakudari*) but they also served to extend ministerial powers and increase administrative jurisdiction (namely 'territory'). The connections established between the ministries' officials posted in Special Corporations, their subsidiaries and their branch offices throughout Japan effectively link the ministries to the private sector. Additionally, through their officials posted at branch offices of Special Corporations and their subsidiaries, the national ministries can monitor local government policies and guide the planning of policies. A number of Special Corporations continued operations for years despite bearing large debts, which would never be repaid to FILP.

Prime Minister Hashimoto (1996–8) was a charismatic LDP politician who was known for his penchant for green leather trousers and who was popular with the female electorate. He was groomed in politics by his father who was a member in Kishi's cabinet. Elected to the House of Representatives in 1963 as a member in the Tanaka and Takeshita factions he was able to begin forming his own powerful faction in the 1990s, which was the largest among the LDP. While he was the Minister of Transport in Yasuhiro Nakasone's cabinet in 1986 he was profoundly influenced by Nakasone's neo-nationalism. When he was MITI Minister in Murayama's administration he was known in international political circles for his stormy negotiations with the USTR on behalf of the automobile industry.

Hashimoto was committed to structural reforms of the political economy. He streamlined government administration by reducing the number of ministries from twenty-one to twelve as of 2001. The merger of some of the ministries, the integration of minor agencies into the existing ministries and the creation of agencies that had previously been connected to the ministries as independent agencies did not go smoothly due to historic institutional differences. Furthermore, the mergers served no more than to change the names of various ministries and to create turmoil within the newly merged ministries regarding the restructuring of management of the institutions and territorial issues and objectives. Some officials were very concerned about how the mergers would impact on their ranking and promotion and chose to leave the civil service in favor of the private sector or starting their own businesses. The newly merged ministries managed jointly the Special Corporations which had been established and managed by a single ministry prior to the merger.

During his administration Hashimoto raised the consumption tax from 3 to 5 percent and was blamed for prolonging the recession that had continued since 1992. Approval of government support to the mortgage companies which were burdened with toxic debt also proved an unpopular policy. Hashimoto lost the election for LDP president in 1998. However, he continued to oversee administrative reform until 2001 when the mergers of the ministries were initiated. He retired from politics in 2004 after being implicated in a $1 million personal political fund-raising scandal. During Hashimoto's administration, efforts were made to implement structural reforms of FILP in order to stop the automatic supply of funds from the PSS and the state pensions and halt indiscriminate and wasteful spending.

Prime Minister Junichiro Koizumi (2001–6), who was the Finance Minister in Hashimoto's cabinet, continued to pursue reforms of the public sector. He was committed not only to downsizing FILP, but also to the privatization of the PSS, which provided a major source of funding to FILP. He also was determined to reduce the number of Special Corporations, continuously fed by FILP agency bonds. In other words, in order to end the Special Corporations' gravy train, not only was it necessary to restructure FILP, but also to privatize the PSS which included Postal Life Insurance (Kampo). This task would prove to be a drama played out over five years to culminate in superficial reforms as assessed by former Prime Minister Noda 2009 in his book.[1]

FILP reforms: breaking up is hard to do

Until 2001 FILP received its capital from the Trust Fund Bureau (TFB) where deposits from the PSS and Kampo had been transferred for public financing. However, the TFB was terminated in 2001 and the PSS, as a part of its reorganization, was not obliged to transfer money to FILP. The Fiscal Loan Fund (FLF) replaced the TFB and Special Corporations were pressured to access capital through FILP bonds which were issued by FLF. The FLF bonds were guaranteed by government. Furthermore, corporations unable to access capital independently could issue bonds independently, which were similar to JGB but not guaranteed by the government. And even though the PSS was no longer required to invest in public corporations, since 2002 the postal savings have been used to purchase FILP bonds and FILP agency bonds at the discretion of management.

Koizumi pledged to slash public spending in order to reduce government deficit, which was 130 percent of GDP at the time, and intended to downsize FILP by 17.7 percent ($218 billion). Nevertheless, during 2007–8 loans from FILP increased 14 percent and from 2008 to 2009 loans increased 72 percent. Although the MOF chart on the FILP website shows that loans have been decreasing, FILP can be regarded as 'Japan's secondary budget' through the issuance of long-term, low-interest rate loans.

State banks too

Koizumi's reforms of Special Corporations included the privatization of state banks which, while supporting Japan's rapid economic growth, were regarded as serving similar functions. The Japan Finance Corporation (JFS) was established on October 1, 2008 by MOF under the Japan Finance Corporation Act. The JFS is a FILP designated institution which entitles it to issue FILP agency bonds which are guaranteed by government.[2]

One of the banks placed within the JFS was the Japan Corporation for Small & Medium Size Enterprises (JASME) established by MOF in the 1950s to provide loans and services to independent small and medium-sized businesses. In the late 1990s the corporation had about ¥410.9 billion in capital resources and was the primary lender to small businesses, offering long-term loans at interest rates that were lower than those from private financial institutions. JASME was the result of the consolidation of the Small Business Credit Insurance Corporation, Japan Small Business Corporation and the Textile Industry Restructuring Agency. The capital resource was approximately ¥3.5 trillion funded by FILP. JASME helped small businesses upgrade operations by providing finance, but the business owners had to apply through their local government authority for the loans, which, in turn, requested loans from

JASME. JASME then distributed the money to local government, which then passed it on to applicants. JASME supported its budget through FILP agency bonds. Over the years, the agency had based the loans to small businesses on the same collateral and similar to the commercial banks, but JASME lacked the skills to assess properly credit risks of borrowers. Consequently, the bank was burdened with toxic debt and was unable to repay FILP.

Two other state banks integrated in the FSC, which provided loans to small businesses, were the People's Finance Corporation, established in 1959 by MOF, and the Corporation for Agriculture and Forestry and Fisheries also established in the 1950s by MAFA.

In 2008, the three banks were revised as special corporations or *tokushugaisha* and placed within the JFS. The difference between 'Special Status Corporations' or *tokushuhoujin* (referred to in this book as 'Special Corporations') and the 'special corporations' established in 2008 is that Special Status Corporations are public corporations that were established by the ministries under a special law (as explained previously). The 'special corporations' established in 2008 according to a separate law are still completely government funded but the law specifies that these corporations will eventually be privatized. The three state banks still provide loans to SMEs engaged in agriculture and manufacturing.

Initially, the government, which owns 100 percent of the banks, had planned to sell all of the shares within a five- to seven-year period. However, privatization was postponed for three-and-a-half years because of the financial crisis in 2009. The state banks are essential to the support of SME business and big businesses for the construction of infrastructure overseas because, unlike the private banks, they can carry more risk.

The privatization of some of the *tokushugaisha* was again postponed for three years to deal with the aftermath of the Great Northeast Earthquake in March 2011 because the banks were needed to support the regions affected by the earthquake.

The government will reconsider the process of selling shares and the degree of influence it will reserve over banking operations by the end of FY 2014.[3]

The Nippon Telephone and Telegraph Company (NTT), established as a Special Corporation by the former Ministry of Telecommunications, was privatized but the government owns one-third of shares of the NTT Holding Company. NTT is a *tokushugaisha* or special corporation. *Tokushugaisha* can also receive funds from FILP but MOF must assess the proposed work before the funds are approved. The corporations can also issue their own corporate bonds which are not government guaranteed.

The 2012 FILP Plan issued by MOF called for continued loans to state banks such as the Japan Bank of International Cooperation (JBIC) which was the result of the merger of METI's Japan Export/Import Bank (EXIM) and the Overseas Economic Cooperation Fund (OECF) in October 1999. In October 2008, JBIC became the international arm in the JFS to provide loans to small and medium-size companies and to larger companies for the construction of infrastructure overseas and for such operations as oil mining. JBIC can issue JBIC bonds which are not guaranteed by government or FILP agency bonds which are guaranteed by government.

The predecessor of the Japan International Cooperation Agency (JICA) was the Japan International Cooperation Agency which was established as a Special Corporation by the Ministry of Foreign Affairs (MOFA). The corporation merged in 2008 with the division of JBIC which provides concessional loans to developing countries. The state bank finances economic development in developing countries as a part of ODA. It can issue FILP agency bonds. There are ninety-eight overseas offices.[4]

In October 1999 the MOF's Japan Development Bank (JDB) merged with the bankrupt Hokkaido-Tohoku Development Finance Corporation, a regional public corporation managed by MOF. The JDB was established in 1952 by MOF to finance Japan's industrial development by providing loans to heavy industries to support both domestic and overseas expansion. The merger was celebrated with a new name, the Development Bank of Japan (DBJ). The bank's former name in Japanese translates as 'Japan Development Bank' (*Nihon Kaihatsu Ginko*). Although the new name in English appears to be almost identical, the English translation of the Japanese is 'The Investment Strategy Bank of Japan' (*Nihon Seisaku Toshi Ginko*). DBJ is also a *tokushugaisha*.

The DBJ was one of the institutions that helped in January 2010 to rescue Japan Airlines which was on the verge of bankruptcy. The DBJ is set to be privatized in 2015, assuming a key role in supporting Japan's domestic economy and industrial expansion abroad. However, these plans are still in the discussion stage and may be postponed as well in order for the DBJ to assist companies that have been adversely affected by the Great Northeast Earthquake or from the recession.

On the surface it appears that there has been a massive restructuring of Special Corporations (*tokushuhoujin*) with stricter guidelines regarding the use of public revenue and how the corporations justify their budgets. However, although FILP has been downsized, it can be argued that in the case of many of these corporations, the pay-as-you-go government gravy train system is still intact.

Reform of the PSS

Japan's postal service system, initiated during the Meiji period, was modeled on the British postal service system. Until 2003 all services, including mail and parcel delivery, postal savings and postal life insurance were provided at the post offices. Postal savings with a cap of about $122,700 are offered to individual depositors at the post offices. Since the postal savings business is regulated under the Postal Savings Act and not under the Banking Act, the bank cannot offer loans to businesses or individuals. Also, the postal savings cannot participate in inter-bank transfers and depositors are required to transfer from postal savings by check.

In 2003, the three services were reorganized as a single public corporation, the Japan Post Public Corporation (JPPC) and managed by the state. The corporation was the nation's largest employer with 400,000 employees (one-third of all government workers) and a nationwide network of 24,000 post offices, which provided all of the services. Until it was reorganized again in 2007 JPPC held 25 percent of household assets. The corporation also held 20 percent of Japan's debt through JGB.

Koizumi contended that a privatized JPPC would serve to curb government spending and the growth of public debt. The proponents of privatization also claimed that it would help to eliminate a large source of corruption and pork-barrel patronage as well as allow greater efficiency and flexibility in the use of company funds. But Koizumi's privatization efforts met with stiff opposition from members of his own party, the LDP, and from postal service employees. Politicians relied on the postal savings' significant resources to fund FILP and many of their constituencies in rural regions were concerned about reduced postal services. The rural postmasters traditionally collected substantial funds for LDP campaign coffers from depositors in the postal accounts. Postal service workers, who were an influential lobbying group and who rallied rural voters, were concerned about job losses if the JPPC were privatized.

Koizumi's bill was initially voted down in the Upper House in August 2005. Determined to push the bill through the Diet, Koizumi immediately dissolved the more powerful Lower House on August 9 and called for a snap election (the Upper House cannot be dissolved). Also, as the president of the LDP he exercised the power to kick out thirteen members of the LDP who were opposed to privatization, and succeeded in persuading friends and colleagues in the public and private sector who had high profiles in the media to stand for election. Nationwide elections were held on September 11 and Koizumi won the majority by 288 to 233.

One of Koizumi's friends, Takafumi Horie, supported by the LDP, ran as an independent in the Hiroshima Sixth District, but he lost and his fortunes further declined when he was arrested for fraud the following January.

The privatization bill was passed in October 2005 and two years later in October 2007, the JPPC was divided into four companies and managed by a holding company. The JPPC was renamed Japan Post (JP). The government planned to privatize and sell by 2017 the savings and the life insurance company. However, the government would retain one-third of the holding company – enough to allow a veto of any changes in the company. In 2014 Japan Post Insurance held $846 billion in assets and Japan Post Bank held $208 trillion in assets. Together, Japan Post Bank and Postal Insurance hold approximately $2 trillion in JGB, making it Japan's largest creditor.

The sale of Kampo no Yado: enter Yoshihiko Miyauchi

The JPPC built the Kampo no Yado nationwide resort network as accommodation for Postal Life Insurance policy-holders. The sixty-nine inns and seventy-nine facilities were built to promote health and welfare for the policy-holders and to promote postal savings at the cost of ¥240 billion which was financed by life insurance premiums.

Yoshihiko Miyauchi, a close friend of Koizumi, collaborated with the president of Sumitomo Bank, Yoshifumi Nishikawa, in the design of the privatization scheme. Nishikawa was appointed the first president of Japan Post Holding Co. When the JPPC was privatized in 2007, Japan Holdings Co. decided to dispose of ninety-seven hotels because of the debts in FY 2003 which totaled ¥18 billion. Twenty-three facilities established to promote postal savings were also to be sold because of debts which totaled ¥10.1 billion during the same period. Japan Holdings opened bids for the resort on its website and received bids from twenty-seven companies. According to the JP, two companies, one of them Orix, remained in the running and when the other company pulled out, Orix won the bid with an offer of ¥10.9 billion.

However, the sale was vehemently opposed by Prime Minister Aso's cabinet Minister of Internal Affairs and Communications (MIC), Kunio Hatoyama, who viewed the proposed sale as 'a race whose results had already been decided', questioning the competitive nature of the bidding procedure as well as a conflict of interests. Hatoyama, who was also Aso's campaign manager and his key cabinet minister, demanded that Nishiyama resign but Nishiyama refused. Aso was placed in an untenable position because if Hatoyama resigned, he would become the third minister to depart from his cabinet, weakening the LDP in the coming September election. If Aso, who had not been in favor of Koizumi's reforms of the JPPC, backed Hatoyama's demand for Nishikawa's resignation he would be perceived as a politician involved in the operation of a company that was in the process of undergoing privatization.

In the end, Hatoyama submitted his letter of resignation from the cabinet in June. On June 30, Nishikawa was reappointed by the JP board at a meeting of general shareholders. Orix later withdrew its bid.

Hatoyama's departure from Aso's cabinet dealt a blow to the Aso administration, which had been beleaguered by political scandal. On August 30, the DPJ won a landslide victory in the Lower House election, paving the way for Hatoyama's brother Yukio Hatoyama to become Japan's first DPJ prime minister. He pledged a 'drastic revision' of the postal privatization plan, which was opposed by some members of the DPJ.

Prime Minister Hatoyama suspended the JP privatization plan, the rationale being that the plan ignored the needs of consumers by focusing too much on profits. Privatization would force the closure of some local post offices, resulting in job losses. Another motivation for preferring to keep the postal service in government hands was the need to finance government spending by returning money from the private sector to the public sector (e.g. FILP).

When the LDP returned to power, Abe's government pulled forward the schedule for beginning the privatization from 2017 to 2015. In April 2014, MOF, which owns a 100 percent share of Japan Posts Holdings Ltd. and a 100 percent share of Japan Post Bank and Japan Post Insurance (Kampo), began discussions regarding the process of selling shares in the Holding Company as well as the number of shares to be sold. Revenue from the sale would be used to fund the resuscitation of the regions impacted by the Great Northeast Earthquake. The government plans to initiate the first public offering of shares in the holding company by 2015. On September 5, 2014 MOF released a shortlist of fifteen security firms to manage the first phase of public offerings, among them Nomura Holdings Inc., Goldman Sachs Group Inc., Mitsubishi UFJ Morgan Stanley Securities Co, Daiwa Securities Group Inc. and Citigroup Inc. Ten companies will be selected.[5]

Special Corporations: a tug of war

Koizumi's administration devised a scheme that would convert a number of Special Corporations into Independent Administrative

Institutions (IAIs) with the expectation that eventually financing from FILP bonds and tax revenue would no longer be necessary and that there would be more transparency with regard to accounting methods. Many of the loans were not repaid and Seiji Ota, who was the director of the LDP office for the promotion of reforms, contended that one-third of the funds allotted to Special Corporations by FILP were wasted. Since MOF had been reticent to use the formal budget and tax revenue to finance the increasing number of loans throughout the 1990s, FILP was burdened with toxic debt.

Similar to the 'law for the establishment of Special Corporations', the Incorporated Administration Law for the establishment of independently administrative institutions was implemented on December 13, 2002. The law is neither civil nor corporate.

The Ministry of Public Management, Home Affairs, Post and Telecommunications released an explanation in English that outlines the concept of the new IAI system:

> The IAI system lies on the basic concept of public welfare, transparency, and autonomy of activities as Article 3 of the Law of the General Rules provides that (i) the IAIs must make efforts for just and effective operation under the consideration that the fulfillment of their undertaking is indispensable to people's lives, society and the economy; (ii) the IAIs must make efforts to open to the public the status of their organizations and the operations by such means as the announcement of the content of their activities as provided by this law; (iii) the autonomy of each law must be respected in accordance with the application of the Law and the laws establishing the IAIs.

Unwelcome publicity: Special Corporations on center stage

In February 1997 Japan's biggest business weekly magazine *Nikkei Business* did a cover story on Special Corporations, interviewing Hiroshi Kato in the process. Kato, who was the president of Chiba Commercial College and the chairman of the government's Tax Commission in the 1980s, emphasized that public funding of Special Corporations was a serious problem because the ministries had the power to use the money at their discretion without seeking consent from the Diet. Indeed, the politicians supported this behavior because they solicited contracts from the corporations involved in public works for their constituencies.

Kato complained that there was no public disclosure by Special Corporations for accounts indicating profit/loss balances and that the accounting system used was difficult to fathom because it differed from the system used by private corporations. He recommended privatization. Some of the corporations had already been dismantled prior to 1996, when the number stood at ninety-two.

Nikkei Business claimed that while Special Corporations had been founded on the precept that the work executed would serve the national interest the opposite was true for the following reasons.

 (i) Special Corporations received funding from sources that were difficult to trace.

 (ii) Special Corporations could set up subsidiaries ('children' and 'grandchildren' corporations) that showed profits even though the parent corporations were in debt.

(iii) The ministries established Special Corporations as their subsidiaries to provide temporary employment for staff and post-retirement positions for retired senior officials before they moved to the private sector.

(iv) Special Corporations used funds to do work that was in the best interests of the corporations.

As of October 1999 the number of corporations had been reduced to eighty-four through mergers of insolvent with solvent corporations. Some Special Corporations began opening their books to reveal more than had been available before 1999. However, many of the corporations, including their subsidiaries, did not provide financial statements but due to the government's investigation of accounting practices, by 1999, the financial sheets of giant corporations, including JH and the Japan National Oil Corporation (JNOC), revealed massive debt.

The privatization of the Japan Highway Corporation: a soap opera

Koizumi planned to reduce the number of Special Corporations through dissolution or converting them into IAIs. Koizumi focused his initial efforts on the dissolution of the former MOC's debt-ridden JH, which was referred to as 'the world's largest general contractor'. The expenditure in 1998 of Osaka Media Port in 1998 was $60 million, the highest of the JH's subsidiaries.

Originally, Koizumi wanted to merge the JH with three other corporations – the Hanshin Expressway Corporation, the Metropolitan Expressway Corporation, and the Shikoku-Honshu Bridge Authority, which carried massive debts. In total, the accumulated debt was $488 billion. He then wanted to privatize the single entity by 2005 and have it repay the outstanding loans within forty-five years. He also wanted to cut government investment in future road construction by 40 percent because costs had ballooned to $2.46 billion annually.

The plans were admirable but the implementation of them was hindered by the vested interests of LDP law-makers, who relied heavily on contributions from their constituencies, who depended on public works projects for contracts and employment, and the bureaucrats who relied upon post-retirement positions in construction-related businesses. They demanded that the debts of the Shikoku-Honshu Bridge Authority, which could not repay the FILP loans, be separated from the other corporations, and that those prefectures where the bridges were located share the burden of the repayment with central government. Koizumi's administration was pressured to produce a watered-down version of the original package that Koizumi had hoped to get through the National Diet.

The diluted version only focused on the completion of a 9,342 km expressway, courtesy of a proposal from the Ministry of Land, Infrastructure, and Transportation (MLIT was the result of the merger in 2001 of MOC, the Land Agency and the Ministry of Transportation). The cost was estimated to be $214 billion. The repayment of the debt was doubtful. Two of the five-member advisory panel, who Koizumi appointed to review the reform and who had prioritized repayment of the debt, resigned in protest on December 23, 2003, accusing the prime minister of failing to adhere to his objectives. They claimed that the new version of the bill contradicted the purposes of the original bill, which had favored the repayment of the debt over the construction. Also, the revised bill would permit the continuation of state involvement in wasteful road construction and delay debt repayment.

The process of the privatization of the JH was turbulent. The last president was Haruhiko Fujii who had taken the post in 2000 after retiring as vice-minister of the former MOC. During the period he was in both offices he was popular among LDP politicians because he expanded highway networks considerably and because of his close relationship with road construction firms. He was dismissed by the land minister Nobuteru Ishihara (Shintaro Ishihara's son) after a much-publicized heated confrontation with Ishihara who accused him of not cooperating in the process of privatization.

On April 14, 2004, Ishihara replaced Fujii with his LDP colleague, Takeshi Kondo, who was a member of the Upper House. Kondo had previously been an executive of Itochu Corporation, a major trading firm. He retired in April 2006 and was succeeded by a former CEO of Toshiba Europe and a director of the Japan Federation of Economic Organizations.

The four public corporations were privatized on October 1, 2005. But instead of one entity there are three, each with a new name. Nevertheless, the Ministry of Infrastructure (the former MOC), Land and Transportation continues to manage the highway networks. FILP agency bonds fund the Japan Expressway Holding and Debt Repayment Agency.

The image of reform: Japan National Oil Corporation

Japan has to import over 80 percent of its fossil fuel. METI oversees the energy-producing industries, among them oil. The ministry manages imports and refining through federations of oil importers. The former MITI established JNOC in 1967 to assist Japanese oil companies with exploration and drilling for oil. The corporation received funding from FILP and had 142 subsidiaries and branch offices overseas. The federation connected METI to the oil refineries, which distributed to retailers. The domestic companies cooperated with foreign firms, usually holding the larger share of the investment.

Koizumi wanted to privatize JNOC because in 1998 when the corporation was targeted for restructuring the president, Kuni Komatsu, who was a former MITI Administrative Vice-Minister, divulged that the company carried outstanding debt of $1.23 billion. However, Japan's oil refiners were opposed to private companies taking over JNOC and wanted the government to continue JNOC's operations because the corporations were financially too weak to take on the risks of oil exploration.

In August 2003, JNOC declared a net loss of $1.9 billion for fiscal 2002 and an accumulated debt of $6.17 billion due to the failure of its subsidiary, the Japan Oil Development Co. (JODCO). In 2004 METI began to dismantle JNOC, privatizing some of its subsidiaries such as the Japan Petroleum Exploration Co. and the Indonesian Petroleum Co. (INPEX Corp.), a major upstream oil and gas company that was established in 1966 of which it owned a 53.96 percent share. INPEX had expanded operations internationally and was popular among foreign investors.

METI agreed to clear JODCO's debts in order to convince INPEX to take over the money-losing JODCO. INPEX merged with Teikoku Oil in March 2006, receiving 81 percent of its shares. By 2008, JODCO was fully integrated into IMPEX Holdings.

METI retained JNOC's oil and exploration units when it was merged with its Special Corporation, the Metal and Mining Agency, which in 2004 was christened the Japan Oil, Gas and Metals National Corporation (JOGMEC)[6] as an Incorporated Administrative Agency under the 'Incorporated Administrative Agency Act' initiated in 2002. Prior to the nuclear crisis, nuclear energy was supplying 30 percent of Japan's electricity while fossil fuels were providing over 60 percent of electricity. In 2013 the utilities used 8 percent more liquid gas than the previous year and coal increased 26 percent. JOGMEC is engaging jointly with oil companies such as INPEX Corp. in the exploration and production of oil and natural gas, which has become a major source of energy since all of the nuclear power plants are currently off-line. On July 25, 2014 JOGMEC signed a 'memorandum of understanding' with Mexico's state-led PEMEX on technical cooperation and personnel exchange, using Japanese technologies and finance to support the increase of Mexico's oil production and shale gas development.

One of the major complaints lodged against the JNOC was poor management by officials who did not have the expertise to direct oil exploration and production, pointing to MITI officials who took temporary positions for two years and forged relationships with domestic and foreign oil companies, which led to permanent post-retirement upper management positions in these companies. Traditionally, a retired administrative vice-minister from the ministry filled other top management positions such as vice-president or the director of finance. Before his resignation, Komatsu had served as president for six years. Although Komatsu had climbed to the position of MITI Administrative Vice-Minister, he had no experience in energy administration. There were a number of such migrations of officials from the JNOC and from other MITI Special Corporations to such companies as Indonesia Oil, Japan Steel Pipe Co., Mobil, Shell and Abu Dhabi Oil. The trade-off for the privatization of JNOC was that *amakudari* was allowed to continue in JETRO.

A number of Special Corporations were re-established as IAIs or as Incorporated Administrative Agencies in 2003 under a special law as stated on METI's website:

An incorporated administrative agency is a judicial person that acts independently of the state and manages business operations such as research, inspection and trade insurance that were formerly performed by the state. A particular feature of such agencies is that they can independently consider how to perform their operations, and run these operations in a better, more efficient manner on their own responsibility. Specifically, each minister sets objectives to be attained by agencies under his or her jurisdiction, and each agency draws up a plan to achieve the objectives and carry out operations in line with the plan. The results obtained are evaluated by outside experts and the evaluation is reflected in management plans for subsequent years.

The explanation does not report that the government intends to review all of these agencies within a period of five to seven years in terms of efficiency of operations and management. If it is determined that the corporations are no longer viable, they may be terminated or downsized. Nevertheless, it is difficult to envision that ministries such as METI, MOF or MLIT would willingly part with their agencies.

In addition to JOGMEC, METI manages the following Incorporated Administrative Agencies that are directly related to the energy sector and which employ retired METI officials in upper management positions or as directors on the boards.

1. The New Energy and Industrial Technology Development Organization (NEDO)[7] was established by the former MITI as a Special Corporation in 1980 for the promotion and funding of projects related to renewable energy and the development of industrial technologies. With a budget of $2.8 billion (FY 2009) NEDO employs 1,000 staff and engages in projects overseas with offices located in Silicon Valley, Washington, DC, Paris, Beijing, Bangkok and New Delhi.
2. The Japan Nuclear Energy Safety Organization (JNES).[8]
3. The National Institute of Advanced Industrial Science and Technology (AIST)[9] was established in 2001 as an amalgamation of fifteen research institutes that were managed by the former MITI. Its predecessor had been established in 1982. The new AIST is the largest government-supported research institute in Japan with forty autonomous research institutes employing 2,400 researchers and 700 administrative staff.

METI's other Incorporated Administrative Agencies include:

1. Research Institute of Economy, Trade and Industry (REITI).[10]
2. National Center for Industrial Property Information and Training INPIT).
3. Nippon Export and Investment Insurance (NEXI).[11]

4. National Institute of Technology and Evaluation (NITE).
5. Japan External Trade Organization (JETRO).[12]
6. Institute of Developing Economies, Japan External Trade Organization (IDE-JETRO).[13]
7. Japan Water Agency (HWA).
8. Japan International Cooperation Agency (JICA).[14]
9. Information-Technology Promotion Agency, Japan (IPA).
10. Japan Organization for Employment of the Elderly, Persons with Disability and Job Seekers (JEED).
11. Organization for Small & Medium Enterprise and Regional Innovation, Japan (SMRJ).

The Government Housing and Loan Guarantee Corporation

The former MOC established the Government Housing and Loan Guarantee Corporation (GHLC) as a Special Corporation in 1950 to provide finance for the rebuilding of homes devastated by the Second World War. It was the biggest home lender, financing 30 percent of all houses since the war. Retail banks were unable to compete with the GHLC because of asset liability risks. In 2001, the GHLC provided 27 percent of all new loans. In 2002, 40 percent of all mortgage debt was from GHLC loans. The repayment period was up to thirty-five years for long-term, fixed-interest rate loans. The funding was mainly through FILP.

Koizumi resolved to liquidate the GHLC because it was heavily in debt. Also, FILP reforms would make the provision of long-term, fixed-rate loans by the GHLC difficult. The GHLC was converted to an Incorporated Administrative Agency on April 1, 2007 and christened the Japan Housing Finance Agency (JHF).[15] The corporation is 100 percent government funded and managed by MLIT.

The corporation does not engage in direct housing loans to the general public. Its main business is scrutinizing mortgage debt to enable private financial institutions to create a steady supply of long-term, fixed-rate mortgage loans. In other words, asset liability management (ALM) is passed on to the market by securitization, reducing the ALM risk for the JHF.[16] So far, there have been no signs of success in the reorganization of the GHLC because of the soft real estate market.

The image of reform: Urban Development Corporation

Another Special Corporation targeted by Koizumi for reform was the Urban Development Corporation (UDC), which was established by the former MOC in 1955 to engage in the supply and maintenance of housing. Funded by FILP, it had constructed 1.5 million homes in 1999. The corporation was reorganized into an Incorporated Administrative Agency in July 2004 and renamed the Urban Renaissance Agency (UR). Theoretically, the organization's work is no longer inclusive of urban projects and projects providing housing. Its principal work is to build public facilities to stimulate private sector investment in public works projects. The URO is 100 percent government funded and managed by MLIT.[17]

Despite Koizumi's objectives to cut public spending through structural reforms, at the time he left office in 2006 the government debt was 145 percent of annual GDP.

Holding on to a good thing: the 'Fantasia' phenomenon (i.e. the Sorcerer's Apprentice)

Why Japan Can't Reform: Inside the System (2008) updated the reforms planned during Prime Minister Koizumi's administration to illustrate that the reforms were no more than the image of reform: (i) the ministries' institutions still perpetuated the interests of the ministries, thus inhibiting structural reforms of the economy; (ii) the fundamental characteristics of the Japanese political economic system gave the bureaucracy the power to continue operating their organizations, despite political opposition; (iii) the organizations functioned to extend ministerial control over local government; (iv) successive government administrations since the 1990s had struggled to dismantle the institutions but had failed; and (v) the efforts by successive administrations since the 1990s to implement crucial structural reforms of the political economy had proven futile.

In March 2007 a survey released by the Lower House reported the number of IAIs (including subsidiaries) maintained by the ministries and the number of 'retired' bureaucrats, including officers on loan to these entities:

1. The Ministry of Land, Infrastructure and Transport: 834 entities, 6,386 bureaucrats.
2. Ministry of Health, Labor and Welfare: 709 entities, 4,007 former officials.
3. Defense Ministry: 207 entities, 3,917 former officials.
4. Ministry of Education, Culture, Sports, Science and Technology: 934 entities, 3,007 former ministry officials.

On November 8, the secretariat of the cabinet's headquarters for Administrative Reform released documents to a government panel of experts on streamlining public corporations. Originally, fifty-seven corporations were set up to take over part of the operations of the ministries and agencies but this number had increased to 101, a similar pattern to that which evolved as the ministries were establishing their Special Corporations. The report showed that 40 out of 101 IAIs awarded contracts to their subsidiaries with more than 90 percent of the contracts completed without competitive bidding.

The documents also revealed that the 101 IAIs altogether had 260 affiliates. Companies where one-third or more of their posts were occupied by former directors and senior officials of the IAIs were among the affiliates. Also, 230 officials at the 101 corporations had assumed directors' posts at affiliates in fiscal 2005 through *amakudari*.

On October 24, 2009, Kyodo News Service reported that ninety-eight IAIs hired retired officials for top management positions. Forty of the entities hired officials who had retired from the ministries which managed their respective IAIs. Eleven were operated by METI and seven of them, including JETRO, were headed by former METI bureaucrats. Of the seven, six were officials who had left the ministry to work as executives and advisors at major private companies. The average annual salary of twenty-nine chiefs for FY 2009 was $226,470.

When Abe took office in 2012 he did a U-turn on his previous plans to curtail *amakudari* in 2007 by giving top posts to elite ministry officials. As an example, the CEO of the FSC was replaced by Koichi Hosokawa, a former MOF administrative vice-minister, who had also served as the FSC Deputy Director before assuming his current post. To equalize ministerial territory, Hideji Sugiyama, a former METI vice-minister was appointed president of the Shoko Chukin Bank in July 2013. The bank was established in the 1950s to fund loans to SMEs and managed jointly by MITI and MOF. The current Shoko Chukin Bank continues as a financial policy instrument for SMEs.[18]

In his book *Minshu no Teki* former Prime Minister Yoshihiko Noda stated that he had anticipated that Koizumi's administration would implement reforms and cut public debt but assessed the reforms as being no more than the image of reform of Special Corporations and Japan Posts. He condemned Special Corporations (Noda refers to IAIs as Special Corporations) as a waste of tax revenue, as a haven for retired bureaucrats who landed comfortable jobs with high salaries, and as impediments to the implementation of structural reforms.[19] During Noda's administration, a bill was passed to merge JETRO with a corporation managed by the Ministry of Foreign Affairs in 2014, which was recommended in *Special Corporations and the Bureaucracy* (2003). However, now that Abe and the LDP have returned, it is doubtful that the merger will take place.

Ministry officials work long hours without receiving overtime pay and, therefore, the ministries' corporations offer an incentive to enter the civil service. The ministries still rely on their corporations as a means of taking care of their officials after they retire. Most officials are trained as generalists and do not have specific skills which are pertinent to the private sector. Since officials want to continue earning income for their families, the ministries' corporations provide positions where they can conveniently rely on financial support.

Mr. Noda was correct in his assessment of Special Corporations but if he had worked as a ministry official, he may have concluded that there must be something at the end of officials' careers that will provide post-retirement salaries besides benefits. Despite the name change to Independent Administrative Institutions or Incorporated Administrative Agencies or 'special corporations', the Japanese will still refer to the ministries' public corporations as Special Corporations (*tokushuhoujin*). My 2003 book states:

> Special Corporations are illustrative of the basic nature of Japan's political economy. The ministries' determination to maintain territory and thus protect vested interests can be seen in the continued operations of Special Corporations despite Koizumi's plans to dissolve them.[20]

12
The Skill at Disguising

An In-depth Research of the Bureaucracy (*Kanryou Dai Kenkyuu*) by Tetsuo Ebato was published in 1990. Ebato graduated with a degree in economics from Tokyo University before entering Mitsui Bank. He left the company to become a freelance writer. His book regards the Defense Agency, the Supreme Court, the former Ministry of Health and Welfare, the Ministry of Agriculture and Fisheries and MITI.

His chapter concerning MITI revealed the views of many Japanese civil servants at the time. For example, Ebato reported that MITI was known as an 'aggressive' agency and that MITI officials felt that they had to continuously squeeze out new policies. The officials had the reputation of being skillful debaters, arguing to promote their policies and actively seeking new territory. On the other hand, although MITI officials were said to be skillful analysts, their policies were often hastily planned and incomplete (i.e. half-baked).[1]

The survey of bureaucrats in *A Creaking Giant Power* (*Kishimu Kyodai Kenryoku*) in 1993 included questions regarding which agencies they thought were no longer necessary or would no longer be necessary in the future. The Hokkaido Development Agency took first place (subsequently dismantled). The reasons given were that the period of development in Hokkaido had long passed and that the agency was ineffective.

MITI took first place among the ministries. Although the respondents acknowledged that the ministry had done good work during the period of rapid growth, they felt that it lacked a clear vision and was now groping for an industrial policy that would assist Japanese businesses to internationalize. There was criticism concerning MITI's tug of war with the Ministry of Transportation (renamed in 2001 Ministry of Land, Infrastructure and Transportation, MLIT) and the Ministry of Posts and Telecommunication (renamed in 2001 the Ministry of Public

Management, Home Affairs, Posts and Telecommunications) over their administrative jurisdiction of the transportation and high-tech industries and information networks.

In 1995, Prime Minister Murayama's efforts to convince the ministries to consolidate some of the smaller Special Corporations attracted media attention. The former Ministry of Agriculture, Forestry and Fisheries balked at dissolving its Raw Silk and Sugar Price Stabilization Corporation and Livestock Industry Promotion Corporation. The ministry contended that the corporations would continue to protect consumers by planning strategies that would stabilize prices. However, it was willing to merge the two corporations and in 1996 the entities were united and named the Agriculture and Livestock Industries Corporation (ALIC).[2]

The opinion page of the *Asahi Shimbun* ran an article on January 9, 1995 reporting that when Murayama's administration conducted hearings on the restructuring of Special Corporations, the former MITI was reluctant to participate and wanted to know if the restructuring concerned the number of corporations or if the discussion was related to the financing of the corporations. The article also claimed that the ministries were changing the objectives of the corporations by contriving new roles. The paper called this 'skill at disguising' (*henshin no gijutsu*), pointing to the Japan External Trade Organization (JETRO) as an example of a Special Corporation that had been established in 1956 for the purpose of promoting Japanese exports: 'Now when you phone JETRO headquarters the receptionist answers, "JETRO, import promoter".'[3]

Inside/Outside Japan: 'Is JETRO Out of Control?'

On June 13, 1995 the front page of the *Sankei Shimbun* published an article by its Washington, DC correspondent Yoshihisa Komori titled 'Is JETRO Out of Control?' (*Jetero Boso?*) Next to the story was a photograph of JETRO's Tokyo headquarters. Komori pointed to the editorial of the April edition of a monthly newspaper *Inside/Outside Japan* published by JETRO New York and sent unsolicited to opinion leaders in business, government and academia. In his editorial, the president of JETRO New York who was a MITI official wrote positively about former US Secretary of Defense Robert McNamara's book *In Retrospect: The Tragedy of Lessons of Vietnam*. He wrote in part:

> Finally, on this 20th anniversary of the end of the war, he [McNamara] has made public his examination of how he and other policy makers were gradually pulled into a dubious war. It is in this

process that he repeatedly admits his mistakes. This is a courageous act. I cannot recall a single instance from among Japanese policy makers who, following Japan's defeat, did anything remotely similar.

According to Komori, William Triplet II, an aide to Republican Senator Robert Bennett, who was a member of the Senate Committee of Foreign Relations and a recipient of the paper, took exception to the article, protesting that the president of an organization that was established to promote foreign trade and economic cooperation should not be involved in commenting on political issues.

Komori claimed that there was opposition in the National Diet to the continuation of JETRO because (i) it no longer served its original function as a trade organization; (ii) JETRO was an underground MITI (*kakure gaimusho*); and (iii) JETRO had in effect become the 'Number Two Ministry of Foreign Affairs' (*dai-ni Gaimusho*). The accusations that JETRO was no longer functioning as a trade promotion organization but was being maneuvered into other areas supported the *Asahi Shimbun*'s contentions that MITI was 'disguising' JETRO in order to continue operations. Also, by alleging that JETRO had become a secondary Ministry of Foreign Affairs, *Sankei Shimbun* implied that MITI was using JETRO to wrest territory from MOFA.

Coincidentally, in the same issue there was an article about the upheaval in Cambodia with the Khmer Rouge and the argument in the National Diet to extend the operations of the Self-Defense Forces.

The monthly political magazine *Sentaku* followed with an article in its July 1995 issue. The story carried a photograph of *Inside/Outside Japan*. The article claimed that the reason Triplet was displeased was because JETRO's activities in the United States were a source of irritation to the CIA and the FBI. *Sentaku* asserted that the CIA and FBI were watching closely the activities of the directors of industrial research in JETRO New York when they visited other JETRO offices in the United States. The agencies regarded the MITI officers as CIA-type agents from Japan and since the representatives could not be classified as either foreign diplomats or as scholars, their status was ambiguous. Also, there was a suspicion among members of congress that the officers engaged in industrial espionage.

Another article reporting JETRO's involvement in industrial espionage in the United States followed in the October 10, 1995 edition of *Nikkei Report*. Steven L. Harmon reported that the *New York Times* had alleged that the CIA and the National Security Agency had tapped the conversations of Japanese trade representatives and automobile manufacturers during the 1995 trade negotiations in Geneva, providing evidence that Japan was engaging in industrial espionage in the United States. Harmon discovered that the FBI was focusing its investigation on JETRO's offices in Los Angeles and San Francisco, questioning former staff about their bosses' activities. Harmon stated that a female staff member had told the FBI that espionage was 'a routine part of the jobs of such Japanese posted in the United States'.

Manipulation of operations to maintain JETRO

JETRO, which was converted to an Incorporated Administrative Agency in 2003, is a superb representation of how the ministries use their corporations to serve their best interests and the interests of the corporations as stated in the *Nikkei Business* article published in 1997. Chalmers Johnson credited Osaka Mayor Bunzo Akuma, Michisuke Sugi, the chairman of the Osaka Chamber of Commerce and a former official from MCI, for establishing the Japan Export Trade Research Organization, JETRO's predecessor in 1951. Their objective was to encourage small businesses to export goods to lucrative foreign markets such as the United States. The organization offered services for export promotion and the provision of information on foreign markets. In 1954, it was reorganized and renamed the Japan Export Trade Recovery Organization.

Johnson wrote that MITI accepted the organization and posted its officials in upper management. In 1956, MITI took over and chartered the organization as a Special Corporation, the Japan External Trade Organization. In 1958, JETRO created the Institute of Asian Economic Affairs, which two years later was converted into a public corporation and renamed the Institute of Developing Economies (IDE) but it was merged with JETRO in 1998. In 1971, yet another organization was established – the International Economic and Trade Information Center.

JETRO opened its first overseas offices in London and New York City in 1959, registering in the United States as a public corporation and not as an agency of a foreign government under the Foreign Agents Act of 1938, which caused some consternation among Americans officials. In 1976, the US Department of Justice sued the JETRO Trade Council (established in Washington, DC in 1958) for civil fraud, charging that MITI contributed 90 percent of the Council's funds through its JETRO New York office. Soon afterwards, JETRO registered as a foreign agent.[4]

In 1975, JETRO was operating twenty-four trade centers and fifty-four offices in fifty-five countries, testimony to the fact that not only had

Japan become a major player in world markets, but also that MITI was expanding territory by putting down roots overseas. Besides the JETRO offices, MITI officers were seconded as trade attachés to Japanese consulates, embassies and Japan Chamber of Commerce offices for periods of two to three years.

MITI made use of the JETRO offices as listening posts, monitoring foreign trade regulations, foreign and domestic policies that would affect the import of Japanese goods, environmental and industrial standards, government patent applications (in anticipation that the new inventions would be applicable to Japanese industries), and investment opportunities for Japanese business. JETRO staff also collected macroeconomic data and surveyed markets on behalf of Japanese small businesses.

In 1981 MITI established the Japan Economic Foundation (JEF) as a JETRO subsidiary.[5] The JEF published the bi-monthly journal *The Journal of Trade and Industry* which is now known as *Spotlight*. The JEF website states its mission as:

> to deepen mutual understanding between Japan and other countries through activities aimed at promoting economic and technological exchanges. With this goal in mind, JEF engages in a broad range of activities; it provides information about Japan and arranges opportunities to exchange ideas among opinion leaders from many countries in such fields as industry, government administration, academia and politics in order to break down the barriers to mutual understanding.

The members on the JEF board of trustees also serve as chairmen or presidents of METI's industrial associations: the Japan Automobile Manufacturers' Association, Japan Electronic and Information Technologies Industrial Association, the Japan Iron and Steel Federation, and the Japan Society of Industrial Machinery Manufacturers. Yasuo Hayashi, who was JETRO's former chairman and CEO (2007–11), is also on the board.

Hayashi entered MITI in 1966 after graduating from Tokyo University. A career officer, he was a Director-General of the Small and Medium-Size Enterprise Agency and Director-General of the International Trade Policy Bureau. Hayashi's migration pattern (*amakudari*) to chairman and CEO of JETRO is typical of the migration pattern of elite bureaucrats to the corporations in their ministries' portfolio. After retiring from METI he lectured at Saitama University and worked at the International Energy Agency in Paris before assuming the post of vice-president and managing director at Mitsui & Co. Europe PLC. Hayashi migrated to JETRO in 2007. After retiring as JETRO chairman, he remained as Special Advisor to the agency.

Noboru Hatakeyama was JEF's chairman and CEO from 2007 to 2011. His path to JEF is also specific to how elite officials migrate between public corporations. After graduating from the Law Faculty at Tokyo University in 1959, Hatakeyama entered MITI. After assuming positions which included Director-General of International Trade Policy, he retired from MITI as International Vice-Minister. In June 1998 he was appointed the Chairman and CEO of JETRO.

For better or for worse

By the early 1980s, Japan, whose economy was export-driven, was showing a marked trade surplus with its leading trading partner, namely the United States, which was in recession. There was significant pressure from the US government to deregulate domestic markets and raise import quotas for such goods as agriculture products, electronics and motor vehicles as was discussed in previous chapters. Realistically, JETRO's role as a promoter of Japanese exports was no longer relevant to Japanese businesses as it had been in the 1960s and 1970s. Also, JETRO's role as a surveyor of foreign markets and a collector of economic and political data had, in part, become extraneous because research was being conducted by large Japanese multinationals, research institutes and MITI officials posted in embassies and Japan Chamber of Commerce offices.

However, MITI intended to continue operating a corporation that had effectively resulted in creating more territory for its officials. As a gesture of compliance with US demands, MITI began the process of re-orchestrating JETRO's function so that the organization would serve as a promoter of foreign imports and foreign investment. In 1983, JETRO set up a task force to look at import promotion. In 1984, import promotion activities such as trade fairs were held in Nagoya, Yokohama and Kitakyushu. In the same year, a second task force was set up to promote international economic cooperation for industry. In 1989, MITI completed the conversion of JETRO export promoter to JETRO import promoter with the establishment of yet another organization, the Institute of Trade and Investment. The number of foreign offices increased to eighty in fifty-seven countries while the domestic offices increased to thirty-eight. JETRO's 2002 website explains: 'JETRO made a 180-degree reversal and began promoting imports entering Japan, a primary mission that continues to this day.'

On November 22, 2002 Koizumi's Cabinet State Minister of Administrative and Regulatory Reforms, Nobuteru Ishihara (Shintaru Ishihara's son), told reporters at a press conference that he hoped that Diet members would understand that the continuation of Special Corporations was problematic. He gave JETRO as an example, stating that he and the Minister of Economy, Trade and Industry were amazed to learn that the corporation issued a pamphlet advertising import promotion, insinuating that some corporations were no longer serving the functions they were originally established to serve and that the ministries were contriving work for them in order to justify their budgets and continue operations.[6]

The brochure titled 'JETRO in America' identified JETRO as a 'nonprofit, government-supported organization dedicated to promoting mutually beneficial trade and economic relationships between Japan and other nations'. The brochure listed seven offices in the US – New York, Atlanta, Chicago, Houston, Denver, San Francisco and Los Angeles – where 'each has a comprehensive information center on US–Japan business and economic relations and offers American business people a variety of consulting services and other assistance':

> By far the major focus of our activities in the U.S. is helping American companies develop exports to Japan. Promotion of U.S.–Japan industrial cooperation, technology exchange and direct investment in Japan are also areas of significant activity. Over the years, JETRO has become a valued resource of thousands of American companies, particularly small and medium-sized businesses new to the Japanese market. In addition to directly assisting private companies, we cooperate closely with national, state and local economic development agencies, as well as with industrial and trade associations seeking to promote exports to Japan.

The brochure related the types of services available to potential exporters:

> With a wide array of effective export promotion services, a cadre of seasoned Japanese business experts and an extensive information infrastructure, JETRO is ideally suited to help American companies take advantage of burgeoning opportunities in Japan. From providing comprehensive market information to personalized consultation, representing products at key Japanese trade fairs to offering free temporary office space in major Japanese cities, we have what it takes to help American businesses get on the road to success in Japan.

Promises and more promises

JETRO's import promotion programs and literature are packaged to give the corporation a glossy professional image of a Japanese government-supported agency that is earnest in its efforts to help small businesses enter Japanese markets. JETRO's services are directed to small and medium-size businesses whose owners would like to do business in Japan but who are unfamiliar with regulations, the markets and consumer culture. From the late 1980s, JETRO began publishing a series of market reports for products that found consumer acceptance such as foods, alcoholic beverages, clothing, sports equipment, cosmetics, electronic equipment, jewelry and organic products. More than a hundred reports had been published by the end of the 1990s.

In 1989, JETRO released *A Survey on Successful Cases of Foreign-Affiliated Companies in Japan*. Claiming that foreign direct investment had been liberalized because the Foreign Trade Control Law had been amended in 1980, JETRO presented thirteen case studies of successful ventures in Japan. The thirteen manufacturers who were questioned about how they had prepared for operating in Japan answered very positively about their experiences. However, they were not identified by company names but by product, the location of headquarters, location of operation in Japan, and the amount of capital investment.

In 1990 a colorful magazine was issued describing companies that had entered Japan successfully. *The Challenge of the Japanese Market* pointed to companies, such as Baccarat, Bausch & Lomb, Cartier, Jaeger, Peugeot, Rolex and Reebok, that had been accepted in Japan. However, JETRO did not advise small-business owners that the main reason these companies had successful ventures in Japan was that they already had brand-name recognition among Japanese consumers before entering, and that Japanese people had traditionally been eager buyers of luxury goods when they travelled overseas. The majority of the companies mentioned had originally joined with a large Japanese trading company which routinely scouted for companies with products that were ready for the market, as was the case for Mercian Inc.

The 1996 edition of *Success is Yours* reassured small-business exporters of processed food that entry into Japan was not difficult if certain procedures were followed. The American confectioner and maker of the famous Jelly Belly jellybeans, Herman Goetlitz Inc. was held up as an example of how a processed food producer was able to enter the Japanese market successfully. Since Jelly Belly was already popular among Japanese consumers who purchased the product in the United

States, Goetlitz could count on instant name-recognition and success. Also, Sony Corporation was the distributor and would not have taken a risk with a manufacturer that did not have a solid track record. Here again, JETRO did not explain that if foreign businesses do not have a strong brand loyalty among Japanese consumers before entering the market they would have difficulty surviving unless a Japanese company was willing to take on an unknown. Although JETRO did not participate in facilitating Goetlitz's entry, readers may have assumed that JETRO was involved, since it did not state otherwise.

Success 1996 Case Studies continued to tout the success of large foreign companies in Japan that had prior recognition among Japanese consumers before entering the Japanese market. Case study 5 was entitled: 'L.L.Bean Japan Entering the Japanese Market without Capital Investment'. The company's outerwear was popular among the Japanese who were on extended visits to the United States.

According to the case study, in 1992, L.L.Bean joined the giant retailer Seiyu and Matsushita Electric Industrial to form L.L.Bean Japan. Seiyu put up 70 percent of the investment and Matsushita the other 30 percent, the total capital investment being ¥490 million. The study explained that L.L.Bean, a company with a large mail-order business in the US, researched the Japanese market through a consulting firm and found that Japanese consumers preferred retail outlets to mail-order. Therefore, it had to rely on large companies to market and distribute its goods in Japan. Matsushita imported L.L.Bean goods and Seiyu retailed them. Although Bean did not provide any capital and did not take any risks, it sold its rights to sell its products to Seiyu and Matsushita, who ultimately controlled the business in Japan. As discussed in previous chapters, this type of business tie-up is common in Japan, but mainly among well-established foreign companies. Small businesses rarely get the opportunity to participate in these kinds of ventures.

JETRO offers a number of support services. In 1991, the Senior Trade Advisor Program was inaugurated in the United States, whereby former executives from Japanese multinational companies or JETRO staff were posted to the International Economic Divisions of state governments. They visited small businesses operating in their states to find products that would suit the Japanese market. By 1994, there were twenty-one advisors who could also serve MITI as information-gatherers. When small-business owners visit a JETRO office in the US to inquire if their products are suitable for the Japanese market, they are referred to a trade advisor assigned to the office. Owners are often advised to revise the product to meet either the Japan Industrial Standards (JIS) or consumer preferences to such an extent that the capital investment necessary for revising a product can often be far more than the business owners can afford, given the risks of entering unknown territory.

In 1993, the Foreign Investment in Japan Corporation (FIND) was established as a private corporation, promoting itself as 'Your Foothold in the Japanese Market'. Its services included the contribution of funds to foreign businesses that wanted to operate in Japan. The corporation claimed:

¥500 million in capital provided by the Japanese government (Structural Fund) and a further ¥445 million was invested by powerful businesses in the private sector and industry associations.

Among the thirty-one stockholders were MITI industrial associations such as the Electronics Industries of Japan (EIAJ). A MITI subsidiary, the Industrial Structure Improvement Fund, was also a stockholder. The majority of private companies were in industries that MITI regulated, including Toyota Motors, Mitsubishi Chemical Corp., Nissho Iwai Corp., Kobe Steel Ltd. and Nissan Motors Corp.

There are trade fairs in larger cities in Japan that focus on specific industries where businesses exhibit products and meet potential buyers. There are also JETRO Support Centers located in Foreign Access Zones (FAZ), providing information to foreign businesses about Japanese markets, doing business within FAZ.

In 1993, Business Support Centers (BSCs) opened in Tokyo, Yokohama, Kobe, Nagoya and Fukuoka to assist foreign small-business owners during their visits to Japan to find buyers for their products. The BSCs offer exhibition space, temporary office facilities and consulting services free of charge.

JETRO organizes seminars throughout the year for foreign business owners and foreign dignitaries and for the Japanese business community when foreign trade delegations visit Japan to promote investment in their countries.

Two programs were introduced in 2000. The Tiger Gate Program introduces Japanese venture capital companies to American incubator-size businesses involved in high-tech areas. One of the Tiger Gate incubators is located in Silicon Valley, California. JETRO assists Japanese nationals to finance the venture while the tiny companies contribute the intellectual property.

In the 1990s trade directories of Japanese companies who were interested in ventures with foreign businesses were available in the JETRO overseas offices. The Trade Tie-up Promotion Program (TTPP) initiated in 2000 offers the same database to promote joint ventures between foreign and Japanese business via the Internet.

Does JETRO promise more than it delivers?

Karel van Wolferen wrote an article entitled 'The Japan Problem' in 1986 when Japan and the United States were engaged in heated trade talks. His article analyzed how Japan was dealing with US demands to reduce the surplus by opening up markets to American goods, and stated:

> In Japan quite often – and always more frequently than the West – what is true on paper is not true in practice. Japanese spokesmen widely advertise the fact that a number of foreign firms that have tried hard enough have been successful in the market. These firms are well-known because they belong to a small sample always in this context. A select few foreign firms receive assistance to serve as fresh examples of Japanese openness.[7]

Foreign business owners who have engaged in Japan will undoubtedly recognize that the information released by JETRO does not include details that would have given the uneducated business owner a more realistic picture of doing business in Japan. In addition, the Business Support Centers have received poor reviews from small business owners because they are not centrally located and visits from potential buyers are too few to justify the trip and the expense.

The June 16, 1997 issue of *U.S. News and World Report* continued to probe JETRO's authenticity as an import promoter. An article by Senior Writer William J. Holstein entitled 'With Friends Like These' questioned JETRO's function in the United States. In his article, Holstein described JETRO as 'a uniquely flexible organization that defies American definition'. He contended that JETRO America did not serve to promote imports into Japan, but rather was a sophisticated commercial intelligence-gathering agency. He suggested that the promotional materials served to disguise the true reason for JETRO's presence. Edward J. Lincoln told Holstein: 'At best the Japanese are being disingenuous when they say that JETRO's primary job is promoting American exports.' Lincoln suggested that JETRO's 'core mission' was to collect American technology and political intelligence.

In his article Holstein stated that there was a risk that products invented by small businesses would be appropriated by Japanese companies to whom they had been introduced by JETRO. He provided as an example the experiences of a Clearwater, Florida entrepreneur, Donald Lewis, whose electronic device JETRO claimed in its publication *Success in the Making* it had marketed in Japan. Holstein contended that JETRO's support led to Lewis losing control over his invention to an automobile manufacturer. Lewis claimed that Toyota had agreed to use his device, and when Toyota had used it for a few days, the Japanese distributor told the inventor that it would be best to sell his stake to Toyota. Lewis felt under pressure to sell because Toyota was a giant manufacturer and very influential.

JETRO chairman Toru Toyoshima painted a different picture when he addressed an audience of the New York Japan Society in 1993. He reported that a senior trade advisor had come upon Lewis' electronic anti-rust system and thought that it would do well in Japan. According to Toyoshima, the Export-Import Bank of Japan loaned Lewis US$1.5 million to expand his operations. Toyoshima said, 'As some of you know, in April 1990 the EXIM Bank of Japan introduced a lending program designed to increase imports into Japan and provide financing to American companies with products that are likely to sell well in Japan. The Florida company became the first to have such financing.' Coincidentally, Toru Toyoshima was Hatakeyama's predecessor at the JEF.

When Holstein asked the JETRO New York chairman Kazunori Iizuka about JETRO's activities in the United States, Iizuka insisted 'We are promoting U.S. exports to Japan to reduce the trade gap between us.' The JETRO website at the time was advertising requests from Japanese companies for such items as 'used medical beds' and 'primary coat stripper for optical cable'. FIND was terminated on March 31, 2002. Edward J. Lincoln wrote in his book *Troubled Times* that it had been expected that FIND would assist in a concrete way with foreign investment, but the corporation was criticized because it did little more than propose joint ventures with Japanese firms that were members of FIND. It also charged a fee for introductions. Lincoln argued that since FIND was a government corporation, it was not free to give advice on mergers and acquisitions. He concluded: 'Foreign firms were less in need of advice or introduction to potential businesses than the dismantling of the real obstacles to acquisitions.'[8]

In 2007, the United Nations Conference on Trade and Development (UNCTAD) inward FDI performance index ranked Japan 137th among 141 countries, which constituted 2.5 percent of the GDP. Peter Mandelson, the former European Union Trade Commissioner, complained in a speech given at the EU–Japan Center for Industrial Cooperation on

April 21, 2008 that Japan was 'the most closed investment market in the developed world'. Ironically, the event was sponsored by METI and JETRO. Mandelson suggested that Japan, whilst taking advantage of the openness of foreign markets was creating barriers to foreign investment. He cited figures showing that 3 percent of Europe's total $300 million outward investment was invested in Japan, comparing it with Japan's outward investment. 'For every dollar Japan invested in the UK and the Netherlands alone, European companies were able to invest a net total of only 3 percent in Japan.' Since then inward investment in Japan has fallen to 2 percent of annual GDP.

The same old story: Invest Japan

The Manufactured Imports & Promotion Organization (MIPRO)[9] was established in 1978 by MITI. As of April 1, 2013 MIPRO was renamed the Manufactured Imports & Investment Promotion Organization. MIPRO operates an office in Washington, DC where METI officials and Japanese trade delegations visit regularly.

The MIPRO 2012 website includes a message from the president Tsutomu Higuchi, director of Policy Planning Division, Energy, Conservation and Renewable Energy in ANRE:

> Inward direct investment in Japan accounts for less than 2% of Japan's nominal GDP, which is much smaller than similar shares in other major advanced countries, and nearly 80% of such investment is made in Kanto and Koshin-etsu districts. Therefore, extending foreign investment in Japan and promoting the penetration of foreign capital into Japan are urgent tasks. In cooperation with affiliated organizations, MIPRO is supporting global business activities and secondary investment in local areas by foreign companies in Japan. The investment branch wants to promote inward investment with a program called INVEST JAPAN.

MIPRO's services are designed specifically to support small-lot business imports and foreign small business start-ups in Japan. MIPRO's investment division promotes inward investment in twenty designated cities in Japan's six regions.

Although MIPRO's services are relevant to manufactured goods they overlap with JETRO's services. For example, MIPRO published information regarding industrial standards, regulations, market information and market trends, direct investment into Japan, activities of foreign firms in Japan, Japanese lifestyles and consumption trends and so forth. MIPRO offers consulting services, seminars about how to do business in Japan and introduction to Japanese firms for potential investment.

JETRO provides most of the services it provided in the 1990s. Market information published in the 1990s can be accessed on JETRO's current website. There are the same small business support services, the same database (TTP) of prospective importers and Japanese business partners, expert business consulting services, and 'a global network of company executives, advisors and more': 'Because JETRO is an independent agency of the Japanese government we are able to provide many of our services for free.'

Inside/Outside Japan: 'creative MITI, aggressive MITI'

The article in *Nikkei Business* in 1997 stated that the ministries established Special Corporations as their subsidiaries to provide temporary employment for staff and post-retirement positions for retired senior officials before they moved to the private sector, that Special Corporations used funds to do work that was in the best interest of the corporations and that Special Corporations received funds from sources that were difficult to trace. *Sankei Shimbun* alleged that JETRO operated as an 'underground MITI' and as a version of the MOFA.

The national ministry officials cynically alluded to MITI as 'aggressive MITI' and 'creative MITI' because MITI no longer had a cogent industrial policy since the end of the Cold War in 1989. In order to justify its budget and protect its existing administrative territory, MITI officials pursued the territory of other ministries. *Inside/Outside Japan* provided a façade contrived to support MITI's objectives; to pursue other ministries' turf such as MOF and MOFA; to promote and defend MITI's industrial policy; and most importantly, to present JETRO as the Japanese government's trade promotion organization. The paper was a vehicle which MITI used to present itself in different ways, depending on what the audience wanted to hear, while furthering its own interests.

Inside/Outside Japan was a monthly newsletter that was launched in 1992 by JETRO New York. The newsletter promoted Japan's industrial and trade policies and JETRO as a trade promotion organization in an innovative format. The Executive Director of Research and Planning conceived of a monthly newsletter that would serve as a platform for articles regarding US–Japan politics, economics, trade and social issues and which was sent unsolicited to both Japanese and American government officials, well-known academics and business leaders.

The president, an elite MITI official who served as the figurehead of JETRO New York for a period of two years, was very creative in his use of the paper in the promotion of his government's trade and foreign policies. He succeeded in creating a positive image of both MITI and JETRO, using methods that differed from past presidents, who primarily relied on networking personally with national and state government officials, businessmen and academics. The president preferred to supplement his networking activities with *Inside/Outside Japan* and used the paper for disseminating information about Japanese business and promotion of government policy.

The paper was also an effort to encourage the perception among foreign readers that JETRO was a multifaceted government-funded organization which promoted trade and investment in Japan and was managed by officials who understood Americans, their political economy and America's relationship with Japan (MOFA territory). Simultaneously, the paper's tone promoted to readers the importance of 'mutual understanding' and acceptance of the Japanese way of governing and doing business. Although the paper was, in effect, an attempt to revise JETRO's image and, therefore, maintain and increase its budget, it equally gave MITI officials the opportunity to answer US officials and the US media's contention that Japan's markets were closed to foreign business and investment.

Although some of the articles were quite biased in defending Japan's position at the US–Japan trade negotiations and flexing Japan's muscle in the international political arena, the articles were cleverly conceived and relatively informative. The paper provided an excellent representation of Japan's economic conditions at the time, government policies regarding US–Japan trade relations and promises to deregulate and open markets.

Although published during the 1990s, many of the articles portend the consequence of Japan's unfulfilled promises to deregulate markets on Japan's current economic conditions. As an example, inward investment is still at the same level as in 1992 at 2–2.5 percent of GDP and structural reforms have yet to be implemented. Indeed, a number of the articles relate to current events and Japan's continuing economic problems. To demonstrate how the paper served to promote MITI's interests and relevance to current events excerpts from some of the articles are presented here.

In the second issue (July 1992) the president promised in his editorial that Japan's economy would recover within seven years which agreed with the prognosis of many government officials at the time. It was also the mainstream view in the international business community:

> Real estate prices continue to drop, vacancy rates of new office build-ings remain high, banks are competing among themselves trying to dispose of bad loans, manufacturers are struggling to reduce excess capacity and personnel ... This is not a description of the United States a few years ago, but Japan today ...
>
> Seven-Five-Three is a traditional Japanese festival for congratulat-ing children on turning seven, five, or three years of age. But the term is now used to forecast Japan's economic recovery: real estate will take seven years, banks five, the securities market three before regaining their footholds ... The bursting of the economic 'bubble' seriously injured the United States: now it is injuring Japan no less.

The president acknowledged that his government was too optimistic in its original forecast of economic recovery and was now going to release a recovery package to ignite the economy:

> The recovery plan, announced on August 28 provides for $86 billion to achieve four main goals: (1) expand spending on public hous-ing; (2) increase loans to small businesses; (3) promote investment in plant and equipment; (4) to give financial institutions incen-tives for depreciating bad debts. The package includes $250 million earmarked for promoting imports.

In the same issue was an article about Japan's quasi-military entrance into international peacekeeping operations (PKO) with the passage of a PKO bill in June allowing Japan to send troops overseas to engage in UN operations. The vote in the Lower House was an overwhelming 329–17 and in the Upper House 137–102. However, the LDP wanted the SDF to assume the role because it was equipped to perform UN peacekeeping activities. The article, which illustrated MITI's role as the No. 2 MOFA, stated the following:

> A basic fear that remains is that this law might open the door to milita-rism in Japan. It is important to remember, however, that the new law allows the Japanese government to dispatch only lightly armed contin-gents abroad on narrowly defined missions. Japan's participation will be limited to non-military activities such as election monitoring ...

Clearly Japanese leadership is committed to supplying personnel for the protection of international order.

The November 1992 issue trod on MOFA territory with an article about Japan's leadership in Asia and its attempts to promote peace and improve relationships among Asian countries through regional trade agreement (ASEAN). The article reports that Japan was trying to repair relations with China and Korea to demonstrate its commitment to this end. While admitting that Japan must promote China's ties with the West, the article also reveals Japan's defensive stance and paranoia regarding China's rapid economic development in Asia and its economic and political influence in the international community. The article expresses concerns that issues such as China's human rights violations and arms dealings would serve to frustrate Japan's efforts to help China internationalize.

Crazy about Clinton: the honeymoon

Some of the officers seconded by prefecture governments and by MITI's other Special Corporations regarded MITI as a ministry which had weakened during the previous decade because it no longer had an effective industrial policy. However, the December 1992 issue of *Inside/ Outside Japan* was a tour de force with the president promoting MITI's industrial policy by praising President Bill Clinton for his determination to fix the US economy through the restructuring of its industrial policy and for his seemingly liberal attitude towards Japan's trade surplus with the US.

The president was positive about Bill Clinton's recent election in November and his initial speeches before his inauguration in January regarding the restructuring of the US economy by rethinking its industrial policy:

> As the new administration contemplates ways of strengthening U.S. competitiveness, 'industrial policy' seems to be on the lips of many policy makers. In devising and pursuing industrial policy, however, it is important to recognize that a government's role in fostering industrial competitiveness is limited ... In speaking about Japan's industrial policy, the impression is often given that its function is to 'pick the winner'. And in noting this, it is stressed that since the government can't work better than the market, industrial policy can produce mainly errors ... As has been the experience of some

countries, the government arbitrarily choosing potential 'winners' can lead to market distortions, as well as collusion and corruption.

No reference was made to the recent scandals of collusion between the MOC and construction companies or on some of the elements specific to Japan's industrial policy, which, in contrast to America's industrial policy, covered all of Japan's industrial sectors. It is well documented that Japan's industrial policy protected domestic companies from foreign competition through recession cartels, production rationalization and tax incentives to Japanese corporations who procured from domestic suppliers. The policy was implemented by administrative guidance enforced through built-in control mechanisms such as *amakudari* and MITI's industrial associations.

The president attempted to persuade readers that MITI had a softer side, as the promoter of R&D for environmental protection and as a ministry which took only a peripheral role in guiding industry: 'One vital point that tends to be missed, though, is that industrial policy is not the matter of choosing winners. Instead, it is a joint effort between government and industry to respond to it appropriately.' He suggested that a government 'may introduce tax breaks and low-interest loan for the producers of such equipment. In such government–business working schemes, competitive vitality of each industrial sector is indispensable and taken for granted. The main actor is always the industry.'

The Executive Director of Research and Planning contributed a piece to the same issue which lauded Clinton's recognition that the US's trade deficit with Japan was not entirely Japan's fault nor due to Japan's 'misconduct' (i.e. protected markets and non-tariff barriers) while stressing that the US must get its act together and revive its economy.

Japan's import promotion measures or MITI's promotion of MITI and JETRO?

The February 1993 issue of the paper announced a series of measures which would support the flow of exports to Japan's markets:

Japan's worry about its trade surplus is not a recent phenomenon. When the surplus continued to swell after rounds of tariff reductions and other measures to reduce procedural hurdles, Japan introduced steps unprecedented in world history and began actively promoting imports. The government's current efforts expand similar measures, with the stress on encouraging foreign businesses to come to the Japanese markets or to increase their imports to Japan. Among such import-promotion programs are:

(1) Special lending rates provided by the Japan Development Bank (JDB) for import-enhancing facilities and the Export-Import Bank of Japan for importation of manufactured goods.
(2) Set-aside-for-imports programs in government procurement.
(3) Business Support Centers (BSC), to be added to JETRO. Intended to provide free 'business centers' to foreign people who actually visit Japan to find leads or establish contacts.
(4) Foreign Access Zones (FAZ). By March 1993 a total of seven air- and sea-ports will have expanded facilities for encouraging imports.
(5) Expansion of the activities of the office of Trade and Investment Ombudsman (OTO). Established to resolve problems faced by foreign markets in Japan.

The president's editorial in the same issue was clearly in MOFA territory as he lauded former President Clinton's support for George W. Bush's military entry into Iraq:

Future historians are likely to rate President Bush high for shaping a clear direction for the 'new world order'. His decision to take military action against Iraq just a few days before handing his post over to Mr. Clinton gained worldwide support, and significantly reduced the sense of instability and uncertainty in the post-Cold War international order that people began to have not long ago after the East–West schism ended in a victory for Western philosophy.

While welcoming Clinton's continuation of American foreign policy, the president took the opportunity to emphasize that there was also the need for Japan to change from 'a passive participant to an active player in the global system' and that the country was obliged to 'dedicate itself to the betterment of the world with a far greater vigor than it has in the past'.

Promotion of industrial policy with a Scottish twist

The president was extremely 'creative' in his promotion of MITI's Vision for the 1990s, 'Creating Human Values in the Global Age', in a speech which he delivered on March 10, 1993 to the members of the Carnegie Council on Ethics and International Affairs. In his address 'MITI and Human Values' he managed to connect MITI's Vision and the release of another fiscal stimulus package with Andrew Carnegie's 'Gospel of Wealth' while simultaneously presenting his ministry as a compassionate and caring agency determined on helping the Japanese realize a better quality of life.

Although it would take some stretch of the imagination, comparisons can be made between MITI, a Japanese bureaucracy, and Andrew Carnegie, a Scottish immigrant from Dunfermline who became the father of the American steel industry. He founded Carnegie Steel, the forerunner of US Steel, in 1869, a year after the beginning of the Meiji Restoration. He made his fortune in iron, coke and chemicals. The Ministry of Agriculture and Commerce (MAC) began nurturing Japan's steel industry in the late nineteenth century. However, here any similarity between Carnegie and MITI ends and dissimilarities begin because Carnegie's wealth came out of his own pocket and not from tax revenue. The parks, libraries, schools, hospitals, meeting halls, universities and concert halls were personally financed. Japanese government fiscal stimulus packages were funded by Japanese tax-payers.

The president introduced himself to his audience by mentioning his recent visits to the Carnegie-Mellon Institute in Pittsburgh and Carnegie Hall in New York, both highly visible examples of Andrew Carnegie's philanthropic activities. Then he got down to the subject of his speech, 'creating human values as a form of industrial policy'. Describing his ministry as a firm but gentle guide of Japan's industry, he said that MITI was sometimes called 'notorious' but that he was unaware of the term's origins:

> Perhaps it has to do with the way Japan's economy developed rapidly in the past five decades and MITI's supposed role in that development, which is often expressed by the very term 'industrial policy'.

The president spoke of Japan's competitive spirit as the driving force behind Japan's industrialization after the Meiji Restoration quoting the first sentence of the first essay in Carnegie's 'Gospel': 'The problem of our age is the proper administration of wealth.' He reflected:

> Though Mr. Carnegie was a great philanthropist, in his gospel he did not preach a 'kinder, gentler' attitude, he was hard-nose arguing, at one point that 'no substitute [for the law of competition] has been

found: and while the law may sometimes be hard for the individual it is best for the race because it insures the survival of the fittest'.

The president's reference to Carnegie's generous but hard-nosed character was savvy because it connected with MITI's use of administrative guidance. He insisted that Japan's post-war industrial policy included cooperation but there was a catch: 'Competition is important, but a body of people – be it family, a company, or a society – cannot hope to function and grow without cooperation among its members.'

The president was inferring that companies cooperated with MITI's guidance to form cartels, to rationalize production, to fix prices and to procure from domestic suppliers in order to ward off competition from foreign firms.

Carnegie's tract on distribution of wealth had a Socialist tone to it:

> under its sway we have an ideal State, in which the surplus wealth of a few becomes, in the best sense, the property of many, because administered for the common good, and this wealth, passing through the hands of a few, can be made a more potent force for the elevation of our race than if distributed in small sums to the people themselves.

Likewise, MITI's Vision and MITI's role could be characterized as Socialist. The president reminded his audience that post-war industrial policy had focused on catching up with the Western powers and on increasing Japan's competitiveness in the global marketplace. Each of these visions, in that sense, was a 'how-to' guide on a grand scale.

He assured the audience that 'creating human values' was very much a part of industrial policy: 'after all, industrial policy ... at least as practiced by MITI ... is aimed to increase prosperity or a sense of well-being in the nation'. He claimed that MITI was aware that the Japanese were not enjoying the fruits of their labor and that the Vision for the 1990s was to shift the focus from 'how-to' to 'what-for'. He listed some of the objectives of the Vision:

> greater consumer-orientation and protection, further promotion of recycling, creating greater employment opportunities and increasing security for the elderly, and pushing for advancement of women's social and professional status. The vision calls for vast improvement of social infrastructure, including housing (no more rabbit hutches,

please), and a massive attempt to reduce excessive concentration on Tokyo and encourage regional development ... the vision sets forth goals that must be achieved to secure long-term economic development that is essential to the enhancement of human values.

As a government spokesman, the president stated a recurring theme; although Japan's economy might be regarded as stagnant, Japan was still experiencing growth of 1.5 percent GDP and that the first stimulus package of $87 billion was proving an effective measure to spur the economy.

The speech was given two weeks prior to the release of the second fiscal stimulus package, which the president explained in his editorial in the April issue of *Inside/Outside Japan*, putting a spin on Japan's role in the global economy:

The Japanese economy, which has remained in the doldrums since the 'bubble' burst two years ago, is finally beginning to brighten. Improvements in machinery orders which began last October are continuing ...

In mid-April the Japanese government will introduce a new stimulus package. Following the $87 billion measure that went into effect early this year, the new package will aim to boost 'new social capital' by inducing investments in things such as telecommunications and university laboratories ... The effect of the previous stimulus package on the construction industry was evident in January, when top 50 construction companies reported a 60% increase in new orders from a year earlier ...

Internationally, the continued recovery of the U.S. economy remains the key to worldwide growth. But Japan's role is no less great, especially when European countries are reeling with serious recession. Japan is implementing large stimulus measures to increase domestic demand and help the world economy grow with stability.

The year 1993 is going to be a historic one when the foundations for a new international order will be laid. Both the United States and Japan are prepared to undergo fundamental change – the United States with the keyword 'sacrifice', to rebuild the domestic economy, and Japan with 'global responsibility', to strengthen its international role. It is our hope that during the U.S.–Japan Summit in mid-April President Clinton and Prime Minister Miyazawa will solidify the partnership of the two nations.

When interviewed in 1994, a MITI official answered the question of whether he thought that Japan could internationalize. His reply revealed the real picture and not what Americans wanted to hear:

> I don't think that the Japanese can internationalize. 'Internationalization' is spoken about but Japanese go abroad, have experiences but return to Japan and their same way of life. Unfortunately, things from the outside will never enter Japan smoothly. I really don't understand what 'internationalization' is, but I think that for Japanese to achieve a level that enables them to negotiate and interact with various nationalities is difficult.

An officer from a prefectural government was also interviewed during the same period. His reply is relevant today:

> Japan is a small island nation and insular. People are not open to outsiders. They build stone fences and close themselves off. Japan has internationalized in some areas like trade but for the general population, Japan has not internationalized at all.[10]

Getting hotter

The increasing trade friction between Japan and the US was covered daily by both American and Japanese media. Although in his December 1992 editorial the president entertained high hopes for the Clinton administration trade policies regarding Japan's trade surplus, he expressed in the April 1993 issue of *Inside/Outside Japan* some concerns, ending his editorial with a subtle warning:

> In the new era following the Cold War, we certainly hope our amicable relationship will continue, with the United States changing itself to affect basic economic restructuring, Japan to further facilitate access to its markets and take on greater global responsibilities. This is all the more reason we must oppose demands that deliberately interfere with market mechanisms.

The president was not entirely forthright when he insisted that Japan's economy was based on market mechanisms. Even though Japan was the second largest economy in the world and the world's largest net creditor, Japan's mercantilism was already creating problems in the economy that would prove to be insurmountable unless deregulation and basic structural reforms were implemented quickly.

The president devoted his editorial in the May 1993 issue to the Clinton–Miyazawa Summit which was held the previous month. He protects MITI's administrative territory by stating that Clinton was unrealistic about 'result-oriented trade' or 'managed trade' and that Japan was the submissive underdog at the negotiation table. He speaks of:

> The United States' position as the senior partner and founder of Japan's post-war democracy, and Japan, because of its inherent politeness and reluctance to offend ...
>
> There is undue emphasis on select aspects of bilateral trade and ignores, for example, the fact that the imbalance in trade between Japan and the United States fundamentally results not from allegedly closed markets but from macroeconomic factors and differences in export capabilities. Forcing numerical import targets on a trading partner would be the ultimate form of market intervention – as Japanese corporations and Mr. Miyazawa forcefully argued.

The June 1993 issue included a special MITI report presenting the US as the culprit:

> The Japanese Ministry of International Trade and Industry (MITI) has issued the second annual report on unfair trade policies of Japan's major trading partners. The report examines U.S., Canada, Australia, and Asian nations, as well as Japan, and finds that the United States most violates GATT rules and resorts to unilateral actions.

The November 1993 issue titled 'Urgency in Import Expansion' introduced EXIM Bank's intention to extend to Japanese distributors of imports 'import-promotion credit lines' to cover increased import costs and total import costs. The credit line could also be used to import machinery and equipment and pharmaceuticals. And JETRO received publicity as well: 'JETRO has set up special facilities to exhibit imported houses.'

America bashing

The president took a more aggressive stance in his Special Supplement for the March 1994 issue of *Inside/Outside Japan*. *For a Better U.S.–Japanese Relationship* protests the Clinton administration's negotiation tactics at the meeting between Clinton and Hosokawa in February when Hosokawa refused to agree to setting numerical targets on certain Japanese imports:

> What concerns me the most is that both U.S. and Japanese negotiators are deepening their mistrust of each other. Evidently, American negotiators have come to believe in two things. One is that 'Japan is an odd man out.' In this view, the stubborn persistence of the trade imbalance between Japan and the United States derives directly from the nature of the Japanese market that is radically different from those of other industrialized countries. The other is that Japan's market liberalization cannot be achieved because of Japan's 'entrenched bureaucracies' and wayward corporate practices.

In the following sentence the president stated the obvious, while unaware of the future consequences:

> Today, U.S. industry has regained competitiveness through restructuring and bold innovations, whereas Japanese industry has stumbled badly – in part as a result of what American industrialists call 'overinvestment'.

But he expressed his hope for reducing the US–Japan trade imbalance by promoting JETRO as one of the solutions:

> There are encouraging signs. The U.S. Commerce Department is starting ambitious export-promotion programs. Meanwhile, JETRO has various arrangements for promoting the importation of U.S. products into Japan. To mention only two, the trade agency at present maintains a total of nineteen senior trade advisors throughout the United States who identify products with potential in Japanese markets and guide their producers every step of the way. Not long ago, it opened a Business Support Center in Tokyo which provides free space and business equipment to business people who wish to explore Japanese markets. It plans to open another such center soon.

The president followed with an attack on two well-recognized journalists who pointed to Japan's bureaucrats for inhibiting social and economic change in Japan:

> In this, Messrs. Karel van Wolferen and R. Taggart Murphy completely missed the point when they asserted, in their joint OP-ED

article in the *New York Times* (20 February), 'It was the bureaucrats who stopped Mr. Hosokawa from going along with specified trade targets.'

The Executive Director of Research and Planning also took offense in a letter to the editor of the *New York Times* a week after the van Wolferen article was published:

> The 'failure' of the latest round of United States–Japanese trade talks shows the simplistic and self-centered approach the United States often takes toward its 'most important' international trading partner; unrealistic demands such as numerical targets, failure to obtain agreement or fulfillment, followed by threats to retaliate or a retaliatory action.

The director accused the United States of not understanding:

> the complexity of economic mechanisms and the workings of Japanese society ... Take one administration official's pronouncement to the effect that Japanese bureaucracy is now the 'enemy of the United States' ... It is naïve to assume, as the Clinton Administration apparently does, that by reshaping Japan's bureaucracy to its own liking, the United States can eliminate its deficit with Japan.

Does every little bit help?

On January 26, 1994 JETRO New York hosted an event sponsored by the New York State Department of Economic Development (NYSDED), the National Minority Business Council and JETRO to announce the formal presentation of New York State's Global Export Market Service (GEMS) grants to ten members of the council. The grants for the members were aimed to help the small businesses that were engaged in apparel, accessories and tableware production export to Japan. The event was orchestrated to promote JETRO as Japan's primary promoter of foreign small business exports to Japanese markets.

An article in the April edition of *Inside/Outside Japan* reported that the president spoke briefly about the JETRO senior trade advisors who were posted at nineteen state governments 'in order to help small firms export to Japan by, for example, introducing their products in JETRO's Import Frontier'. The president also spoke about how the Business Support Center in Tokyo served to encourage companies to explore

Japanese markets. 'The huge trade imbalance between the United States is real but, it is these small but practical steps that help reduce the U.S. trade deficit.'

The GEMS companies had already exhibited their products at the JETRO Business Support Center in Tokyo the previous October. Hiranobu Sekiguchi, the owner of a boutique in a popular, youth-oriented section of Tokyo, visited the center one day, liked what he saw and promised to place an order in January when he would be in New York. He also attended the news conference at JETRO New York, courtesy of JETRO.

The craftware company Monoco Design was chosen for a gallery exhibition in Kobe. According to the artist upon his return to New York, the exhibition was well attended and he managed to sell some of his work. However, USTR representatives may have questioned whether a few pieces of pottery exported to Japan could be considered a step to reduce the US trade deficit.

In the same issue the president's perspective on 'Mr. Hosokawa's Sudden Resignation' dealt with Prime Minister Hosokawa's resignation after only eight months in office which the president explained 'was to take responsibility for the irregularities allegedly found in financial transactions that he had long entrusted to his personal aide'. The president praised Hosokawa for his efforts to reform the political system and to deregulate Japanese markets.

Don't bash us bureaucrats

The Special Supplement in the March 1994 issue was a diatribe by the president who, while defending Japan's position in the US–Japan trade talks, was also defending his fellow bureaucrats and protecting MITI's territory. In the president's view, the meeting a month earlier between President Clinton and Prime Minister Hosokawa who mutually agreed to postpone decisions about numerical quotas amounted to a 'breakdown' in negotiations.

His lecture to his readers is relevant to: (i) the fundamental reasons for Japan's current political economic situation; (ii) Japan's continuing reluctance to open markets to foreign competition and inward investment; (iii) Japan–US trade relations; and (iv) the ministries' use of their corporations to promote their interests.

The president bemoaned the United States' tendency to impose sanctions on countries 'whenever it fails to achieve its own goals'. He requested more understanding about Japan's position in trade relations and the role of Japan's bureaucracy which he felt was maligned in the American press and by the USTR. The president avoided addressing the reasons for Japan's protected markets and trade surplus, but offered:

> In the decades since [Japan's post-war rapid economic growth period] Japan has had a trade surplus. This is mainly the result of the stupendous efforts of its manufacturing sector to improve itself and excel – although there have been macro-economic factors such as the high savings rates that enabled Japanese industry to maintain high investment levels ...
>
> Today, U.S. industry has regained competitiveness through restructuring and bold innovations, whereas Japanese industry has stumbled badly – in part as a result of what some American industrialists call 'overinvestment'. No one knows as yet whether this reversal of fortune is extensive enough to reverse the trade-balance positions of the United States and Japan. But with the compounding factor of the high yen continuing and Japanese corporations continuing to invest overseas, the trend is evidently toward a reduced imbalance. It certainly will be helped by U.S. industry's seriousness in exporting to Japan – as evident, for example, in the production of compact cars with the right-side steering wheel.

To ensure that JETRO's role as the government-funded promoter of inward investment and imports was duly publicized the president declared:

> JETRO has various arrangements for promoting the importation of U.S. products into Japan. To mention only two, the trade agency at present maintains a total of nineteen senior trade advisors throughout the United States who identify products with potential in Japanese markets and guide their producers every step of the way. Not long ago, it opened a Business Support Center in Tokyo which provides free space and business equipment to business people who wish to explore Japanese markets. It plans to open another such center soon.

The president again pursued American bureaucrat bashers to protect MITI's turf. Without divulging the real story regarding the mechanisms which served to protect Japan's market from foreign competition and foreign investment, the president explained to uninformed readers that during Japan's rapid economic growth period in the 1960s and 1970s it was necessary for the government to regulate industrial production:

> But if there was a honeymoon period between business people and bureaucrats, it was becoming a thing of the past by the early 80s ... I think that it is a mistake to say, as some Americans do, that the bureaucrats are the roadblock to any social and economic change in Japan ... I must emphasize that Japan has dismantled a range of barriers against imports.

The president promised:

> But it is necessary to keep making these efforts, for Japan must reduce its persistent and large trade surplus. Keenly aware of this, the Japanese government is pursuing important programs: further deregulation, an aggressive implementation of antitrust statutes, large-scale public investment to enrich people's lives [e.g. FILP and stimulus packages] and promotion of imports and investment from abroad.

He concluded the article by going for the jugular:

> In all these efforts, change must come from within. Short-sighted and self-serving pressure from the United States can be counterproductive. This is because it only breeds mistrust and discontent on the side that gives pressure and alienation and resentment on the side that is [being] pressured.

In 1999, Dr. Edward J. Lincoln, an advisor to Walter Mondale, a former ambassador to Japan, stated in his book *Troubled Times*: 'The *amakudari* system provides substantial reason to be skeptical of the extent of deregulation and the unilateral market opening in Japan because of the manner in which this practice establishes a formal web of personal ties between government and Japanese firms.'[11]

Although other countries may sympathize with the president's evaluation of the United States, they do not understand the unfortunate economic consequences of Japan's unwillingness to open its markets. Japan's current economic problems are the result of mercantile policies during Japan's post-war period as also was contended in 2003 by A. Mikuni and R. Taggart Murphy:

A mercantile regime may enjoy a period of success at it accumulates specie – or, in today's terms, claims on other countries. But it usually runs into some monetary train wreck. The mercantilist's efforts to convert its claims on others into its own currency drive up the exchange rate because foreigners, whose sales to the mercantilist country are restricted, have few ways of accumulating the mercantilist's currency in the first place, so little of its currency is held outside its borders. The mercantilist exporters then find that no one can afford to buy their goods.[12]

Abe isn't the only one

The president was again treading dangerously on MOFA territory with his editorial in the September 1994 issue titled 'The Matter of Article 9'. But the editorial could well have been written in 2014 and is worth quoting here:

For over four decades now, the 'war-renunciation' clauses of Article 9 of the Japanese Constitution and the actual existence of military forces have cast a duplicitous shadow on the minds of the Japanese people. Like many of my generation, I have had some painful experience in this regard.

As a law student a quarter of a century ago, I knew I faced a dilemma when the time for taking the test on the Constitution came. The professor who administered it was a constitutional authority well-known for his unadorned view that the Self-Defense Forces were unconstitutional. What if a student had, as I did, a different view? Given in the first term, the test was regarded as the first hurdle to be cleared. After pondering the thought, I decided to hold on to my view.

The president reported that his test result was a disappointing 'B'. He blamed the Socialist Party, which occupied one-third of the house seats since the 1950s, for its opposition to any constitutional change:

Once this irrational opposition is lifted, we might be able to secure more dispassionate, realistic debate on a wider range of security issues. More important, the removal of blind opposition of a party representing a sizable segment of Japanese people should usher in a new age in which similar debate is extended to all issues. If this comes to pass, Japan can claim to have changed in one crucial way.

The president concentrated on trade and industry with his editorial in the September 1995 issue 'Japan's Industry in Peril' in which he states that the yen valued at ¥100 per dollar should be depreciated further to ¥160–200 per dollar:

> Outside the manufacturing industry, Japan still has few industries that are internationally competitive. The nightmare for Japanese policy planners is the prospect of getting stuck with the excessively protected and therefore the least efficient industries after the most efficient parts of Japan's vaunted manufacturing industry have left the country. To correct the dangerously high yen, Japan could do one of two things. It could sharply cut its trade surplus by accepting imports and curtailing exports. Or it could drastically deregulate its economy, open up the uncompetitive sectors of its industry, and increase imports in order to sharply reduce the gap between domestic and foreign prices. Since the first is no choice at all, the question is: Will the Murayama government seriously set out to deregulate its economy?

Open house

The Japanese and American press had targeted JETRO as an organization which did not engage in trade promotion but in covert activities and which served to expand MITI's territory. However, the allegations regarding covert activities by the media were inconsequential compared to far more pressing issues: the use of tax revenue and human resources. The JETRO New York president told Holstein that JETRO's annual budget was supported with 70 percent tax revenue but he did not divulge the source of the remaining 30 percent. He also reported that JETRO's annual budget for the operation of JETRO's seven offices in the United States was $30 million. This amount covered the salaries and benefits for local staff but did not include the relocation expenses and salaries for JETRO officers and MITI officers. The sum may have covered promotional expenses and seminars but not all of the import promotion materials.

The negative press resulted in opening the JETRO New York office to investigation by the FBI and the CIA as well as to public observation. JETRO New York was the largest JETRO USA office but reflected the structure and management in other large branch offices located overseas. JETRO New York had moved its office to the McGraw-Hill Building from a smaller office that was located in the Time Life Building on the Avenue of the Americas a few blocks down from the McGraw-Hill Building. And due to the increase of representatives sent from Japan (the 'bubble' effect) the office had to be enlarged. JETRO managed to secure the office next door that had been rented by another company and refurbished the premises to meet the requirements of new representative offices. Mitsubishi Estate owned both buildings at the time.

The offices were a microcosm of officials seconded by their government agencies, prefectural governments and industrial associations. Ensconced in the New York office during the 1990s before the consolidation of some agencies, were officials seconded from MITI's corporations such as the Japan Corporation for Small & Medium-Size Enterprises (JASME) and EID/MITI, EXIM's Import and Investment Insurance Department. There were officers from MITI's industrial associations such as the Japan Automobile Manufacturers' Association (JAMA). MITI officials represented industrial machinery to monitor American EPA regulations, small machinery production and such industries as aeronautical and automotive, and MITI officers monitored US politics. The Industrial Research Division was manned by the two officials. There also were representatives from the Economic Planning Agency (EPA), which collects macroeconomic statistics in Japan.

The former Ministry of Transportation (as of 2001, MLIT) loaned officers to represent the ship building and ship machinery industries. The Ministry of Agriculture, Forestry and Fisheries loaned officers to JETRO.

Since JETRO USA is registered with the US State Department, it is able to host various agencies and organizations that are not registered. During the economic bubble a number of prefectures, anticipating economic expansion, opened one-man offices at JETRO's overseas offices to establish a presence without considering fully the objectives of the 'presence'.

The prefectural governments represented at JETRO New York included Kyoto, Osaka and Ehime. The public corporations such as the Japan Highway Corporation and prefectural governments which were not attached to MITI were required to pay JETRO substantial fees for office space and secretarial support, which helped JETRO pay the rent as well as justify its budget. Regardless, these officers were expected to cooperate with MITI in research projects and promotional events that were not related to their responsibilities for their respective agencies.

The offices were managed by JETRO staff posted from Japan for three years, and MITI elite officials managed operational budgets. JETRO staff cared for the needs of all representatives, including facilitating visas for the agents, applying for social security, health insurance, and procuring local staff to assist the officials with research and administration. The officers seconded from JETRO Japan engaged in public relations and promoted JETRO as an organization that assists American small businesses to enter the Japanese market and do business in Japan and organize seminars.

All of the officers, including MITI officials, who were on loan to both JETRO's domestic and JETRO's overseas branches, were regarded as JETRO staff, although they worked primarily as representatives of their agencies in one-man offices. As an example, an officer posted by the Kyoto Prefecture government would identify himself first as a member of JETRO staff. Most of the officers' previous careers were not related to their work at JETRO New York and they received little preparation regarding their future work before leaving Japan. The requests from their home offices to investigate trade regulations, laws, current government policies, environmental issues and industrial standards were forwarded to consulting companies, some of which had been on contracts that had continued for years from director to director without any regard for the quality of work. Other duties included guiding delegations of Japanese businessmen on tours of their regions, arranging meetings with businessmen and government officials for their organizations' officials and entertaining Japanese government officials.

A number of the officials posted in the JETRO USA offices had never lived abroad and their comprehension of English was superficial. The complex Japanese language is rarely spoken outside of Japan and some of the officers could feel at a distinct disadvantage and on the defensive because they were unable to easily communicate with Americans. Furthermore, all of them had worked as members of divisions and had never worked independently, which for some officers can be very stressful. JETRO management exacerbated a latent xenophobia among the officers by releasing news bulletins about crimes perpetrated against Japanese tourists throughout the United States. The officers were continuously cautioned about racism, drugs and the proliferation of gun-related incidents in the United States. Consequently, the officers were always anxious about living in a country where they could be victims of violent crime.[13]

The posting of representatives overseas in the ministries' public corporations like JETRO may not be based entirely on merit. Civil servants from both prefecture governments and the national ministries, who have displayed loyalty through their work and to their superiors, are sent abroad. Civil servants may be sent because a family member is an elite official in government or a father-in-law is an elite ministry official. But officers may also be chosen for duty abroad because their behavior is considered outside the norm and disruptive in the workplace. The officers could be suffering from a mental disorder, or, in some instances, alcoholism, and posting them overseas serves to isolate them from their division and their colleagues.[14]

Nice work if you can get it

In general, the officers' workload was far less strenuous compared to their responsibilities in Japan and they enjoyed a two- to three-year hiatus from the pressures of the home office where overtime was usual. Despite the relaxed atmosphere at JETRO New York and despite the fact that the officers were from separate organizations, the hierarchical structure of Japan's governing system, with the national ministries on top and prefecture government towards the bottom, was well defined, as is also the case in the majority of Japanese government offices overseas.

For the majority of the officials, a posting in the United States was an opportunity afforded to a minority of Japanese civil servants, offering a luxurious life-style and the opportunity to live abroad for a few years, courtesy of the Japanese tax-payer. Similar to foreign corporate executives who are sent abroad by their firms and officials from foreign government agencies, the bureaucrats who were married were relocated with their families and they enjoyed a standard of living they would never experience in Japan. Homes were spacious, often with gardens, an unusual phenomenon in Japan where land is at a premium, especially in the metropolitan areas. The officers also received allowances for their children's educational needs.

Ironically, despite their concerns about safety in the United States, and, in some cases, ambiguous attitudes regarding US–Japan relations and American mores, they recognized that America offered a physically easier and mentally calmer life-style than the Japanese civil service. Some of the JETRO officers used their stay at JETRO New York as a means of escape from their system. However, the majority of elite MITI officers seemed satisfied with their status, knowing that upon return to their ministries they would receive a promotion. But some of the other officers such as JETRO staff, and representatives from prefecture governments and agencies coveted 'green cards'.[15]

Nothing much changes in this system

METI officials who are posted abroad at JETRO overseas offices promote Japan's economic and trade policies to governments, businesses, media and educators. The officials lobby governments on behalf of Japanese businesses, search for patents considered applicable to Japanese business interests and for small businesses with technologies which are in need of capital investment for R&D. Most countries post commercial attachés from the ministries of commerce and industry in embassies and consulates. However, even though they serve as commercial attachés, METI officials' interfacing duties give them the semblance of foreign attachés. Also, JETRO offices dispense to the public both commercial and cultural information, duplicating some of the literature released by the MOFA.

What about the budget for operating seventy-eight offices abroad and thirty-eight offices in Japan? *Special Corporations and the Bureaucracy* (2003) recommended that in order to cut costs some of JETRO's functions should be consolidated with MOFA and MOF overseas operations thus eliminating some of the offices:

> For example, the research of foreign political economies by officers in overseas offices run by MOF and by officials in consulates and embassies is regularly contracted to local research and consulting companies and their reports are transmitted to the ministries' headquarters. Since METI staff is posted in embassies and consulates, in order to cut costs and the drain of public funds they could engage jointly with MOFA and MOF officers in research projects as well as share the duties of interfacing with foreign business and political communities. The Japanese Chamber of Commerce and Industry is managed by METI's Industrial Policy Bureau and, like JETRO, maintains offices around the world. The transfer of some of JETRO's activities to these offices would serve to cut costs.
>
> Nevertheless, even though opponents of Special Corporations regard JETRO's duties as extraneous it is likely that METI will not consider the above options and continue to operate JETRO as a signature piece and one of its power bases in Japan.[16]

Since many civil servants migrate regardless to positions in private corporations which are in their ministries' administrative jurisdiction, the two-year period of grace bureaucrats spend in IAIs or in affiliated agencies serves no more than to provide a respite from the pressures of the workplace and a good salary plus retirement benefits, courtesy of Japanese tax-payers.

Evidently former Prime Minister Noda read the book and took action during his administration, targeting JETRO for a merger with an MOFA organization in 2014. However, now that the LDP has returned to power there may be a U-turn because METI elite officials are considered specific to the promotion of exports of nuclear and other technologies and to escorting executives of the heavy industries to foreign markets to meet with government officials and corporate executives for possible joint ventures. In other words, the LDP wants to ensure that METI officials remain content.

13

The Price of Pork-Barrel Patronage: Beggars Can't be Choosers

In 2001, although 53 percent of the Niigata electorate voted against the use of mixed oxide fuel (MOX) METI refused to budge on its long-term objectives for the use of MOX and fast breeder reactors and began looking for other prefectures to build pluthermal plants. Ehime Prefecture was fair game because there was already a nuclear power plant hosted by the small fishing village of Ikata, which is located on Japan's narrowest peninsula and the westernmost point of Shikoku, Japan's fourth largest island. Its industry is limited to fishing and citrus farming. The mountainous terrain prevents urban development but the substantial investment from the nuclear industry has supported infrastructure and tourism. Ikata Nuclear Power Plant is Shikoku's only nuclear installation and provides much of the islands' electricity. No. 1 reactor, built by Mitsubishi Heavy Industries, began commercial operation in September 1977. No. 2 reactor was commissioned in 1982. No. 3 reactor, which is partially loaded with MOX, began operations in March 2010 and was built jointly by Mitsubishi and Westinghouse.

Although Governor Iga was expected to maintain control over Ehime politics, the recession prompted dissatisfied voters to replace him in January 1999 with Moriyuki Kato, a high-ranking official in the Ministry of Education who retired from office to enter politics. The initial reaction from local businesses was positive because Kato's close ties to the national ministries would hopefully serve to facilitate the procurement of public works contracts and subsidies. However, by Kato's second term in office, Ehime residents had come to realize that Kato's connections brought more than they had bargained for.

Kato's connections to MEXT and METI: textbooks and MOX

The Ministry of Education was merged with other agencies in 2001, a result of the reorganization of the national ministries. The Ministry of Education, Culture, Sports, Science and Technology (MEXT) was also engaged with the development of the nuclear industry.

In 2001, Prime Minister Koizumi supported MEXT's approval of the controversial *New History Textbook* (edited by Kato's former ministry) for high-school students which glosses over the wartime atrocities committed by Japanese military in Asia in the Pacific such as the abduction of 'comfort women'. The textbook refers to the war in the Pacific as 'The Greater East Asia War', the term used by Japanese nationalists.

Besides Koizumi, other proponents of the textbook included former METI vice-minister Keiji Furuya and former Tokyo governor Shintaro Ishihara. *Sankei Shimbun*, which owned the same ultra-conservative media group that also owns the textbook's publishers, ran a series of editorials supporting the textbook. The book's authors were academics who were members of the right-wing Society of Textbook Reform and who believed that Japan had entered Asia to liberate the region from the control of white colonists and that the so-called atrocities were merely 'normal excesses' committed by all armies. Despite China's and South Korea's anger over the manipulation of facts, negative reactions from the foreign press, heated debate in the Diet and strong resistance in local governments, by 2004 the book had been adopted by a number of prefectures. In April 2004, the Tokyo Metropolitan Board of Education officially adopted the textbook, thanks to the persistence of Ishihara.

Kato endorsed the textbook publicly in 2002, announcing that he felt that the textbook was 'most appropriate to deepen people's appreciation of the history of our country'. Although many local citizens were opposed to the textbook, Kato received more support from Koizumi and Abe on May 15, 2004 at an Ehime town meeting for the revised education bill. The hall was packed with 100 educators with links to MEXT. A subsequent investigation of the event revealed the following November that sixty-five educators had been paid ¥5,000 each for attending the meeting and that one member was given the task of spouting statements in support of the textbook and asking questions prepared by the ministry. Despite a lawsuit filed in December 2005 against Kato by 1,000 people, including South Korean and Chinese, demanding the rejection of the textbook, it was distributed to schools in 2006. Koizumi admitted to organizing town meetings and paying educators to give rehearsed speeches favoring the textbook.

Ehime residents had not anticipated that the election of a former MEXT official would also lead to a pluthermal reactor with MOX fuel. METI's Japan Nuclear Cycle Development Institute and MEXT's Japan Atomic Energy Research Institute (both Special Corporations that were merged in 2005 to form the Japan Atomic Research Agency) developed MOX fuel for fast breeder reactors. In October 2006 when METI requested that Ehime host a pluthermal plant to become fully operational by 2010, in spite of vehement protests from civic groups, Kato welcomed the project since Ehime's economy would undoubtedly benefit from substantial government subsidies of ¥6 billion ($51.7 million) which was a hefty sum, especially for a prefecture which generated only about 36 percent of its tax revenue. On October 13, 2006, after obtaining the consent from Ikata mayor Kazuhiko Yamashita, the governor presented a written agreement to the president of Shikoku Electric Power Company (YODEN) which owns and operates the power plant. Six months earlier, Saga Prefecture in Kyushu had given permission to the Kyushu Electric Power Company to build a pluthermal reactor at its Genkai plant.

Three years later, refusing to capitulate, on January 18, 2009 the Association of Ehime Prefectural People for Cooperation as well as other citizen organizations requested that METI's former Nuclear Industrial Safety Agency (NISA) force YODEN to cancel its plans for the pluthermal reactor. Their demands were ignored and YODEN began commercial operations in March 2010. Kato expressed confidence about YODEN's safety measures and his belief that the central government's pluthermal policies were practical.

At the age of 76, Kato decided not to campaign for a third term in office and to retire from politics. His successor was Torihiko Nakagawa, a local lawyer, who won the 2010 election on the LDP ticket. He also applauded the initiation of a pluthermal plant and agreed with Kato that the government's screening methods and government nuclear policy were reliable.

On August 2, 2011 *Mainichi Shimbun* reported that a retired METI official who headed the public relations in NISA admitted that NISA had asked YODEN senior officials to request that staff attend a seminar in Ikata in June 2006 where there was discussion of using MOX in Ikata's No. 3 reactor in order to influence a positive response from attendees.

No. 3 reactor went offline in April 2011. Abe's administration has targeted Ikata as one of the first plants to go online as soon as the Nuclear Regulatory Agency (NRA) gives the all-clear. Although they are very concerned about the safety issues, the majority of Ikata residents, many of whom worked in nuclear-related jobs and who were adversely affected financially due to the loss of subsidies and jobs, are clamoring for the restart of the reactors. In an interview in March 2014 Mayor Yamashita said that he would accept the restart of the plant if the NRA confirmed that the plant was safe. YODEN has submitted an application to government to restart the reactor.

Where oh where did the money go?

Ehime is representative of other prefectures where public works projects implemented during the 1990s have not had the anticipated affect on their economies. On the contrary, it resulted in the draining of both central and local government coffers.

In the 1990s, the government continuously released huge fiscal stimulus packages, allocating a large portion to public works. Hundreds of miles of roads, expressways, dams and bridges were built, providing construction companies with lucrative contracts and employment for thousands of workers, while no consideration was given to how the new infrastructure would serve the local population in the future. Ultimately, the infrastructure was built for the sake of building.

The brochure released by the Foreign Access Zone Co. Ltd. claimed that I.T.E.M. Ehime was built to 'promote local industries that serve Japan's increasingly international society'.

Between 1997 and 2001 there were a total of eleven international trade fairs but generally the halls of I.T.E.M. Ehime remained vacant. There was no noticeable change in the range of foreign imports in the World Mart. Foodstuffs, wine, toys, sporting equipment and other items on display overshadowed industrial goods.

Within I.T.E.M. Ehime is an Ehime Products and Tourism Center divided into three areas where products from local industries are exhibited The industries represented are paper and paper products, towels, canned and bottled *mikan* juice, and extruded fish paste (*chikua*). China's cheaper towel exports to Japan are undercutting the price of the towels produced in Ehime and 'Made-in-China' paper products are also out-selling Ehime paper products.

The I.T.E.M. World Mart displays foreign goods that are purported to have been introduced to Ehime consumers. The products exhibited include colorful African textiles, which, given the conservative nature of the Ehime population, may not be on consumers' wish-lists. Other products on display include confections and Marmite from New Zealand and Vegemite from Australia, a bicycle made in South Africa – even though the bicycle industry in Japan is highly protected – honey and jams, and a Swiss cuckoo clock.

There is a JETRO Support Center which promotes FAZ to foreign business owners on their visits, providing information on doing business within FAZ, market reports on foreign products that found consumer acceptance, and regional business reports.

A second FAZ was planned for construction during the last decade. According to the Ehime Foreign Access Zone Co., the construction would 'involve building a new port and roads connecting the facilities to the expressway system. The result will be a comprehensive upgrading of industrial infrastructure.'

Although the first FAZ was underutilized, Iga's friends in the ministries considered that the investment in public works projects would be justified by Ehime's future expanding economy and that the project would spur small-business growth. The allocation of subsidies for infrastructure also provided lucrative contracts to big business and employment to hundreds of workers.

Traffic is relatively light on the network of highways and tunnels that were carved through Ehime's beautiful mountainous terrain. The international airport is also underutilized much of the year. The modern museum is a beautiful structure with luxurious mahogany toilets, but the small collection of art housed in the museum questions the justification of the expenditure.

The Kurushima Bridge was under the management of the Honshu-Shikoku Bridge Authority, the debt-ridden corporation that was one of the entities merged with the JH. Commuters to Hiroshima preferred riding the ferry rather than using the Kurushima Bridge because the toll was too expensive, which was a key reason for debts. In other words, much of the public works such as the bridge, highways and convention center are not being utilized enough to have warranted their construction in the first place and the Japanese refer to them as 'empty boxes'.

Devolution?

The books published by Mainichi and Nikkei in 1994 reported the surveys conducted in 1993 of ministry officials concerning the ability of local government civil servants to plan policies independently. The surveys revealed that the majority of respondents considered that the national ministries must always bear the responsibility of governing the regions. Both of the books contended that *amakudari* and the temporary posting of elite officials in branch offices of Special Corporations in the prefectures (*shukko*) helped the ministries to monitor local government policies. Since the bureaucratic hierarchy places officers from the national ministries above local government officers, the positioning of ministry officials at the local government level automatically induced acquiescence by local government to ministerial guidance.

The ministries monitor local government policies via their officials who are 'loaned' to the branches of the ministries' corporations or to local government offices. They also assist local government officers in planning local government policies as well. The prefectures with inadequate tax bases were unable to finance welfare and educational services and contracts for the construction of infrastructure projects to local businesses and thus were in the ministries' pockets. Compliance with ministerial 'recommendations' encouraged more subsidies for public works contracts to those prefectures. The consequence of the reliance on the ministries for continuous support was the inefficiency of local government and the inadequate training and development of local government officers who lacked the confidence to act independently.

The Japanese have been urging government for years for more regional autonomy and more power to plan and implement policies at the local level. During the 1990s there were some reforms at the local level.

But at this time the push for devolution to the local authorities should be considered within the context of Japan's severe economic conditions. The reforms are being promoted at the executive level (Cabinet Office). Following the recommendations by an advisory committee, the government requested that local authorities assume more of the financing of infrastructure, public works projects, education and welfare in order to downsize central subsidization and conserve national budget outlays.

Local government officials are assuming more of the responsibility for planning policies and for providing financing for health and welfare programs and for public works projects, thus reducing the dependence on government subsidies. MIC explains on its website, published in 2010, that its remit is 'to realize a government that can adapt to changing circumstances in an economic society in such a severe financial situation'.[1]

Prior to March 2011, the MIC was already beginning to cull personnel in public administrative bodies at both the national and local levels which is defined as 'a series of head count rationalization programs' in order to structure a 'simple and efficient administrative organization, and optimizing its number of personnel placements'.

It was intended to incorporate the administrative agencies (104 corporations by March 2011) in order to separate the planning of policies from the implementation of the policies and to 'make the implementing departments efficient and better in quality'. MIC plans to review each incorporated agency's organization and programs in order to consider whether or not it should be abolished 'with expenses being reduced and task management made more efficient'. Since the assessment is from the top, local authorities must still adhere to ministerial edict. It appears that local governments are expected to assume more of the finances because they are being given more 'autonomy'.

The MIC acknowledges that Japan's economy has been in a state of recession since 1992:

> Regional finance therefore plays an extremely important position, so to speak, as one of the two wheels of a vehicle together with national finance. Increasingly important will be the roles of local governments and accompanying financial measures, such as promoting regional sovereignty reforms, supporting nursing, medical and parental care designed for the society with a declining birthrate and ageing population ...

> Regional finance totals the finance of about 1,700 local governments, most of which are financially weak municipalities. The shortage of funds for regional finance increased swiftly in and after fiscal 1994 due to the decline in local tax revenue ...

Moreover, the balance of loans in regional finance grew rapidly in recent years due to the decline in local tax revenues, compensations for tax cuts, and the increased issuance of local bonds for stimulating the economy. The end of fiscal 2011 saw the loans growing to 200 trillion yen, accounting for 41.4 percent of GDP. This marked a 2.9-fold increase since fiscal 1991, showing an increase of 130 trillion yen.

Local governments, especially the weaker localities, shared with central government about 30–40 percent of tax revenue, the costs for public works, educational programs and social welfare. However, the tables are turned to accommodate 'such a severe financial situation'. The MIC states: 'To ensure financial balance ... the ratio of the state to regions on a final spending basis is opposite the ratio of the state to regions in terms of distributing tax revenues. Thus, the funding for local public entities to run their projects has been shifted from the state to the regions.'

Local governments must issue their own bonds to raise funds for public works, which is a struggle given the economic conditions of small businesses in some regions. Also, the decreasing population through the consolidation of local authorities as well as a rapidly aging population may also impact on bond sales. But MIC assures local governments that in emergency situations they will be rescued by a state bank

In fiscal 2009, the Financial Organization for Local Public Enterprises was reorganized to establish the Japan Finance Organization for Municipalities as 'a financial organization for joint use by regions designed to grant loans for general accounting, in order to respond to the financial needs of local public entities in a timely and appropriate manner'.

The ministries are not pleased with the arrangement for a variety of reasons. The Ministry of Internal Affairs and Communications (MIC) which is in charge of managing the operation is reluctant to delegate too much of the burden to the local authorities. MOF is unhappy with the transfer of central government control over revenues to local governments. Elected officials and the ministries, which are in charge of implementing the projects, namely MLIT and MOFA, are very concerned about the cuts in revenue allocated for the subsidies for specific projects.

Currently local governments must submit applications for subsidies for public works (e.g. infrastructure projects) which explain the objectives and necessity in their region and in the context of national priority. The applications are assessed before revenue is allocated for the projects.

Mayors can exercise a great deal of influence over the operations of some local governments and their priorities evolve to encompass their local governments' agendas. The mayors of large metropolises have been promising drastic reforms within their local governments but whether or not these reforms are implemented is another issue. Furthermore, the Association of Prefectural Governors has proposed a set of reforms but the results of the implementation are limited because there must be a consensus with the ministries and the association of municipal officials (to name a few of the parties involved).

The civil servants' salaries in the national ministries are generally lower than the salaries of civil servants in prefectural governments. In 2012 Abe's administration cut the wages of national ministry officials 7.8 percent with the objective of using the savings to support the reconstruction of the Northeast. However, salaries were restored in 2014 because of the effect on civil servants' morale and of the need to equalize the wages with those offered by the private sector.

Nevertheless, 'a government that can adapt to changing circumstances in an economic society in such a severe financial situation' will take decades to take shape because of the structure of Japan's governing system as previously discussed. Additionally, the current consolidation of villages and towns is promoting a continued loss of population and a decrease of local tax revenue. Again, MIC is confident: 'Through local allocation taxes and local bonds, along with other means, the LPFB ensures funds for the local public governments.'[2]

However, these measures may come too late to wean local governments off central government's subsidies and to instill an effective self-governing system at the local level.

14
Still Bubbling

After the bursting of the inflated real estate bubble in 1990 the weaker non-bank financial institutions such as leasing companies and credit associations began to fail. In addition some regional banks also failed. These institutions were closely connected to the large city banks because deposits in the city banks were used to finance loans to clients of local banks. The MOF pressured the metropolitan banks to bail out the banks that were in distress. For example, four major city banks were forced to take over the collapsing Taiheiyo Bank and the Tokai Bank acquired the failing Sanwa Shinkyo Ginko.

Nonetheless, despite the cumulative effects of the continuing recession and the continuing fall of real estate values through the 1990s, Japanese banks continued aggressively to loan large sums to Japanese producers in India, Thailand, Indonesia, Singapore and Malaysia at low or no interest rates in order to gain market shares. The MOF reported that the number of Japanese banks operating in Asian countries increased from 83 in 1990 to 161 by the end of 1995. In 1993, Japanese banks, in seeming denial of the risk of accumulating additional loads of NPL, made $72 billion in loans. By the end of June 1996 Japanese banks had increased the amount to $116 billion.

Many banks suffered tremendous losses due to aggressive lending during the 1990s but the banks simply denied the bad-loan problem. Although the official declaration of non-performing loans in 2004 was ¥35 trillion, the private sector put the figure at ¥87 trillion. The Japanese government stated that through the 1990s it injected ¥9,000 billion ($83.5 billion) into banks in order to avoid a banking crisis. Although a substantial amount, this was a very small proportion and considerably less than 10 percent, even on government estimates, of the total of non-performing loans held by the banks. The Japan Economic

Institute, an organization under the auspices of the Ministry of Foreign Affairs, reported in August 2000 that the Financial Services Agency (FSA) declared the amount of problem loans for all banks as of March 2000 to be ¥81.8 trillion ($743.6 billion at ¥110 = $1.00) compared with ¥80.6 trillion in 1998.[1] In his address to the Japan–US Business Conference on February 17, 2002 the chairman of Keidanren Takashi Imai claimed that the banks had disposed of ¥75 trillion.

Due to conflicting reports it is difficult to estimate the actual amount of NPL but the government estimate of NPL for the end of September 2002 was ¥40 trillion ($330 billion) and that during the decade 1993–2003 the banks had written off ¥83 trillion (about $700 billion) of NPL. However, there was speculation in the private sector that the 'real amount' of these disposed NPL could be double or triple the official report. Edward J. Lincoln claimed in 2003:

> Even the large amount of loans that has been written off does not necessarily represent loans that have been resolved. In many cases, the banks have simply set aside reserves equal to the amount of the loan while taking no action against the borrower to recover collateral, leaving 'zombie' borrowers – effectively still in business.[2]

Kobayashi contended in 2004 that during the 1990s the banks simply denied the bad-loan problem and that, although the official declaration of non-performing loans in 2004 was ¥35 trillion, the private sector put the figure at ¥87 trillion.[3]

The Asian economic crisis in 1997 triggered more action by the government. In the period from March to September 1998 the government injected $180 billion into the banking sector.[4] But some institutions were already on the verge of collapse. The failure in 1996–7 of two major financial institutions – the Nippon Credit Bank (NCB) and the Long-Term Credit Bank (LTCB), both Special Corporations that had been established in the 1950s by MOF – revealed the severity of the non-performing loan problem.

After the collapse of the asset-inflated bubble the LTCB was riddled with $19.2 billion of debt. After the Asian financial crisis in 1997 the government nationalized it and pumped $2 billion into the failing bank. The deregulation of financial markets in 1998 allowed the purchase of a Japanese bank by a foreign consortium. Ripplewood, a $300 billion American private equity firm, Goldman Sachs Group, Deutsche Bank and General Electric purchased the bank in March 2000 for $1 billion after the government was unable to find a suitable domestic bank for merger. The bank was renamed Shinsei ('new life'). Diet members were not pleased with Ripplewood's purchase of a state bank. The media also expressed displeasure at the entry of foreign venture capital firms in Japan. The contract called for government to pay at least $45 billion to cover bank losses.

In February 2004 when Goldman Sachs sold 35 percent of Shinsei equities for $2.4 billion[5] and Ripplewood sold more shares for $3 billion in March 2005, earning over $6 billion for its investors, there was public outcry since government investment in the bank to seal the transaction was twice that of the American consortium. It was the first and last time that a foreign company purchased a state bank.

The NCB (also known as Nippon Fudosan Bank or 'Japan Real Estate Bank') made loans to real estate companies. When the asset-inflated bubble burst, many of the companies became insolvent. The NCB was said to be among the world's top fifty banks in 1997 but it was heavily burdened with toxic loans after the bursting of the asset-inflated bubble and continued to accrue NPL throughout the 1990s. After the Asian financial crisis the debt had escalated to $27 billion and the government was forced to nationalize it despite the pleas from management. In September 2000, following Ripplewood's lead, Softbank Corp., Japan's major Internet investor, organized a consortium to purchase the NCB for approximately $907.1 million. Similar to the LTCB purchase, the consortium requested that the government inject funds to cover the bank's remaining NPL. Orix Corp., Tokio Marine and Fire, Cerberus Capital Management, Pacific Capital Group and Lehman Brothers were the major shareholders. The bank was renamed Aozora Bank ('blue sky') in 2001.

Softbank, which controlled almost 49 percent of shares, had intended Aozora as an investment bank for Internet-related companies but the Financial Services Agency (FSA) was not cooperative and Softbank decided to offload its shares in 2002 in order to secure funds for the expansion of its core broadband business. It offered its stake to Cerberus, which owned 12 percent of Aozora. Since foreign investors were not allowed to control more than 20 percent of a financial institution, the FSA was initially reluctant to approve the transaction. However, Softbank succeeded in persuading FSA to give approval and the sale was concluded in September 2003.

Toxic loans lurking beneath the surface

Although the government poured ¥10.433 trillion into bankrupt financial institutions during the four-year period 1999–2003,[6] NPL still remained a problem for banks that were a result of previous mergers. Resona Holdings, Japan's fifth-largest bank, was the result of a merger between Daiwa Bank and Asahi Bank in 1998 and 1999. The government had injected ¥1.17 trillion into these banks prior to the merger. Resona Holdings includes in its group Resona Bank (the core banking unit), Saitama Resona Bank, Kinki Osaka Bank, Nara Bank and Resona Trust & Banking Co. On May 30, 2003 the Resona Bank, whose clients were mainly small businesses, announced that it had sustained a ¥549.4 billion loss. The following day it formally applied to government for public funds of ¥1.96 trillion, promising to restructure under the guidance of FSA officials. On June 11, 2003 the government approved Resona's application. It purchased 5.6 billion common shares worth ¥280 billion and 8.4 billion shares of preferred stock worth ¥1.68 trillion. Government owned 50.1 percent of the bank. Since the government had 70 percent of the voting rights Resona Holdings was effectively nationalized.

Another example is United Fund Japan (UFJ Holdings Inc.), Japan's fourth-largest banking group, which was created through the merger of Sanwa Bank and Tokai Bank on January 15, 2002. UJF's creditors were primarily from depressed industries. Among them were two heavily indebted large trading firms, Nissho-Iwai and Nichimen.[7] UFJ's other debt-ridden clients included the retailer Daiei and condominium builder Daikyo. At the end of 2004 UFJ posted a net loss of ¥400 billion. Mitsubishi Tokyo Financial Group merged with UFJ in October 2005 to assume the leading role in operations.

Although the focus of major intervention in respect of NPL has been on the major banks, 53 percent of NPL were held by a number of banks among the 600 regional financial institutions. The enormity of the problem was brought into focus when the government in December 2003 took over the insolvent Ashikaga Bank, the eleventh-largest regional bank in Japan. Founded in 1895, it had a negative net worth of ¥102.3 billion. Ashikaga Bank (a part of Ashikaga Financial Group) is located in Utsunomiya City, Tochigi Prefecture, a popular resort area among both Japanese and foreign tourists. The hotel and inn business expanded in the 1980s, estate and securities prices increased rapidly and the bank made a large number of loans to inn keepers and hotel owners. Many of the loans eventually became NPLs. The bank had been engaging with North Korean financial institutions for 30 years as a main intermediary of funds to North Korea with contracts allowing it to remit money and settle accounts to North Korean financial institutions. Kyodo Press reported on March 27, 2002 that Ashikaga had remitted

$1million on 333 occasions during 2001–2. The bank cancelled its contract in April ostensibly to downsize its overseas operations but it was rumored that nationalization was due in part to the bank's relationship with North Korea.

In December 2003, fifteen regional lenders that had received injections of public funds reported that their combined NPL as of September 2003 (including Ashikaga Bank) totaled ¥2.98 trillion.[8] This was a decrease of 4 percent since March 31. On the other hand, Japan's seven major banks had achieved a 13 percent fall in their NPL for the same period.

The IMF issued a warning on April 7, 2004 that the non-performing loans held by the regional banks whose clients are mainly small to medium-size firms were endangering Japan's economic recovery and should be disposed of as quickly as possible. Only 5 percent of NPL held by the regional banks had been disposed of between January and September 2004, while the major banks had reduced NPL by 14 percent. Although the government's target was to bring NPL down to just below 4 percent of total loans, this figure did not reflect the NPL held by regional banks, which were 7.5 percent of total loans.[9]

In May 2005 credit rating companies Standard & Poor's, Moody's Investor Service and Fitch Ratings Ltd. revised the credit ratings for the four mega-bank groups to ratings established before the 1997 banking crisis and on May 26, 2005 the FSA announced that Japan's bad-loan crisis was over.[10] In a preliminary report released by the BOJ on July 9, 2005 the balance of bank lending for city banks, trust banks and regional banks had decreased by 2.6 percent year on year for June. This represented the ninetieth continuous month in which a decrease had been recorded.[11]

Despite the positive news, the problem of the regeneration of loans to sustain struggling companies continued to lurk beneath the surface. As an example, an investigation by the FSA of Sumitomo Mitsubishi Financial Group (SMFG) in the later part of 2004 revealed that the banking group had greater exposure to struggling companies than it had previously admitted. The investigation pressured the banking group, which had previously forecast a net profit of ¥180 billion, to announce it suffered a net loss of ¥234 billion ($2.17 billion) for 2004. Consequently the FSA rated SMFG as the weakest of the seven major banks. However, the SMFG assured the FSA that the bad-loan problem was under control but like its peers the bank was finding it difficult to persuade corporations to borrow despite the low interest rates offered.

As a result of acquisitions of the state banks by foreign firms, further foreign takeovers of businesses are being frustrated by the implementation of new laws. In October 2004 METI began to contemplate establishing a law that would discourage hostile takeovers of Japanese firms, which would include such measures as the so-called poison pill (the issuance of new shares to prevent hostile takeovers) and employee stock ownership plans. These strategies were regularly used in the US during the 1980s. METI's plans mirrored many Japanese business owners' anxieties that foreign firms would buy struggling domestic businesses. On February 22, 2005, the Justice Ministry announced that it planned to amend a current law to allow companies to revise their corporate charters before mergers take place, which would give companies more power to withstand hostile takeovers. On March 19, 2005, the cabinet approved a new bill that would delay for one year the easing of restrictions on foreign involvement in Japanese corporate takeovers.

The scandal in 1997 surrounding the entertainment of MOF and BOJ officials at expensive restaurants and clubs by banks brought to public attention that the non-disclosure of non-performing loans by the banks was partly the consequence of the intimate relationship between the BOJ, MOF and the banks that had been promoted through the *amakudari* system. In their defense, the banks insisted that they had been pressured by the officials to provide the entertainment. With the appointment by the Abe government of Kuroda as the governor of the BOJ, *amakudari* continues to compromise the banks' independence from the MOF and the BOJ.

Enter the FSA

The Financial Services Agency (FSA) was established in 2000 to deal with the regulatory problems in the financial industry that had been accruing during the 1990s. Established by MOF, the agency was the result of the integration of the Financial Supervisory Agency and the Financial System Planning Bureau. The FSA's objective is to ensure proper regulation of banking activity and, thus, the stability of financial markets. The FSA's website states the objectives of the FSA:

1. As the financial system constitutes a basis for all economic activities, the FSA seeks to develop a vigorous financial system and to promote competition so as to revitalize the national economy.
2. Development and proper implementation of regulations to protect users.
3. Ensuring transparency and fairness in financial administration based on clear rules, market discipline and the principle of self-responsibility.[12]

Consolidation may sort out debt but not bad behavior

There were also a number of mergers between undercapitalized banks (less than 8 percent assets) and the stronger banks. Daiichi Kangyo (DKB), the first bank to be established in Japan after the Meiji Restoration, was Ajinomoto's corporate bank. In 1971, the DKB merged with the Nippon Kangyo Bank (NKB) that had been established in 1897 by government to issue long-term, low-interest rates loans to light industry and agriculture. During the Second World War the NKB was the lead underwriter for war bonds. The bank became a quasi-commercial bank in the mid-1950s.

By 1988 at the peak of the asset-inflated economy the DKB was the world's leading retail bank. When the asset-inflated bubble burst in 1989, the bank carried a load of non-performing loans (NPL) because of risky loans to corporate clients and to Yakuza crime syndicates. Despite the scandals involving MOF's monitoring of banks in the early 1990s, the DKB continued to cover up the extent of its NPL problem and continued to provide loans while not calling in the bad debts. In 1997 during the Asian financial crisis public prosecutors uncovered DKB loans to criminal organizations and Kuniji Miyazaki, the chairman and former president, committed suicide. In 2002 the government urged the DKB to consolidate operations with the IBJ and Fuji Bank.

One of the IBJ's key clients Sogo Co. Ltd., which operated a chain of upmarket department stores, had invested in real estate during the 1980s and also fell victim to the collapse of the asset-inflated bubble. By the time the corporation declared bankruptcy in 2002, it owed its main bank, the IBJ, $17 billion. IBJ president Masao Nishimura had testified before the Diet that even though the IBJ knew that Sogo was insolvent by 1994 it continued to loan substantial sums. Furthermore, Sogo's president had held a top position at the IBJ which served to forge a tight relationship between the bank and the corporation. If the IBJ called in the loans, it would be tantamount to admitting publicly that it was in trouble. Sogo's acute distress in the second half of the 1990s and its imminent collapse prompted the government to urge the retail Fuji Bank to purchase IBJ equity in a stock-swap transaction in August 1999.[13]

Fuji Bank was a major post-war bank which also suffered severe losses after the bursting of the bubble. To counteract the losses, the bank established Yamaichi Securities, an asset investment affiliate to compete with Nomura Securities, and Yasuda Trust Banking. However, Fuji was unable to support the operations. Yamaichi, which was Japan's fourth-largest broker, declared bankruptcy in 1997 and Fuji was forced to lay off several thousand staff while borrowing trillions of yen in public funds. In 1999 Yasuda Trust collapsed.

In April 2002, together Fuji Bank and the IBJ merged with Dai-ichi Kangyo Bank. The new bank was renamed Mizuho Financial Group and claimed to be the largest bank in the world with assets of ¥140 trillion ($1.35 billion).[14]

However, the merger did not alleviate the bad-loan problem and Mizuho was obliged to sell 20–30 percent of its shares worth ¥100 million to foreign financial institutions. The DBJ purchased 10 percent of Mizuho shares. The government's efforts to accelerate the disposal of NPL through the resuscitation of corporate borrowers gave the DPJ the authority to purchase shares.

Also, the merger did not go smoothly because of the vast differences in the respective institutions' corporate cultures and because individual corporate strategies also differed. The IBJ was considered a traditional government bank that financed industrial development and was closely connected to METI. Management style was bureaucratic and the managers were deemed arrogant who wanted to control operations. The DKB was revered as a bank whose ancestor was Japan's first bank established during the Meiji Restoration and the biggest commercial bank during Japan's post-war period. Fuji Bank was Japan's largest retail bank until the formation of the DKB after the war.

Despite the establishment in 2011 of a state agency, the Deposit Insurance Corporation of Japan, to help financial companies erase from their books their links with gangsters, the culture of financial institutions' connections with gangsters still continues as does the lax regulatory system. The agency purchases the loans at discount rates from the banks or the credit card companies. Since 2011, the agency has purchased debts worth ¥300 million for ¥11.7 million.

In September 2013, Yasujiro Sato, the president of Mizuho Financial Group admitted that he, along with his predecessor and fifty-four current and former executives knew that the bank had processed 230 loans worth $2 million to the Yakuza and other gangster groups. Most of the loans were for automobiles. Sato relinquished his salary for six months and Takashi Tsukamoto resigned as Mizuho Bank chairman. On the back of Mizuho's revelations, Mitsubishi UFJ Credit Card division came forward as well and admitted to loaning to mobsters.

Aozora?

Aozora was the No. 1 unsecured creditor to Lehman Brothers. When Lehman filed for Chapter 11 bankruptcy in 2008, Aozora held $463 million in bank loans. Aozora was also the second-largest net creditor to Mizuho with $289 million in loans and Citibank's Hong Kong branch with $275 million in loans. A few months after Aozora announced on December 16, 2008 that it held $157 million loans to the Bernard Madoff fraudulent investment (ponzi) scheme, Aozora began negotiations with Shinsei Bank for the integration of operations by 2010 followed by a merger. However, negotiations broke down and Aozora purchased Japan Wealth Management Fund in 2011 to merge it with its Aozora Securities.

Nevertheless, Cerberus, wanting to reduce its exposure in Japan, decided to sell its stakes in various Japanese enterprises, including Aozora Bank. The American private equity firm announced in January 2013 that it planned to sell most of its Aozora shares for $1.9 billion.

Merrill Lynch: the second time around but why?

Due to the Asian financial crisis (1997–8) in April 1998 the deregulation of the foreign exchange law (foreign transactions could be executed by anyone) and the opening up of the financial sector prompted foreign firms to come to the rescue of bankrupt security firms and banks. Two examples of this type of infusion of venture capital activity were:

- Merrill Lynch bought Yamaichi Securities in 1999 which had collapsed in 1997. Despite ¥114 billion in special loans made by the BOJ, the firm formally announced bankruptcy in 1999.
- The Travelers Group purchase 25 percent of Nikko Securities.

These types of purchases were considered beneficial by government because they helped to revitalize the financial sector. Furthermore, the purchases were significantly beneficial to the purchasers because they opened up further investment opportunities in the market.

Merrill Lynch's decision to enter Japan for the second time in 1998 to snatch up the failing Yamaichi Securities at a bargain was based on the company's previous exposure in Japan when in 1993, as the world's largest underwriter of debt and equity, it had entered Japan with the intention of offering the Japanese the same services it was offering customers in the US. Merrill Lynch, hungrily eyeing Japanese household savings, which amounted to $10 trillion at the time, salvaged Yamaichi with the objective of becoming, as Merrill Lynch Japan chairman pledged, 'Japan's most trusted broker'. Merrill Lynch invested $200 million in starting operations and retraining Yamaichi staff.

The firm presumed that since Yamaichi and Nomura had treated investors badly in the past, Merrill Lynch could reform and reinvent

Yamaichi. However, trying to compete with Japan's four largest brokers proved to be problematic. Government regulations, which protected domestic firms from foreign competition, dictated the kinds of services that international firms could provide while prohibiting Japanese from investing in financial services outside Japan. And Yamaichi's clients would not forget or forgive Yamaichi for failing to deliver and misrepresenting its financial solvency. Furthermore, Japanese tend to be loyal to a company with whom they have had a long-term relationship but not with a particular salesperson.

Although Merrill Lynch Japan Securities brought in $14 billion of assets, the company's outflows equaled its inflows by FY 2002. Merrill Lynch decided to quit its retail banking business and concentrate on private banking, which proved more pragmatic.

The birth of big zombie companies

The Daiei Group and Kanebo Inc. are examples of how Japanese companies, despite experiencing a huge debt burden after the bursting of the asset-inflated economy, continued to borrow from their trusted and trusting creditors to diversify into businesses that deviated from their core competencies. A number of large companies struggled to survive the recession after the asset-inflated economy collapsed. In order to cut costs large producers began to source cheaper parts rather than procuring from their long-term contracted suppliers, many of them small businesses. The larger corporations managed to survive due to the loans from their main lenders who also held shares in the companies and whose executives were among the board of directors.

By 2000, lenders were no longer able to continue providing loans to companies that had become essentially zombie companies and whose loans were based on questionable collateral. By 2003, it had become clear to the FSA and to the ministries whose administrative jurisdiction included these bankrupt firms that further state action had to be taken to address the issue and to deal with NPL. It was against that background that the Industrial Revitalization Corporation of Japan (IRCJ) was created. The IRCJ was launched on April 16, 2003 by the Japanese government as an attempt to resuscitate failing companies and to deal with the problems associated with non-performing loan problems held by banks.

The official function of the IRCJ was to purchase loans from creditors and remove the conflict of interests between the main bank and other creditors. In this way, the rehabilitation of the borrowers would be facilitated. The IRCJ acquired the liabilities of selected failing firms, persuaded the banks to forgive a substantial amount of the debt, thus eliminating NPL, selected a firm or firms deemed appropriate for sponsoring capital investment in the floundering company and, together with the sponsoring firm, implanted a restructuring program. The IRCJ was given two years (until March 31, 2005) to accept applications from banks and their major clients and to approve assistance of the firms, and three subsequent years to dispose of all liabilities. The success of the IRCJ and the speed with which it pursued its aims depended to a considerable extent on both the cooperation of the banks and the extent to which they were addressing directly through their own activities the problems with non-performing loans.

The initial target of 100 firms appeared to be attainable when, within a month of the launch, twenty banks, and their borrowing firms, had presented applications for loan-sales. The chairman of the IRCJ, Atsushi Saito, warned against seeing the IRCJ as an easy route to disposal of loans when he told BOJ officials on June 2003 that most of the parties involved did not have clear restructuring strategies and so would not be considered eligible. Since the evaluation of the restructuring plans would take two to three months the process of choosing which firms were eligible for acceptance into the process would take time. But Kotaru Tsuru, a senior fellow at the Research Institute of Economy Trade and Industry (REITI), a METI Incorporated Agency, gave an alternative reason for the initial slow start:

> Under a typical rehabilitation scheme, IRCJ purchases loan assets from creditor banks of a troubled company, but does so only after the creditors have taken a share of the losses, specifically waving loan claims in excess of the value of assets held in collateral. If the IRCJ's assessment of the collateral is less than that of a creditor bank, the bank must relinquish a greater portion of its loan claims than it would in a scheme with no IRCJ involvement. Naturally banks do not want to have their 'hidden wounds' exposed, especially if the wounds are serious. Thus, large borrowers – with whom creditor banks might be forced to drop claims large enough to threaten their management under an IRCJ-led claim – tend to be subjected to a bank-prescribed rehabilitation scheme that seeks to put off the day of reckoning.[15]

Originally the IRCJ was authorized to 'only lend funds, provide guarantees to financial institutions and to approve businesses after the completion of debt repurchase'. This proved to be a severe limitation to activity. On December 1, 2003 the IRCJ was given ministerial authorization to undertake the following activities:

1. Lend to businesses approved for assistance and provide guarantees to financial institutions and others that lend to approved businesses during the period between deciding to provide assistance and deciding to purchase debt.
2. Arrange financial support for businesses under assistance.

These additional provisions in effect enabled the IRCJ to make loans and guarantees as the process of reconstruction of the finances of the firms was progressing rather than wait until plans had been finalized. This change was important in providing more flexibility to the IRCJ process.

In effect from December 2003 the process became:

1. The failing company and its main creditor apply to the IRCJ for assistance.
2. The IRCJ evaluates the company's losses and potential for sound restructuring and future profits before approving assistance.
3. The IRCJ agrees to purchase the debt, buying up to 95 percent of the original stock.
4. The IRCJ transfers the debt to other banks who then deal with requests for repayment by the company's creditors.
5. Solvent companies bid to take over the company and manage its restructuring.
6. The IRCJ sells the equity (the IRCJ could choose to retain some shares) to the approved bidders and exits operations.

The IRCJ took temporary custody of failing firms, found banks that would purchase the debts and, finally, chose firms that would buy the existing shares and manage the company. The role was therefore one of being catalyst and facilitator rather than executive.

The sectors of the firms being assisted by the IRCJ represented construction and transportation (administered by MLIT) and manufacturing, retailing and hotels (administered by METI). The choice of firms ostensibly was based on whether the companies were salvageable and whether they were willing to adhere to restructuring strategies laid out by the IRCJ and by the sponsoring firms who were taking on the debt. Realistically, the IRCJ's choice of firms was linked to assisting banks that had a particular need of assistance with non-performing loans.

Daiei Inc.: delaying the inevitable

A major firm chosen in 2004 was Daiei Inc. The Kobe Earthquake in 1995 had impacted severely on Daiei's finances with a net loss of ¥50.7 billion. The company's finances continued to falter during the remainder of the decade. Daiei's declining sales of over a decade were only partly due to the slowdown in consumer spending and over-diversification. It was also competing for supermarket dominance with Ito-Yokado (Seven Eleven) and Aegon. Prior to the earthquake, Daiei had been experiencing a bumpy ride. Although profits had risen to over ¥3 trillion, its net income was said to have plummeted from ¥10 billion in 1992 to ¥5.4 billion in 1994. Nevertheless, Isao Nakauchi was determined to keep control of his company.

In 1997, the government lifted the formal ban, initiated in 1947 by SCAP, on the formation of holding companies. Also, cross-shareholdings in the *keiretsu* were again sanctioned. The reinstatement of holding companies permitted Nakauchi to create Daiei Holdings K.K. for Daiei's non-retail businesses. Although Nakauchi postponed further expansion operations, Daiei's sales and net income continued to fall because consumer spending domestically was adversely affected by the Asian financial crisis that same year. When the Asian crisis continued into 1998, Tadasu Toba, Daiei vice-president, assumed the presidency and began selling real estate assets and unprofitable stores. In August 1998 Daiei announced plans to divest itself of the Ala Moana Shopping Center in Honolulu, Hawaii as well as other assets in an effort to reduce interest-bearing debts that were estimated at ¥2 trillion and to restructure the company.

Nakauchi, in denial about Daiei's rapidly declining fortunes, refused to relinquish Daiei's assets and was constantly at odds with Toba. By February 1999 fifteen Daiei companies had fallen into debt. Although originally Daiei had predicted a ¥500 million net profit for the fiscal year, in August it forecast a ¥9.8 billion loss. On September 1, it announced its intentions to sell the major portion of its shares in the real estate-information provider Recruit Co. A number of companies expressed a keen interest, including Kadokawa, Toshiba, Sumitomo Trading Company, CSK, Mitsui Heavy Industries, Toyota, KDD and Softbank but the sale was hampered by commercial legalities. Daiei's plans were formalized on January 21, 2000 with the announcement that 25 percent of the shares would be sold back to Recruit firms for ¥100 billion.

In 1999, Daiei also agreed to sell Ala Moana Center to General Growth Properties for $810 million. Despite efforts to stem losses Daiei's fortunes continued to decline. In October 2000 Toba admitted that he had purchased 100,000 shares of Daiei OMC Inc., Daiei's credit-card firm, for ¥21 million in May 1999 prior to the company's announce-ment the following August that it would write down its non-bank financing affiliate. The proposed disposal of bad loans boosted OCM's share prices and Toba realized a ¥16 million profit when he sold his shares in December 1999. Vice-President Kazuo Kawa, who was also involved in the insider trading scandal, was demoted to a Daiei board member.

The tell-tale sign that Daiei's financial woes were being monitored by the state was the announcement in October that Nakauchi was retiring as chairman and that on January 1, 2000 a former METI official, Jiro Amagai, would replace him. Amagai resigned as the head of the Equity Bureau of the National Personnel Authority (NPA) to assume the post. Ironically, when Amagai joined MITI in 1968 he was in charge of the implementation of the Large-Scale Retail Stores Law. Kunio Takagi, who had joined Daiei in 1966 and who was seconded to Recruit in 1992 to serve as executive director, took over the post as president. Takagi and Amagi announced a massive three-year restructuring plan that called for thirty-two store closures and the lay-off of 4,000 staff.

In November 2000 Daiei announced the losses for the year at ¥240 billion and predicted an additional net loss of ¥130 billion. Daiei asked Tokai Bank, Sanwa Bank, Sumitomo Bank and Fuji Bank to buy ¥120 billion in new Daiei shares in order to help Daiei deal with ¥310 billion in losses ($9 billion). The trade-off was that officers from the banks would replace some of Daiei's existing directors to aid in the restructuring. On February 1, 2001, Marubeni Corp. agreed to pur-chase 5 percent of Daiei shares and an additional 10 percent of shares in Maretsu Inc., a supermarket chain that is a Daiei affiliate, bringing Marubeni's stake in Maretsu to 20 percent. Daiei previously owned 14.5 percent of Maruetsu.

Despite restructuring efforts Daiei's debts did not disappear. On March 20, 2002, Daiei asked the government for aid under the industrial revi-talization law. Tax breaks would amount to ¥600 million. The firm also applied to METI for grant subsidies to the parent company. Daiei asked its three main lenders, UFJ Bank, Sumitomo Mitsui Banking Corp. and Fuji Bank, for ¥520 billion in loans. The banks had no choice but to acquiesce because Daiei's potential default on loans could portend losses of ¥2 trillion. In other words, the banks were deeply indebted as well. The loans granted amounted to ¥400 billion and on April 27, METI granted Daiei preferential treatment so that the firm and its 109 companies could receive tax breaks and be eligible for loans at lower interest rates from the DBJ. In October 2002 the DBJ announced that it would invest ¥10 billion in Daiei.

Meanwhile Daiei continued to pare down its operation by selling off Hub, its English pub chain subsidiary, in December for ¥4 billion. In January 2003 it sold four of its hotels to Goldman Sachs Group Inc. for ¥45.4 billion. It also had to divest itself of Lawsons Inc., Japan's second-largest convenience store chain and its Japan franchises of Wendy's and Big Boy restaurants after failing to raise funds through the initiation of an IPO.

Nevertheless, despite the aid from Marubeni, and bail-outs from its banks and from the government, the group continued to be plagued with interest-bearing debt and net losses. On October 18, 2003 the group announced that net profits plummeted 98.4 per cent to ¥2.3 billion during the first half of 2003. The company, together with the UFJ Bank (to which Daiei owed ¥400 billion), Mizuho and Sumitomo Mitsui began to pressure Daiei to seek assistance from the IRCJ but Daiei refused and tried to raise capital from private sources. By wiping off Daiei's loans from its books UFJ would be able to dispose of NPL by 50 percent.

The IRCJ to the rescue

Daiei's three main lenders approached the IRCJ for help in August 2004 but Daiei, concerned that the IRCJ would pressure it to sell off its baseball club, the Hawks, to corporations proposed by the IRCJ, would not cooperate and tried to raise funds from the private sector. The IRCJ attempted to assess Daiei's assets in September but Daiei management, again, was uncooperative. Finally Daiei's management agreed to join its main lenders and formally applied to the IRCJ for assistance in October 2004. On October 22, Takagi resigned, publicly taking responsibility for the failure of the restructuring plan.

To the IRCJ's dismay, Daiei gained the acceptance from Colony Capital to sell the Hawks to Softbank in December 2004 (coincidently, Ripplewood was a partner in Softbank). Daiei had managed to attract a foreign investor, when it reached an agreement with Colony Capital, an American investment fund, to sell its Fukuoka Dome stadium that stood next to its Sea Hawk Hotel and Resort. As part of the deal, completed in April 2005, Capital took over ¥60.5 billion of Daiei's ¥110 billion debt in the Fukuoka business.[16]

The expansion into other businesses that deviated from their core competence, as well as growing competition, was the primary reason why the majority of companies in the IRCJ roster had overextended themselves. The IRCJ's business restructuring plan for its ailing companies was to attempt the resuscitation of the companies' core competencies. The business plan for Daiei called for the termination of the unprofitable and money-losing operations such as in commercial real estate. The Daiei Group had significant unrealized losses resulting from its previous policy of buying land used to expand its network and other strategies such as developing operations nationwide without any consideration of efficiency, diversifying outside of retailing with only limited success, and placing undue reliance on low pricing strategy.

After five months of delays, on December 28, 2004 the IRCJ formally approved the 'application for assistance' that had been made in June from the Daiei Group companies and its main lenders, UFJ Bank Ltd., Mizuho Corporate Bank Ltd. and Sumitomo Mitsui Banking Corporation. The retailer's debts totaled ¥1 trillion. The retailer's tumultuous and somewhat reluctant journey to the IRCJ was widely covered by the media.

The corporate information regarding Daiei is as follows:

1. Daiei was established in 1957 as Daiei Inc.
2. The company's headquarters is located in Kobe City, Hyogo.
3. The capital assets as of August 31, 2004 totaled ¥119,510,560.
4. Daiei's debt was assessed at ¥1 trillion, 20 billion, 562 million.
5. The Daiei Group of 109 firms is divided among twelve main companies. The majority are engaged in retailing (182 general merchandise stores, 63 supermarkets, and 18 discount stores in 38 regions in Japan). Several companies engage in commercial real estate leasing and finance.
6. As of August 2004 the parent company employed 10,091 full-time staff.

The 'rationale' given by the IRCJ for accepting Daiei for revitalization was that its core retail operations, selling everyday essentials, could be revitalized. The scale and profitability of its food business placed it in Japan's leading group of operators, and its drug store-related operations enjoyed similar scale. The Minister of Economy and Industry also commented in the same report that he hoped that the IRCJ in its business restructuring plan for Daiei would take into consideration that the Daiei Group was a large employer throughout Japan and that the IRCJ 'gives full consideration to the impact on local economies, employees and vendors, while endeavoring to make effective use of existing outlets'.

The IRCJ requested that the major creditors forgive ¥405 billion in debts. ¥192 billion in preferred shares or 82.8 percent that were held by the three main lenders would be canceled.

The IRCJ would invest ¥50 billion in Daiei (¥40 billion would be a 'debt-equity-swap' and ¥10 billion would be in cash) and a sponsor would invest ¥60 billion. The two organizations would each acquire one-third of the controlling rights of Daiei and subsequently cooperate in its management. The IRCJ would hold the remaining one-third of the voting rights. Applications from companies seeking to sponsor Daiei ('debt repurchase') had to be received between December 28, 2004 and February 28, 2005.

Daiei's directors would resign by the end of March 2005 and would 'forgo any retirement bonuses'.

The bidding game: keeping it in the family

Marubeni, the major stock holder in Daiei's supermarket operations, was reportedly unhappy when the IRCJ stepped in because companies other than Marubeni might be chosen as the sponsor and the trading company would lose control of its investment. Aeon, which joined with Kyocera to bid for Daiei, had experienced success in rehabilitating companies. Kiacon entered a bid with Itochu Corp. and Orix Corp. Wal-Mart, the world's largest retailer, which owned 37 percent of Seiyu Inc., a competitive bidder, was committed to taking full ownership of Daiei US.

But Wal-Mart was not included on the shortlist. Marubeni, together with Aeon, Japan's leading retailer, and Kiacon were chosen as the three main candidates. The safest choice was the firms that had the closest ties to Daiei. Marubeni and its bidding partner Advantage Partners Inc., an investment firm, who had developed products with Daiei in the past and was experienced in running supermarkets, were chosen by the IRCJ as sponsors on March 7, 2005. Advantage Partners also owned 17 percent of Maruetsu Corp., a grocery chain affiliated with Daiei.

Although MOF and UFJ agreed with IRCJ's decision, METI which was directly involved in Daiei's revitalization was vehemently opposed to Advantages Partners' participation. Nevertheless, pressure from the prime minister's office ultimately pushed through the deal. The opinion among retailers and distributors was that METI wanted to preserve its *amakudari* posts. METI was able to save face because the IRCJ accepted Marubeni's initial proposals that Daiei would be revitalized relatively independently of Advantage Partners.

Marubeni intended to invest ¥62 billion in Daiei and in return gain 34.3 percent of Daiei's voting rights shares. The IRCJ held another 33 percent while Daiei shareholders held the remaining voting rights.

On March 30, 2005, Daiei shareholders, the value of their shares considerably diluted, voted in favor of the IRCJ reconstruction plan. Marubeni planned to concentrate restructuring efforts on Daiei's grocery business. In April 2005 Marubeni recruited Yasuyuki Higuchi from outside the corporation to replace him. Higuchi resigned as president of Hewlett-Packard Japan on May 31 to assume the post. Marubeni also named Fumiko Hayashi, the former president of BMW Tokyo Corp. as chairwoman and CEO. The new management faced monumental problems in their quest to salvage Daiei. On April 15, 2005, the same day that Marubeni announced the hiring of Higuchi and Hayashi, Daiei Group posted a net loss of ¥511.2 billion.

Both Higuchi's and Hayashi's days were numbered because they were regarded as outsiders who were neither from Daiei nor from Marubeni and not in a position to implement Daiei's restructuring. Higuchi stepped down as president eight months after assuming the position. Toru Nishimi, Marubeni's senior vice-president took over as president of Daiei, giving Marubeni more control over Daiei operations. The trading house, realizing that Daiei would be an albatross, also sought assistance from Aeon Co. Ltd. in 2006. Japan's top retailer purchased 20 percent of Daiei shares from Marubeni and in 2013 purchased the remaining 29 percent of Marubeni's shares for a reported $105.15 million.

Kanebo Ltd.: delisted from the TSE

Kanebo's upper management anticipated stable growth during the 1990s but the end of the bubble economy and the ensuing recession impeded Kanebo's expansion plans and subsequently eroded profit margins. In FY 1992 although the sales in cosmetics and toiletries increased, Kanebo experienced a decline in profits in its other divisions. In FY 1994 it reported losses in all divisions and Kanebo was forced to reduce wool production by 30 percent and nylon and polyester filament by 20 percent. Over a period of three years, Kanebo gradually laid off 2,000 staff and limited hiring to reduce overheads. 1995 was not a good year for Kanebo due to the appreciated yen which reduced the volume of exports, and also the Kobe Earthquake which impacted negatively on domestic spending.

Kanebo struggled to restructure operations and cut costs by terminating its relationship with the National Starch and Chemical Company in 1994 and abandoning its polyester business and establishing a new subsidiary to produce resins in the same plant. Kanebo moved production facilities from Japan to countries with cheaper workforces. The company acquired full control of Kanebo Cosmetics Europe in 1998 but sold its pharmaceutical R&D operations.

Kanebo signed a licensing agreement with the French fashion house Jean Lanvin after Christian Dior terminated its licensing agreement to produce and distribute women's ready-to wear apparel in Japanese department stores. However, to compete with its rival Shiseido, Kanebo Cosmetics Division was still expanding its cosmetics markets with large capital investment, entering the United States for the first time in 2000 to sell new lines of expensive skin-care products in Bergdorf Goodman in New York. The new lines were also introduced to the European market.

The IRCJ to the rescue again

In 2004 when Kanebo was saddled with debts of $6 billion, Kao, Japan's leading manufacturer of toiletries and household and industrial cleaners, offered to take over the cosmetics division for $4.9 billion. Kanebo refused the offer and asked creditors to forgive $1.2 billion in loans. When the banks refused, the conglomerate sought the help of the IRCJ, which purchased its core cosmetic division for $3.2 billion.

A primary mission of the IRCJ was to encourage more transparency in auditing practices. But the IRCJ's intention to address issues of financial analyses and accounting practices did not necessarily relate to the firms that were selected to sponsor the restructuring of failing firms. Realistically, the IRCJ's choice of firms was linked to assisting the banks that were experiencing difficulty recovering loans from zombie companies.

Apparently, the IRCJ did not recognize the need to investigate Kao's corporate finances prior to making the decision to choose the company to restructure Kanebo. The efforts by Kao to restructure Kanebo were hampered by the accumulation of further debt and consequently, Kao was burdened with more debt. Standard & Poor's placed the company on a negative Credit Watch in February 2004 after the company had announced its decision to purchase Kanebo. The company had been in the black for seven years prior to the acquisition but in December 2005 Standard & Poor's again issued a Credit Watch report that Kao's debt level had increased due to the refinancing of Kanebo's debt.

Cooking the books

Kanebo's decision was not entirely in its best interests or in the best interests of Price Waterhouse Coopers, Kanebo's auditors. In May 2005, the IRCJ charged Kanebo with accounting fraud. Evidently, Kanebo had a negative net worth for at least the previous nine years, but it had disguised its financial troubles by altering its books. Furthermore, Price Waterhouse Coopers Aoyama, Kanebo's auditors, had cooperated in the effort. On June 13, 2005, the Tokyo Stock Exchange (TSE) delisted Kanebo, whose stocks had been publicly traded for 114 years. PWC Aoyama was sanctioned and suspended from auditing for two months.

The investigation into the auditing fraud also confirmed the inter-personal network between METI and the IRCJ. In June, a high-ranking METI official and the former head of METI's policy planning office admitted that in 2004 he withdrew $270,000 from the bank accounts where funds for the IRCJ research projects were deposited. He topped up those funds with his personal funds to purchase Kanebo shares in 2004. However, he had since returned the money plus $24,000. METI Vice-Minister Hideji Sugiyama denied that there was insider trading and asserted that the official did not have access to special information. Although the official resigned, he was not arrested.

The IRCJ disbanded in May 2007, regarding its mission as successfully completed.

The end of Mercian Inc.: follow the leaders

On November 26, 2010 Mercian Inc. was delisted from the TSE for the false reporting of net worth. As an affiliate of a multinational corporation Mercian was not in the same league as Kanebo. Nevertheless, it is an excellent example of how the BOJ's post-Plaza Accord monetary policy, the MOF's sloppy regulation of financial institutions, along with the institutions' willingness to provide questionable loans culminated in a frenzy of over-expansion and over-diversification of core businesses.

Mercian's demise also represents the mistaken consensus among business leaders in the 1980s that Japanese business model was the secret to success.

In 2000 Yoshihiko Miyauchi and Shunsuke Inamori, the chairman of Ajinomoto Corporation, had taken posts as board directors. In the same year Glenfiddich, dissatisfied with sales, transferred the third-party arrangement to Suntory.

The 2001 Annual Report portended Mercian's rocky conditions and that the company was under financial duress:

> the stagnant economy hurt sales of wine to restaurants, market recovery remained slow, and there was insufficient inventory

consolidation in the market. Consequently, sales fell, and it was primarily low-priced products for individual users that saw increased sales this fiscal year.

The sales of *shochu* increased from 2000, continuing to be a Mercian best seller. The Château Mercian series – Mercian's wine – again received high praise in international competition, an example of Mercian's technical merit in achieving a high standard of quality.

Previously it was stated that domestic wines in Japan are usually 90 percent imported reconstituted grape juice. Mercian's domestic wines were considered inferior to Suntory's and despite Suzuki's forecast, the *shochu* market had become very competitive. Suntory was leading market share.

Regardless, in the 2002 Annual Report Suzuki continued to put a positive spin on Mercian's conditions by touting Mercian's management overhaul and the change to Japan's new corporate accounting standards:

We achieved the above [reduction of interest-bearing debt] ... despite a harsh operating environment, including persistent deflationary conditions in the domestic economy and the global economic slow-down, which depressed exports. These successes were made possible by the dedication and teamwork of our management and employees striving toward common goals.

Again, Mercian was focusing on wine and its own Château Mercian and other lower priced wine produced at its domestic facility. But *shochu* continued to be its best-seller.

Suzuki's message to stockholders in the FY 2003 and 2004 Annual Reports focused on the success of Mercian's restructuring and its core domestic liquor business. He pledged to improve operations in the feedstuffs business.

In March 2002 the firm of Deloitte Touche Tohmatsu was hired as independent auditors for FY 2001, 2002, 2003 and 2004. The auditors reported that they considered Mercian's consolidated statements to be accurate. Nevertheless, the final pages in these reports carry a 'Cautionary Remark Regarding Forward-Looking Statements':

Statements made in this document with respects to Mercian's plans, strategies, expectations about the future, and other statements except for historical statements are forward-looking statements. These forward-looking statements are subject to uncertainties that could cause actual results to differ materially from such statements. These uncertainties include, but are not limited to, general economic conditions, demand for and price of Mercian products, Mercian's ability to continue to develop and market advanced products and currency exchange rates.

The 2004 report displayed color photographs of skin-care products Mercian was producing from grape extract labeled 'Visage'. But the exit of Miyauchi as a director could suggest an escape from a burning building. Takei Shiina, who had been the vice-president and chairman of IBM Japan Ltd., had become a director after retiring from IBM.

It should be noted that Mercian's Annual Reports in English do not include the list of primary stockholders which is included in the Japanese version. The lack of continuity in the list of primary shareholders listed in the Japanese version was ominous.[17]

Fire sale

The primary stockholders in 1999 were the financial institutions that provided loans to Mercian. The 1999 Annual Shareholders Report in Japanese shows that there were 17,012 stockholders and that there were ten main stockholders: Ajinomoto with 11.1 percent equity, Daiichi Life Insurance Company owned 5.5 percent, Daiichi Kangyo Bank (Mercian's corporate bank) and Mitsubishi Trust with 4.7 percent each, Yasuda Life Insurance and Tokyo Mitsubishi Bank with 3.8 percent, Fuji Bank owned 3.4 percent, and Sumitomo Maritime and Fire Insurance Co. Ltd. and Greater Tokyo Marine and Fire Insurance Co. Ltd. owned 2.3 and 2 percent respectively.

The major stockholders remained the same in 2000 but due to the merger of Daiichi Kangyo, Fuji Bank and the IBJ, the shares were transferred to Mizuho. Ajinomoto had owned 11.1 percent of its affiliate's shares until 2002 when the percentage of shares increased to 11.6 percent as indicated in the 2003 Annual Report. Also, Nihon Master Trust, a bank that was established in 2000, became a new shareholder with 12.5 percent. Additionally, the list of key shareholders had changed from the previous year with other financial institutions holding smaller percentages of equity.

In 2002, Ai Oi Nissei, an Asset Administration Services took equity and in 2003 Ajinomoto's shares increased to 11.6 percent. Nihon Master Trust came on board, purchasing 12.5 percent of shares.

Mercian's annual report for 2005 is not available.

In 2006, Kirin Holdings, Japan's top beverage producer, announced that it had purchased a 50.1 percent stake in Mercian to diversify assets outside of beer brewing.

Printed on the first page of Mercian's Annual Report for FY 2009 is a 'Note Regarding Revision of Financial Statements':

> In 2010, an internal investigation conducted by Mercian revealed major deficiencies in internal controls pertaining to Companywide management processes, financial accounts settlement and reporting processes, and business processes in the Fish Feedstuffs Division. As a consequence of this investigation, Mercian was obliged to revise its consolidated financial statements for fiscal 2009 and the preceding four fiscal years and to have the revised statements audited by its independent auditor, Deloitte Touche Tohmatsu.

Hiroshi Ueki, the president and CEO, who was also the president and CEO of Kirin Holdings, stated that in July 2007 Mercian had become a member of the Kirin Group of companies and that one of his primary responsibilities was to:

> reinforce Mercian's corporate structure in terms of management, stimulating horizontal and vertical communication and promoting management that mirrors the perspectives of our customers. To these ends, we have implemented a broad range of measures designed to fortify our operating foundation ...
>
> Despite the positive impact of a value-based sales approach and efforts to optimize inventory and reduce sales, general and administrative costs in the wine business, and increased sales in the Pharmaceuticals and Chemical segment, the operating loss swelled to ¥1,579 million, from ¥1,303 million (¥93.50 = $1). This reflected a persistent downward trend in sales in other businesses, notably alcoholic drinks and feedstuffs segment and the worsening impact of rising prices for raw materials used in fish feed. Mercian's net loss also worsened to ¥2,117 million, from ¥1,871 million ... This was due to the application of a new accounting standard of inventories, as a result of which the differences between inventories at the beginning and the end of the fiscal year (¥795 million) was accounted for as a loss on write-down of inventories and included in extraordinary losses.[18]

The TSE, which had been watching the company for a possible delisting, took action and delisted Mercian Inc. On the same day that

Mercian was delisted, Kirin Holdings announced that it would purchase Mercian Inc.'s remaining shares for $132 million in order to gain tighter control over the company, which had confirmed in May that it had inflated profits over losses for several years, booking a loss of ¥6.5 billion (¥87.10 = $1). Kirin was forced to revise down its forecast for annual net profits by 27 percent, partly to accommodate the loss. Kirin's shares dropped 1.1 percent and the Nikkei 225 average fell 1.1 percent. Ajinomoto took over Calpis in the 2010 deal with Kirin.

At a press conference Ueki told reporters that Mercian would decide whether to shut down the fish-feed division. He included that he would take a 50 percent salary cut for three months to take responsibility for the false transactions and that five executives and an auditor would have their pay reduced. In 1999, Mercian employed 2,000 staff. In 2014, Mercian was employing 500 staff.

Mr. Suzuki, who died in 2010, was a man with a mission but, like many CEOs in Japanese companies, he was remote from Mercian's daily operations. Mr. Suzuki was the Chairman of the Corporate Governance Committee of the Corporate Governance Forum of Japan. He also had served as vice-chairman of the Japan Federation of Employers.

Conclusion: The Third Lost Decade?

Abe's brew of reckless monetary policies combined with a revved-up version of tired fiscal policies mixed with a good dose of neo-nationalism may prove disastrous. *Why Japan Can't Reform* detailed the brief administrations of Prime Ministers Abe, Fukuda and Aso (2006–9) in their attempts to drag Japan's floundering economy out of deflation, to lower public debt and to initiate institutional reforms. However, their administrations were plagued by political scandals and factional bickering and initiatives for structural reforms were postponed.

Economic statistics up to July 2008 lent to the evaluation of continued economic deterioration at the regional level. The book predicted that the economy would stay in mild recession and that regional development would stagnate due to SME bankruptcies with regional banks burdened with defaults as well as a load of non-performing loans.

Fiscal policies were also detailed in order to emphasize that government policies mimicked the policies that were implemented in the 1990s. There was the state recapitalization of banks, fiscal stimulus packages that poured state funds into public works projects, long-term, low-interest rate loans and credit guarantees to small businesses, and so forth. But the policies did little more than postpone tackling the root problems in the economy and prepare Japan for dealing with domestic crises such as the recent nuclear event and the impact on its export-driven economy by the current economic slowdown.

Continuing mercantile policies resulted in an unremitting dependency on consumer economies, historically the US. Protectionist policies resulted in the highest current account balance and one of the lowest rates of FDI among the OECD countries (2 percent of the annual GDP). Japan had a massive public debt that was recorded in mid-2008 as 190 percent of the annual GDP (the highest among the member nations in the OECD).

Innovative policies to revive small businesses and regenerate beleaguered prefectures were likely to be dismissed in favor of past policies. The release of a $51 billion stimulus package in October 2008, the sixteenth since 1993, 'topped up' the $18 billion stimulus package released in September by former Prime Minister Fukuda. However, it had minimal effect on growth and served only to guarantee loans and credits to SMEs, subsidies to businesses affected by rising energy and commodities costs, medical benefits to the elderly, large tax breaks to mortgage holders, lower road tolls, etc. Domestic consumption, which accounted for 60 percent of the GDP, lagged as consumers conserved. The IMF and the OECD continued to pressure the government to raise consumption tax to 10 percent and to initiate structural reforms. The forecast stated in the book:

> Even if the Democratic Party of Japan (DPJ) were to be swept into the majority in both Houses by a rising tide of discontent among voters and even if structural reforms are initiated, the effort would be akin to plugging holes in a dyke to stem the flood of problems that are a consequence of years of reliance on an antiquated system and pork-barrel policies.[1]

The Japanese are resigned to mercantile policies in order to survive, but they also feel vulnerable because of their dependence on the United States and China. The dependence on these two economic powers will intensify Japan's insecurity since its economy is extremely fragile. Furthermore, Japan's weakened economic environment together with its adherence to mercantile policies will determine how Japan reacts to the demands of other trading partners to open markets to imports, to foreign business ventures and to FDI.[2]

The Japan system: indestructible but destructive

The Introduction in *Japan's Nuclear Crisis* (2012) states:

> The challenges that the Japanese were facing prior to the triple disaster were numerous. External pressures on the economy were also increasing. Despite fiscal policies that focused on the continuous release of stimulus packages and supplementary budgets, resulting in a burgeoning public debt and despite the Bank of Japan's soft

monetary policies as well as the efforts by successive administrations to implement structural reforms of the economy, Japan was stuck in deflation. Nevertheless, it was still widely believed that the Japanese government would be able to resolve the problems that had been inhibiting stable economic growth and excavate Japan out of fifteen years of deflation. But even if some reforms are implemented it may be too late to bring Japan's economy back on track. The Japanese political society is conservative and risk-averse and reforms may be put aside in favor of the familiar status quo.[3]

The chapter reviewed the problems that plagued Japan's economy since 2000 and the issues that continued to frustrate the implementation of fiscal and monetary policies since the 1990s. Japan's pre-nuclear crisis' micro and macro economy were also reviewed in order to emphasize the reasons for the precariousness of Japan's economy and to forecast that deflation would continue, validating the predictions made in the previous books and, thus, enabling a reasonable assessment by readers regarding the pace of Japan's post-March 11, 2011 economic recovery.

Since there has been no effort by government to implement structural reforms, since public debt is continuing to spiral (currently 243 percent of GDP), and since Abenomics may serve to spur inflation rather than economic growth, some of the same subtitles apply.

Sovereign debt: out of sight – out of mind

On June 23, 1997 the late Prime Minister Ryutaro Hashimoto gave an address at Columbia University at a luncheon sponsored by the Foreign Policy Association and Columbia's Department of International Relations. 'Japan-US Relations: A Partnership for the Twenty First Century', which was delivered in Japanese, regarded Japan's economy and planned reforms of the financial sector. The speech was simultaneously translated into English. When a trader from Wall Street questioned Hashimoto about what would happen if Japan's economy began to deteriorate rapidly, Hashimoto jokingly replied that Japan would be pressured to sell some of its US securities. Evidently the translation implied that Hashimoto was serious. That afternoon, the DOW plummeted forty points and Hashimoto was reprimanded by the Japanese press.

In 1997 Japan was the world's second largest economy and the largest net creditor. Although there had been a barrage of fiscal stimulus packages and the banks were still burdened with non-performing loans, public debt was still manageable. The BOJ had yet to lower interest rates to almost zero. In 2014 Japan's sovereign debt of 243 percent of GDP is the highest ratio compared to Greece (179 percent) and to the US (101 percent).

Fiscal rebalancing is not being given serious consideration as Abe's fiscal policies continue to mirror policies initiated during the last two decades with huge stimulus packages and secondary budgets to support infrastructure projects, benefiting the larger construction companies. So far, Abenomics, which promises to expand growth, has seen the release of an enormous QE package equal to one-third of the Japan's GDP which is creating more liquidity, putting downward pressure on the yen, raising equity prices and distorting the domestic economy. In December 2013, reporting that Japan's money supply had reached $1.83 trillion, just short of the $200 trillion targeted, the BOJ purchased additional assets while the government launched a $910 billion package to compensate for the April 2014 rise in the consumption tax from 3 percent to 8 percent. The metropolitan banks announced in May that they were raising mortgage interest rates and, even though BOJ Governor Haruhiko Kuroda is not concerned about a 2 percent rise in long-term bond interest rates, credit rating companies are warning that regional banks do not have sufficient assets to withstand a 2 percent rise. The regional banks are now steering away from JGB and purchasing foreign government securities for their portfolios.

Abe's growth strategies lack the 'third arrow' of structural reform and the glow of Abenomics is fading. Former BOJ Governor Masaaki Shirakawa who retired from office in April 2012, two months before Kuroda assumed office as governor, was opposed to further purchases of JGB but he promoted BOJ purchases of riskier assets such as exchange traded funds, real estate investment trusts (REIT) and long-term JGB. Nevertheless, Shirakawa expressed concerns in May 2011 that Japan would lose market confidence if the government failed to deal with its finances. He also worried that the weakening of confidence in private sector financial firms, which are heavily invested in JGB, would lead to higher borrowing costs. The economy would suffer, tax revenue would fall and the government would have difficulty paying off its debt. The following July 2011, the BOJ was not prepared to guarantee more JGB to fund growth because it would undermine the trust in the currency, increase long-term interest rates and pose difficulties selling JGB on the market. However, Abe was determined to install a new governor who was enthusiastic about QE as a means to end deflation and to depreciate the yen.

Shirakawa, an economist, emphasized the limits of an enormous increase in the monetary base particularly within the context of Japan's deflation and other economic problems and that fiscal policies must complement monetary policies. He urged the government to address Japan's slowing growth rate and low productivity as well as the rapid decrease of the working population and to implement structural reforms. Kuroda, who is pro-QE and who wholeheartedly supports Abenomics, set an inflation target of 2 percent within two years, which seemed an overly optimistic prediction. Some of the bonds are so-called *Zaito* bonds, also referred to as FILP bonds or FILP agency bonds (as described in a previous chapter) and issued by designated *Zaito* institutions such as the FSC. However, these bonds are not guaranteed by the government.

On February 18, 2014, a day after the government announced that Japan's GDP growth for the last quarter grew by 1 percent, which was far lower than the 2.8 percent anticipated, the BOJ doubled the size of two funding for lending programs to $68 billion which enabled banks to borrow twice as much at low interest rates. However, so far, the funding for the lending program for businesses at 0.1 percent interest rate has yet to receive an enthusiastic reception from firms which are reticent to invest capital in new installations and equipment because of tepid growth in Japan's primary markets.

Kuroda was beginning to sound like his predecessor in an interview with *The Wall Street Journal* in May 2014. He told managing editor Gerard Baker and correspondent Jacob Schlesinger that Japan's medium-term growth rate was less than 1 percent: 'Unless this growth potential is raised, the end result may be only the 2% inflation target achieved, but real growth is meager.'

In early May, the OECD downgraded its November forecast of Japan's 1.5 percent GDP to 1.2 percent for FY 2014. Although the BOJ's loose monetary policies were helping to raise inflation, Japan's economic recovery would be undermined if wages were not simultaneously raised. The OECD urged Abe to pursue structural reforms and to raise the consumption tax in 2015 from 8 to 10 percent.

In his interview, Kuroda expressed his concern that despite 2 percent inflation, growth would be tepid and urged Abe not to rely on monetary policy alone but to implement structural reforms that coincided with BOJ's policies. He has followed Shirakawa's lead, purchasing riskier assets such as REIT and long-term government bonds.

Nevertheless, economists have argued over the years (as the government debt continues to escalate) that JGB are held domestically by state and retail banks and that, because interest rates are so low, the government can easily service the debt. However, with two decades of the continued release of fiscal stimulus packages and burgeoning welfare costs to support an aging population, Japan's sovereign debt has topped $10.46 trillion, double the size of its economy. According to the MOF, the government will spend 24 percent of the budget or $257 billion and half of the total tax revenue on servicing its debt compared to the US total interest payments at about 10.2 percent of the budget by end of September 2013. The BOJ has estimated that the potential unrealized capital losses to the large banks if matured bond yields climbed one percentage point would be ¥3.2 trillion.

BOJ officials expressed concern in April 2014 that Japan's ten-year JGB yield at 0.615 percent had remained stagnant since March 2013 and failed to reflect the recent rise in the CPI. The stagnation was the result of the BOJ's exceptional JGB purchases which served to support the bond market and keep debt-servicing costs low after its 2 percent inflation target was achieved. At a news conference on April 8, Kuroda told reporters that, although the BOJ was not considering exiting from QE, spare capacity in the economy was 'approaching zero'. His hint that the BOJ might cut asset purchases caused bond interest rates to spike momentarily. The cost of risk is dangerously low as investors are seeking yield rather than security. And as investors seek safer havens, Japan's thirty-year government bonds at 1.67 percent yield seem to some a better bet.

On June 18, 2014 the BOJ announced that at the end of FY 2013 the bank was Japan's biggest debt holder with 20.1 percent of JGB or $1.97 trillion, the highest on record. According to the report, insurance companies held 19.3 percent of JGB, followed by small and medium-size financial institutions with 13 percent, government public bodies with 8.9 percent and households holding only 2.1 percent. In recent months the trade of ten-year bonds remained flat and there were days when two- to five-year bonds went untraded. If this trend continues bond yields could rise from the current 0.49 percent for ten-year bonds to 2 or 3 percent resulting in the MOF struggling to finance the huge sovereign debt.

The BOJ was purchasing 70 percent of JGB monthly as QE continued, effectively transferring interest-risk from the private sector to the bank and bringing the relationship between the BOJ and government much closer. On July 2, 2014, the BOJ announced that Japan's monetary base had increased to a record-breaking ¥233.25 trillion in June.

QE: desperate measures for desperate times

Quantitative Easing (QE) is a policy tool used by central banks to create money through large purchases of assets such as government bonds and corporate bonds in order to increase the money supply (also referred to as 'money stock') in the economy. Economists closely measure money supply at a given time in order to gauge economic conditions. The BOJ's primary purchases have been JGB.

In 2000, the yen–dollar average exchange rate was ¥106 per dollar. QE 1 occurred in March 2001 which served to increase the BOJ's monetary base 60 percent and depreciate the yen against the dollar to ¥122.37. The policy continued until 2006 (¥116.12 per dollar) when the BOJ reversed policy. In 2009 the yen–dollar average exchange rate was ¥99 per dollar, reflecting the impact of the financial crisis.

QE 2 in March 2010 was implemented with purchases of JGB. However, the yen's depreciation was negligible at ¥94.58 per dollar due to the continuing recession. In November 2012 the yen had appreciated to ¥80.80 per dollar. The BOJ's QE 3 in April 2013 put downward pressure on the currency and acted to devalue the yen to the extent that its value fell 10 percent against the dollar during 2013–14.

In 2001, Japan's sovereign debt was 130 percent of the annual GDP, already among the highest of the OECD countries. In 2006 the debt had climbed to 145 percent of GDP. Currently the debt is 243 percent of GDP. If QE continues without the implementation of fiscal policies such as raising taxes and reducing the government debt, QE can be regarded as 'monetizing debt' which is generally believed to be inflationary. Although Abe's enthusiasm for aggressive QE was related to expanding growth and spurring inflation, the cheap yen was posing numerous problems for Abe's economic policies. Although the larger exporters, such as automobile manufacturers, were originally profiting from QE, they have not adjusted overseas prices to remain competitive in international markets. Additionally, Japanese manufacturers, prior to 2011, reacting to a strong currency, moved production outside of Japan and, therefore, there is little room for Japan to increase exports. At the time of writing, imports were exceeding exports. Also, since 2013, stock prices had surged 50 percent from the previous year. The BOJ was concerned whether the surge in the Nikkei would trigger a bubble. Nevertheless, high equity prices would guarantee that the LDP would remain in power for the long-haul.

The Nikkei Asian Review published 'Cheap yen increasingly costly for Japan's economy' on May 9 by Professor Eisuke Sakakibara, who otherwise is known as 'Mr. Yen'. Sakakibara joined MOF in 1965 after receiving a degree in economics at Tokyo University. He received a doctorate in economics from the University of Michigan in 1969. Professor Sakakibara became the director of the Finance Bureau in 1995 before assuming the post of Vice-Minister of Finance for International Affairs.

In his article Professor Sakakibara stated that the government had miscalculated the effectiveness of a weak yen as exports rose only 0.6 percent in volume. He estimated that Japanese overseas manufacturing output would be 37.3 percent of the total output in FY 2013. Sakakibara argued that there have been 'dramatic changes in the structure of manufacturing' (by Japanese companies) and that although a cheaper currency would benefit countries where oil and gas are extremely cheap, a stronger currency benefited Japan which must import most of its raw materials.

Reuters reported in May that Sayuri Shirai, who was a member on the BOJ board, was urging Kuroda not to try to achieve his 2 percent inflation target by 2015 but to continue aggressive monetary stimulus until FY 2016 in order to avoid creating excessive distortions in the economy and to give households and companies time to adapt to price rises. She also warned that household spending would deteriorate unless wages were increased to accommodate the tax increases. Although large companies are increasing wages, smaller and medium-size companies are still reticent to accommodate.

In an interview with Bloomberg on September 19 Kazuma Iwata, former deputy director of the BOJ (2003-8) and currently the president of the Japan Center of Economic Research, expressed concerns that Japan was in danger of a recession because of the weak yen. Iwata told reporters that realistically the yen's value was 90-100 yen per dollar 'reflecting Japan's economic fundamentals' and that 'Abenomics entails the risks of "beggar thyself" consequences and signs are already emerging.' He recommended that the BOJ abandon its inflation target of 2 percent and extend its current policy to five years and abide by it. 'That's the most that monetary policy can do.' Iwata warned that if the consumption tax was not raised to 10 percent investors would lose confidence in the market and avoid purchasing JGB.

Jens Hagendorff is the Martin Currie Professor in Finance and Investment at the University of Edinburgh Business School. Professor Hagendorff's research and publications regard the factors behind bank risk-taking and systemic risk, and bank regulation, especially capital adequacy under Basel. Prior to entering academia, Hagendorff worked at the Financial Stability Department of the Bank of Spain and served as visiting fellow at the Federal Reserve Bank of Atlanta and the Bank of Spain in Madrid. When he was interviewed in June he kindly contributed his insights on the use of QE policy.

Professor Hagendorff defined Quantitative Easing as the purchase of assets with electronic money created for that purpose:

> The central banks in many countries do not monetize it but purchase assets on the secondary market. The governments or corporations issue bonds and the central banks collect the funds to finance the government debt. The banks swap the hard assets with cash and there's a big 'liquidity preference' which is what economists like to call it in times of crisis. People prefer cash to cash-like assets such as government bonds or high-grade bonds. It is a strong force in creating a large monetary aggregate (big money supply). When bank lending goes down, as it has almost everywhere in the world during the last few years, QE is partly making up for it, but only partly.

Hagendorff spoke about the positive and the negative effects of QE:

> There comes a point when standard monetary instruments have no traction. Interest rates cannot be lowered further. In Europe the ECB cannot do much to the extent of monetary instruments but they can use QE. The larger monetary aggregates have really fallen off a cliff in the last few years. People are worried that QE will cause inflation. But the money supply now is much lower than in 2007 simply because bank lending is a key component of money supply. They can create a lot of money at a push of a button by guaranteeing loans. This isn't happening at the moment and there is a big drop in money supply. QE partially takes care of that but it has to be short-term. We don't want it to be too long. That's the downside.
>
> We must be careful what we do when those losses occur. The public does not pay attention to QE policy when it is implemented but the public will care when double-digit billion dollar losses pile up. To hide the losses (which might be what some central banks do) could be to simply wipe out the bonds. This is not good because it blurs the line between fiscal and monetary policy and financing the government which QE shouldn't be about. There is a risk that governments try to hide the losses and cross the line of what central banks shouldn't really be doing, which is monetizing government debt. QE policy should only finance the private sector that needs liquidity but mainly funding for bank loans. However, QE can create new asset bubbles.

Hagendorff's assessment of Japan's sovereign debt and the BOJ's QE policy was that if domestic households had high savings rates and purchased government bonds, the debt would be sustainable for a long time. On the other hand, QE becomes expensive in the long run:

> The point about QE is that when the bonds are sold the price will fall and central banks make huge losses. People believe in an independent central bank and when politicians tell them that they have made $30bn in losses people's beliefs are shattered, which concerns me. At the moment I don't see what else the BOJ can do. The ECB has yet to engage in substantial QE on a scale similar to that of the Bank of England or the FED. If the lack of meaningful QE were to continue, this would hurt southern European countries especially. The reason for the lack of QE is back-room politics. The ECB does not want to explain in the future to Germany why they are losing money on bond purchases.

How long would Hagendorff engage in QE if he was a central banker?

> It depends upon the size of the monetary aggregate. Basic bank lending matters a lot. Now it is fashionable to go by unemployment figures. I think that it is important to keep people's expectations low because there is the risk that once expectations are lost they are lost for a long time. The BoE and the Fed like to talk a lot about unemployment as being important, but if you create inflation for too long, [people's expectation of inflation] will change. The decades of work by the central banks will be lost because the public won't trust them any longer.

Hagendorff agreed with Shirakawa and Kuroda:

> QE and monetary policy can only achieve so much and needs to go hand-in-hand with structural reforms. I do not know much about Japan's labor market but Japan is moving towards a demographic catastrophe. Since the working population is decreasing productivity must increase to compensate. Kuroda can do very little without structural reforms but at least QE is better than nothing. But it will not perform miracles.

What about consistently low interest rates?

> Low interest rates must be implemented even for a long time but bubbles of some kind are created like the housing bubble in the UK

currently. If there were high interest rates now, economic conditions would be much worse. In a way, the UK has similar problems to Spain which has a very indebted private sector and it helps a lot to make the situation more bearable.

When asked if he considered central banks to be independent of government he replied that in most countries they were but added a caveat:

Bankers must watch the political situation. Quite a few people in the Fed were very concerned during the last election. One of the conservative political candidates was launching a campaign to abolish the Fed which coincided with the revelation that the Fed had loaned huge amounts of money to foreign banks in dollars where there were dollar shortages. It was thought at one point that the amount equaled a quarter of the US GDP. The Fed will make good money in the end because the banks pay nice interest rates on these amounts.

But the central banks have to maintain legitimacy. In the US I think that a law is required to repeal independence. The German Bundesbank is similar because it would take a simple bill in Parliament to revoke independence. The only central bank I am aware of is the ECB whose independence is based on a treaty. A country can leave the euro but it cannot repeal the independence of the ECB. Legitimacy cannot be stretched too much, otherwise, there are concerns.

If Hagendorff managed a fixed-interest pension fund would he invest in JGB?

Not government bonds because the yields are so low but I like Japanese corporations because they are quite cheap given the fundamentals.[4]

According to a report also issued in June 2014 by the Official Monetary and Financial Institution Forum (OMFIF), besides public pension funds like the GPIF central banks, including European ones, are also among the public entities which have been diversifying into private equities in order to counteract the loss of reserves due to low interest rates. The OMFIF calculated that central banks have lost $200–250 billion in interest income as a consequence of the fall in bond yields. Whether or not public sector investment in private equities will create an asset bubble is still undetermined but the amount is said to be 'at least $1 trillion'.

In June, Masayoshi Amamiya was reappointed as BOJ executive director of the Monetary Policy Department. Amamiya is known as one of the chief planners of Quantitative Easing and of the new aggressive QE since Kuroda entered the BOJ as governor. Since the reappointment of officials in the BOJ is rare it can be assumed that the central bank will continue to engage in aggressive QE.

But the struggle for growth was eluding Abe as exports in May 2014 for the first time in fifteen months fell 2.7 percent from the same period in the previous year. Exports to the US fell 2.8 percent and exports to Asia, which total more than 50 percent of Japan's exports, fell 3.4 percent, signifying a global decline in external demand. Although the BOJ was confident about the recovery of demand in Japan's major markets, the demand was deemed insufficient to help Japan cope with its current economic slump. It was also doubtful that Abenomics would be able to stimulate domestic demand to make up for the decline in exports and, inevitably, the BOJ would continue aggressive QE. On September 9 the BOJ took an unprecedented step by purchasing three-month and six-month bonds giving a negative yield. The amount of the purchase was estimated at $4.7 billion. On September 18 the bank purchased negative yield one-year bonds. By increasing its QE purchasing program, the BOJ was clearly 'monetizing' government debt. On September 26 the government announced that inflation fell from 1.3 percent to 1.1 percent in August, a ten-month low due primarily to a drop in global crude oil prices, signaling another round of stimulus. Although BOJ officials considered that inflation would not sink below 1 percent, Japanese economists were not ruling out that possibility.

And the moral of Japan's QE story? 'Once you start you can't stop!'

The big squeeze

Why Japan Can't Reform (2008) argues that an aging population together with decreasing population and the rise of welfare costs would increase public spending and raise the government debt. The low fertility rate was causing major concern at that time since 25 percent of the population was over 65 and the longevity rate was the highest in the world. In 2005, Japan began to lose population and the National Institute for Population and Social Research predicted that the portion of the population aged 65 and older would rise to 27.8 percent in 2020 while those aged 15–64 would fall to 60 percent. There were also concerns in Japan at that time that with little immigration and a birth-rate that was below replacement (at 1.32), the population of 127 million had already started to shrink. Pension and health-care payouts were swelling as the number of elderly was increasing. Furthermore, the productive population was shrinking and premium payments were decreasing.

According to a survey released by MIC on April 15, 2014 the main working population fell below 80 million as of October 1, 2013, for the first time in thirty-two years. The survey confirmed the forecast of the National Institute for Population's report. The total population of Japan fell 0.2 percent from the preceding year to an estimated 127,298,000. The decline in the working population aged 15–64 was significant. The total workforce (including foreign nationals) was 79,010,000, down 1,165,000, signifying the third consecutive year of decline. The population aged 65 and older totaled 31,898,000, an increase of 1,105,000. Inevitably, current wage-earners will be burdened with the responsibility of paying for the social welfare costs of retirees. MIC released yet another report on June 24 stating that Japan's population had fallen to 126.7 million or 0.19 percent, a decline for a fifth straight year.

Professor Hagendorff was particularly concerned about the repercussions of an increasing aging population and over-capacity on economic growth. When informed of Japan's refusal to increase immigration (at 2 percent) in order to solve labor shortages he replied:

The more we speak about Japan the more similarities I see with Germany. Germany and Italy have the fastest aging population in Europe. Although Germans don't think of it as a blessing, it is a blessing because immigration can occur across borders more easily. Germany can't do anything about the influx of immigrants from other parts of the EU because Germany is doing rather well and the other countries are not. If it weren't for free movement of immigrants, Germany would be in the same situation as Japan. The birth rate among people with university degrees is exceedingly low (approximately 1.5). Half of the women with university degrees will not have children in order to pursue careers.

In 2002, as a part of Koizumi's reforms of the public sector, the pension systems of farm, forestry and fisheries personnel were consolidated into a single IAI. In April 2004 a major scandal erupted when the prime minister, seven cabinet ministers, Naoto Kan, the leader of the DPJ, and 113 Diet members admitted that they had missed payments to the National Pension scheme. The future prime minister Yasuo Fukuda, who was the Chief Cabinet Secretary at the time, resigned from Koizumi's cabinet when it was revealed that he had also withheld payments.

The fact that even the highest officials in government had failed to contribute to the pension scheme aggravated the concerns among Japanese that paying into a pension scheme would not necessarily give them full benefits upon retirement simply because there would be fewer young people to contribute.

Former Prime Minister Noda, who criticized Abenomics as 'vodoo' economics in 2014, stated in his book in 2009 that consumption tax must be raised to 15 percent by 2013. Nobel Laureate economists together with such venerable institutions as the IMF and the OECD were positive about Abenomics, although tempering their enthusiasm by urging the government to implement structural reforms, which they have been urging for over fifteen years. The MOF reported in August 2013 that the government debt hit $10.3 trillion, the highest in history.

Japanese economists were taking it a step further, warning the government that consumption tax must be raised to 20 percent by 2020 to afford funding burgeoning welfare costs and to balance the books. Nevertheless, the government was wary of raising the 8 percent tax to 15 percent because of the events which followed the increase from 3 to 8 percent in April.

In March 1997, a month before the government had raised the sales tax from 3 to 5 percent, retail sales rose to 12.4 percent, compared to the previous month. After the tax hike was implemented sales fell 3.4 percent and remained in the doldrums for the rest of the year as the economy went into recession. After the sales tax hike in April 2014, retail sales fell 4.4 percent. It was the sharpest drop since March 2011. Industrial output also fell.

Some politicians were concerned that the sales tax hike to 8 percent would cut the GDP by 1 percent and that Japan's economy was in danger of experiencing the same recession as in 1998. Their concerns were justified. Japan's GDP contracted an annualized 7.1 percent in the second quarter, the fastest pace since 2009. Consumption fell 5.1 percent. Although BOJ officials remained confident that the tax hikes would not have a negative impact on inflation targets and economic growth and predicted that retail sales would recover by year-end, it was a foregone conclusion that further monetary stimulus and government expenditure would continue.

In its biannual report released on May 6, 2014, the OECD cut its forecast for Japan's 2014 GDP from 1.5 percent to 1.2 percent, cautioning the Abe government to implement structural reforms and raise the consumption tax to 10 percent in 2015 as was planned to cover burgeoning social welfare costs. Also, growth will undoubtedly weaken unless wages coincide with the rise in inflation. On June 27, the Statistics Bureau reported that in May prices rose 3.4 percent from a year earlier, the fastest rate in thirty-two years due to the tax hike and higher utility bills because the gas and electricity companies had raised their prices 5.3 percent in May, which was the highest rate since the pricing system was initiated in 2009. Household spending fell 8 percent. Consumer spending on cars and communication equipment also dropped significantly. Nevertheless, wages, excluding overtime and bonuses, continued to fall for the twenty-third consecutive month.

Abe, at a press conference on June 13, announced that the government would decide by year end whether to raise the consumption tax to 10 percent in October 2015. However, due to pressure from both business leaders and cabinet ministers who were strongly promoting the 10 percent tax, Abe pushed forward his decision to November. By the end of September, cabinet ministers were making necessary preparations for submitting a bill in the Diet. If the tax hike is implemented the BOJ will provide the appropriate stimulus.

Pension funds are severely affected by low interest rates. Abe pledged to restructure the Government Pension Investment Fund (GPIF), the world's largest pension fund manager, which declared its smallest gain in three quarters because of JGB losses. The GPIF is following the lead of global public sector funds in the diversification of its portfolio and reducing its exposure to JGB by 40 percent and increasing investment primarily in domestic equities by 12 percent, which may be increased to 20 percent. On 3 September, Abe appointed Yasuhisa Shiozaki, who served as Abe's Chief Cabinet Secretary in 2006–7, to the post of Health Minister and as the head of the GPIF. Shiozaki, who represents Ehime Prefecture in the Lower House is in charge of revamping the $1.2 trillion fund.

However, Japan Post Insurance (Kampo), Japan's largest insurer with $846 billion in assets, regarded Abenomics (e.g. QE) as a recipe for higher returns from equity purchases. It was rumored that the government insurer was investing $3.5 billion in the TSE, a rise of 50 percent from a year earlier. Kampo was also planning to invest $6.4 billion in foreign bonds instead of purchasing JGB.

Managers of the private pension funds were avoiding investing in domestic debt and seeking riskier but higher performing assets such as real estate and catastrophe bonds. The change served to drive the real estate market, bank loans and new investment in infrastructure. On the other hand, there were concerns that the market could plummet due to growing inflation and the tightening of interest rates.

Going nuclear again

Japan's Nuclear Crisis predicted that the nuclear power plants would be reactivated as soon as new safety regulations had been established but due to the vociferous public protest and the reticence of political parties to take a stance (even though both the LDP and DPJ were pro-nuclear prior to the Fukushima crisis), all of the plants remain off-line.

As was forecast, the LDP are back with Abe at the helm who is determined to restart the reactors. His 'Basic Energy Package' declares that nuclear power is an 'important base load electricity source' but it does not state specifics about the development of alternative energy sources, suggesting a long-term commitment to nuclear energy. The government, while planning to restart a number of reactors, is also planning to scrap approximately 25 percent of reactors because they are deemed too old to continue operating. Due to high maintenance costs KEPCO is considering decommissioning two reactors in Fukui Prefecture that were commissioned in the 1970s. However, it intends to restart two other reactors in Fukui after safety inspections are completed.

In May, Abe replaced two outgoing commissioners of the NRA with advocates of nuclear power in order to ensure that the NRA will approve the restarts of some reactors by the autumn. Satoru Tanaka, a professor of nuclear engineering at Tokyo University, and Akira Ishiwatari, a professor of geology at Tohoku University, are pro-nuclear. However, the independence of the NRA from government and the impartiality of the commission are being questioned because Tanaka received funding for research during the past decade from nuclear-related bodies. Reuters reported on June 10 that Tanaka had received over $100,000 for funding his research from J-Power, Hitachi Nuclear Ltd. and GE Nuclear Energy Ltd. He also received funds from TEPCO Memorial Foundation for judging research grants.

One major reason for the U-turn is that Japan's trade deficit in FY 2013 climbed 70 percent to ¥13.4 trillion ($134 billion), the third consecutive year that exports fell behind imports. MOF reported that as of

March 31, 2014, exports totaled 10.8 percent at $690.5 billion while imports rose 17.3 percent to $825 billion. The currency's depreciation of 10 percent against the dollar since the beginning of QE in April 2013 has been a double-edged sword. While raising the profits of the large exporters, it has simultaneously increased the cost of imports, including oil and liquid natural gas (LNG). The postponement of the restart of domestic reactors is forcing Japan to import more than three times as much liquid gas while simultaneously increasing Japan's current account deficit.

Japan's era of huge trade surplus is over. The trade deficit as of the end of January 2014 rose to $112 billion, escalating 65 percent from the previous year due to soaring energy prices as a consequence of the termination of the nuclear power plants. Besides fossil fuel, the overall cost of imports has risen significantly.

A second factor is that power utility companies are lobbying the government to restart the plants, which they had relied upon to supply electricity. Currently the utilities are substituting thermal power from their thermal power plants to compensate for the loss of nuclear power. In July 2011, Japan, which was already the world's third-largest importer of crude oil, would be importing an additional 350,000 barrels per day, which was selling at $100 per barrel. The Chubu Electric Power Company (CHUDEN) forecast in July 2011 that the substitution of thermal power to generate electricity would cost the utility $3.25 billion in purchases of LNG and that the importation of oil would raise costs by $3.1 billion. Consumers' utility bills, already among the most expensive of the industrialized countries, would rise considerably by the winter.

Thirdly, CHUDEN, which owns and operates Hamaoka Power Plant in Shizuoka Prefecture, announced on July 26, 2011 a consolidated operating loss in the order of ¥100 billion ($1.28 billion) in FY 2012. In addition, CHUDEN needed ¥300 billion ($3.9 billion) to refinance bonds that would mature in FY 2011. Considered too big to fail, CHUDEN's chief lenders the DBJ, Tokyo-Mitsubishi UFJ and Mizuho Corporate Bank loaned a total of ¥350 billion to the utility. In August, the Bank for International Cooperation (JBIC), whose remit is to grant loans to companies and institutions that are investing in the construction of infrastructure and resource management in other countries and not for increasing capital, came to CHUDEN's rescue and provided an emergency loan of ¥100 billion. JBIC justified the loan by claiming the loan was for funds to cover costs of fuel imports from other countries.

The power of the state and the power of money

LDP politicians whose constituents reside in towns that host the reactors and where the population depends primarily on the nuclear industry for employment are also pushing for the restart of the reactors. The majority of local governments hosting the plants are anxious that the plants go online again in order to sustain their economies that are heavily dependent on nuclear-related activities.

The Japanese media reported in January that a taxi service in one town that hosts three reactors refused to chauffeur an LDP politician who was running for office on an anti-nuclear platform.

When the pro-nuclear governor of Tokyo Naoki Inose resigned from office in December 2013 after admitting to receiving funds from a medical political lobby group for his election campaign, former Prime Minister Morihiro Hosokawa stood for governor on an anti-nuclear platform. Ironically, even though he was strongly pro-nuclear during his administration, Junichiro Koizumi, Abe's former mentor, jumped on the anti-nuclear band wagon to back Hosokawa's anti-nuclear campaign. The main opposition was former Minister of Welfare Yoichi Mazuoe whom Abe robustly supported. Mazuoe won a landslide victory on February 9. Toshio Tamogami, who also entered the election, pulled in 6,011,000 votes or 12 percent of the ballots. He ran on a platform that denied the 1937 Nanking Massacre and the use of 'comfort women' by the Japanese military before and during the war.

Several weeks later Tsugumasa Muraoka, a former official from the Ministry of the Interior and Communications who was supported by the LDP and the Komeito, during the gubernatorial campaign in Yamanashi Prefecture, won against two anti-nuclear opponents who were against the construction of a new power plant, which had been planned prior to Fukushima. The utilities who routinely purchase reams of tickets to the political parties' campaign events are lobbying for the construction of new nuclear reactors for the domestic market. The *Asahi Shimbun* reported on August 15, 2014 that seven utilities were continuing to spend billions of yen to promote nuclear power to the public at visitor centers located at the nuclear power stations despite the decrease of visitors to the centers. The operating expenses were said to be funded by consumers' utility bills. Even though advertising budgets in FY 2012 decreased 56 percent, seven utilities were still spending billions to promote nuclear at the centers, which had been established to reassure the residents in the towns which hosted the plants.

Since FY 2010 TEPCO and Tohoku Electric Power Co. (TODEN) has donated $1.95 million to Rokkasho village, which hosts a nuclear reprocessing plant. On July 14, the village sent a request to the utilities for the continuation of the donation for the refurbishment of port facilities and for supporting a program to prevent fish poaching. According to the *Asahi Shimbun*, TEPCO and TODEN agreed to the request on July 22. In 2012, TEPCO had intended to end the donation in order to use the funds to pay compensation to residents affected by the Fukushima meltdown.

All of the ten utility companies had filed for safety inspections by August 2013 but the utilities which applied earliest were expected to receive permits for restarts first. On September 10, 2014 the NRA announced that the Sendai plant No. 1 and 2 reactors met the new safety standards. The plant, hosted by Satsuma-Sendai, Kagoshima Prefecture in Kyushu, was expected to go online at the beginning of 2015 after KYUDEN's submission of paperwork detailing operations and accident responses. The company also had to gain the formal consent from the local government. METI intends to send staff to fully engage central government in the process. The restarts of Ehime's Ikata as well as a number of other power plants such as Hamaoka and Kashiwa-Kariwa were delayed for one year because the new emergency headquarters constructed to protect workers from radiation did not meet the new safety standards for withstanding earthquakes. TEPCO, the operator, was relying on the restart of the Niigata plant in order to avoid raising electricity bills. According to a public survey conducted by the *Asahi* and released on July 28, 59 percent of the Japanese interviewed were opposed to the restart.

The ongoing concern among anti-nuclear activists and pacifists that the Japanese government was storing plutonium for military purposes was justified when it was revealed by the Kyodo News Service on June 7 that Japan had omitted declaring 640 kg of unused plutonium to the International Atomic Agency (IAEA) in 2012 and 2013. Since Japan possesses the largest amount of plutonium among countries with nuclear weapons it is closely monitored. According to *Kyodo*, Kakujo, a nuclear information website, first reported the undeclared plutonium. Tatsujiro Suzuki, a professor at Nagasaki University and the former vice-chairman of the Japan Atomic Energy Commission, said that apparently the commission 'had overlooked' the omission and would try to improve its reporting. On September 17 the cabinet office reported that Japan's stockpile of plutonium was 47.1 tons, up 2.9 tons from the end of 2013. 10.8 tons is stored in Japan while the remaining plutonium is stored in the UK at Sellafield and in France where spent fuel was reprocessed.

Japan's Nuclear Crisis predicted that the Japanese government would aggressively promote the export of nuclear technologies to emerging markets. Although some DPJ party members were keen to end Japan's dependency on nuclear power, which provided 30 percent of Japanese electricity, the DPJ manifesto did not include the phase-out of nuclear power plants. Furthermore, prior to Fukushima, Naoto Kan, who was the prime minister at the time, had actively promoted the export of nuclear technologies to Vietnam, Turkey and Lithuania. *Japan's Nuclear Crisis* argued that even if Japan's nuclear village did not construct nuclear reactors domestically, undoubtedly it would manage to survive because of the exportation of nuclear technologies.

In April 2014, the government reached an agreement with Turkey and the United Arab Emirates for the construction of nuclear power plants. It was anticipated that Mitsubishi Heavy Industries, as a member of a consortium which included Itochu and Frances's GDF Suez, would build the plant. The French company Areva, which is the largest spent fuel reprocessor, and Mitsubishi Heavy Industries have been engaging in joint fuel reprocessing in Japan since 2006. In May 2013, Areva shipped the first load of reprocessed fuel (MOX) since the Fukushima disaster to the Takahama power plant in Fukui Prefecture, which is operated by the Kansai Electric Company (KEPCO). Also in May, it was announced that Areva was engaging the Japan Nuclear Fuel company in the commercial reprocessing of spent fuel at Rokkasho, Niigata.

Closer to home, in January Toshiba announced that it will acquire a 60 percent share in the UK nuclear power company NuGeneration for $166 million. NuGen is a joint venture between France's GDF Suez and Spain's Iberdrola. Plans are for three reactors to be commissioned in 2024 or 2025 at Sellafield. The reactors will be built by Westinghouse Electric, which is Toshiba's US subsidiary. Sellafield already hosts a spent fuel reprocessing plant which, until the Fukushima crisis, reprocessed the spent fuel from Fukushima and other plants in Japan. In October 2012 Hitachi acquired Horizon Nuclear Power from EOAN and RWE, Germany's two largest utilities, to build plants on two existing sites in the UK. And in July 2014 GE-Hitachi Nuclear confirmed that an agreement had been reached with the Lithuanian government to build a power plant. Nevertheless, Japan's nuclear village is experiencing not only fierce competition from foreign companies but, also, prolonged periods of negotiations and the additional costs of training local technicians and staff.

But where did the money go?

The Fukushima nuclear reactors are still plagued with overwhelming problems, including the containment of nuclear contaminated water, nuclear waste and decommissioning. In December 2013, the government doubled the size of its interest-free lending program to TEPCO to fund radiation cleanup and compensation expenses. The package, which is currently $96 billion, is to be financed with government bonds and included in fiscal 2014 budget. Although it is expected to take TEPCO forty years to repay the loan, the government wants to ensure that the utility will invest in power plants and transmission lines to ensure a stable power supply. Ironically, revenue from the tax levied on consumers' electric bills, which is targeted to fund the development of alternative energy sources, will also be used to pay TEPCO's bills.

The book predicted that the majority of evacuees would be unable to return to their homes due to the continuing problems at Fukushima and to the delays in the construction of public housing. In June the government issued dosimeters along with instructions to the evacuees that they could return to their homes but that they would have to take responsibility for their health. On August 4, the prefectural government announced at the Reconstruction Promotion Council meeting that the construction of 40 percent of the 3,700 initial units would be delayed for nine months because the pace of transactions with the owners of farmland and forest was not progressing as rapidly as had been intended.

On July 28, *Kyodo Press* reported that the Reconstruction Agency announced that due to labor shortages, surging prices for materials and coordination difficulties with residents, 35.2 percent of the FY 2012 budget allocated for the reconstruction of damaged areas went unused and 35.3 percent of the budget for FY 2013 was unused. In 2014 higher construction costs were impacting negatively not only on public work tenders but on commercial construction in other regions such as Tokyo which is preparing for the Tokyo Olympics. Furthermore, the government revenue originally allocated for the reconstruction of the northeast in 2011 was depleted as ministries competed for funds to support their own projects rather than reconstruction.

Local government officials in Fukushima municipalities rejected central government's initial offer of grants to allow the temporary (thirty years) storage of nuclear debris from the Fukushima power plant. Nevertheless, the concerns about the funding for the 2016 reconstruction budget, because of the planned cuts in corporate taxes and Abe's intention to focus more revenue on the development of other local economies, prompted the decision in July 2014 by the local municipalities to accept the government's offer to double the amount of the grants totaling $301 billion. $150 billion was to be used for the construction of the intermediate facilities, $100 billion was targeted for the reconstruction of Fukushima and $15 billion would go to towns which host sources of electricity. On August 30, Fukushima Governor Yuhei Sato formally accepted the government's plan to construct the storage facilities in Okuma and Futaba.

The DNA of Japan's political system: ultra-conservative to the core

At the time of writing *Japan's Nuclear Crisis* former Prime Minister Noda, who was the Finance Minister in Naoto Kan's cabinet had succeeded Naoto Kan as prime minister in August 2011. Although Noda was hoping that the LDP would form a coalition government to pass a 10 percent consumption-tax bill I predicted that the LDP would not cooperate and in September, only a month after Noda took office, the LDP was calling for a snap election. The chapter forecast:

> After only two years in power the DPJ was imploding and the LDP was making a comeback. The constant inter-party bickering and squabbling resulted in institutional paralysis. The Japanese system of government administration was in meltdown and the Japanese were falling into an economic and political morass.[5]

In August 2012, the electorate, frustrated with the DPJ's handling of the nuclear crisis and the economy, in desperation, returned to their roots, reinstating the LDP with Shinzo Abe as prime minister and Taro Aso at his side as deputy prime minister. The Japanese were once again in their comfort zone.

Since the 1980s, a breed of neo-nationalist politicians, who did not experience the war, has become a force in Japanese politics. *Japan's Nuclear Crisis*, while reiterating the facts made in the 2008 book regarding the strong neo-nationalist mind-set in government, laid bare growing neo-nationalism among government officials and the electorate, and continued the narrative in the previous two books regarding Koizumi and Abe and the government's upgrade of the Defense Agency and the re-establishment of the Ministry of Defense. In October 2007, a bribery scandal involving the vice-minister of the MOD, the defense minister in Abe's cabinet and the managing director of a large trading company was widely covered by Japanese media.

The book details the incident in connection with the relationship between the Japanese and American defense industries because several of the participants in the bribery incident actively participated in the Japan–US Center for Peace and Cultural Exchange, an MOFA-linked organization that was established in 1968. The members of the organization are American and Japanese politicians who lobby for the defense industries and are experts on national security issues. Members of the board included former Prime Minister Yasuo Fukuda, former defense minister Fumio Kyuma (a former director) and Seiji Maehara, a China hawk, who was the former DPJ president, the minister of transport and minister of foreign affairs in Prime Minister Kan's cabinet.

There is discussion about the heated territorial disputes with China and South Korea over the Senkaku and Takeshima Islands that have become more antagonistic since 2012 and have promoted the deterioration of Japan–Sino and Japan–ROK political and economic relationships.

The detention of the captain of a Chinese trawler triggered mass demonstrations in three major Chinese cities on October 16, 2010, which quickly spread to other cities. Shouting 'Defend the Senkaku Islands', 'Overthrow Japanese Imperialism!' and 'Fight Japan' protesters smashed Japanese retailers' shops. The Japanese answered with student marches in Tokyo's Aoyama Park which stands on a former military shooting range. Two thousand Japanese, waving Japanese flags, shouted 'We will not permit China to invade the Senkaku Islands! We will not permit China to invade the Senkaku Islands! We will not permit China to invade Japan and other Asian countries!'

One of the organizers of the Tokyo rally was General Toshio Tamogami who was the chief of the SDF Agency (2007–8) before he was dismissed for publishing an essay that insisted that Japan was not an aggressor in the Second World War. He maintained that the war brought prosperity to the Asian nations which Japan had occupied and that there had been no acts of brutality. Tamogami also had organized a march on October 3 in which 2,700 protesters participated.

Former Prime Minister Noda and his cabinet were also defense hawks. His foreign policies concerning Japan's East Asian trading partners were strikingly similar to Abe's government. In his 2009 book, Noda wrote about his primary school days when his father was serving in Japan's SDF. Even as a child, Noda disagreed with the views of his pacifist teachers and fully supported the return of the military. Noda also described his visit to China in 2003 when he defended Japan's territorial rights to the Senkaku Islands.

Nine years later, during his administration, the government purchased the islands from the Japanese owner in order to end China's territorial claims. Shortly after he assumed office, the prime minister expressed concern regarding the lack of transparency in China's military budgetary spending. Although Noda made a two-day state visit to China on December 25, 2011 to meet with Premier Wen Jibao he did not succeed in ameliorating Japan–Sino relations.

Prime Minister Abe and his cabinet's hawkish policies continue with its two important trading partners, China and the ROK. In his keynote address at the May Singapore Shangri-La Asian regional summit attended by ASEAN members and the United States, Abe spoke about Japan's expanding role in the region as a counter-deterrent to China's aggression in the territorial dispute with the Philippines in the East China Sea, where China established an air defense zone, similar to the air defense zone it established around the Senkaku Islands. Abe presented his plans for resolving the territorial disputes and offered coastal boats to countries which were concerned about China's threat. The United States Secretary of Defense Chuck Hagel fully supported Abe's stance.

In February 2014 Abe's Chief Cabinet Secretary announced that Japan was considering the re-examination of the study made twenty years earlier which preceded the formal apology to South Korea for Japan's war-time sex-slave system, known commonly as 'comfort women'. On July 25, 2014, the government rejected the request issued by the UN human rights regulatory committee to accept responsibility for the use of sex slaves before and during the war. The continuing visits to Yasukuni Shrine by Abe and his cabinet ministers also served to inflame the tensions with China and the ROK. Although said to be in a private capacity, in April Abe had sent a letter of condolence to a Buddhist temple in Wakayama Prefecture hosting a ceremony honouring the servicemen who died in the war and convicted Class A Criminals who were executed. A monument stands in tribute to the one thousand 'Showa Martyrs' whom Abe referred to in his letter as 'the foundation of the fatherland.'

Abe's army

It was announced in May 2014 that Abe, determined to take more control over the bureaucracy, had established the Cabinet Bureau of

Personnel Affairs which would choose the appointments of 600 elite ministry officials for positions in their respective agencies. Deputy Cabinet Secretary Katsunobu Kato, a close aide of the prime minister, was serving as the bureau's director-general and Tomomi Inada, Minister of Administrative Reforms, was managing the bureau. The old system allowed the prime minister and his chief cabinet secretary to select 200 elite ministry officials for top posts in the ministries but the new bureau gives Abe and Chief Cabinet Secretary Yoshide Suga the power to screen and appoint 600 elite ministry officials for top positions in the ministries. At a news conference Suga explained that the objective of the bureau was to 'cope with various issues quickly and in a united manner'. Suga, who is Abe's closest ally, is known for his penchant for interfering in personnel affairs. Realistically, Abe and his ultra-conservative right-wing colleagues are creating an ultra-conservative, right-wing environment in the bureaucracy through the appointment of senior elite officials who have similar political views and objectives.

As an example, traditionally, a senior official in the Cabinet Legislation Bureau was appointed to the position of director-general but Abe preferred to bring in an official who would promote the reinterpretation of the Constitution to allow collective self-defense. Ichiro Komatsu, a former MOFA official, was appointed for the job. Another example is Suga's dismissal of Atsuo Saka, a former elite MOF official, from the post of president and CEO of Japan Post Holdings Co. as a means to take over the control of Japan Post from the bureaucracy. In May 2013 Taizo Nishimuro, aged 77, who served as a former Toshiba Corp. Chairman (2000–5) was appointed to the post. Suga purportedly sacked Saka, aged 66, because MOF had traditionally appointed senior officials to the post under the *amakudari* system.

In the autumn of 2013, Abe appointed four ultra-conservative officials whose politics corresponded with his as members of the NHK board. The four then assisted Abe to appoint Katsuto Momii as governor who succeeded Masayuki Matsumoto after Matsumoto suddenly announced that he would not seek another three-year term as had been anticipated. The media reported that he had been admonished by Abe's administration for allowing National Broadcasting System (NHK) coverage to be too critical of nuclear energy and American bases on Okinawa. Abe also established a new NHK Management Board in 2013 and appointed Michiko Hasegawa, a right-wing nationalist, to the board.

Right-wing nationalist sentiments are now being expressed openly not only by senior officials in government, but also by the directors on the board of the NHK. After only two days on the job as the governor of NHK, Momii stated at a news conference that the 200,000 women who had been forced to serve as sex slaves during the war was common practice in any country engaged in war. Momii cited France and Germany as examples. He later retracted his statement when he was grilled in Parliament. But Momii refused to retract his other statements, which included his support of Japan's territorial right to the Senkaku Islands, and rejected the view that NHK should cease criticizing the secrecy law. Despite the controversy sparked by Momii's remarks, two days later Naoki Hyukuta, a novelist who also was chosen by Abe as one of the twelve governors of NHK, stated that in 1938 Chiang Kai-shek had blamed the Japanese army for the Nanjing Massacre and that the event did not occur. Hyutaka also reiterated Momii's statement regarding 'comfort women'.

The NHK is a public broadcasting system and, similar to the BBC, is supported by license fees collected from everyone who owns a television. Although the NHK is ostensibly an independent broadcaster, the twelve-member board of directors is appointed by Parliament, which also approves the NHK annual budget. The media are now concerned that Abe and his right-wing colleagues are interfering with freedom of the press and freedom of speech through the political appointment of people who will silence criticism of government policies, including restarting the nuclear reactors and denial of Japan's wartime atrocities. There is also deep concern that Abe is using the NHK as an organ to control the flow of information and as a mechanism which supports his political agenda.

Immediately after receiving approval from his cabinet for the reinterpretation of Article 9 to allow collective self-defense, Abe created a new ministerial post for security to revise existing laws and to introduce new laws in order to produce a legal framework regarding the right to exercise collective self-defense.

On September 3, 2014, in order to boost his public approval rating, which had slipped to below 50 percent for the first time since he had entered office, Abe reshuffled his Cabinet. In order to preserve his right-wing power base, he kept Suga and Aso by his side, and appointed Justice Minister Sadakazu Tanigaki as LDP President. He also increased the number of female cabinet members to five, which proved popular among the female electorate. Although Abe's approval rating immediately climbed to 64 percent, Japanese media revealed that two of the new female cabinet members had links to the neo-Nazi party in Japan, allegations which they vehemently denied. LDP policy chief Tomomi Inada had supported a 2006 film denying the Nanking Massacre. She annually visited Yasukuni Shrine privately but intended to continue as a member of the cabinet.

Too little too late?

Although METI's organization was slightly restructured, METI bears a striking resemblance to the former MITI. METI is taking on a broader role in Japan's regional economic development. Its mission statement on its website reads that it aims:

> to be a navigator in support of a diverse range of players and to create socio-economic systems for these diverse players to exercise their capabilities to the fullest. As its mission METI will propel the Japanese economy by providing information and analytical insights, creating systems that support society and the economy and enhancing Japan's technological foundations, so that companies, communities, individuals, non-profit organizations, and other players can exercise their capabilities to the fullest and maximize their potential.

As well as the promotion of commerce and trade, METI plans microeconomic policy for industries, protection of industry and ensuring that there is a steady supply of energy. The protection of industry may imply that the policy tool 'administrative guidance' is used as often as before in order to ensure compliance with ministerial guidance.

In June 2010 METI released its 'Industrial Structure Vision' which stated the ministry's objectives to 'launch a nation-wide effort to boast its industry's global competitiveness' to stimulate Japan's economic recovery. METI's aim included a shift in industrial structure to encourage 'potential strengths in businesses', the creation of jobs 'by aggressive globalization and by building world-class business infrastructure' and to change the government's role to 'win the fierce competition to acquire added value among countries'.

The vision, which described Japan as a 'deadlocked economy', included data from the IMF World Economic Outlook Database that showed the general deterioration of Japan's competitiveness in global markets and the effects on the stagnated economy. IMF figures revealed that Japan's global ranking in terms of GDP per capita was third in 2000, falling to twenty-third in 2008. In 1990, Japan's share of the global GDP was 14.3 percent while in 2008 its share had decreased to 8.9 percent.

The METI vision reported that, although the economy was growing during 2000–7, wages remained stagnant or had declined. The number of companies going out of business exceeded the number of start-ups. MOF data revealed that while outward investment had increased, domestic capital expenditure had decreased. From 2006, domestic investment plummeted 37 percent. There was a significant shift by businesses to produce abroad. In 2011, Toyota was producing 50 percent of cars outside of Japan and Honda and Nissan were each producing 70 percent of their vehicles abroad.

Abe's third arrow: let's call the whole thing off?

On June 24, Abe released his long-awaited 'Industrial Revival Plan' that he claimed was the foundation of his 'third arrow' of structural reforms and would promote long-term economic growth. The plan was long on promises but short on specifics. The 'arrow' appeared to be veering away from full-fledged structural reforms and taking a far easier and less politically contentious route to invigorate the economy through the stimulus of domestic business with the reduction of corporate taxes, long-term, low-interest loans to budding entrepreneurs, putting more women in the workplace and doubling annual inward investment to $345 billion by 2020 in time for the Tokyo Olympics. To persuade foreign investors to participate in public works projects Abe was offering $30 billion in contracts to manage infrastructure projects. There were also designated special zones where foreign businesses could operate with tax incentives and fewer restrictions on visas.

To the delight of Japanese businesses Abe's administration was committed to lowering corporate taxes, which at 35.6 percent was the second highest figure among the OECD countries after the US, to below 30 percent within a few years. However, due to numerous tax breaks and tax loopholes that businesses could take advantage of, Japan had a narrow tax base. According to the MOF, only 70 percent of corporations paid corporate taxes, putting the burden on the larger companies for footing the bill. The proposed tax cut was scheduled for FY 2015.

In FY 2013, Japan's corporate tax revenue was $9.67 billion, due to high earnings by larger listed companies which had benefited from the depreciation of the currency. However, according to the MOF each percentage point of tax cuts would reduce government revenue by $4.61 billion annually.

Deputy Prime Minister and Finance Minister Taro Aso was opposed to corporate tax cuts in September 2013 but by the following May he was more open to cuts on the condition that alternative sources of finance were found to make up for the lost revenue. Abe promised that there would be alternative revenue sources to offset the decline in corporate tax revenue but he provided no details. Abe also hoped that the lowering of corporate taxes would promote inward investment.

Abe's corporate tax cut would also serve to instill a cozier relationship between business and government and the 'revival' of Japan Inc. Sadayuki Sakakibara, the chairman of Toray and the new chairman of Keidanren, Japan's largest business lobby organization, is forging a strong relationship with Abe. Sakakibara's predecessor, Hiromasa Yonekura, had criticized Abe's monetary policy as reckless, leading to a strained relationship between Keidanren and the government.

Sakakibara, who was pressing for taxes to be lowered to 25 percent, supported Abe, praising him for his decisive political actions. Sakakibara, who believed that the country would recover from the drop in consumption directly after the tax hike in April, also urged for the implementation of the planned rise in consumption tax to 10 percent in 2015.

But politicians expressed concerns that corporate tax cuts would be difficult to justify to consumers, who were hit with an 8 percent consumption tax, when they had been told that the increase was vital to lowering the deficit and stabilizing the sovereign debt. The BOJ reported on June 19 that, although the depreciated yen had prompted overseas investment to rise 21 percent from the previous year, households were risk-averse with more that 50 percent of assets in cash and deposits. Furthermore, by the end of FY 2013, non-financial corporations' cash deposits had risen 4.1 percent from the previous year and borrowing from private banks had been the slowest since the last quarter of 2012, signifying that domestic spending was low and that Abe's push for growth was far from being realized.

Govinda Finn assessed the planned cut:

> In Japan there is an assumption that taxes will have to rise. Whether the cut benefits Japanese corporations is another issue because 70 percent of them don't pay taxes. But it may give an indication of where the tax burden may fall going forward over the next five to ten years. That's why the relevance of the corporate tax cut debate is higher. The Cabinet office has some estimates about the impact of a 10 percent reduction would have on growth. I think that it is 0.4 percent reduction on growth and a 2 percent rise in capital expenditure.[6]

Abe's 'Industrial Revival Plan' promised a long-awaited overhaul of the public pension investment fund (GPIF), which, as stated above, is planning to reduce exposure to JGB and invest in other assets that promise higher returns. However, the overhaul may be a politically contentious issue and arriving at a consensus will take time.

Although Abe's administration promoted the corporate tax cut as a means to attract foreign businesses to Japan and inward investment there are real concerns among offshore investors about the lack of reforms of corporate governance and a decreasing workforce which will not engender confidence in foreign firms in terms of long-term commitment and investment. Japanese corporations are not required to appoint external directors as supervisors (as was the case at Mercian until 2000 when Miyauchi served as an external) and, as a consequence, there is insularity among board members who will accept all business decisions and operations without question. In most foreign countries companies are legally required to appoint the majority of directors from outside the corporations.

Abe's plan also promises that the TSE would construct a 'corporate governance code' by mid-2015 to bring listed companies' policies up to international standards. But offshore investors will not be pleased with the results of Abe's promise because his draft plan calls for the appointment of only one external director to serve on banks' boards and there is no mention of corporations engaged in the other industries. As of 2014, of 1,813 firms registered on the TSE, 39 percent had one external director on their boards, 39 percent had no external directors and 22 percent of firms had two or more.

Finn also spoke about the dissatisfaction expressed by the TSE listing department about the set of proposals for changes in corporate governance such as the requirements around external board members looking like a compromise solution:

> There is a lot of excitement about the new TSE index and the implications of corporate governance and the return of equity which is a key metric. Corporate governance has clearly been delayed and not prioritized.[7]

Foreign corporations which are considering establishing a subsidiary in Japan or engaging in a public works project to take advantage of government contracts, may find that hiring skilled workers is problematic due to the decreasing workforce. Indeed, Japanese construction firms were experiencing difficulties finding construction workers who were under 65. Although Abe was in favor for raising quotas for immigrants who were deemed appropriate for blue-collar jobs such as construction workers and restaurant staff and to ease restrictions of technical and skilled professionals to enable full-time residency, the insularity and ever-present xenophobia within the general population would pressure the government to strictly control the influx of immigrants. Regardless, the United States' report on human trafficking released in June condemned government-funded programs that train foreign workers declaring that workers were underpaid and forced to work in very poor conditions while receiving no training to develop skills.

In the meantime...: internal and external impacts on Japan's economic growth

Besides the domestic issues discussed in previous chapters and in this chapter, the internal impacts that can also destabilize Japan's economic recovery include natural disasters such as earthquakes or tsunamis or unnatural events such as the Fukushima nuclear disaster. In these circumstances the reaction time dealing with national emergencies will be slow because agencies protect their administrative territory and communication with the cabinet office can be sporadic. There is also the problem of 'information-sharing' which frustrates the coordination of operations as was the case after the Kobe earthquake and, most visibly, after the nuclear crisis. Recovery time is also delayed by the indecisiveness in government because arriving at a consensus about the routes to recovery tends to be a prolonged process.

The external impacts are numerous. Among them, Japan's economy is based on the importation of raw materials for manufacturing goods and exporting the goods to primary markets. Even though the larger Japanese companies are producing abroad to take advantage of ready supplies of raw materials, cheap labor, etc., the global economic slowdown and growing competition from foreign companies in the same industrial sectors will undoubtedly impact on Japan's economic growth. As importantly, geopolitical crises, such as in the Middle East and the Ukraine, will affect consumer markets globally.

The further deterioration of Japan–Sino and Japan–ROK relations may result in regional conflicts as Japan becomes more isolated through its neo-nationalist policies, which is unfortunate since trade relations with its East Asian neighbors play a crucial role in Japan's economic stability. Even though the United States formally supports Japan's territorial rights to the Senkaku, a public survey in 2013 by the research firm Harris Interactive, a survey which has been conducted annually since 1996, revealed that the percentage of Americans who were in favor of maintaining the US–Japan Security Treaty had decreased significantly. The January 17 article in *Nikkei Asia Review* reported that 67 percent of US citizens surveyed by Harris Interactive as well as 77 percent of intellectuals polled responded that the treaty should be maintained but the percentage in favor of the treaty had fallen 22 percent from the previous year. According to Richard Samuels, professor of political science at MIT, who is a renowned scholar on Japanese politics, the steep fall in support was due to Americans' reluctance to become involved in a conflict over the Senkaku Islands. Furthermore, only 35 percent of Americans polled considered Japan important to the United States' interests; 65 percent regarded China as the US's most important trading partner in Asia as was predicted by ministry officials who were interviewed in 1994. Finn voiced his concerns about the mechanisms in Japan's political economy that have so far failed to promote economic growth:

Abe has managed to change the tone of the conversation and made people move away from the question of fiscal sustainability and start to focus on other issues like growth and inflation. However, the fiscal issues in Japan are the primary challenge to the economy and to some extent are paralyzing economic activity and political activity. There has been a failure in politics over the past decade – perhaps bigger than ever than even Japan is used to. Abe presents a different if still uncertain proposition.

During the past decade Japan's economic relationship with the outside world has also changed, which has been partly motivated by external forces such as the rise of the yen, the rise of China and also the result of technological and product innovation in places such as the US which has made Japan no longer as relevant in terms of its export sectors. Japan's share of global exports has declined. It has also happened at the time of the fluctuating exchange rate.[8] Japan's global share of exports has declined partly because of the emergence of China and EM [emerging markets]. Of course, the US and European nations have suffered similarly but Japan is the only one that has seen a sustained fall in its real effective exchange rate as well.[9]

Seeing is believing

In September economists had predicted a 4 percent growth in GDP for the third quarter. However, Japan's economic recovery was at a standstill due to a number of factors, including the drop in consumer demand since April and the continued build-up of inventory, forcing automobile and electronic manufacturers to slash production in order to shed stock. There was also a fall in industrial output, and a decline in exports. A month later economists and the IMF were lowering their expectations to 2 percent growth in GDP. When the yen depreciated to 109.30 per dollar on October 7 Yoshihide Suga concluded that the cheap yen was not helping Japanese exporters and that corporations had stopped overseas expansion completely. He suggested that corporations were considering returning production to Japan. Despite the pressure to raise the consumption tax to 10 percent in 2015 and despite the continuation of QE, there were concerns that a further hike could trigger a recession. As Abe struggles with the need for growth versus the need for cutting the public debt, the IMF emphasized that the tax hike was 'critical to establish a track record of fiscal discipline'.

Abe's 'Industrial Revival Plan' implies a METI-like vision of an innovative, open and more transparent Japanese economy. However, it is difficult to visualize the restructuring of the labor market without the liberalization of immigration laws. When former Prime Minister Noda offered to engage in the Trans-Pacific Partnership, the multilateral trade agreement spearheaded by the US and which includes eleven Asian economies, the outcome of the US–Japan negotiations was predictable. In September negotiations stalled due to Japan's refusal to drop tariffs on automobile and agricultural imports. It is equally difficult to imagine a revival plan centered on sustainable growth without the opening up of Japan's markets to imports and FDI and the removal of an array of invisible non-tariff barriers and the deregulation of more industrial sectors to allow healthy competition with foreign firms. These fundamental structural reforms of the economy are vital to promoting inward investment and economic expansion.

Nevertheless, the institutional mechanisms in the system of government administration to implement these fundamental reforms do not exist. Sadayuki Sakakibara emphasized that the government and business were inseparable 'like car wheel', promising to strengthen the ties between Keidanren and government. A well-recognized method of 'strengthening ties' is the reinstatement of corporate political donations, which was discontinued in 2009 by the DPJ government. Until 1993, Keidanren had advised member companies the amount which they could contribute to political parties. From 2004–10 Keidanren conducted a five-grade policy assessment of each party for members who independently selected the parties they wished to support. In September Keidanren announced that it would again advise members on political donations. It was back to basics.

The conclusion of *Special Corporations and the Bureaucracy: Why Japan Can't Reform* (2003) states:

> Japan's economic woes were originally attributed to macro-economic difficulties resulting from inflated real estate and stock prices. The possibility that structural problems and flaws in the Japanese system itself were contributory factors was generally not considered until fiscal stimulus packages not only failed to ignite the economy but also sent government debt skyrocketing. Japan's prolonged economic stagnation has finally revealed the fundamental reasons for the inability of the Japanese to take decisive measures to bring about an economic recovery. What we must understand is that in order for substantial reform to occur, Japan's socio-political system must be able to adapt to change – and the process will take many years.[10]

As an example of the difficulty in promoting social change even in his own government, just six weeks after Abe appointed five female politicians to serve as ministers in his cabinet, scandals over the misappropriation of political funds forced METI Minister Yuko Obuchi and Justice Minister Midori Matsushima to resign. A third female minister's days may be numbered as well. Eriko Yamatani, who is responsible for the North Korean abduction problem was photographed with members of a right-wing group accused of spouting hate speeches against the ethnic Korean community.

Abenomics is failing to promote growth or dig the economy out of deflation despite the continuation of QE. While exports were rebounding in September, Japan's trade deficit also rose. Although Abe's public approval rating is shrinking (48.5 percent in October), the LDP power base remains intact. A new generation of LDP politicians are waiting for the opportunity to run for office. Nevertheless, their economic policies are unlikely to deal with the magnitude of Japan's problems as contended in *Why Japan Can't Reform*:

> and even if structural reforms are initiated, the effort would be akin to plugging holes in a dyke to stem the flood of problems that are a consequence of years of reliance on an antiquated system and pork-barrel policies.[11]

Notes

Introduction

1. S. Carpenter, *Special Corporations and the Bureaucracy: Why Japan Can't Reform* (Basingstoke: Palgrave Macmillan, 2003), p. 119.
2. C. Johnson, *Japan's Public Policy Companies* (Washington, DC: American Enterprise Institute for Public Policy Research, 1978).
3. S. Carpenter, *Japan's Nuclear Crisis: The Routes to Responsibility* (Basingstoke: Palgrave Macmillan, 2012), p. 25.
4. S. Carpenter, *Why Japan Can't Reform: Inside the System* (Basingstoke: Palgrave Macmillan, 2008), p. 35.
5. Carpenter, *Japan's Nuclear Crisis*, p. 72.
6. Ibid., p. 73.
7. Ibid., p. 74.
8. Ibid., p. 74.
9. Carpenter, *Why Japan Can't Reform*, p. 33.
10. Interview, 10 June 2014.
11. Carpenter, *Japan's Nuclear Crisis*, p. 78.
12. S. Abe, *Utsukushii Kuni E* (Tokyo: Bunsho Shinso, Bungei Shinju, 2006).

1 Back to Basics?

1. S. Carpenter, *Why Japan Can't Reform: Inside the System* (Basingstoke: Palgrave Macmillan, 2008), p. 120.
2. S. Carpenter, *Japan's Nuclear Crisis: The Routes to Responsibility* (Basingstoke: Palgrave Macmillan, 2012), p. 135.
3. Carpenter, *Japan's Nuclear Crisis*, p. 136.
4. Japan's Constitution is often referred to as the Pacifist Constitution.
5. Y. Noda, *Minshu no Teki* (Tokyo: Shincho Shinsho, 2009).
6. *Kyodo*, February 5, 2006.
7. All governments plan industrial policies to support industries that are considered vital to national interests through a set of policy instruments that may include the regulation of production, tax incentives to domestic companies that procure from domestic suppliers, subsidizing of R&D, long-term, low-interest rate loans to businesses for expansion, and the protection of industry from foreign competition from imports through tariffs.
8. C. Johnson, N. Schlei and M. Schaller, 'The CIA and Japanese Politics', Asian Perspective, 24(4) (Kyungnam University, Portland State University, 2000): 79–103.
9. Johnson, Schlei and Schaller, 'The CIA and Japanese Politics'.
10. R. J. Samuels, 'Kishi and Corruption: An Anatomy of the 1955 System', *JPRI Working Paper*, No. 83, Japan Policy Research Institute (Cardiff, CA, December 2001).

2 The Sign of the Times: Japan Inc. (1955–1974)

1. A. Mikuni, 'Why Japan Can't Reform the Economy', *JPRI Working Paper*, No. 44, Japan Policy Research Institute (Cardiff, CA, April 1998).
2. R. Katz, *Japan: The System that Soured* (New York: M. E. Sharpe, 1998), p. 45.
3. S. Carpenter, *Why Japan Can't Reform: Inside the System* (Basingstoke: Palgrave Macmillan, 2008), pp. 117–119.
4. Ibid., p. 157.

3 The Route to Heaven-on-Earth

1. K. Calder, 'Elites in an Equalizing Role: Ex-Bureaucrats as Coordinators and Intermediaries in the Japanese Government–Business Relationship', *Comparative Politics*, 21(4) (1989): 379–403.
2. S. Carpenter, *Special Corporations and the Bureaucracy: Why Japan Can't Reform* (Basingstoke: Palgrave Macmillan, 2003), p. 89.
3. S. Carpenter, *Why Japan Can't Reform: Inside the System* (Basingstoke: Palgrave Macmillan, 2008), p. 152.
4. *Nikkei Shimbun* Editorial Staff, *Kanryo Kishimu Kyodai Kenryoku* (*The Bureaucracy: A Giant Creaking Power*) (Tokyo: Nikkei Shimbunsha, 1994), pp. 245–6.
5. Ibid.
6. *Mainichi Shimbun* Editorial Staff, *Kasumigaseki Shindororum* (*The Kasumigaseki Syndrome*) (Tokyo: Mainichi Shimbunsha, 1994), pp. 296–308.
7. Y. Noda, *Minshu no Teki* (*Enemy of Democracy*) (Tokyo: Shincho Shinsho, 2009), pp. 84–110.

4 Pork-Barrel Politics in the Prefectures: The Winners

1. C. Johnson, *MITI and the Japanese Miracle* (Stanford, CA: Stanford University Press, 1982), p. 24.

5 The Japanese Economic Miracle: Japan Inc. on Center Stage

1. www.mskj.org.jp.
2. 'In the globalized world we have a number of pockets of fixed exchange-rate systems within a broadly flexible or floating exchange-rate regime combined also with broadly open capital markets. Although the general economic cycle, specifically relative interest rates, is the main driver for foreign exchange flows it is also true that expectations of policy differences across the globe can interfere with these flows for quite extended periods even though they may be counterproductive from a longer term macro-economic perspective. Expected changes in currency policy, especially direct foreign exchange intervention, obviously affect participants' views in the foreign exchange markets as these players seek to understand the impact of changes in the supply of, and demand for, currencies. Intervention in EM currencies can also feed back into developed currency demand through the Reserves recycling mechanism.

This is one of the reasons that the Euro's value remained high during periods of weak inflation and easier monetary policy. In particular, it is still important to note that not all countries are equal in importance. Despite all the sins of benign neglect and despite a growing hope in the developing world that the predominance of the dollar as a reserve currency will come to an end, US policy making is still key to how the global economies interact and, therefore, to how exchange rates fluctuate. Whilst some currencies' regimes are less fixed than they were ten years ago nevertheless the Middle Eastern, the Far Eastern and Latin American countries largely still have to accept the monetary policy of the US through the exchange rate transmission mechanism. Somewhat surprisingly, given its increased size and still strong economic growth, China has yet to establish a truly independent domestic monetary policy. Foreign exchange analysts still need to look less at the US economy and more at the USD economy, taking into account the degree of "fixedness" other economies have with the US through their exchange rate regimes, when developing views on the outlook for the currency market.' (Comments from interview with Ken Dickson conducted on June 10, 2014 at Standard Life Investments.)

6 The Roaring 80s: The Bicycle Economy Out of Control

1. www.suntory.com
2. www.otsuka.co.jp
3. B. Hu, 'Ex-Daiwa Rogue Trader Says Most Unauthorized Trades Hidden' (*Bloomberg News*, April 30, 2014).

7 The Metamorphosis of Sanraku Inc.

1. Elite civil servants were most likely to have graduated with a law degree from Tokyo University (Todai) formerly known as Tokyo Imperial University, which was established in 1897 specifically for training students who expected to enter the ministries. For example, Haruhiko Kuroda, the current Governor of the Bank of Japan, graduated with a law degree from Todai before entering MOF. He served as MOF's Vice-Minister of International Affairs from 1999 until he retired from the ministry in 2003. He was appointed as the President of the Asian Development Bank in 2005.
2. S. Carpenter, *Why Japan Can't Reform: Inside the System* (Basingstoke: Palgrave Macmillan, 2008), p. 135.

9 Marketing and Advertising Strategies: What's it all About?

1. www.mercian.co.jp/company/annual.html

10 Bubble, Bubble, Turmoil and Trouble

1. T. Ishikawa, *Akuto: Ozawa Ichiro ni Tsukaete (The Scoundrel: Serving Ichiro Ozawa)* (Tokyo: Asahi Newspaper Publishing Company, 2011).
2. Eneken.ieej.or.jp

3. S. Carpenter, *Why Japan Can't Reform: Inside the System* (Basingstoke: Palgrave Macmillan, 2008), p. 134.
4. Ibid., p. 135.
5. Ibid., pp. 132–3.
6. Ibid., p. 134.

11   Special Corporations: Insatiable

1. Y. Noda, *Minshu no Teki* (Tokyo: Shincho Shinsho, 2009).
2. www.jfs.co.jp
3. www.mof.go.jp/pri/publication.zaikin_geppo/hyou
4. www.mof.go.jp/filp/publication/filp_report/zaito2013
5. http://biz-journal.jp/2014/04/post
6. www.jogmec.go.jp
7. www.nedo.go.jp
8. www.jnes.go.jp
9. www.aist.go.jp
10. www.reiti.go.jp
11. www.nexi.go.jp
12. www.jetro.co.jp
13. www.jetro-ide.co.jp
14. www.jica.go.jp
15. www.jhf.co.jp
16. Asset liability management (ALM) is a tool used to manage risk, such as liquidity risks, interest rate risks, credit risk and operational risk.
17. www.ur-net.go.jp
18. www.zakzak.co.jp
19. Y. Noda, *Minshu no Teki*.
20. S. Carpenter, *Special Corporations and the Bureaucracy* (Basingstoke: Palgrave Macmillan, 2003), p. 123.

12   The Skill at Disguising

1. T. Ebato, *Kanryo Dai-Kenkyu* (*In-depth Research of the Bureaucracy*) (Tokyo: Chikuma Shobo, 1990), pp. 234–41.
2. www.alic.go.jp
3. S. Carpenter, *Special Corporations and the Bureaucracy: Why Japan Can't Reform* (Basingstoke: Palgrave Macmillan, 2003), p. 107.
4. C. Johnson, *MITI and the Japanese Miracle* (Stanford: Stanford University Press, 1982), pp. 231–2.
5. www.JEF.co.jp
6. Carpenter, *Special Corporations and the Bureaucracy*, p. 31.
7. K. van Wolferen, 'The Japan Problem', *Foreign Affairs*, 65(2) (1986/7), p. 293.
8. E. Lincoln, *Troubled Times: US–Japan Trade Relations in the 1990s* (Washington, DC: Brookings Institution, 1999).
9. www.mipro.co.jp
10. S. Carpenter, *Why Japan Can't Reform: Inside the System* (Basingstoke: Palgrave Macmillan, 2008), p. 135.

11. Lincoln, *Troubled Times*, p. 190.
12. A. Mikuni and R. Taggart Murphy, *Japan's Policy Trap* (Washington, DC: Brookings Institution, 2003), p. 96.
13. In 1997, a prefectural government officer arranged a large exhibition for old and well-established small businesses engaged in industries in his prefecture in order to introduce their products to New Yorkers, with the expectation that there was a market for their products in the United States. Some of the firms had been in operation since the eighteenth century. Although partially subsidized by government, the tradesmen assumed a sizable portion of the costs of shipping their wares to the exhibition and setting up exhibition stalls. The exhibition continued for three days and many Americans enjoyed their first exposure to the elegant products presented to them. At the end of the final day, the officer spoke at length to the firms' owners about the viability of their products in the American marketplace. Perhaps influenced by the news bulletins about crimes perpetrated against Japanese circulated in the office and by Japanese media coverage of the US, the officer characterized American consumers as couch potatoes who sat all day watching television while eating spaghetti out of cans and drinking vast quantities of beer. His analysis did not include other market information that may have given the tradesmen a more positive perspective.
14. Carpenter, *Why Japan Can't Reform*, pp. 109–12.
15. Ibid.
16. Carpenter, *Special Corporations and the Bureaucracy*, p. 118.

13 The Price of Pork-Barrel Patronage: Beggars Can't be Choosers

1. www.soumu.go.jp
2. Ibid.

14 Still Bubbling

1. J. Choy, *Japan's Non-performing Loan Problem Refuses to Go Away* (Tokyo: Japan Economic Institute Report, 2000).
2. E. Lincoln, *Making Some Sense of the Japanese Economy* (Cardiff, CA: Japan Policy Research Institute, 2003, Working Paper, No. 94). www.jpri.org/publications/workingpapers/wp94.html
3. K. Kobayashi, 'The 15-Year War on Non-Performing Loans and Deflation' (Tokyo: Research Institute of Economy, Trade and Industry, 2004).
4. G. Melloan, *Japan Banks Remain a Drag on Economic Recovery* (New York: The Wall Street Journal, 1999).
5. *Asahi News* (February 21, 2004).
6. *Nikkei News* (May 30, 2003).
7. Nissho-Iwai merged with Nichimen in April 2000 to form Sojitz Corp. but at the end of March 2004 Sotjitz held ¥1.56 trillion in interest-bearing loans.
8. *Nikkei News* (December 4, 2003).
9. *Asahi News* (May 29, 2004).
10. *Financial Times* (May 26, 2005).

11. *Nikkei News* (July 9, 2005).
12. www.fsn.go.jp/en
13. A. Mikuni and R. Taggart Murphy, *Japan's Policy Trap* (Washington, DC: Brookings Institution, 2002), pp. 61 and 173.
14. *Thomson Financial* (September 1999).
15. K. Tsuru, *Daiei's Rehabilitation* (Tokyo: REITI, March 4, 2005).
16. www.mercian.co.jp/company/ir/annual
17. Ibid.
18. www.kirinholdings.co.jp/news/2010

Conclusion

1. S. Carpenter, *Why Japan Can't Reform: Inside the System* (Basingstoke: Palgrave Macmillan, 2008), p. 147.
2. Carpenter, *Why Japan Can't Reform*, p. 137.
3. S. Carpenter, *Japan's Nuclear Crisis: The Routes to Responsibility* (Basingstoke: Palgrave Macmillan, 2012), p. 26.
4. Two days after Professor Hagendorff's interview the ECB announced that it was lowering its deposit rate to minus 0.1 percent and will charge banks for holding their funds overnight. The negative rate on deposits will allow the ECB to keep money at the bank instead of paying out interest. The ECB also reduced its benchmark policy rate to 0.15 percent from 0.25 percent, to an historic low. It was the first time that the rate on deposits fell into negative territory. Recognized as an unconventional instrument since it is new and untested, it is one of a set of measures the ECB was using to pull the Eurozone out of deflation and to stimulate the European economy without resorting to QE. The ECB was also concerned about banks' reticence to lend and was planning to implement a $544 billion scheme to supply low-interest funds to banks for up to four years in order to promote lending to Eurozone businesses.
5. Interview conducted with Govinda Finn at Standard Life Investments on June 10, 2014.
6. Interview with Govinda Finn, June 10, 2014.
7. Ibid.
8. The BOJ defines Real Effective Exchange Rate or REER as: 'an indicator that captures the international competitiveness of a currency, which cannot be measured only by examining bilateral exchange rates. The EERs of the Japanese yen are calculated as follows. The weighted average of the yen's exchange rate against other currencies is calculated using the relative importance – which is measured by the total value of trade, etc. – as its weights.' The weighted average of a country's currency is related to an index of other major currencies which is adjusted for the effects of inflation. Trade weights are measured according to a country's leading trading partner and in Japan's case not only is the US considered the biggest market, but also the dollar is the reserve currency.
9. Interview with Govinda Finn, June 10, 2014.
10. S. Carpenter, *Special Corporations and the Bureaucracy: Why Japan Can't Reform* (Basingstoke: Palgrave Macmillan, 2003), p. 147.
11. Carpenter, *Special Corporations and the Bureaucracy*, p. 124.

Select Bibliography

Abe. S., *Toward a Beautiful Country* (*Utsukushii Kuni E*) (Tokyo: Shinso Bunsho, Bungei Shunju, 2006).

Calder, K., 'Elites in an Equalizing Role: Ex-Bureaucrats as Coordinators and Intermediaries in the Japanese Government Relationship', *Comparative Politics* 21(4) (1989): 379–403.

Carpenter, S., *Japan's Nuclear Crisis: The Routes to Responsibility* (Basingstoke: Palgrave Macmillan, 2012).

Carpenter, S., *Special Corporations and the Bureaucracy: Why Japan Can't Reform* (Basingstoke: Palgrave Macmillan, 2003).

Carpenter, S., *Why Japan Can't Reform: Inside the System* (Basingstoke: Palgrave Macmillan, 2008).

Choy, J., 'Japan's Non-Performing Loan Problem Refuses to Go Away', Japan Economics Institute (2000).

Dower, J., *Embracing Defeat: Japan in the Wake of World War II* (New York: W. W. Norton, 1999).

Iishi, K., *Bureaucrat Heaven: The Bankrupting of Japan* (*Kanryo Tenkoku Nihon Hassan*) (Tokyo: Michi Shuppansha, 1999).

Iishi, K., *The Parasites that are Gobbling Up Japan: Dismantle All Special Corporations and Public Corporations!* (*Nihon wa Kuitsuku Kiseichu: Tokushu Houjin Koeki Houjin wo Zenhai Seiyo!*) (Tokyo: Michi Shuppansha, 2001).

Johnson, C., *Blowback: The Costs and Consequences of American Empire* (New York: Little, Brown, 2000).

Johnson, C., *Japan: Who Governs?* (New York: W. W. Norton, 1995).

Johnson, C., *Japan's Public Policy Companies* (Washington, DC: American Enterprise Institute for Public Policy Research, 1978).

Johnson, C., *MITI and the Japanese Miracle* (Stanford: Stanford University Press, 1982).

Kan, N., *What on Earth in Japan Will Change Once You Have Become Prime Minister?* (*Anata Ga Souri ni natte, ittai Nihon no Nani Ga Kawaru no?*) (Tokyo: Gentosha, 2010).

Kobayashi, K., 'The 15-Year War on Non-Performing Loans and Deflation' (Tokyo: Research Institute of Economy, Trade and Industry, 2004).

Lincoln, E., 'Making Some Sense of the Japanese Economy', JPRI Working Paper No. 94 (San Francisco, CA: Japan Policy Research Institute, September 2003).

Lincoln, E., *Troubled Times: US–Japan Trade Relations in the 1990s* (Washington, DC: Brookings Institution, 1999).

Mainichi News Paper Corp., Editorial Staff, *The Kasumigaseki Syndrome* (*Kasumigaseki Shindoromu*) (Tokyo: Mainichi Shimbunsha, 1995).

Mikuni, A., 'Why Japan Can't Reform Its Economy', JPRI Working Paper No. 44 (San Francisco, CA: Japan Policy Research Institute, April 1998).

Mikuni, A. and Murphy, R. T., *Japan's Policy Trap: Dollars, Deflation, and the Crisis of Japanese Finance* (Washington, DC: Brookings Institution, 2002).

305

Nikkei News Paper Corp., Editorial Staff, *A Creaking Giant Power* (*Kishimu Kyodai Kenryoku*) (Tokyo: Nikkei Shimbunsha, 1995).

Noda, Y., *The Enemy of Democracy* (*Minshu no Teki*) (Tokyo: Shinchosha, 2009).

Samuels, R., 'Kishi and Corruption: An Anatomy of the 1955 System', JPRI Working Paper No. 83 (San Francisco, CA: Japan Policy Research Institute, December 2001).

Werner, R. A., *Princes of the Yen: Japan's Central Bankers and the Transformation of the Economy* (Armonk, NY: M. E. Sharpe, 2003).

Index

Printed and bound by CPI Group (UK) Ltd, Croydon, CR0 4YY